This book presents a representative collection of state-of-the-art papers on international trade, one of the most dynamic sub-fields in economics. The contributions range over all the major areas of current research, including articles on the geographical aspects of international trade by Paul Krugman and Alan Deardorff, on dynamic stochastic economies by Avinash Dixit, and on endogenous growth by Gene Grossman and Elhanan Helpman. In addition to the theoretical contributions, the book also contains work on important policy issues such as auction quotas, discussed by Kala Krishna, and the role of government in economic development, by Anne Krueger and David Orsmond. Also included is an assessment by Bill Ethier of the theoretical achievements of a leading authority in international trade theory, Ronald Jones, in whose honor the essays were written.

**Theory, policy and dynamics in
international trade**

Theory, policy and dynamics in international trade

Essays in honor of Ronald W. Jones

EDITED BY
**Wilfred J. Ethier, Elhanan Helpman and
J. Peter Neary**

CAMBRIDGE
UNIVERSITY PRESS

CAMBRIDGE UNIVERSITY PRESS
Cambridge, New York, Melbourne, Madrid, Cape Town, Singapore, São Paulo

Cambridge University Press
The Edinburgh Building, Cambridge CB2 2RU, UK

Published in the United States of America by Cambridge University Press, New York

www.cambridge.org
Information on this title: www.cambridge.org/9780521434423

First published 1993
First paperback edition 1995

A catalogue record for this publication is available from the British Library

Library of Congress Cataloguing in Publication data
Theory, policy and dynamics in international trade – edited by
Wilfred J. Ethier, Elhanan Helpman, and J. Peter Neary.
    p.   cm
ISBN 0 521 43442 4
1. International trade.   I. Ethier, Wilfred J.
II. Helpman, Elhanan.   III. Neary, J. Peter.
HF1379–T48   1993
382 – dc20   92-20680   CIP

ISBN-13 978-0-521-43442-3 hardback
ISBN-10 0-521-43442-4 hardback

ISBN-13 978-0-521-55852-5 paperback
ISBN-10 0-521-55852-2 paperback

Transferred to digital printing 2005

Contents

IV   Policy towards international trade

V   Trade, growth and dynamics

Conference participants

ERIC W. BOND	Pennsylvania State University, U.S.A.
HAROLD COLE	University of Pennsylvania and International Monetary Fund, U.S.A.
W. MAX CORDEN	Johns Hopkins University, U.S.A.
ALAN V. DEARDORFF	University of Michigan, U.S.A.
AVINASH DIXIT	Princeton University, U.S.A.
WILFRED J. ETHIER	University of Pennsylvania, U.S.A.
RONALD FINDLAY	Columbia University, U.S.A.
GENE M. GROSSMAN	Princeton University, U.S.A.
ELHANAN HELPMAN	Tel Aviv University, Israel
RONALD W. JONES	University of Rochester, U.S.A.
CARSTEN KOWALCZYK	Dartmouth College, U.S.A.
KALA KRISHNA	Harvard University, U.S.A.
ANNE O. KRUEGER	Duke University, U.S.A.
PAUL KRUGMAN	Massachusetts Institute of Technology, U.S.A.
JAMES R. MARKUSEN	University of Colorado, U.S.A.
WOLFGANG MAYER	University of Cincinnati, U.S.A.
JAMES MELVIN	University of Waterloo, Canada
ROBERT MUNDELL	Columbia University and University of Pennsylvania, U.S.A.
J. PETER NEARY	University College Dublin, Ireland and University of Ulster Northern Ireland
MICHIHIRO OHYAMA	Keio University, Japan
DAVID W. H. ORSMOND	Duke University, U.S.A.
ROY J. RUFFIN	Houston University, U.S.A.
LARS E. O. SVENSSON	Institute for International Economic Studies, Stockholm, Sweden
AKIRA TAKAYAMA	Southern Illinois University, U.S.A.
YASUO UEKAWA	Chukyo University, Japan
MAKOTO YANO	Yokohama University, Japan and University of Southern California, U.S.A.

Part I

Introduction

1   Scope of the volume

WILFRED J. ETHIER, ELHANAN HELPMAN
AND J. PETER NEARY

This volume has two interrelated purposes: to present a selection of important contemporary work in international trade theory at the beginning of the 1990s, and to honor Ronald Jones, one of the leading post-war figures in international economics. Although Jones is still as active and innovative a researcher as ever, his sixtieth birthday in 1991 provided an opportunity to assess and honor his contributions. With this in mind, a conference was organized at the University of Pennsylvania in November 1990, at which drafts of the papers in this volume were presented. The result, we hope, is a collection of papers which shows both the continuing influence of Jones's work and the increasing diversity and maturity of international trade theory.

Chapter 2, by Wilfred Ethier, attempts to assess Ronald Jones's contributions to international trade theory, while the remainder of the book contains representative work from the frontier of the field. The remainder of the present chapter introduces the subsequent contributions and attempts to place them in context. We have arranged them so that they form a natural progression, starting in Part II with the spatial and historical context of international trade and moving through positive and normative issues in static models of trade (in Parts III and IV respectively) to work on dynamics and growth in Part V.

In chapter 3 Paul Krugman continues his recent work on geography and trade. Whereas previously he developed a theory of industrial specialization based on agglomeration effects in production and a regional dispersion of demand, here he builds a theory of industrial specialization based on agglomeration and transportation "hubs." The main idea is that transport costs differ across pairs of countries and regions. Some locations have a transport advantage in servicing many other regions. A location of this sort becomes a natural attractor of industries with economies of scale in manufacturing. The result is that in the presence of dispersed demand the structure of transport costs interacts in important ways with economies of scale in determining the pattern of specialization and trade.

3

In chapter 4 Ronald Findlay applies trade theory to a major historical episode: the discovery of the New World. He models the Old World as a region that produces food using land and labor, and manufactures using resources, capital and labor. Available resources are limited in supply. Taking a long-run view, however, capital accumulates in response to profit opportunities. Labor is allocated between the sectors to equalize wage rates and total labor supply is fixed. The discovery of the New World as a "Great Frontier" provides a vast pool of additional land, except that the use of this land entails rising marginal costs; i.e., an extension of the frontier by a single acre is more expensive the further it is pushed out. Labor that migrates to the New World can produce food and raw materials. Among the many issues examined in the paper, particular interest attaches to the effects of an industrial revolution in the Old World, modeled as a productivity increase in manufactures biased towards capital and labor. Findlay shows that this raises capital intensity in manufactures, leads to an increase in the price of raw materials in terms of manufactures, to migration of workers to the New World and to an expansion of the frontier in the New World. He thereby provides an explanation of an important historical episode.

Alan Deardorff develops in chapter 5 an extension of the factor proportions theory that accounts for bilateral trade flows. He focuses on the observed phenomenon that a country may export capital-intensive products to a more capital-rich trade partner. The idea behind this extension is that countries are composed of regions across which factor mobility is imperfect. An extreme case would be a country with no interregional factor mobility whatsoever. In this event each region specializes according to standard forces of comparative advantage and international trade becomes the outcome of interregional trade. Thus, for example, a country with two regions, one with a very high capital to labor ratio and the other with a very low capital to labor ratio, may end up exporting the most labor- and the most capital-intensive products, and importing a middle range of products. Naturally, its exports of the most capital-intensive product will most likely be directed to a country with lower capital abundance while its exports of the least capital-intensive product will most likely be directed to a country with higher capital abundance. This helps to explain observed patterns of trade.

In chapter 6 Roy Ruffin takes up the role of equalizing differentials in labor markets in the theory of international trade. Trade theorists have traditionally paid little attention to the structure of labor markets. Ruffin points out that this neglect may be costly. If workers have preferences over occupations beyond monetary rewards, these preferences affect the relative structure of costs across industries. It follows that, in addition to differences in technologies and relative factor endowments, cross-country differences in occupational preferences determine comparative costs and thereby specialization in production and trade. Ruffin explores this insight in simple models.

Wolfgang Mayer and Jun Li take up, in chapter 7, the problem of indivisibilities in production. They focus on the labor market in which technological features (such as the need to operate entire production lines) interact with institutional features (such as labor laws and union attitudes) to limit short-run output adjustments to discrete changes that result from changes in the number of shifts. Employing a two-sector structure, they show that a number of standard relationships in trade theory are affected by these constraints. Thus, for example, the response of the wage rate to changes in relative commodity prices is not monotonic. For, suppose that as long as the number of shifts remains constant the wage rate increases with the relative price of the unconstrained sector. Given, however, that it cannot reduce employment only slightly but by a whole shift, the constrained sector maintains the same level of labor employment in the face of rising labor costs. But when labor costs become sufficiently high an entire shift of workers lose their jobs. This discrete drop in employment brings about a discrete drop in the wage rate in order to induce the unconstrained sector to employ those workers. The result is that, as the relative price of the unconstrained sector rises, the wage rate rises continuously for a while, drops discretely subsequently, and continues to rise afterwards (at least for some time). The authors also discuss welfare and a variety of other phenomena.

The revival of interest in economies of scale and imperfect competition has generated a voluminous literature that examines their implications for international trade. Michihiro Ohyama contributes further to this line of thought in chapter 8. Allowing for U-shaped cost curves, departures from marginal cost pricing and entry costs in the two-by-two model, Ohyama shows that a variety of standard trade theorems continue to hold in modified forms. He then goes on to identify a hysteresis phenomenon that is driven by entry costs. These elements have a bearing on the structure of comparative costs and gains from trade.

Peter Neary examines taxes on trade in goods and inputs in chapter 9. Using modern methods of analysis he is able to shed new light on the structure of second-best policies. Thus, for example, he shows that in a small country that has irremovable trade taxes the optimal second-best tax on a mobile factor is positive if and only if on average that factor is used intensively in sectors subject to higher tariff rates. He also characterizes welfare-enhancing proportional shifts in tax rates and the welfare costs of taxes on traded goods as a function of the taxes on international factor movements relative to their second-best values, and vice versa. Finally, he shows the implications of market power for the optimal structure of a country's trade taxes.

The issue of auction quotas has occupied the attention of economists in recent years more than in the past, especially as part of the research program on trade policy in the presence of market power. It has, of course, been known for many years that quantitative restrictions affect an economy differently from trade taxes. The question of whether one can improve on free trade with quantitative restrictions, has, however, not been satisfactorily answered. In chapter 10 Kala Krishna continues her line of research on this subject. She first examines a country with a competitive import-competing sector that faces a foreign oligopoly and shows that in her example an import quota does not raise domestic welfare. In addition she studies the determination of quota rents under a variety of circumstances, including domestic oligopoly.

Avinash Dixit extends in chapter 11 the study of the relationship between commodity prices and factor rewards on the one hand and the intersectoral allocation of resources on the other to a dynamic stochastic framework. Prices evolve over time according to a stochastic process while the resulting stochastic process of factor rewards is derived from the model. Labor can be sector specific or move freely across sectors. But the intersectoral reallocation of capital is costly. Therefore small changes in prices induce small changes in factor rewards without inducing a reallocation of capital. When the price deviation is large enough, however, capital moves in response to differentials in rental rates. Dixit's simulations show that small adjustment costs may significantly reduce capital's mobility across sectors and that there is less adjustment in capital when labor is mobile across sectors than when it is not. In addition he reports interesting results about the rewards to inputs, such as the fact that labor is not helped when the mobility of capital is restricted.

Eric Bond adds, in chapter 12, a new contribution to the evolving literature on the role of informational constraints in the design of policies for infant industries. He considers an economy with an infant industry that can be entered by entrepreneurs and non-entrepreneurs. All new entrants lose money during the first period. Entrepreneurs have, however, a positive probability of learning enough during the first period to be sure of earning positive profits in the future. This probability is revealed during the first period. Non-entrepreneurs never make positive profits. Financial institutions cannot distinguish between the two groups, nor can they identify an entrepreneur's probability of success that is revealed during the first period. Both are private information. In view of these constraints financial institutions design optimal lending contracts that build on collateral. Bond shows that whenever the government faces the same informational constraint as the financial institutions it cannot improve on the outcome by intervening in the capital markets. In this event a subsidy to loans, that has been defended for infant industries, proves not to be helpful. On the other hand a variety of policies that intervene in product markets and change the distribution of collateral raise overall efficiency.

Kazuo Nishimura and Makoto Yano devote their essay to a discussion of the international transmission of economic fluctuations. They develop, in chapter 13, a neoclassical two-sector model of capital accumulation in which one sector manufactures consumption goods while the other manufactures capital goods. Installed capital provides productive services with a one-period lag. In autarky the accumulation path can be stationary, monotonic or fluctuating. The last possibility arises when the capital goods sector is labor intensive. When two countries with different technologies trade freely with each other in consumption and capital goods, and they also maintain free international flows of financial capital, the pattern of worldwide capital accumulation depends on whether one or both countries completely specialize in production (at least one has to specialize). In the former case the pattern of accumulation is dictated by the autarky pattern of the country that produces both goods. In the latter case it is always monotonic. Finally, the authors describe the patterns of accumulation of individual countries in terms of their co-movement with the worldwide stock. This sheds light on the degree to which international trade can induce fluctuations in a national economy.

With the recent revival of the theory of economic growth researchers have identified a variety of factors other than those emphasized by the neoclassical theory, which affect a country's dynamic evolution. Prominent among them are government policies. In chapter 14 Anne Krueger and David Orsmond focus on the effects of government policies on the growth of less developed countries. Some policies, such as inflation-prone macroeconomic management, are expected to hurt growth, while others, such as the development of infrastructure, have growth-promoting potential. But in order to realize this potential policies should be applied in the right measure. The authors report cross-section estimates for a sample of countries, including many developing countries, of the relationship between the growth rate and government policies. Thus, for example, high public employment relative to non-agricultural employment reduces the rate of growth as does a distorted trade and payments regime. On the other hand an increase in the share of publicly owned enterprises in non-agricultural output raises the growth rate. In addition to the direct effects the paper reports a variety of indirect effects of policies on the performance of the private sector thereby providing valuable new insights on a major problem.

In chapter 15 James Markusen and Richard Manning consider long-run versions of the specific-factors model. Capital is taken to be the sector-specific input, but the nature of the capital stock may differ across sectors. In any case capital that has been designed for one sector cannot be used in the other. On the other hand a sector can raise over time its capital stock by means of investment. They consider two types of economies. In the first type only one sector can accumulate capital. In this event an expansion of labor supply in a small country (where labor is costlessly mobile across sectors) brings about capital accumulation in the sector that permits it up to the point at which this sector absorbs the entire increment in labor at an unchanged capital–labor ratio. Labor employment in the other sector does not change in the long run. This is an example of a long-run result that emerges from this framework. The authors also discuss other issues, such as the relationship between the short-run and long-run transformation curves and long-run factor price equalization. In the second type of economy, where capital can be accumulated in both sectors, the long-run transform-ation curve is linear.

In the last chapter Gene Grossman and Elhanan Helpman take up the problem of technological competition between two innovating economies. Each country can invest resources in the development of new products and the system affords an innovator indefinite monopoly power. The products are, however, close substitutes which limits the profitability of innovation. There also exists free entry so that in equilibrium the present value of oligopoly profits just covers innovation costs. Cumulative experience in innovation reduces a community's innovation costs via learning, and this learning process is country specific. The authors show that when countries are of similar size the country that has an initial advantage in innovation (as a result of larger cumulative experience) wins the technology race, in the sense that it attains in the long-run a 100 percent market share in the innovating sector. This result does not depend on the size of the initial advantage. They also compare the welfare of representative individuals in leading and lagging countries and discuss the effects of an industrial policy.

As the reader can judge from this introduction the collection of essays in this volume covers much ground at the frontier of research in international trade. And each essay pays tribute in its own way to Ronald Jones's contribution to the field.

2 Ronald Jones and the theory of international trade

WILFRED J. ETHIER

Ronald Jones enters his sixties as productive as ever. This renders a summary evaluation of his contribution impossible: not only is that contribution apparently far from complete, but any judgment today about an accomplishment yesterday might well be nullified by a superseding accomplishment tomorrow. So I attempt no retrospective overview. A collection of article-by-article comments is likewise impractical. Instead I indulge myself with a subjective selection of some of his more important earlier contributions, which offer the most hope for a mature perspective, and which together suggest the nature of the larger body of work.

Trade theory has always been "model oriented." Indeed, for about half a century debate over which was the "best" model preoccupied a substantial portion of theoretical activity. Even today trade theorists can be usefully classified by their attitudes toward modelling. One group stresses the advantages of consistent application of a single theoretical structure to diverse issues.[1] At the other extreme are those who emphasize basic ideas while giving little emphasis to the framework(s) in which those ideas are exploited. A third group emphasizes models rather than ideas but allows the choice of model to vary with the task at hand. Jones clearly belongs to this third group. Therefore it is convenient to approach his work by using choice of model as an organizational principle (but not the exclusive principle). This is not to say that his papers have been driven by a concern for model structure at the expense of economic issues. They are, in fact, typically driven by economic issues, but the hard work of choosing the appropriate model has been done before the paper has been written.

Ricardian trade models

The constant-cost model used by Ricardo to illustrate the principle of comparative advantage has been a staple of the pure theory of international

I thank Elhanan Helpman and Peter Neary for useful comments and suggestions.
[1] John Chipman and Ivor Pearce have independently argued this view to great effect.

trade ever since. The model was employed extensively by the classical authors to discuss trade theory, and a central goal was to formulate Ricardo's comparative-cost doctrine to be applicable to many goods and countries (but, of course, just one internationally immobile factor of production). Trade theory's use of the model remained widespread even in the face of the triumphs of neoclassical marginalism. Interest grew further in the forties when Frank Graham (1948) used the higher dimensional version to construct the numerical examples with which he assailed the classical theory to futile yet stimulating effect.

The development of linear programming and activity analysis at last furnished economists with adequate tools, and they were soon put to work by many writers. Notable results include McKenzie's (1954) proof of the existence of competitive equilibrium and his treatment (1955a, 1955b) of efficient patterns of specialization. In *Comparative Advantage and the Theory of Tariffs: A Multi-Country, Multi-Commodity Model* (1961) Jones stated the many-commodity, many-country version of the Ricardian comparative-cost expression and proved that it does indeed determine the efficient patterns of specialization. Thus he in effect completed the major research project of this area of trade theory, a project that had been outstanding since the time of Ricardo.

Generalizing the Ricardian comparative-cost criterion to higher dimensions can be approached as characterizing the world production-possibility frontier – the collection of efficient world outputs obtainable subject to the constraint that labor be internationally immobile. This frontier in turn equals the frontier of the collection of all nonnegative linear combinations of outputs obtainable when each country specializes in the production of a single good. The efficient specializations are those that lie on this frontier, rather than strictly inside it. To trace out the frontier we must first find these efficient specializations.

The various specializations can be grouped into separate *classes*, where a class is defined by how many countries are specialized to each good. For example, one class can be defined by having good 1 produced by all n countries and all other goods produced by no countries – this class contains only one possible assignment. If the number of goods is also n, another class can be defined by having each good produced by exactly one country specialized to it – this class contains $n!$ possible assignments. The problem is to characterize the efficient specializations within each class.

In the standard two-country, two-commodity case, country 1 will have a comparative advantage over country 2 in good 1 relative to good 2 if

$$\frac{a_1^1}{a_2^1} < \frac{a_1^2}{a_2^2}$$

where a_i^j denotes the amount of labor required to produce a unit of commodity i in country j. This inequality can be written equivalently

$$a_1^1 a_2^2 < a_1^2 a_2^1$$

In this form the condition generalizes to higher dimensions. For example, suppose there are the same number of goods as countries, and consider the class that assigns each good to exactly one country. The assignment of good 1 to country 1, good 2 to country 2, etc. will be efficient if and only if

$$a_1^1 a_2^2 \ldots a_n^n \leq a_{i(1)}^1 a_{i(2)}^2 \ldots a_{i(n)}^n$$

where $i(j)$ denotes the commodity assigned to country j in an alternative assignment in the class. That is, within each class the optimal assignment minimizes the product of the associated labor requirement coefficients.

Jones made ingenious use of the Hawkins-Simon conditions of input–output analysis to prove that the Ricardian comparative cost criterion does indeed generalize in this fashion. Intuition can be gained by examining the conditions for a competitive equilibrium. If the specialization of country i in good i, for all i, is efficient, we can construct preferences for the n countries so that production with this pattern of specialization is consistent with a competitive free-trade equilibrium. Suppose that the international commodity price vector $(p_1, p_2, \ldots, p_n)$ and the vector $(w^1, w^2, \ldots, w^n)$ of national wage rates support this equilibrium. Then $p_i = a_i^i w^i \leq a_i^j w^j$, for all i and j. Consider an alternative specialization, say country i in good $i + 1$ for $i = 1, \ldots, n - 1$ and country n in good 1. Then,

$$1 = \frac{p_2 \cdots p_n p_1}{p_1 p_2 \cdots p_n} \leq \frac{a_2^1 w^1 \ldots a_n^{n-1} w^{n-1} a_1^n w^n}{a_1^1 w^1 a_2^2 w^2 \ldots a_n^n w^n} = \frac{a_2^1 \ldots a_n^{n-1} a_1^n}{a_1^1 a_2^2 \ldots a_n^n},$$

which gives the desired inequality.

The transfer problem

A discussion of the transfer problem is hard to avoid because Jones has been unable to resist returning to the topic again and again. In doing so he has displayed several distinct facets of his research personality.

The transfer problem has been one of the most intensely discussed issues in international trade theory for over a century. Though of some intrinsic importance, the inherent significance of the problem is much less than the magnitude of its discussion would suggest. Part of the reason no doubt is the unusual prominence given to a number of major transfers over the years.[2] But part of the reason must also be the remarkable confusion propagated by generation after generation of eminent trade theorists.

---

[2] To the transfers themselves, not to the issues addressed in the literature on the transfer problem.

In the fifties a pair of articles by Paul Samuelson (1952, 1954) left the essence of the basic problem quite transparent and set the directions for most discussions since. The central concern of the long literature on the subject has been the effect of an unrequited transfer payment by one country to another on the terms of trade of the paying country. At the initial terms of trade, a one-dollar transfer of expenditure abroad will reduce by m dollars the home excess demand for importables, where m denotes the home marginal propensity to import. In a two-commodity, two-country world the foreign excess supply of home importables will fall by $1 - m^*$, where m^* denotes the foreign marginal propensity to import.[3] Thus the transfer will generate an excess demand for the home (paying) country's imports if and only if $1 - m^* > m$. In this case the home country's terms of trade must deteriorate to clear international markets.

Samuelson endorsed the view that the *orthodox presumption* $m + m^* < 1$ was no more compelling, other things equal, than its anti-orthodox alternative. He then proceeded to study the consequences of barriers to trade that might be expected to bolster the orthodox case.

Jones has contributed to the literature on the transfer problem in several ways. No doubt his most attractive contribution was a simple but ingenious argument for the anti-orthodox presumption in the basic 2 × 2 model. The essential idea, published in *The Transfer Problem Revisited* (1970), was that, other things being equal, countries tend to import what they need relatively more. Consider a simple two-agent exchange model where the agents each have homothetic (but not identical) tastes. Then the contract curve between them must lie entirely on one side of the diagonal of the endowment box. Suppose God randomly determines an initial allocation of the given world endowment by choosing a point within the box. If the divinity is sufficiently well-behaved to employ a uniform distribution for this purpose, the allocation point is more likely than not to lie on the same side of the contract curve as the diagonal. But this is the set of allocations generating trading equilibria in which the sum of the marginal propensities to import exceeds one. At last, a concrete result concerning what can be presumed about the terms-of-trade effects of a transfer! This simple argument essentially constitutes what has been accomplished, for the basic 2 × 2 model, regarding the most prominent concern of this very long and very large literature.

Another contribution of Jones to this literature, addressed in *Trade with Non-Traded Goods: The Anatomy of Inter-Connected Markets* (1974) and *Presumption and the Transfer Problem* (1975) was to analyze the effects of nontraded goods. One might suspect that the addition of a nontraded good

---

[3] Foreign excess demand for their importables rises by m^* and their excess demand for their exportables (i.e., the paying country's importables) accordingly rises by $1 - m^*$, so their *excess supply* of exportables *falls* by this amount.

would favor the orthodox case by rendering an m that exceeds one-half less plausible. But such an intuition ignores the supply and demand responses required by the necessity that the markets for nontraded goods clear internally, though Viner and Samuelson had seemed to suggest that the orthodox case would nonetheless be strengthened. Jones's analysis sorts out the role of relative demand and supply responses and in fact does not establish an orthodox presumption. A case for the anti-orthodox presumption also emerges if the transfer is of productive capacity rather than of expenditure, a possibility of practical importance. In the "neutral" case where such a transfer induces, at the initial prices, equiproportional changes in consumption and in production of each good in each country, the paying country's trade vector shrinks and that of the receiving country enlarges, thereby causing an excess demand for the payer's exportables and an excess supply of its importables.[4]

The possibility that the receiving country's terms of trade might deteriorate sufficiently to reduce its welfare has for some reason generated a remarkable recent boomlet of professional interest. In the standard 2×2 model this outcome is inconsistent with the familiar Marshall–Lerner condition (if substitution elasticities are nonnegative) and is therefore commonly ruled out by stability considerations. Examples where the outcome occurs can accordingly be constructed if the basic model is altered so as to sever the link between the Marshall–Lerner condition and stability. Perhaps the most straightforward way to do this is simply to add (national) external economies of scale to one of the sectors in the textbook 2×2 Ricardian trade model. For consider an equilibrium in which one country specializes in production of the good subject to increasing returns to scale and the other country diversifies. If this equilibrium is stable and if $m + m^* < 1$, any transfer from the specialized country to the diversified one that leaves this pattern of specialization unchanged must improve the payor's terms of trade; further, it must benefit the payor and harm the receiver for some intermediate range of degrees of economies of scale. The example "works" because the Marshall–Lerner condition, which fails here, is no longer a plausible stability condition.[5] However, the recent literature has for some reason instead followed the more tortuous path of increasing

---

[4] See Caves and Jones (1981). Apropos of quixotic orthodoxy, the Caves–Jones text itself (currently Caves–Frankel–Jones) is a significant link in the orthodox line of succession of international economics textbooks. Taussig produced the first modern-style text devoted exclusively to international economics. His student Angell wrote a text that was also prominent for many years, and Angell taught at Columbia when Kindleberger was a graduate student there. Kindleberger in turn produced a leading text and was teaching at MIT when Jones did his own graduate study.

[5] Indeed, the *Marshallian* stability of this equilibrium is equivalent to violation of the Marshall–Lerner condition. Note also that the orthodox presumption $m + m^* < 1$ is in this case associated with an *improvement* of the terms of trade of the paying country.

14   Wilfred J. Ethier

the dimensionality of the model. In particular, the number of countries has been increased by considering countries that are trading partners of the paying and receiving countries (but not directly involved in the transfer). Jones cannot be blamed for initiating this literature. Rather his contribution – see *The Transfer Problem in a Three-Agent Setting* (1984) and *Income Effects and Paradoxes in the Theory of International Trade* (1985) – was to dissect the transfer process in this higher-dimensional environment to make clear exactly what circumstances are associated with a situation where it is truly better to give than to receive. Moreover, the latter paper shows that this outcome can be reinterpreted as arising from the same forces which give rise to other well-known phenomena such as immiserizing growth.

Heckscher–Ohlin trade theory

Jones's paper *Factor Proportions and the Heckscher–Ohlin Theorem* (1956) is one of the classic contributions to the development and refinement of the basic Heckscher–Ohlin–Samuelson model of trade. Jones's contribution was essentially to do for the Heckscher–Ohlin theorem itself what Samuelson had done for the Stolper–Samuelson (1941) theorem and for factor-price equalization (Samuelson [1948, 1949]) and what Rybczynski (1955) was doing for the Rybczynski theorem.[6] The paper developed and clarified the distinction between the price and quantity versions of the Heckscher–Ohlin theorem and the implications for that theorem of factor-intensity reversals – standard textbook fare ever since. Indeed, this contribution is so basic that to describe it now would be not merely redundant but ridiculous.

In the sixties Jones's algebraic approach to the Heckscher–Ohlin–Samuelson model set the tone for how a whole generation did trade theory. This will be discussed below.

Lower dimensional trade theory

Geometry (and/or its corresponding algebra) was the predominant analytical technique employed in trade theory during the sixties, in good part a reflection of Harry Johnson's influence. Though he himself could wield the technique to clear and powerful effect, Johnson also generated a disdain (even a contempt) for contemporary microeconomics that was both to inhibit the development of trade theory and also to contribute powerfully to the low esteem within economics that our field acquired at that time.

[6] Actually Jones himself independently and contemporaneously proved what has come to be known as the Rybczynski theorem. This illustrates what Jones would no doubt regard as a Gresham's Law of Names.

Jones's contribution, in retrospect, was to transform trade theory from a backwater to a vibrant branch of microeconomic theory. This, of course, is a methodological contribution, not a treatment of an economic issue. But it was to have more influence on how trade theory was pursued than any other contribution in the preceding half-century.

The crucial step here, of course, was Jones's celebrated 1965 paper, *The Structure of Simple General Equilibrium Models.* Profiting from the dissertation of his student Akihiro Amano, Jones in this elegant paper set out the essentials of the "hat" comparative-statics analysis of the basic $2 \times 2 \times 2$ model.[7] Elasticities and relative shares were used with great effect to render transparent the structure of the model and to make obvious its basic duality properties. The result was a framework allowing trade theorists to continue to analyze issues as they had been doing in a context specifically related to how economists actually did microeconomics. The framework was sufficiently seductive that for over fifteen years the lion's share of significant contributions employed it. It was also employed for countless forgettable exercises, but this is yet still another (though perhaps unwelcome) testimonial to its usefulness.

Influential though the 1965 *JPE* article was, it is more accurately viewed as a single episode (and not among the more substantive episodes) in an extended research project to formulate the basic (low-dimensional) theory of international trade in terms consistent with contemporary micro-economics yet accessible to traditional trade theorists. The project can be said to have commenced with the 1961 *IER* paper, *Stability Conditions in International Trade: A General Equilibrium Analysis.* Curiously, a high point is the short piece, *Tariffs and Trade in General Equilibrium: Comment* (1969). Though ostensibly nothing more than a comment on a justifiably forgotten paper, this artful note remains today the basic statement of the traditional theory of tariffs.

All of this raises the question of the practical relevance of low-dimensional trade models. The empirical literature has not been kind to factor-endowment models. The Leontief Paradox and its succeeding contributions have convincingly demonstrated that the 2×2 framework is inadequate to deal satisfactorily with reality, and higher dimensional factor-endowment models simple enough to be empirically implemented have not been supported by the data (see Bowen, Leamer and Sveikauskas [1987]). At the same time, factor endowments are clearly important in practice, factor-endowment models can usefully describe reality with only moderate disaggregation (see, e.g., Leamer [1984]), and we constantly find ourselves thinking about trade problems in factor-endowment terms. Thus

---

[7] Actually this paper did not use circumflexes at all, but rather asterisks, apparently because of a typesetting constraint.

the robustness of its basic results, especially with regard to dimensionality, is a key issue for the usefulness of the larger part of international trade theory. Jones addressed the issue in his Frank Graham Memorial Lecture, published as *"Two-Ness" in Trade Theory: Costs and Benefits* (1977).

The issue is in fact pertinent to a large share of Jones's work, and implicitly addressed by that work, in light of his knack for deploying just the right model for a particular task. When he explicitly addresses the issue, Jones in effect explains much of his own past modelling decisions. The two-dimensional version of the factor endowments model has turned out to be an effective research tool because the insights it provided in the form of its basic theorems have been shown to extend in fundamental ways to higher dimensions (and significantly to survive other forms of generalization as well). On the other hand, the generalization of the Ricardian comparative-cost criteria discussed above was in its very essence an affair of higher dimensions, and indeed dimensionality had played an important part in the examples Graham had used earlier to propel his polemics. Significant aspects of the transfer problem revolve around higher dimensionality: of commodities, regarding the role of nontraded goods, and of countries, regarding the role of trading partners not direct parties to the transfer. Further, one of the key differences between the Heckscher–Ohlin–Samuelson and specific-factor models concerns dimensionality.

Specific factors

Since the seventies the Heckscher–Ohlin–Samuelson model has shared center stage with another low-dimensional factor-endowments model, one that differs from the former in that one of the two factors is immobile between sectors. Thus there are in effect three factors, two sector-specific and one intersectorally mobile. This model was introduced independently in 1971 by Jones in *A Three-Factor Model in Theory, Trade, and History* and by Samuelson,[8] being christened the "specific-factors" model by Jones and the "Ricardo–Viner" model by Samuelson.[9] Actually, 1971 witnessed a return, rather than an introduction: until Stolper–Samuelson came along the model had been a standard work-horse of trade theory, and its basic properties had been clearly spelled out in textbooks.

The wide popularity of the specific-factors model is evidently due to two of its properties, each of which has been emphasized by both Jones and Samuelson. First, it is just very useful: a simple general equilibrium model

---

[8] See Samuelson (1971).
[9] Each name is revealing but neither is completely satisfactory. While specific factors are critical to the model, so is a mobile factor; while Ricardo and Viner can be associated with the model, as compelling a case can be made for some intermediate writers.

whose structure is transparent and which exhibits much of the intuition originating with partial equilibrium. Jones himself has made use of the model to analyze a number of diverse issues. Second, it breaks the rigid link between commodity prices and factor rewards that the Heckscher–Ohlin–Samuelson model imposes whenever production is diversified.

Making one of the factors sector-specific produces three qualitative effects on the Heckscher–Ohlin–Samuelson model. It increases the model's dimensionality, it causes the number of factors to exceed the number of goods (or transforms the model from an "even" one to an "odd" one in Jones's terminology) and it adds zeros to the technology matrix (each sector makes zero use of one factor for all input prices). These three effects influence the commodity-price, factor-reward relation in two important ways.

First, the fact that there are more factors than goods means that commodity prices will generally not suffice to determine factor rewards. That is, even if the economy remains diversified, a change in factor endowments will cause factor rewards to change at unchanged commodity prices. Thus the factor-price equalization theorem fails. This property of the model was of primary concern to Samuelson.

The second influence can be grasped by looking at the relation between commodity and factor price changes implied by the model:

$$\hat{r}_1 > \hat{p}_1 > \hat{w} > \hat{p}_2 > \hat{r}_2.$$

Here a circumflex indicates logarithmic differentiation, p_i denotes the price of commodity i, r_i the reward of the factor specific to commodity i, and w the reward of the mobile factor. The latter is influenced in an ambiguous way by relative price changes: it always rises in terms of one commodity and falls in terms of the other. This behavior – so unlike Stolper–Samuelson – is made *possible* by the fact that the model is of higher dimensionality than 2×2; it is made *necessary* by the greater number of factors than goods and by the zeros in the technology. This property of the model was of primary concern to Jones, with the concern culminating in Jones's 1977 paper with Roy Ruffin, *Protection and Real Wages: The Neo-Classical Ambiguity*. This paper argued for a presumption (but not a certainty) that an import tariff would lower the real reward of the mobile factor.

Factors are distinguished from goods in two distinct ways in this model – they are inputs rather than outputs, and they are traded on national markets rather than on international markets. When an excess of factors over goods is significant, as with factor-price equalization, it is generally because of the latter distinction, not the former. To see this, allow one of the factors to be internationally mobile.[10] Suppose first that this is labor, v_L the factor that is also intersectorally mobile. Then p_1, p_2 and w will be

[10] This possibility was discussed in Dixit and Norman (1980), pp. 124, 125.

determined on world markets, and the question is whether this will serve to equalize r_1 and r_2 across countries. Clearly it must – with positive quantities of both specific factors, v_1 and v_2, trapped in each country, each must produce both goods; with producers of a good in the two countries receiving the same price for it and paying the same for one input, competitive equilibrium requires that they pay the same for the remaining input as well. Thus factor-price equalization is a necessary property of international equilibrium if labor is internationally mobile. Another way of thinking of this is that the two countries are always in a common diversification cone in the v_1–v_2 plane of immobile factors: the two positive axes represent the techniques chosen by the respective industries, so the diversification cone coincides with the positive quadrant.

If instead one of the specific factors, say v_1, is internationally mobile (a case explored by Jones in *Tax Wedges and Mobile Capital* [1987]), the result is similar, but the diversification cone in the v_2–v_L plane is now a subset of the positive quadrant depending on the equilibrium prices. If both countries produce the first commodity, x_1, in equilibrium, they must have the same wage, with p_1 and r_1 directly equalized in international markets. But this implies that r_2 is also equalized, since x_2 must be produced in both countries. These common values of w and r_2 determine the least-cost technique of producing x_2, which corresponds to a ray in the v_2–v_L plane. The diversification cone for this equilibrium is the cone formed by this ray and the v_L axis: if the endowments of both countries lie in this cone they will have equal factor prices; otherwise all of v_1 will locate in one country, inducing specialization and severing the link between those prices determined in world markets and those determined in national markets.

Thus adding an international market for any factor causes the specific-factors model to have exactly the same factor-price equalization property as the Heckscher–Ohlin–Samuelson model: factor prices will be equalized in an international equilibrium if and only if both countries' endowments lie in a common diversification cone corresponding to that equilibrium. Of course the special features of the model have implications for those cones: as always, the production functions determine the shapes of the diversification cones.

This result is fortunate because having critical properties of the model sensitive to such a casual property of the technology[11] as the relative number of goods and factors would be a distinct embarrassment. Having

---

[11] To paraphrase a complaint of Robert Solow about the importance of the factor-intensity condition for the stability of two-sector neoclassical growth models. Of course either the number of goods exceeds the number of factors or not; we just don't know the proper way to go about counting them (or if there is a proper way).

them sensitive to how many markets exist should by contrast seem natural to economists.

One would not expect the addition of an international factor market to help much in dealing with the model's prediction about the effect of commodity-price changes on real factor rewards, for two reasons. First, in this case we really do care about the distinction between goods and factors as outputs and inputs – that's related to why real factor rewards are of interest. Second, the departure from Stolper–Samuelson results is a reflection of not just the excess of factors over goods but also of the higher dimensionality and the zeros in the technology, and adding an international factor market will not help in regard to these features. The chain of inequalities of relative price changes is independent of which international markets exist, and the reinterpretations of that chain allowed by adding another international market are of little interest.

The factor-price equalization property, though, offers hope for a Rybczynski-type result. Suppose we allow one factor to be internationally mobile (it doesn't matter which one) and consider the effects of an exogenous change in the endowments of the other two factors, at given international prices. Suppose, as in the usual experiment, that this endowment change keeps the economy within the diversification cone. Then the earlier argument implies that factor prices, and therefore the techniques of production in both sectors, do not change. Then it is easy to see that such a change must produce the following (or its alternative where all inequalities are reversed).

$$\hat{x}_1 = \hat{v}_1 > \hat{v}_L > \hat{v}_2 = \hat{x}_2$$

In this expression two of the factor changes reflect the hypothesized exogenous change in endowment while the third reflects the endogenous change in the economy's use of the internationally mobile factor. This comes within a whisker of the conventional result, with relative factor intensities predicting the direction of output changes, and with those changes (almost) magnifications of the endowment changes. Note also that the economy's use of the internationally mobile factor must change in such a way as to give v_L a middle role analogous to that of w regarding price changes.

Concluding remarks

This essay has addressed subjectively selected peaks of Jones's contributions. So most of the rich terrain has been neglected. The neglect is considerable. For four decades Jones has pondered almost every significant issue addressed by trade theory. Very often his treatment has been

20   **Wilfred J. Ethier**

definitive; invariably it has set the artistic standard. Although we have not managed to follow this standard,[12] he has taught us what economics should be. In trade theory Ronald Jones has not only helped to lay the foundations, he has also set a good example.

References

Bowen, Harry P., Edward E. Leamer and Leo Sveikauskas 1987 "Multicountry, Multifactor Tests of the Factor Abundance Theory," *American Economic Review*, December, 1987.
Dixit, Avinash and Victor Norman 1980 *Theory of International Trade*, Cambridge.
Graham, Frank 1948 *The Theory of International Values*, Princeton.
Leamer, Edward E. 1984 *Sources of International Comparative Advantage*, Cambridge.
McKenzie, Lionel W. 1954 "On Equilibrium in Graham's Model of World Trade and Other Competitive Systems," *Econometrica*, April.
    1955a "Specialization and Efficiency in World Production," *Review of Economic Studies*, June.
    1955b "Specialization in Production and the Possibility Locus," *Review of Economic Studies*, January.
Rybczynski, T. M. 1955 "Factor Endowments and Relative Commodity Prices," *Economica*, November.
Samuelson, Paul A. 1948 "International Trade and Equalisation of Factor Prices," *Economic Journal*, June.
    1949 "International Factor-Price Equalisation Once Again," *Economic Journal*, June.
    1952 "The Transfer Problem and Transport Costs: The Terms of Trade When Impediments are Absent," *Economic Journal*, June.
    1954 "The Transfer Problem and Transport Costs, II: Analysis of Effects of Trade Impediments," *Economic Journal*, June.
    1971 "Ohlin Was Right," *Swedish Journal of Economics*, December.
Stolper, Wolfgang F. and Paul A. Samuelson 1941 "Protection and Real Wages," *Review of Economic Studies*, November.

Appendix: Professional publications of Ronald W. Jones

Articles

1. "Factor Proportions and the Heckscher–Ohlin Theorem," *Review of Economic Studies*, October 1956.
2. "Depreciation and the Dampening Effect of Income Changes," *Review of Economics and Statistics*, February 1960.

[12] Paul Krugman must be exempted from this judgment.

3. "Stability Conditions in International Trade: A General Equilibrium Analysis," *International Economic Review*, May 1961.
4. "Comparative Advantage and the Theory of Tariffs; A Multi-Country, Multi-Commodity Model," *Review of Economic Studies*, June 1961.
5. "Economic Growth and the Theory of International Income Flows" (with Murray Brown), *Econometrica*, January 1962.
6. "Variable Labor Supply in the Theory of International Trade" (with Murray C. Kemp), *Journal of Political Economy*, February 1962.
7. "Duality in International Trade: A Geometrical Note," *Canadian Journal of Economics and Political Science*, August 1965.
8. "'Neutral' Technological Change and the Isoquant Map," *American Economic Review*, September 1965.
9. "The Structure of Simple General Equilibrium Models," *Journal of Political Economy*, December 1965.
10. "Comments on Technical Progress," *Philippine Economic Journal*, 5, 2, Second Semester, 1966.
11. "International Capital Movements and the Theory of Tariffs and Trade," *Quarterly Journal of Economics*, February 1967.
12. "Monetary and Fiscal Policy for an Economy with Fixed Exchange Rates," Supplement to *Journal of Political Economy*, August 1968.
13. "Variable Returns to Scale in General Equilibrium Theory," *International Economic Review*, October 1968.
14. "Portfolio Balance and International Payments Adjustment: Comment," in Mundell and Swoboda (eds.) 1969. *Monetary Problems of the International Economy*.
15. "Tariffs and Trade in General Equilibrium: Comment," *American Economic Review*, June 1969.
16. "The Role of Technology in the Theory of International Trade," in R. Vernon (ed.) 1970. *The Technology Factor in International Trade*.
17. "The Transfer Problem Revisited," *Economica*, May 1970.
18. "Effective Protection and Substitution," *Journal of International Economics*, February 1971.
19. "Distortions in Factor Markets and the General Equilibrium Model of Production," *Journal of Political Economy*, May/June 1971.
20. "A Three Factor Model in Theory, Trade, and History," Ch. 1 in Bhagwati, Jones, Mundell and Vanek 1971. *Trade, Balance of Payments and Growth. Essays in Honor of C. P. Kindleberger*, North-Holland.
21. "Activity Analysis and Real Incomes: Analogies with Production Models," *Journal of International Economics*, August 1972.
22. "The Metzler Tariff Paradox: Extensions to Nontraded and Inter-

mediate Commodities," Ch. 1 in G. Horwich and P. A. Samuelson (eds.) 1974. *Trade, Stability, and Macroeconomics* (Essays in Honor of Lloyd Metzler) Academic Press.

23. "Trade with Non-Traded Goods: The Anatomy of Inter-connected Markets," *Economica*, May 1974.

24. "The Exchange Rate and the Balance of Payments," *Information Commercial Espanola*, October 1974.

25. "The Small Country in a Many Commodity World," *Australian Economic Papers*, December 1974.

26. "Trade Patterns with Capital Mobility" (with Roy Ruffin), in M. Parkin and A. R. Nobay (eds.) 1975. *Current Economic Problems*, Cambridge.

27. "Presumption and the Transfer Problem," *Journal of International Economics*, August 1975.

28. "Income Distribution and Effective Protection in a Multi-Commodity Trade Model," *Journal of Economic Theory*, August 1975.

29. "Trade Theory, Trade Policy, and Protection: A Comment," in P. B. Kenen (ed.) 1975. *International Trade and Finance*, Princeton.

30. "Devaluation, Non-Flexible Prices, and the Trade Balance for a Small Country" (with W. Max Corden), *Canadian Journal of Economics*, February 1976.

31. "Terms of Trade and Transfers: The Relevance of the Literature," in D. M. Leipziger (ed.) 1976. *The International Monetary System*, AID.

32. "Import Demand and Export Supply: An Aggregation Theorem" (with Eitan Berglas), *American Economic Review*, March 1977.

33. "Protection and Real Wages: The Neo-Classical Ambiguity" (with Roy Ruffin), *Journal of Economic Theory*, April 1977.

34. "'Two-Ness' in Trade Theory: Costs and Benefits," *Special Papers in International Economics*, No. 12, 1977, International Finance Section, Princeton University, April 1977.

35. "The Relevance of the Two-Sector Production Model in Trade Theory" (with José Scheinkman), *Journal of Political Economy*, October 1977.

36. "Comments on Technology, Technical Progress, and the International Allocation of Economic Activity," in B. Ohlin (ed.) 1977. Nobel Symposium, *The International Allocation of Economic Activity*.

37. "The Export of Technology" (with Eitan Berglas), in K. Brunner and A. Meltzer (eds.) 1977. *Optimal Policies, Control Theory and Technology Exports*, supplement to *Journal of Monetary Economics*.

38. "Comments upon Trade and Direct Investment," in R. Dornbusch and J. Frenkel 1979. *International Economic Policy*, Johns Hopkins University Press.

39. "A Model of Trade and Unemployment" (with Kamran Noman) in Jerry Green and J. Scheinkman (eds.) 1979. *General Equilibrium, Growth, and Trade*, Academic Press.

40. "Temporal Convergence and Factor Intensities" (with J. Peter Neary), *Economics Letters*, 3, 4, 1979.

41. "Demand Behavior and the Theory of International Trade," Ch. 17 in J. S. Chipman and C. P. Kindleberger (eds.) 1980. *Flexible Exchange Rates and the Balance of Payments*, North-Holland.

42. "Taxation Schemes in a World with Internationally Mobile Labour and Capital: A Comment," in P. Oppenheimer (ed.) 1980. *Issues in International Economics*, Oriel Press.

43. "Comparative and Absolute Advantage," *Schweizerische Zeitschrift für Volkswirtschaft und Statistik*, 3, 1980.

44. "The Theory of Trade in Middle Products" (with Kalyan Sanyal), *American Economic Review*, March 1982.

45. "International Trade Theory," in E. C. Brown and R. M. Solow (eds.) 1983. *Paul Samuelson and Modern Economic Theory*, McGraw Hill.

46. "International Differences in Response to Common External Shocks: The Role of Purchasing Power Parity" (with Douglas D. Purvis), in E. Claassen and P. Salin (eds.) 1983. *Recent Issues in the Theory of Flexible Exchange Rates*, North-Holland.

47. "Two-Way Capital Flows: Cross-Hauling in a Model of Foreign Investment" (with J. Peter Neary and Frances P. Ruane), *Journal of International Economics*, May 1983.

48. "Factor Intensities and Factor Substitution in General Equilibrium" (with Steve Easton), *Journal of International Economics*, August 1983.

49. "International Trade and Foreign Investment: A Simple Model" (with Fumio Dei), *Economic Inquiry*, October 1983.

50. "The Positive Theory of International Trade" (with J. Peter Neary), in R. W. Jones and P. Kenen (eds.) 1984. *Handbook of International Economics*, North-Holland.

51. "The Transfer Problem in a Three-Agent Setting," *Canadian Journal of Economics*, February 1984.

52. "Protection and the Harmful Effects of Endogenous Capital Flows," *Economics Letters*, 15, 1984.

53. "A Comment on Comparative Advantage and International Trade in Services," in R. Stern (ed.) 1985. *Trade and Investment in Services: Canada/U.S. Perspectives*, Toronto: Ontario Economic Council.

54. "A Theorem on Income Distribution in a Small, Open Economy," *Journal of International Economics*, February 1985.

55. "Ricardo-Graham World Transformation Surfaces," *Osaka City University Economic Review*, March 1985.

24   Wilfred J. Ethier

56. "Income Effects and Paradoxes in the Theory of International Trade," *Economic Journal*, June 1985.
57. "International Factor Movements and the Ramaswami Argument" (with Isaias Coelho), *Economica*, August 1985.
58. "A Simple Production Model with Stolper-Samuelson Properties" (with Sugata Marjit), *International Economic Review*, 19, 1985.
59. "Relative Prices and Real Factor Rewards: A Re-interpretation," *Economics Letters*, 26, 3, 1985.
60. "(The Dutch Disease): A Trade Theoretic Perspective," in J. P. Neary and S. van Wijnbergen (eds.) 1986. *Natural Resources and the Macroeconomy*, MIT Press, Cambridge, MA.
61. "The Theory of International Factor Flows: The Basic Model" (with I. Coelho and S. Easton), *Journal of International Economics*, May 1986.
62. "Neighborhood Production Structures with an Application to the Theory of International Trade" (with H. Kierzkowski), *Oxford Economic Papers*, 1986.
63. "The Population Monotonicity Property and the Transfer Paradox," *Journal of Public Economics*, 32, 1987, 125–32.
64. "International Capital Mobility and the Dutch Disease" (with J. P. Neary and F. P. Ruane), in H. Kierzkowski (ed.) 1987. *Protection and Competition in International Trade: Essays in Honor of W. M. Corden*, Blackwell, 86–98.
65. "Trade Taxes and Subsidies with Imperfect Competition," *Economics Letters*, 23, 1987, 375–79.
66. "Heckscher-Ohlin Trade Theory," *The New Palgrave*, 1987.
67. "Tax Wedges and Mobile Capital," *Scandinavian Journal of Economics*, 89, 3, 1987, 335–46.
68. "Comment on Current Issues in Trade Policy," in R. M. Stern (ed.) 1987. *U.S. Trade Policies in a Changing World Economy*, MIT Press, Cambridge, MA, 69–72.
69. "Co-movements in Relative Commodity Prices and International Capital Flows: A Simple Model," *Economic Inquiry*, January 1989.
70. "Protection and the Optimal Tariff," *Journal of International Economic Integration*, Spring, 1989.
71. "New Trade Theory and the Less Developed Countries: Comments," in G. Calvo, R. Findlay, P. Kouri and J. de Macedo 1989. *Debt, Stabilization, and Development*, Blackwell, 371–75.
72. "Raw Materials, Processing Activities and Protectionism" (with Barbara J. Spencer), *Canadian Journal of Economics*, August 1989, 469–86.
73. "Perspectives on 'Buy-Outs' and the Ramaswami Effect" (with Steve

Easton), *Journal of International Economics*, November 1989, 363–71.
74. "Should a Factor-Market Distortion be Widened?" (with Masayuki Hayashibara), *Economics Letters*, 1989, 159–62.
75. "Foreign Monopoly and Optimal Tariffs for the Small Open Economy" (with Shumpei Takemori), *European Economic Review*, December 1989.
76. "The Role of Services in Production and International Trade: A Theoretical Framework" (with Henryk Kierzkowski), Ch. 3 in R. W. Jones and A. Krueger (eds.) 1990. *The Political Economy of International Trade: Essays in Honour of R. Baldwin*, Blackwell.
77. "Foreign Investment and Migration: Analytics and Extensions of the Basic Model" (with Steve Easton), *Keio Economic Studies*, 27, 1, 1990.
78. "Appraising the Options for International Trade in Services" (with Frances P. Ruane), *Oxford Economic Papers*, November 1990, 672–87.
79. "The Ramaswami Function and International Factor Mobility," *Indian Economic Review*, July–December 1990, 143–64.
80. "Vertical Foreclosure and International Trade Policy" (with Barbara J. Spencer), *Review of Economic Studies*, January 1991, 153–70.
81. "Wage Sensitivity Rankings and Temporal Convergence" (with J. Peter Neary), in E. Helpman and A. Razin (eds.) 1991. *International Trade and Trade Policy*, M.I.T. Press, Cambridge, MA.
82. "The Stolper-Samuelson Theorem, the Leamer Triangle, and the Produced Mobile Factor Structure" (with S. Marjit), in A. Takayama, M. Ohyama and Y. Otah (eds.) 1991. *Trade, Policy, and International Adjustments*, Academic Press, 95–107.
83. "International Trade and Endogenous Production Structures" (with S. Marjit) in W. Neuefeind and R. Riezman (eds.) 1992. *Economic Theory and International Trade: Essays in Honor of J. Trout Rader*, Springer-Verlag.
84. "Trade and Protection in Vertically Related Markets" (with Barbara J. Spencer), *Journal of International Economics*, February 1992, 31–55.

Books

World Trade and Payments, (with R. E. Caves), Little, Brown & Co., 1973.
   Revised Edition, 1977
   Third Edition, 1981
   Fourth Edition, 1985
   Fifth Edition, 1990 (with R. E. Caves and J. Frankel)

26   **Wilfred J. Ethier**

International Trade: *Essays in Theory*, North-Holland, 1979.

Books edited

Trade, Balance of Payments, and Growth (essays in honor of Charles P. Kindleberger), North-Holland (with J. N. Bhagwati, R. A. Mundell, and J. Vanek), 1971.
Handbook of International Economics,
  Vol. 1 (with P. B. Kenen), North-Holland, 1984.
  Vol. 2 (with P. B. Kenen), North-Holland, 1985.
International Trade: *Surveys of Theory and Policy*, North-Holland, 1986.
The Political Economy of International Trade (with A. Krueger), Blackwell, 1990.

Part II

History, geography and the theory of trade

3 The hub effect: or, threeness in interregional trade

PAUL KRUGMAN

In his delightful Graham lecture Ron Jones mounted a spirited defense of "two-ness" in trade models. So it is with some trepidation that I offer in this paper a model where one cannot even discuss the subject without counting up to three! In justification I can only claim that what Ron meant was not that two is a magic number, but that it is useful to study small models – and in that sense this paper is a (small!) addition to the lovely house that Jones built.

The subject of the paper is that of the role of transportation "hubs" in the pattern of interregional and perhaps international trade. By this I do not mean anything very profound; I simply mean a situation in which the costs of transportation between locations differ in such a way that one location can reasonably be described as a transport "hub." One cannot have a hub in this sense with only two locations, but one can with three, as illustrated in Figure 3.1. In that figure, we suppose that consumption and production take place at the three locations 1, 2, 3. There are some costs of transportation between these locations. Transport costs are, however, lower between 1 and either 2 or 3 than between 2 and 3. Thus 1 is the "hub" of this network. What I want to argue is that (i) transportation hubs are especially desirable places to locate the production of goods and services subject to increasing returns, and (ii) the interaction between increasing returns in production and in transportation leads to the endogenous formation of such transportation hubs.

These ideas are pretty obvious, both to laymen and to students of industrial location. They have, however, to my knowledge never been the subject of formal modelling; certainly they are not part of the standard corpus of international trade theory. The reason for this gap in the literature is that in international trade theory we traditionally avoid dealing with transportation costs as much as we can – we treat countries as dimensionless points, and often assume zero transport costs between countries as well (or segregate goods into disjoint sets of costlessly traded

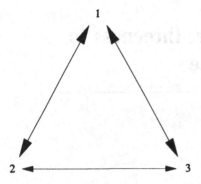

Figure 3.1

and completely nontraded products). While there have been a few efforts to argue that transportation costs matter in a fundamental way for international specialization – Isard (1956) springs to mind – in general the role of transport costs, and more generally of space and location, remains much neglected in international economics.

I view this paper as part of a larger project, which is to recast at least some of the theory of international trade as simply an aspect of the field of economic geography – a field in which transportation costs play a crucial role. In several other papers (Krugman 1991a, 1991b, 1991c) I have explored the way in which increasing returns can interact with factor mobility to produce a differentiation of regions into an industrialized core and an agricultural periphery. The transportation hub effect can be viewed as an alternative, or perhaps complementary, explanation of the same kind of regional differentiation. In the best Jonesian style, however, I will make no effort to stuff everything into one model. In this paper I focus entirely on the transportation hub story, excluding factor mobility by assumption.

The paper is in four parts. The first sets out the basic economic model, a monopolistic competition framework of a kind that has become very familiar. The second provides a brief restatement of a known result, the tendency of increasing returns industries to locate where the market is large. The third part then shows how a similar logic induces such industries to locate in a transportation hub. The final part makes transportation costs endogenous, and shows how such hubs can emerge.

1. The basic model

The basic economic framework I will use is the monopolistic competition model of Dixit and Stiglitz (1977). There are two sectors, monopolistically competitive X and constant returns Y. Everyone shares a common utility function of the form

$$U = C_X^\pi C_Y^{1-\pi} \tag{1}$$

where π is the share of income spent on X, $1 - \pi$ the share spent on Y. C_X in turn is a CES aggregate of spending on a large number of potential products.

$$C_X = [\textstyle\sum_i C_i^\theta]^{1/\theta} \tag{2}$$

There is only one factor of production, labor. Y is produced using constant returns. To produce any variety of X, if it is produced, requires a fixed cost followed by constant variable cost:

$$L_{Xi} = \alpha + \beta\tau_{Xi} \tag{3}$$

There is full employment, with the X and Y sectors using the common factor L:

$$\textstyle\sum_i L_{Xi} + L_Y = L \tag{4}$$

Let us begin by considering a closed economy. The determination of market equilibrium in this model is by now familiar. Given a large number of actual products, each produced by only one firm, each firm will face a perceived elasticity of demand

$$\varepsilon = \frac{1}{1-\theta} \tag{5}$$

Given this constant elasticity of demand, the optimal policy is a constant proportional markup on marginal costs. Let labor be the numeraire, so that prices are measured in wage units. Then the profit-maximizing price of each firm producing a variety of X is

$$p_X = \frac{\beta}{\theta} \tag{6}$$

Next assume that there is free entry and exit of firms, so that profits are driven to zero. Then it can easily be shown that the equilibrium output per firm is

$$q_X = \frac{\alpha}{\beta} \frac{\theta}{1-\theta} \tag{7}$$

In a closed economy, the share of expenditure on X will equal the share of income earned in the production of X; since there are no profits, and wages are equalized across sectors, π will also be the share of the labor force employed in X. It follows that the number of products and firms in X is

$$n = \frac{\pi L(1 - \theta)}{\alpha} \qquad (8)$$

2. Trade between two regions: the home market effect

Let us now consider trade between two regions, given exogenous transportation costs. The basic result derived here, first shown in Krugman (1980), is that if one of the regions is sufficiently larger than the other, the production of the increasing returns sector X will be concentrated there.

Let us suppose, then, that there are two regions, 1 and 2. Each has a labor force, L^1 and L^2 respectively. We assume for the purposes of this paper that labor is immobile between regions. (As noted above, in other recent papers I have emphasized labor mobility as a source of "positive feedback" in interregional trade. The point of the immobility assumption is to put that force on one side; in practice I believe that transportation network effects and the forward and backward linkages resulting from factor mobility are mutually reinforcing.)

There are assumed to be transportation costs between the two regions. More specifically, it is assumed that while Y can be shipped costlessly, part of any shipment of X melts away en route – Samuelson's "iceberg" model of transport costs. We let $\tau < 1$ be the fraction of any X variety shipped that arrives, so that τ is an inverse index of transport costs.

As noted in Krugman (1980), when firms face constant elasticity demand in both countries, and when transport costs are a constant fraction of the price, the aggregate elasticity of demand that firms face is also constant; thus f.o.b. pricing continues to obey (6).

As long as both regions produce Y, their wages will necessarily be equal; we assume that this is the case. With equal wages, f.o.b. prices of firms producing X will also be equal at some common p_X.

I now make the following assertion: If L^1 is sufficiently larger than L^2, all X production will be concentrated in region 1.

To demonstrate this, we hypothesize a situation in which this is the case, then ask whether it would be profitable for a single firm to begin production in region 2.

Suppose, then, that there are n firms producing X varieties in region 1, and earning zero profits. Notice that consumers in both regions will spend a share π of their income on X. In region 2 part of this expenditure will go to transportation, but since transportation costs are incurred in the goods themselves, all of the spending still emerges as firm income. So the value of the sales of a typical region 1 firm, measured in wage units, is

$$p_X q_X^1 = \frac{\pi}{n}[L^1 + L^2]$$ (9)

Now suppose that a single firm considers beginning production in region 2. If it does so, it will be at disadvantage in region 1, because its c.i.f. price will be $1/\tau$ times as high as that of firms located in region 1; but it will be at a corresponding advantage in region 2. Let c^{ij} be the consumption by residents in region i of an X variety produced in region j; we have

$$\frac{c^{12}}{c^{11}} = \tau^\varepsilon$$ (10)

and

$$\frac{c^{22}}{c^{21}} = \tau^{-\varepsilon}$$ (11)

Firms are, however, interested not only in the final sales to consumers but in the goods used up in transit. Let z^{ij} be the direct and indirect consumption of an X-variety produced in region j by consumers in region i; we have

$$z^{12} = \frac{c^{12}}{\tau}$$ (12)

(Local sales, of course, incur no transport cost.)

Let us therefore define the parameter σ,

$$\sigma = \tau^{\varepsilon-1} < 1$$ (13)

It is apparent that the value of the sales of a single firm that produces in region 2 is

$$p_X q_X^2 = \frac{\pi}{n}\left[\sigma L^1 + \frac{1}{\sigma}L^2\right]$$ (14)

When will entry of such a firm be unprofitable? Since by construction firms in region 1 sell just enough to cover their fixed costs, entry in region 2 will be unprofitable if

$$p_X q_X^2 < p_X q_X^1$$ (15)

or

$$\sigma L^1 + \frac{1}{\sigma}L^2 < L^1 + L^2$$ (16)

It is immediately apparent that if L^1 is not sufficiently larger than L^2, the inequality (16) will not be satisfied: Jensen's inequality will see to that. So we must have a larger labor force in region 1. A little rearrangement of (16) leads to the basic criterion for concentration of X production in region 1,

$$\frac{L^1}{L^2} > \frac{1}{\sigma} \qquad (17)$$

From the definition of σ in (13), notice that the relative advantage in market size necessary to sustain industry concentration is less, the *lower* are transport costs (i.e., the higher is τ).

We may note as an aside that even if $L^1/L^2 < 1/\sigma$, the region with the larger labor force will still be a *net* exporter of X. Showing this is fairly intricate; readers are referred to Helpman and Krugman (1985), Ch. 10.

3. A three-region model: the hub effect

I now turn to a three-region model, and show that there is an effect closely related to the home market effect, which we can call the "hub" effect. If one of the three regions has better access to the other two regions than they have to each other, this superior access can lead to concentration of production in the increasing returns sector.

Let us therefore go to the world illustrated in Figure 3.1. The three regions have labor forces L^1, L^2, L^3. We let τ^{ij} be the share of an X variety shipped between regions i and j that survives, and assume an asymmetry in transport costs:

$$\tau^{12} = \tau^{13} = \tau > \tau^{23} = \tau' \qquad (18)$$

So it is cheaper to ship goods to and from the "hub" region 1 than between regions 2 and 3.

Suppose now that the three regions all have the same labor force L, so that there is no home market effect per se. Nonetheless, firms in 1 in effect have better market access than firms in the other regions. When is this sufficient to concentrate production in region 1?

Again we start by postulating concentrated production, then ask whether it is profitable for a single firm to produce elsewhere. The value of sales of a region 1 firm is simply

$$p_x q_x^1 = 3L\frac{\pi}{n} \qquad (19)$$

Without losing any generality, imagine a potential entrant into region 2. That firm is at a disadvantage in selling into region 1, where its product will be $1/\tau$ times as expensive as a local product; but region 1 firms will be at a corresponding disadvantage in region 2. The crucial difference comes in region 3, where the transport costs of hub firms will be less. Keeping in mind that transport costs are incurred in the goods themselves and thus enter into sales, we note that for the potential entrant

$$p_X q_X^2 = \frac{\pi L}{n} [\tau^{\varepsilon - 1} + \tau^{-(\varepsilon - 1)} + (\tau'/\tau)^{\varepsilon - 1}] \tag{20}$$

The criterion for concentration of production is thus that

$$\tau^{\varepsilon - 1} + \tau^{-(\varepsilon - 1)} + (\tau'/\tau)^{\varepsilon - 1} < 3 \tag{21}$$

The hub effect may now be seen. The first two terms of (21) necessarily sum to more than 2. The criterion for concentration can only therefore be met if the last term is sufficiently less than 1. That is, the costs of transportation to and from the hub must be sufficiently less than the costs of transportation between other locations.

It is apparent that given any value of τ, there is a critical value of τ': if τ' is below that critical value, a concentration of X production in the hub will take place. Let us define K as the criterion value (which must be less than 3 for full concentration to take place); we have

$$\frac{\partial K}{\partial \tau} = \frac{\varepsilon - 1}{\tau} \left[\tau^{\varepsilon - 1} - \tau^{-(\varepsilon - 1)} - \left(\frac{\tau'}{\tau} \right)^{\varepsilon - 1} \right] < 0 \tag{22}$$

and

$$\frac{\partial K}{\partial \tau'} = \frac{\varepsilon - 1}{\tau'} \left(\frac{\tau'}{\tau} \right)^{\varepsilon - 1} > 0 \tag{23}$$

So it must be true that a higher value of τ permits a higher value of τ' to be consistent with concentration of X in the hub.

Figure 3.2 shows the relationship between the critical value of τ' and that of τ for the case where $\varepsilon = 4$. Notice that formation of a concentration of X is possible only if τ is not too small, i.e., if transportation costs are not too large – otherwise it will be profitable to produce at least some X in non-hub locations even if transportation between 2 and 3 is impossible! For this case the minimum value of τ consistent with full hubness is 0.84. On the other hand, as τ approaches 1, it is straightforward to show that the gap between τ and τ' necessary to sustain a hub approaches zero – that is, when transport costs are small, even a slight difference in access will turn one location into a hub. Thus in general we expect concentration of production in transportation hubs when transportation costs are low, rather than when they are high – which is the same result that we get in examining the conditions for concentration of X production near the larger market.

So if one location has better transportation access than the other two, it will be a preferred location for production of goods subject to increasing

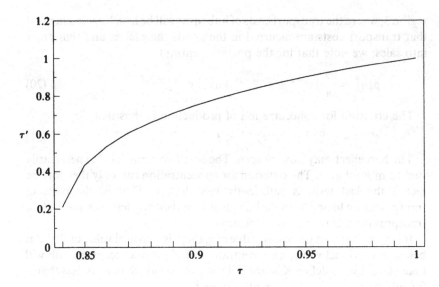

Figure 3.2

returns. Like many propositions involving increasing returns, this is something that is obvious to anyone who has *not* had training in economics; now that we have a model we can see that it is in fact obvious.

4. Endogenous transport hubs

Why should one location have better access to other locations than they have to one another? One possibility would be literal centrality of position. St Louis and Atlanta, for example, are airline hubs, while Boston is not, because St Louis and Atlanta are in the middle of the US, Boston at its edge.

But in the modern world centrality alone does not guarantee hub status. If it did, America's busiest airport would be in Memphis, not Chicago.

The reason that Memphis is not the transportation hub is, of course, that transportation is itself an activity subject to increasing returns. For that reason canals, railroads, and air routes have each in their eras created an "economic space" that, as Perroux (1950) noted, has a geometry that does not match that of space as seen on the map.

This leads to the evident point that a location's role as a hub can be self-sustaining. Consider Figure 3.1 again, and suppose that all X production is in fact concentrated in location 1. Then all interregional trade will flow along the sides of the triangle, as regions 2 and 3 trade Y for X. But if there are economies of scale in transportation itself, this will lead τ to be higher than τ' even if the three locations are symmetrically situated.

If X production had instead been localized at 2, of course, then trade would have flowed along the other sides of the triangle – and 2 would be the hub. So the position of a hub can be self-fulfilling, determined by history; again this is a typical result.

This paper has used a simple model to demonstrate two simple points: that transportation hubs are favorable locations for industries subject to increasing returns, and that a location's role as such a hub can be self-sustaining, giving a potential role to historical accident. In practice, transportation hubs usually reinforce their role by offering both the backward linkages of a large local market, and the forward linkages of local supplies of inputs – both linkages themselves depending crucially on increasing returns. What this paper's model does is to isolate a further reason for geographic concentration of industry that reinforces these other reasons.

References

Dixit, A. and J. Stiglitz 1977 "Monopolistic Competition and Optimum Product Diversity," *American Economic Review* 67, 297–308.

Helpman, E. and P. Krugman 1985 *Market Structure and Foreign Trade*, MIT Press, Cambridge, MA.

Isard, W. 1956 *Location and space-economy*, MIT Press, Cambridge, MA.

Krugman, P. 1980 "Scale Economies, Product Differentiation, and the Pattern of Trade," *American Economic Review* 70, 950–59.

1991a "History and Industry Location: the case of the US Manufacturing Belt," *American Economic Review* 81, 80–83.

1991b "Increasing Returns and Economic Geography," *Journal of Political Economy* 99, 483–99.

1991c "First Nature, Second Nature, and Metropolitan Location," NBER Working Paper.

Perroux, F. 1950 "Economic Space: Theory and Application," *Quarterly Journal of Economics* 64, 89–104.

4 International trade and factor mobility with an endogenous land frontier

Some general equilibrium implications of Christopher Columbus

RONALD FINDLAY

Adam Smith devoted no less than fifty-six pages of his great treatise to the subject of "the Advantages which Europe has derived from the Discovery of America", considering Columbus's voyages, and the almost contemporaneous journey to India around the Cape of Good Hope by Vasco da Gama, to be "the two greatest and most important events recorded in the history of mankind."[1] While the theme of the emergence and expansion of the "The Atlantic economy" has been one of the staple topics of economic historians it is surprising that it does not appear to have made much of an impression in the theoretical literature of international trade, perhaps because of the long Ricardian tradition of *defining* a "country" as a fixed bundle of resources existing independently of trade rather than as emerging in response to the opportunities opened up by trade itself.[2]

An important feature of the Discoveries was that they should not be considered as having made available at an instant a large additional supply of land and other natural resources. Rather they opened up a new "frontier" where land could be extended indefinitely but only at a rising marginal cost in terms of other real resources. Wilderness had to be cleared before crops could be grown, harvested and gathered. The westward movement of this frontier provided the historian Frederick Jackson Turner (1861–1932) with his famous thesis that it was the influence of this factor that was the key to the experience of American history, accounting for such features as "rugged individualism," democratic values and entrepreneurial vigor. Turner's thesis was refined and expanded by the Texas historian Walter Prescott Webb (1888–1963) into the concept of a "Great Frontier" for the core society of Western Europe that comprised not only the

I am indebted to Richard Baldwin, Andre Burgstaller, Richard Clarida, Max Corden, Stanley Engerman, Michael Gavin, Knick Harley, Kevin O'Rourke and Alwyn Young for very helpful comments.

[1] See Smith (1976), Vol. 2, Book 4, Ch. 7, Part III, p. 141.
[2] See J. H. Williams (1929) for a classic critique of the Ricardian model in this regard.

Americas but Australasia, Oceania and Southern Africa as well. Recently, yet another distinguished American historian, William H. McNeill, has integrated these considerations together with the eastern expansion of Russia into the steppes of Central Asia and Siberia into a global version of the original frontier thesis.[3]

Webb saw the Discoveries as a gigantic resource windfall for Western Europe. He estimated the population of that region to be about 100 million in 1500, with a land area of 3.75 million square miles. To this was added a vast potential of about 20 million square miles overseas as the direct result of the voyages, raising the available acres per capita from about 24 to 148, a six-fold increase. It was not until 1900 that the original per-capita ratio was once again attained, after an enormous increase in population.[4] The role of this factor in European development is also stressed in the stimulating work of Eric Jones (1981).

The overseas areas identified by Webb correspond to what the League of Nations statisticians used to refer to as "Regions of Recent Settlement." The aboriginal populations of these areas were decimated by contact with the early European settlers, through warfare but mostly by disease. Initially the New World resources were used for the cultivation and export of tropical products such as sugar, tobacco and cotton. The labor force that produced these crops were African slaves, while European workers were for the most part indentured servants. It is estimated that nearly 8 million Africans were taken to the New World as slaves before 1820, while the corresponding figure for Europeans who arrived free or indentured was less than 2 million, as little as one-fifth.[5] This early phase in the history of the Atlantic economy of the "triangular trade" involving slaves, raw materials and manufactures between Africa, the New World and Europe was succeeded from about the middle of the nineteenth century by an enormous torrent of Europeans going overseas, 46 million between 1846 and 1920.[6] These people produced the wheat, wool, beef and other products of the North American prairies, the Argentine pampas and the Australian outback. Accompanying this vast wave of settlers was the massive export of capital to provide the necessary infrastructure of transportation and housing.

Simultaneously with the opening of the new regions two other changes of great significance were taking place, a massive population upsurge and the technological breakthroughs of the Industrial Revolution. Together these processes fused into the creation of a truly global network of trade and factor

---

[3] See Turner (1920), Webb (1952) and McNeill (1983). Turner's thesis was first advanced in an essay of 1893. Webb's thesis is perceptively discussed in Chapter 3, "The New Frontier," of Elliott (1969).
[4] See Webb, p. 18.   [5] See McNeill, p.19.
[6] See Findlay (1990) for a model of the earlier phase of the Atlantic economy.

flows in the nineteenth century in which manufactures from Europe were exchanged for primary commodities from the "Great Frontier," with both types of output being produced by European capital and labor either at home or overseas. In the words of Alfred Marshall "the splendid markets which the old world has offered to the products of the new, since the growth of steam communication, have rendered North America, Australia and parts of Africa and South America, the richest large fields for the employment of capital and labor that there have ever been."[7] The details of the extent and timing of these unprecedented flows of goods, capital and people are conveniently summarized in Woodruff (1973). A brilliant perspective on the early history of the Atlantic migration is given by Bailyn (1988).

The purpose of the present paper is to provide a simple general equilibrium model that attempts to capture the stark outlines of the economic structure that emerged by the late nineteenth century as a consequence of the European discoveries four hundred years earlier. In addition to the general historical reflections on the significance of the frontier cited earlier, the specific inspiration was provided by the work of Guido Di Tella (1982) on Argentine experience. Kenen (1965) is another relevant contribution on the relation between natural resources, capital and trade. The analytical core of the model presented here, however, as of so much else in the trade theory of the last two decades, is the classic work of Ronald Jones (1971) on the role of "specific" factors in international trade. It is very interesting to note, however, the links between Jones's own work and the "staple" theory of the Canadian economic historian Harold Adams Innis that inspired the contributions of Chambers and Gordon (1966), Caves (1965, 1971) and Easton and Reed (1980). The relation between the approach taken in the present paper and the "staple" theory is provided in Findlay and Lundahl (1992).

1

A necessary prelude to our analysis of the impact of the discoveries is to first specify the closed world of "Europe" that existed prior to that event. There is a fixed endowment of labor and land available to this economy. One of the goods produced, "Food," has labor and land as inputs in a constant returns to scale production function

$$F = F(L_F, T) \tag{1}$$

of the usual neoclassical type, with positive first and negative second derivatives with respect to each argument. The supply of land T is fixed, and

---

[7] See Marshall (1890), p. 669.

used exclusively for Food. Essentially therefore we have the output of Food as a concave function of the labor input L_F.

Labor is also used to produce Manufactures. This good uses two additional inputs, capital K and raw material R. The production function is

$$M = \min \{H(L_M, K), R/\alpha\} \tag{2}$$

where H is a constant returns to scale neoclassical production function with the same qualitative properties as (1), while α is a constant. Thus capital and labor are substitutable in the production of the "final" output of M but there is a fixed proportion between the gross output of M and the intermediate input R.

We assume that capital is in perfectly elastic supply at a constant rate of time preference, equal to the rate of interest, ρ. This is consistent with a long-run view of capital accumulation in which the capital stock eventually adjusts to a level at which its marginal product is equal to the rate of interest or time preference. Capital, as in Ramsey and Solow, is of the same "stuff" as the output of manufactures, and so its marginal product is a pure number per unit time.

Under perfect competition, which we assume throughout, we will have as a result of profit maximization

$$(1 - \alpha p) h'(k_M) = \rho \tag{3}$$

where $h(k_M)$ is the production function H in intensive form, k_M is the ratio of K to L_M and p is the relative price of the raw material in terms of Manufacturers. The left-hand side of (3) is the "net" marginal product of capital.

Profit maximization under perfect competition also provides us with

$$(1 - \alpha p)\{h(k_M) - h'(k_M)k_M\} = w \tag{4}$$

and

$$\frac{\partial F}{q \partial L_F} = w \tag{5}$$

where w is the real wage in terms of Manufactures and q is the relative price of Food in terms of Manufactures. Together (4) and (5) imply that the marginal productivity of labor in Food, evaluated in terms of the *numeraire* good Manufactures, will be equal to the net marginal product of labor in Manufactures.

With Food and Manufactures as the only goods produced within the system we also have

$$L_F + L_M = \bar{L} \tag{6}$$

where $\bar{L}$ is the fixed endowment of labor.

The supply of the raw material R is assumed to be initially in fixed supply, determined exogenously by a monopolistic source of Mediterranean or Baltic supplies such as Venice or the Hanseatic League. This gives us

$$\alpha M = \bar{R} \tag{7}$$

which states that the demand αM for the raw material has to be equal to the supply $\bar{R}$.

We assume that the proceeds $p\bar{R}$ of the sale of the raw material to the Manufacturing sector are all paid in terms of the output of Manufactures and do not constitute income of Europe itself. It would of course be trivial to make part of this income, the "rent" accruing to the trading body, be earned by Europe. With the option that we have chosen national income is

$$Y = (1 - \alpha p) M + qF \tag{8}$$

the sum of "value added" in Manufactures and the value of Food output.

We now turn to the demand side of the model. Taking preferences as given, we have the budget constraint

$$Y = M_D + qF_D \tag{9}$$

and the demand function for food

$$F_D = F_D(Y, q) \tag{10}$$

where F_D and M_D are the demands for the two final goods, which are positively related to income and negatively to "own" relative prices. By Walras' Law we close the model by clearing either one of the two markets. We choose

$$F_D = F \tag{11}$$

Equations (8) to (11) enable us to show that M_D would equal $(1 - \alpha p)M$, which is therefore not an independent equation.

We thus have 11 equations in the 11 unknowns $p, q, w, L_F, L_M, K, Y, F, M, F_D$ and M_D, giving us a determinate system.

The determination of equilibrium is depicted in Figure 4.1. The positive relationship between L_F and F is simply the concave production function (1) for the Food sector. The negative relationship between L_F and F_D depends upon the working of the whole model. To establish this we first derive a positive relationship between L_F and q

$$q = q(L_F) \quad q'(L_F) > 0 \tag{12}$$

To each value of L_F there corresponds, from (6), a value of L_M. The fixed amount of $\bar{R}$ determines M by (7), and the production function H in (2) determines the corresponding value of K for each value of L_M. The ratio k_M

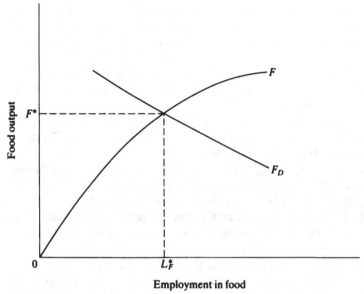

Figure 4.1

of K to L_M is therefore determined and hence the marginal product of capital $h'(k_M)$ as well. From (3) this determines the price p of the raw material. Equating the left-hand sides of (4) and (5) enables us to solve for q since $\partial F/\partial L_F$ also depends only on L_F. Thus we have derived the value of q corresponding to the given value of L_F. Increasing L_F lowers L_M and raises K, so k_M is increased. Raising k_M lowers p by virtue of (3). The higher k_M and lower p result in a higher value of w by (4). The higher L_F lowers $\partial F/\partial L_F$ and so must raise q by (5). This proves that $q'(L_F)$ is positive as required. The negative relationship between q and F_D from the demand function (10) finally allows us to obtain the negative relationship between L_F and F_D depicted in Figure 4.1, if income effects are not strong enough to overcome substitution effects, as we will assume here.

The intersection of the two functions in Figure 4.1 determines the equilibrium price ratio q^* and labor allocation L_F^* and thus the equilibrium values of all other 9 unknowns as well.

Our specification of the closed European economy on the eve of the discoveries has emphasized the effect of the "raw material constraint" in determining the limits of its potential. Capital is in perfectly elastic supply at a fixed interest rate and so is not a limiting factor while technological improvements in industry cannot achieve much in the face of the bottleneck in raw materials. Easing the raw material constraint by an increase in $\bar{R}$

however would raise the output of M directly by virtue of (7). For any given value of L_F the output of F will of course remain constant, i.e. the positive concave function in Figure 4.1 will be unchanged. Since a given L_F implies the same L_M, and M has increased because of the rise in $\bar{R}$, it follows that K must increase and therefore k_M as well. From (3) this means that p must fall since $h'(k_M)$ declines with a rise in k_M. At constant q it follows from (8) that Y must increase since p falls, M rises and F remains constant. Thus, from the demand function (10), the negative relation between L_F and F_D in Figure 4.1 must be shifted upwards for each value of L_F. The new equilibrium must therefore result in higher values of L_F and F. This implies that L_M falls so that K and k_M rise even more than at constant q, and the fall in p is also greater. The fall in p and the rise in k_M imply a higher w in (4), which together with the higher L_F implies a rise in q by (5).

Thus the easing of the raw material constraint results in increases in the outputs of both final goods and in the capital-intensity of production in Manufactures, as well as a rise in the relative price of Food. With limits on production set by the fixed supply of land and the scarcity of raw materials, production increase in Europe was also limited by the prospect of diminishing returns and declining per-capita incomes. The "animal spirits" of entrepreneurs and the flow of inventions would also be constricted in this closed world, as witnessed by the failure of the Eastern societies to develop in sustained fashion despite promising beginnings.

It is time, therefore, following Winston Churchill, to "call in the New World to redress the balance of the Old."

2

Our conception of America or the New World as a "Great Frontier" is that it is initially a vast wilderness from which an economic resource, land, denoted T_A, can be obtained only at an increasing marginal cost in terms of capital. We postulate that

$$K_A = \phi(T_A) \tag{13}$$

with

$$\phi' > 0, \quad \phi'' > 0, \quad \phi(0) = 0$$

In other words, the more the frontier is extended the higher is the marginal cost of an additional acre. Once the land is cleared it can be used to produce either Food F or the Raw Material R, in conjunction with labor. The production functions for these two goods will be of the usual neoclassical type, with constant returns to scale. The only source of labor in the whole system is the original European stock. The production system for

America is therefore summarized by (13) and the following four equations

$$F_A = F_A(L_A{}^F, T_A{}^F) \tag{14}$$

$$R_A = R_A(L_A{}^R, T_A{}^R) \tag{15}$$

$$T_A{}^F + T_A{}^R = T_A \tag{16}$$

$$(L_A{}^F + L_A{}^R) = L_A = \bar{L} - (L_E{}^F + L_E{}^M) \tag{17}$$

where $L_E{}^F$ and $L_E{}^M$ indicate European employment in Food and Manufacturing as described in the previous section. "Capital" is thus used either to produce Manufactures in Europe, according to the production function (2), or to clear land in America, as in (13). Equation (17) for the world economy now replaces equation (6) for Europe in isolation as the constraint on labor. It would of course be trivial to incorporate "native" American labor into the system but we prefer to emphasize the role of immigration from Europe in the starkest possible manner.

We will also assume that Food is land-intensive at any factor price ratio in America, i.e.

$$\frac{T_A{}^F}{L_A{}^F} > \frac{T_A{}^R}{L_A{}^R} \tag{18}$$

for all possible ratios of land rentals to real wages. America therefore has a Heckscher–Ohlin–Samuelson production structure except for the fact that both the endowments of land and labor are endogenous. There is perfect capital and labor mobility in the world economy so that the rate of interest ρ will prevail both in European industry and in clearing land in America, while the real wage will also be equalized on both sides of the Atlantic as well as between sectors in each region.

If we define π as the relative price of Food in terms of the Raw Material the Stolper–Samuelson theorem immediately determines for us the real wage and rent per acre in terms of either of those commodities, with the rent per acre an increasing, and the real wage a decreasing, function of π. In what follows we will vary π as a parameter and then obtain the general equilibrium of the whole system by clearing the world market for Food.

Since we have

$$w_F = w_F(\pi) \quad w'_F(\pi) < 0 \tag{19}$$

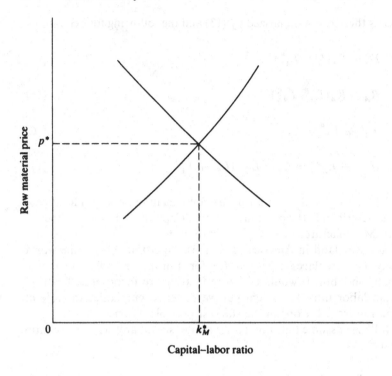

Figure 4.2

from the Stolper–Samuelson theorem, where w_F is the real wage in terms of Food in America, we also obtain

$$\frac{\partial F_E}{\partial L_E^{\,F}} = w_F(\pi) \tag{20}$$

i.e. the marginal product of labor in European production of Food must be equal to this same real wage by the hypothesis of perfect international labor mobility. This determines $L_E^{\,F}$ and F_E, employment and output in the European Food sector, as increasing functions of π.

The Stolper–Samuelson theorem also gives us $w_R(\pi)$, the real wage in terms of the Raw Material. The real wage in terms of Manufactures, w, is equal to $pw_R(\pi)$ where p, as in the previous section, is the price of Raw Material in terms of Manufactures.

Replacing w with $pw_R(\pi)$ in (4), equations (3) and (4) give us two equations in two unknowns p and k_M for any given value of π and hence $w_R(\pi)$. In Figure 4.2 the negatively sloped curve is the relation between p

and k_M given by (3) while the positively sloped curve is the relationship between these variables in (4), for a given value of π. The intersection of the two curves gives us p and k_M corresponding to the given value of π.

The Stolper–Samuelson theorem also gives us the rental per unit of land in terms of the Raw Material as a function of π, which will be denoted $g_R(\pi)$. Since we have just determined p as a function of π we have also determined the rental per unit of land in terms of Manufactures as a function of π, which we will denote as $r(\pi)$.

The hypothesis of perfect international capital mobility requires

$$\rho = \frac{r(\pi)}{\phi'(T_A)} = \frac{pg_R(\pi)}{\phi'(T_A)} \tag{21}$$

Thus, to each value of π, there is a unique value of T_A that makes $\phi'(T_A)$ satisfy (21).

What remains is to determine employment in Manufactures, as well as the capital engaged in that sector, along with the labor force migrating to America and the distribution of employment between the two sectors there and the corresponding output levels.

Suppose all the labor not employed in European agriculture ($\bar{L} - L_E^F$), were to be engaged in Manufactures. Since $k_M(\pi)$ is known we know what K_E^M, the total stock of capital in Manufactures, will be and also the level of output M and the demand for the Raw Material αM less the original exogenous supply $\bar{R}$. This gives us the excess demand for Raw Material which can only be supplied from America. In the absence of any labor force in the New World, however, this excess demand could not be satisfied since production in America would be zero. Enough European labor must therefore migrate to reduce demand for the Raw Material from European industry and increase its supply from production in America until demand is equal to supply in this market. The necessary equilibrium condition is

$$R_A\{\pi, T_A(\pi), L_A\} = \alpha h[k_M(\pi)]\{\bar{L} - L_E^F(\pi) - L_A\} - \bar{R} \tag{22}$$

It can be seen that this equation depends only on L_A, for any given value of π. The right-hand side of (22) gives us the excess demand for R in Europe which is a decreasing function of L_A since the larger is L_A the smaller is employment in Manufactures and hence output, since productivity per worker is determined by the given value of π.

Labor that emigrates to America can produce either Food or the Raw Material. For "small" amounts of L_A America will be completely specialized in Food. Once L_A attains a critical minimum, however, further increase in L_A will raise the output of the Raw Material and reduce the output of Food, by the Rybczynski theorem since the former is more labor-intensive. Given π there is therefore some value of L_A that equates the two sides of (22). This value of L_A also determines the output of Food in America and the allocation of land and labor in America between Food and the Raw Material.

The given value of π has therefore determined the supply of Food in America as well as in Europe. In other words we have a point on the "world supply curve" for Food. We now have to examine how the supply of Food in Europe and America will respond to an increase in π.

Since Food is land-intensive, an increase in π must result in a fall in the real wage in terms of Food in America, by the Stolper–Samuelson theorem, and hence in Europe also by the hypothesis of perfect international labor mobility. Thus employment in European agriculture must rise and hence the Food supply F_E as well.

We now examine the effect of the increase in π on equations (3) and (4) which we solved to obtain k_M and p corresponding to the given value of π. Equation (3) is independent of π so the negatively sloped curve in Figure 4.2 remains unchanged. The rise in π, however, reduces w_R in (4) because $w_R'(\pi) < 0$ by the Stolper–Samuelson theorem. This reduces the right-hand side of (4) for any given value of p and so k_M must fall for (4) to continue to hold, i.e. the real wage in terms of Manufactures must fall in the same proportion as w_R if p is held constant. Thus the positively sloped curve in Figure 4.2 shifts to the left and so p rises and k_M falls in response to the rise in π.

The rise in π must increase g_R, the rental per unit of land in terms of Raw Material in America, by the Stolper–Samuelson theorem, since Food is land-intensive. Because p also rises as a result of the increase in π it follows that $r(\pi)$ must also rise. Thus from (21) it follows that T_A must increase to make $\phi'(T_A)$ rise in proportion to $r(\pi)$ to make the ratio continue to equal ρ, because $\phi''(T_A)$ is positive. This gives us the crucial result that the extent of the frontier in the New World is an increasing function of the relative price of Food, the land-intensive good.

Our next task is to determine the effect of the increase in π on the extent of migration to America and hence on the output levels of Food and Raw Material in America and the corresponding output of Manufactures in Europe. To consider these questions suppose initially that L_A in (22) is constant while π increases. What will be the effect on the excess demand for Raw Material from America? It is immediately apparent that the left-hand side of (22), the supply of R_A, must fall if π rises and L_A is held constant. The rise in π means a fall in the relative price of the Raw Material and thus a decline in its supply if T_A is held constant along with L_A. But, as we have just seen $T'_A(\pi)$ is positive so that T_A goes up, which by the Rybczynski theorem means that the supply of R_A must fall even further. Thus we have a reduction in the supply of R_A at a constant value of L_A.

Turning now to the right-hand side of (22) we see that productivity per worker in Manufactures $h(k_M)$ must fall as a result of the rise in π since $k_M(\pi)$ is negative. Since L_E^F also rises as a result of the rise in π it is clear that the right-hand side of (22) must also fall. European demand and American supply of the Raw Material both fall as a result of the rise in π. We distinguish two cases below corresponding to whether the American supply falls by more or less than the reduction in European demand.

(a) If American supply falls by more than the European demand, migration to America L_A must increase to restore equilibrium. The increase in L_A will raise R_A, by the Rybczynski theorem, while it will reduce European output of Manufactures, and hence European demand for Raw Material, even further than what was induced by the rise in π at constant L_A. In America the higher T_A and L_A, combined with a higher π and a lower output of R_A, must result in a rise in the supply of Food from America F_A.

(b) Suppose, however, that American supply falls by less than the European demand for the Raw Material. Migration to America L_A must therefore fall to restore equilibrium in the market for the Raw Material. By the Rybczynski theorem this must increase F_A even more than by the rise in π with L_A constant.

Thus, in either case (a) or (b), the supply of Food from America F_A must rise in response to the rise in π. Since the supply of the Raw Material R_A also falls in either case it follows that the output of Manufactures in Europe must fall in either case in response to the rise in π and the associated rise in p.

In Section 1 we defined q as the relative price of Food in terms of Manufactures. It can be seen that

$$q = \frac{P_R}{P_M} \frac{P_F}{P_R} = p\pi \qquad (23)$$

and that since p is an increasing function of π it follows that q is also an increasing function of π.

The world economy as a whole can be considered as producing the final goods Food and Manufactures as a function of the relative price q, with the frontier and migration to the New World determined endogenously along with the output of the Raw Material. World income Y_W is determined for each value of π, and hence of q, as world output of Food and Raw Material plus value added in Manufactures. This is readily seen to be the same thing as the wage-bill of the total labor force $\bar{L}$ plus the income of land-owners in America and Europe and the profits of capital in the Manufactures sector

$\rho K_E{}^M$. The total rent of land in America is equal to the interest on the capital cost of clearing $\phi'(T_A)T_A$, evaluated at the margin.

World demand for Food can be specified as before as a positive function of world income Y^W and a negative function of the relative price q. The world supply of Food has been shown to be an increasing function of π, and hence q. We close the model by clearing the world market for Food by the condition

$$F_W{}^D[Y_W, q(\pi)] = F_A[q(\pi)] + F_E[q(\pi)] \tag{24}$$

The value π^* of π that satisfies (24) will also, of course, clear the world market for Manufactures, the supply of which has been shown to be negatively related to π and hence to q.

The general equilibrium of the entire world economy has therefore been determined.

3

The purpose of the present section is to consider the effects of some exogenous shocks on the variables of the system.

(a) *An increase in the labor force*

We begin with an increase in the total labor force $\bar{L}$ available to the system. In terms of the way in which we obtained the general equilibrium solution in the previous section we observe that to each parametric value of π the associated values of the factor prices, k_M and p will remain unchanged since all the relevant functional relationships are independent of the magnitude of the labor force. It is equation (22) that depends explicitly on $\bar{L}$. Thus if π and L_A are unchanged the left-hand side of (22) will remain unchanged. On the right-hand side, however, k_M and $L_F{}^E$ remain unchanged because real wages depend only on π but since $\bar{L}$ is increased employment and output in Manufactures will be higher and therefore the demand for Raw Material from America will also be higher. Therefore L_A has to be increased to increase the supply of the Raw Material from America and reduce the demand for it in Europe until the two are equal. Thus, at a constant π some of the increment in the labor force will migrate to America while the rest will be engaged on Manufactures in Europe. Employment in the Food sector in Europe, and hence output, remains unchanged because w_F depends only on π.

In America π and $T_A(\pi)$ are constant but L_A has increased. By the Rybczynski theorem this causes a reduction in the supply of the land-intensive good Food in America. Thus at each π and therefore q, since p depends only on π, there is a reduction in the world supply of Food, since

European supply is constant while American supply has decreased. World demand for Food has, however, increased since real factor prices are constant, the labor force is higher, and the supply of capital engaged in producing Manufactures is larger because k_M is unchanged and employment has increased. Thus π must rise to restore equilibrium in the world Food market and the system as a whole.

The rise in π will, of course, for reasons already given in the previous section, induce a chain of consequences for the other prices and quantities of the system. First, by the Stolper–Samuelson theorem, will be a fall in w_F and w_R and a rise in g_R. The fall in w_F will lead to a rise in $L_E{}^F$ and therefore Food output in Europe. The decline in w_R will lead to a rise in p and a fall in k_M. The rise in p and g_R raises the rental on land in America and therefore induces an extension of the frontier and an increase in T_A. The rise in π and p means that q must also rise. The rise in π and the extension of the frontier will both tend to increase the output of Food in America.

The increase in population, therefore, despite inducing an extension of the frontier and having the "safety valve" of emigration to America available, will nevertheless manifest itself in a decline in real wages and labor productivity in both agriculture and industry, where it causes a decline in capital-intensity.

For suitable values of the parameters the likely scenario would be for an expansion of output in all four sectors of production F_E, F_A, R_A, and M, and an increase in emigration L_A together with the expansion in T_A. Per capita real income would tend to fall along with real wages on both sides of the Atlantic. The only beneficiaries would be the land-owners, à la Ricardo.

(b) *An industrial revolution in Europe*

The main shock that we intend to subject the system to is an "industrial revolution" in Europe. This is conceived as a Hicks-neutral shift in the production function H for Manufactures, with α constant. A parameter λ, initially equal to unity but now increased can be inserted into all equations involving H or its intensive form h. We now investigate the impact of this shift on the entire system.

As before we hold π constant initially at its original equilibrium value π^*. Consider now equations (3) and (4) involving p and k_M, which give the values p^* and k_M^* corresponding to π^* before the technical change takes place. Inserting λ as a coefficient in front of $h'(k_M)$ in equation (3) and in front of $\{h(k_M) - h'(k_M)k_M\}$ in equation (4), differentiating totally with respect to λ and holding π^* constant the reader can verify that both p and k_M must increase in response to the increase in λ. In other words, the Industrial Revolution would raise the capital-intensity of production and the relative price of the Raw Material in terms of Manufactures. In terms of Figure 4.2 the downward sloping curve shifts to the right and the upward sloping curve to the left. Since λ is now greater than one and k_M rises it is clear that output per worker goes up in the industrial sector.

Holding π^* constant implies that w_F is constant also and hence so is employment and output of Food in Europe. Turning now to equation (22) we observe that if American endowments T_A^* and L_A^* are held constant along with π^* the output of the Raw Material in America, R_A^* will also be constant whereas the demand for the Raw Material from Europe will now be increased, since employment in industry is the same as before and productivity per worker has gone up both because of the increase in λ and the induced rise in k_M. The disequilibrium requires L_A to increase, raising R_A and reducing the demand from Europe until equation (22) is satisfied once more, but at a higher value of L_A than the original L_A^*. The increased migration to America raises R_A because that is the labor-intensive good; the output of the land-intensive good Food in America must therefore contract at π^* by the Rybczynski effect.

The technical progress in European industry and the associated rise in capital-intensity, at a constant value of π, imply an increase in world real income. With homothetic preferences the demand for Food at constant relative prices must therefore be higher. As we have shown, however, the supply of Food at constant π is unchanged in Europe and reduced in America. There is consequently a positive world excess demand for Food at unchanged relative prices. Equilibrium can only be restored by an increase in π and associated increases in p and q.

From equation (21) we see that the rise in π will raise g_R as well and since p increases also the rental $r(\pi)$ in the numerator goes up. This induces an extension of the frontier T_A to drive up the marginal cost $\phi'(T_A)$ of land clearance appropriately to equate the return to ρ. The rise in π thus not only leads to diverting existing resources to Food in America, but induces an extension of the frontier as well. In Europe the rise in π that reduces w_F in America lowers the real wage in European agriculture by the mobility hypothesis and so increases employment and output in Food in Europe.

The rise in migration to America that we noted at constant π cannot be reversed even after the full general equilibrium adjustments to π and T_A have been made. This is because the increase in world real income and the fall in the relative price of Manufactures implied by the rise in q associated with the rise in π mean that consumption of Manufactures must be higher. This means that R_A must be higher. Since π and T_A are both higher, and each has a negative impact on R_A, this implies that L_A must be higher than before for R_A to be higher than originally, because the Raw Material is the relatively labor-intensive good.

The interested reader can work out the effects of other exogenous shocks, such as technical progress in either of the goods produced in America, or in Food production in Europe.

The model as it stands confines the production of Manufactures to Europe, and thus represents a stage prior to significant industrialization getting underway in America. If America has the identical technology for Manufactures available, however, production of this commodity could take place indifferently on either side of the Atlantic, since capital and labor are both "foot loose" in this model.[8] A historically reasonable hypothesis would be that America is initially less efficient, and that tariffs are necessary to launch industrialization as was in fact the case. Protection of European agriculture is another problem that could be studied within the present framework.

We hope therefore to have marked the fifth centennial of the voyage of the "Admiral of the Ocean Sea" by a modest memorial – a small-scale general equilibrium model that attempts to capture the "stylized facts" of the new Atlantic world that it brought into being.

References

Bailyn, B. 1988 *The Peopling of British North America: An Introduction*, Vintage Books, New York.

Caves, R. E. 1965 "Vent for Surplus Models of Trade and Growth," in R. E. Baldwin *et al.* (eds.) *Trade, Growth and the Balance of Payments*, Rand McNally, Chicago.

1971 "Export-Led Growth and the New Economic History," in J. Bhagwati *et al.* (eds.) *Trade, Balance of Payments and Growth*, North-Holland, Amsterdam.

Chambers, E. J. and D. F. Gordon 1966 "Primary Products and Economic Growth: An Empirical Measurement," *Journal of Political Economy* (August).

Di Tella, G. 1982 "The Economics of the Frontier," in C. P. Kindleberger and G. Di Tella (eds.) *Economies in the Long View: Essays in Honor of W. W. Rostow*, 1, Macmillan, London.

Easton, S. and C. Reed 1980 "The Staple Model," mimeo, Simon Fraser University.

Elliott, J. H. 1969 *The Old World and the New – 1492–1650*, Cambridge University Press.

Findlay, R. 1990 "The Triangular Trade and the Atlantic Economy of the 18th Century: A Simple General Equilibrium Model," *Essays in International Finance*, No. 117, International Finance Section, Princeton University.

Findlay, R. and M. Lundahl 1992 "Natural Resources, Vent for Surplus and the Staple Theory," Mimeo, Columbia University (January).

Jones, E. L. 1981 *The European Miracle*, Cambridge University Press.

Jones, R. W. 1971 "A Three-Factor Model in Theory, Trade and History," in J.

---

[8] I am indebted to Alwyn Young for making this important point.

Bhagwati *et al.* (eds.) *Trade, Balance of Payments and Growth*, North-Holland, Amsterdam.

Kenen, P. B. 1965 "Nature, Capital and Trade," *Journal of Political Economy* (October).

Marshall, A. 1938 *Principles of Economics*, Macmillan, London, 8th edn (1st edn, 1890).

McNeill, W. H. 1983 *The Great Frontier*, Princeton University Press.

Smith, A. 1976 *The Wealth of Nations*, University of Chicago Press (1st edn 1776).

Turner, F. J. 1920 *The Frontier in American History*, Henry Holt, New York.

Webb, W. P. 1986 *The Great Frontier*, University of Nebraska Press (1st edn 1952).

Williams, J. H. 1926 "The Theory of International Trade Reconsidered," *Economic Journal* (June).

Woodruff, W. 1973 "The Emergence of an International Economy 1700–1914," in C. M. Cipolla (ed.) *The Fontana Economic History of Europe*, Vol. 4, Part 2, Ch. 11, Fontana, London.

5 Directions of lumpy country trade

ALAN V. DEARDORFF

1. Introduction

The Heckscher–Ohlin Model of international trade makes a strong statement, in the form of the Heckscher–Ohlin (H–O) Theorem, about what goods a country will export and import. These and other implications of the H–O Model have been amply demonstrated by Jones (1956), as well as in his subsequent writings. The H–O Model has very little to say, however, about with whom these goods will be exchanged, even though there is evidence that the bilateral trade of at least some countries has a distinctive pattern that is reminiscent of the H–O Theorem, in that they export goods of different factor intensities to different trading partners. That is, countries are observed to export more capital-intensive goods to less capital-abundant countries, and less capital-intensive goods to more capital-abundant countries.[1]

This behavior, which I will call "cross-over trade," does not arise in the usual H–O model with free trade, although I have, in Deardorff (1987), explored how it can be obtained in such a model by introducing transportation costs of various sorts.[2] Here, however, I will explore the fact

---

[1] This paper arose from a suggestion of Dick Porter who, when told a little about another paper, Courant and Deardroff (1992), jumped to the conclusion that it was about this. It wasn't, but it was a great idea. Thanks, Dick. I have also benefited from comments of Ron Jones, Bob Stern, and other participants in the Conference and in seminars at The University of Michigan and Princeton.

[1] The seminal empirical observation of this phenomenon was for Japan by Tatemoto and Ichimura (1959). They compared the factor intensities of Japan's exports to the two groups of developed and developing countries, rather than looking explicitly at the factor endowments of the trading partners. The pattern was reconfirmed for Japan by Heller (1976) and Urata (1983). However, Urata tested for the pattern using regression coefficients rather than actual factor intensities, and found it in data for 1975 but not 1967. Similar evidence for India is contained in Khanna (1982), which also contains other references to work on this subject.

[2] Deardorff (1987) adds transport costs to the model of Jones (1974), who had shown how a country of intermediate factor abundance will specialize in a small range of goods of intermediate factor intensity. Without transport costs, all goods in this range are exported to

---

that this same behavior is also likely to arise even with free trade within another modification of the H–O Model that Paul Courant and I have dealt with more recently. In Courant and Deardorff (1992) we show that if countries are "lumpy," in the sense of having intra-national regions that differ in their relative factor endowments, then that lumpiness can contribute to a pattern of trade that is contrary to the H–O Theorem. It is straightforward that such lumpiness can also lead to cross-over trade, since a lumpy country is in effect an aggregate of more than one country, each with different factor endowments. Heckscher–Ohlin trade for each is then cross-over trade for the aggregate. I will explore this result in more detail, however, in order to delineate the combinations of factor endowments that will give rise to it.

The lumpy country model of Courant and Deardorff (1992) includes only two goods and two factors of production, identified there as labor and land. Here I will rename the factors labor and capital, so as to correspond to the empirical observation mentioned above, though as usual in models of this sort, the names of the factors have nothing to do with their characteristics. Both labor and land are simply generic factors of production, available in fixed supplies and entering symmetrically into the production functions for producing goods.

I will also allow here for three goods instead of two. With only two goods, as already explored in Courant and Deardorff (1992), while the two regions of the country may individually export different goods, the country as a whole exports only one. Therefore it cannot display the phenomenon of cross-over trade. With a third good, however, each region can export a different good at the same time that both import a third, and this pattern, as it turns out, may well have the property of cross-over trade. Therefore a three-good lumpy-country model seems to be an appropriate place to examine this phenomenon.

With three goods and two factors, there are two fundamentally different cases that may arise on the world market, and the behavior of any country within the world depends importantly on which of these cases obtains. These two cases are laid out in some detail in section 2 of the paper. On the one hand, the prices of the three goods may be perfectly aligned, such that production of all three goods is possible in any country or region with an appropriate factor endowment. Since in that case all such countries would have the same factor prices, I will call this the case of World Factor Price Equalization, or WFPE prices.[3] Alternatively, if prices of the three goods

all trading partners. With transport costs, goods near the ends of this range cannot be profitably exported to countries of very similar factor endowments, giving rise to differences in the country's exports to different trading partners.

[3] This is not to say that factor prices would in fact be the same in all countries in this case. FPE

do not line up exactly in this way, then any country confronting them with free trade will be able to produce at most only two of the three goods. In that case, which pair of goods is produced in a country, as well as the factor prices that support that production, will differ across countries depending on their factor endowments. I will call that the case of World Specialization, or WS prices.[4]

After first elaborating on these two configurations of prices as they relate to homogeneous countries in section 2, I will then consider the case of a lumpy country facing WFPE prices first, in section 3, since this is the case that seems to dominate international trade theory. I will then turn briefly in section 4 to the case of a lumpy country facing WS prices, which is the case that I find to be the more plausible description of the world economy.

2. Price configurations with three goods and two factors

The two possible configurations for world prices in the three-good, two-factor model are shown in panels A and B of Figure 5.1. Both panels show the familiar Lerner–Pearce diagram of trade theory adapted for the case of three goods. Exogenous prices of the goods, p_1, p_2 and p_3, enter the diagram by determining, together with a constant returns to scale technology for producing each good, a set of unit-value isoquants, $X_1 = 1/p_1$, $X_2 = 1/p_2$, and $X_3 = 1/p_3$.

In panel A of Figure 5.1, these three isoquants happen to line up exactly so that a single common tangent touches all three. This common tangent is the unit isocost line consistent with producing any more than one of the three goods, and its intercepts with the axes indicate the reciprocals of the corresponding factor prices, $1/w^0$ and $1/r^0$. If these factor prices prevail, then potential producers in the three industries will employ capital and labor in the ratios k_1, k_2, and k_3 respectively, as shown by the rays from the origin through the respective tangencies with the unit isocost line.

will hold only for those countries whose factor endowments are within the single diversification cone corresponding to these prices, and in a world of many countries there may well be many countries outside the cone. In fact, strictly speaking, there need be no more than one country inside the diversification cone, in which case factor prices would not have to be equalized across any pair of countries, though that possibility has a rather unlikely feel about it. The importance of WFPE, then, is simply the existence of a cone of factor endowments within which all three goods could be produced and factor prices would be equalized for any countries that happen to be in the cone.

[4] Again, the label WS may suggest more specialization than will in fact occur. With free trade, it is still possible in the WS case for every country to produce two of the three goods, so long as their factor endowments lie in one of the two cones of diversification that I will identify below. And with trade impediments of sufficient size, WS prices could be consistent with every country producing every good. The point of WS prices, then, is that producers who face them unprotected by trade impediments will not be able to diversify completely into production of all three goods.

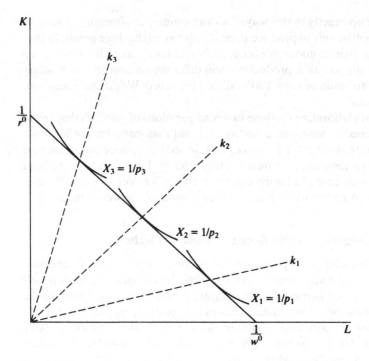

Figure 5.1A

As is well known from the literature on factor price equalization, whether these factor prices will in fact prevail in a particular country depends on whether its factor endowment lies inside or outside of the diversification cone defined by the k_1 and k_3 rays. If endowments lie outside this cone, then only one good – either X_1 or X_3 – will be produced, and factor prices will be given not by the common tangent but rather by the slope of the one isoquant that is in use. If on the other hand endowments do lie inside the diversification cone, then the factor prices will indeed be w^0 and r^0 and production of more than one good will be possible. In this case of more goods than factors, however, the exact outputs of the goods, and even which of the three are produced at all, are indeterminate, as shown in Melvin (1968).

Panel B of Figure 5.1 is quite different. Here, the prices of the goods again determine three unit value isoquants, but they do not now share a common tangent. Instead, there is one unit isocost line tangent to the unit value isoquants for X_1 and X_2, with corresponding factor prices w^1 and r^1, and a second unit isocost line tangent to X_2 and X_3 with factor prices w^2 and r^2. At the first of these sets of factor prices, w^1 and r^1, goods

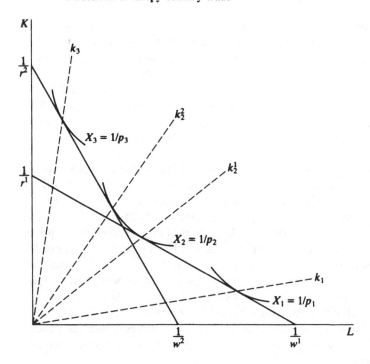

Figure 5.1B

1 and 2 can both be produced – using capital–labor ratios k_1 and k_2^1 – but good 3 cannot. At the second set of factor prices, on the other hand, goods 2 and 3 can be produced together using techniques k_2^2 and k_3, but industry 1 shuts down.

Thus in panel B there are many different possible patterns of specialization and also of factor prices, and which obtains in a given country will depend on its factor endowments. If a country's endowments lie in the first diversification cone, between k_1 and k_2^1, then it will have factor prices w^1 and r^1 and it will produce goods 1 and 2. If its endowments lie instead in the second diversification cone, between k_2^2 and k_3, it will have factor prices w^2 and r^2 and produce goods 2 and 3. Finally, if its endowments lie outside both of these cones, then it will produce only one good, exactly as in the extreme cases of specialization in panel A. However, these possibilities of specialization now include also the intermediate case in which endowments are not extreme at all, but rather lie between k_2^1 and k_2^2 and the country produces only the good of intermediate factor intensity, good 2.

What determines which of these cases occurs? If prices of goods were chosen randomly, then it would seem that the configuration in panel B would be much more likely, since panel A requires the coincidence of prices that line up exactly. However, in a world where all countries share these same technologies it is clear that prices cannot be chosen randomly. If they were, then another configuration, not shown in Figure 5.1, would be just as likely as panel B: a case in which the X_2 unit value isoquant lies further from the origin than the common tangent to the isoquants of X_1 and X_3. However with that price configuration good 2 would not be produced anywhere in the world, and the configuration cannot therefore represent an equilibrium.

Thus the requirements of world market equilibrium impose some constraints on what prices may arise, and these requirements may therefore make the configuration in panel A be much more likely than it at first appears. In fact it is the configuration that has been most commonly assumed in modern trade theory, where cases of international factor price equalization tend to dominate the literature. For notice that in panel A, applied now to all countries of the world, factor prices will be equalized for all countries whose factor endowments happen to lie within the single diversification cone, between k_1 and k_3, and this could conceivably include all countries of the world, if their factor endowments were not to differ too much compared to the differences in factor intensities of the industries. Therefore I have labelled this the case of world factor price equalization, or WFPE prices.

In contrast, in panel B, factor prices *cannot* be equalized for all countries. Factor prices are the same for any pair of countries whose endowments lie within the same one of the two diversification cones. But it is not possible for all countries in the world to lie within the same cone, since that would mean one of the goods could not be produced anywhere in the world. Thus for the prices in panel B to represent an equilibrium there must be at least two sets of factor prices prevailing in different countries of the world. It also follows that goods 1 and 3 cannot be produced in the same country, so that there must be at least a certain amount of specialization in the countries of the world. Therefore I have labelled this the case of world specialization, or WS prices.

There is not space here for me to discuss which of these two cases is the more likely. Twenty years ago there was a flurry of articles addressing this question, starting apparently with Johnson (1967) and culminating in a fascinating paper by Vanek and Bertrand (1971). The latter concluded – based upon a geometric extension of the world transformation curve to three, four, and then higher dimensions – that world factor-price equalization becomes increasingly likely as the number of goods in the economy increases. Fascinating as this argument was, however, I have found myself increasingly skeptical over the years that world factor-price equalization provides the best description of the world economy.[5] Therefore I will deal with each of the two cases in turn in the sections below.

3. The case of world factor price equalization

Suppose then that a small economy faces world prices that are aligned as in Figure 5.1A. To neutralize effects of factor endowments on the trade of the country as a whole, I will first consider the very special case of what I will call zero net factor-content trade. This is the case of a country whose total factor endowments would permit it to produce exactly what it consumes at free trade prices, if these factors were perfectly mobile within the country between regions. With the indeterminancy of output that arises when goods outnumber factors, as they do here, there may still be trade in goods, but the factor content of that trade will be zero. An advantage of this assumption is that any net trade in factor content that then arises when lumpiness is introduced can be attributed to that lumpiness, just as in Courant and Deardorff (1992). And, as will be the case, if lumpiness also forces a particular pattern of trade in goods that would not otherwise arise, that too can be attributed to the effects of lumpiness. How trade patterns in both goods and factor content will vary if this is not the case will be considered briefly later in this section.

Zero net factor-content trade

Figure 5.2 shows the production Edgeworth Box for this country, whose total factor endowments, $\bar{L}$ and $\bar{K}$, are at point E. Since it would be possible to produce all three goods only if this factor endowment lay within the diversification cone, $(\bar{L}, \bar{K})$ must be consistent, at world prices and hence at the factor prices shown in Figure 5.1A, with the use of the techniques of production in each industry indicated in Figure 5.1A as k_1, k_2, and k_3.

Assume identical and homothetic preferences for consumers throughout the country, so that total demand for each good is independent of the distribution of income within the country between regions, so long as total income is constant.[6] Let $\tilde{X}_1$, $\tilde{X}_2$, and $\tilde{X}_3$ be these quantities demanded in the country at world prices. Also let the vectors $\tilde{v}_1$, $\tilde{v}_2$, and $\tilde{v}_3$ represent the amounts of factors needed to produce these quantities in each industry using the techniques of production k_1, k_2 and k_3. These vectors have the

---

[5] My skepticism arises primarily from casual observation, but I have also found additional theoretical reasons for skepticism in Deardorff and Courant (1990) and in Deardorff (1991).
[6] Total income is constant only as long as factor prices remain equalized. See footnote 9 below.

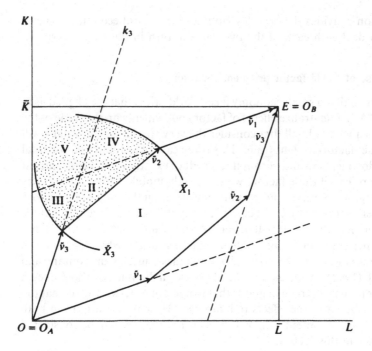

Figure 5.2

same slopes as k_1, k_2 and k_3 respectively, and their lengths are determined by the demands for the goods. Because we are in a special case of zero net factor-content trade, where the country is capable of producing exactly what it consumes in free trade, these three vectors must add up to the country's total factor endowment at E. This is indicated in Figure 5.2 by drawing them into the Edgeworth Box end to end starting with the origin and forming a path through the box that ends just at its upper right-hand corner, E. There are several such paths that could be drawn, depending on the order in which the vectors are selected. Of special interest are the two paths shown in Figure 5.2, $O\tilde{v}_1\tilde{v}_2\tilde{v}_3$ and $O\tilde{v}_3\tilde{v}_2\tilde{v}_1$, where the vectors are arranged in order of increasing and decreasing capital intensity respectively. These two paths, and the factor rays of which their segments are a part, will make it possible to map out areas in factor space where various trade patterns arise once factors are lumpy.

Suppose now that the country is divided into two regions, A and B, each endowed with its own labor and capital in amounts that add up to the country's endowment at E. As in Courant and Deardorff (1992), one can represent the allocation of these factors between the two regions by points within the Edgeworth Box, measuring, say, Region A's endowment from the lower-left corner at O and Region B's endowment from the upper-right corner at E.[7] One can then compare the allocation point to the various factor rays and isoquants to determine the possible outputs of the three goods in the two regions.

Suppose first that the allocation point lies within what is labelled as area I of the box – the hexagonal area formed by the two paths from O to E just described. In that case both regions' factor endowments lie within the diversification cone defined by k_1 and k_3, and they will therefore share the common world factor prices. Furthermore, it is easily verified that the vectors $\tilde{v}_1$, $\tilde{v}_2$, and $\tilde{v}_3$ can be divided between them in such a way that the two together produce exactly what the country demands. Therefore area I corresponds to the possibility of no trade.[8]

Consider, at the opposite extreme, the area of the box labelled V. Here both regions of the country are outside of the diversification cone and cannot share factor prices that are equal to each other's or to those in the world. Instead, Region A must specialize completely in good 3, and have the rather high wage–rental ratio implied by the X_3 isoquant through its endowment point (not shown). Region B, in contrast, specializes in good 1 and has a much lower wage–rental ratio. Furthermore, because both (relative to their respective origins) are above the isoquants $\tilde{X}_1$ and $\tilde{X}_3$ for producing what the country demands, they must produce more of their respective goods than are needed domestically and must export the difference to the world market.[9] In addition, since neither produces good 2 at all, they both must import it from the world market.

Assuming that the rest of the world is composed of many countries of varying factor abundances for which the Heckscher–Ohlin Theorem applies conventionally, this then is a clear example of cross-over trade. Because of its lumpiness in area V of the box, this country exports both the most labor-intensive and the most capital-intensive goods, and imports the

[7] This is not strictly an Edgeworth Box, which would more commonly measure industry factor employments, rather than regional factor endowments, from these opposite corners. The use here is similar to the technique of Dixit and Norman (1980, pp. 110–22) for determining patterns of specialization in two trading countries. It is also somewhat related to a diagram of Lancaster (1957).

[8] Throughout the diversification cone with more goods than factors, outputs are, of course, indeterminate. Therefore, while it is possible in area I for there to be no trade, it is also possible for there to be trade. I will be concerned here only with the trade that *must* arise due to lumpiness, not the trade that *may* arise solely because of the indeterminacy of output.

[9] This conclusion requires the assumption made earlier that preferences in the two regions be identical and homothetic. If that were not the case, then different incomes in the two regions could lead to a level of total consumption of the goods that would differ from the levels $\tilde{X}_1$ and $\tilde{X}_3$. Furthermore, because of the inefficiency of the factor allocation in area V, national income will be somewhat lower than it could have been if factors were mobile between regions. Thus with homothetic preferences, and hence normal goods, the amounts "needed domestically" are actually lower than $\tilde{X}_1$ and $\tilde{X}_3$.

good of intermediate factor intensity. Since more labor-abundant countries will also tend to export the labor-intensive good, this country's exports of good 1 will have to go instead to the more capital abundant countries of the world. And, since the latter will export the capital-intensive good, this country's exports of good 3 will have to go to the more labor abundant countries. With good 2 imported from whomever produces it – presumably countries of intermediate factor abundance – this is exactly the phenomenon of cross-over trade that was identified above.

How general is this phenomenon? Does it only arise when regions of a country are so disparate that they specialize in this extreme fashion? The answer is no, as it turns out, as can be seen by looking at area II of the box in Figure 5.2.

In area II, both regions of the country have factor endowments within the $k_1 - k_3$ diversification cone, and therefore both will share the world factor prices. That is, there is factor-price equalization throughout the parallelogram formed by the two k_1 and k_3 rays, exactly as in the two-good case of Courant and Deardorff (1992). However, it is not true that there can be no trade at these points.

For an allocation in area II, Region A, for example, is so close to the k_3 ray that it must produce a very large proportion of good 3 in order to keep its factors fully employed, and in fact it must produce more of good 3 than $\tilde{X}_3$. This is illustrated in Figure 5.3, where an Edgeworth Box for Region A alone is drawn assuming a regional factor allocation that corresponds to area II in Figure 5.2. As shown, in order to keep its factors fully employed, Region A could produce goods 3 and 2, with an output of the former of X_3^1. Or it could produce goods 3 and 1, with an output of the former of X_3^2. Or it could produce a convex linear combination of these two possibilities. But in any case, its output of good 3 must be at least X_3^1, and this is clearly greater than $\tilde{X}_3$.

By the same reasoning, Region B in area II also must produce an amount of good 1 that exceeds $\tilde{X}_1$, the amount that the country as a whole demands of that good. Therefore, in area II, both regions produce more of a good of extreme factor intensity than can be absorbed at home, and both must therefore export these goods to the world market, exactly as in area V discussed above.

Continuing the argument, it is clear that areas III and IV also have this property, for a mixture of the reasons in areas II and V. Thus, throughout the shaded areas II–V of Figure 5.2, the country displays cross-over trade.

For other unmarked areas in the upper left of Figure 5.2, cross-over trade may still occur, though it is less likely because one of the regions of the country may not produce enough of any good to satisfy the country's demand and still have anything left to export. At the left of the figure, for example, for allocations below the $\tilde{X}_3$ isoquant and above the k_3 ray,

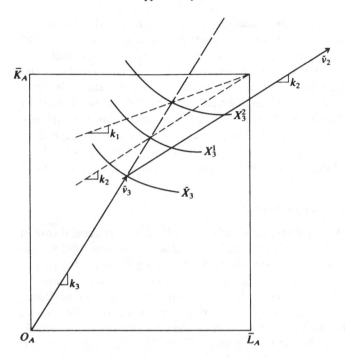

Figure 5.3

Region A produces only good 3, but it produces less of it than would have been demanded with mobile factors. This does not quite preclude its exporting, however, since the inefficiency of specialization will reduce national income somewhat, and also therefore reduce the country's demand for good 3 below $\tilde{X}_3$. Thus there will be a small part of the figure, just below the $\tilde{X}_3$ isoquant (and another above the $\tilde{X}_1$ isoquant) where cross-over trade will still take place. However, for most of the other allocations to the left and above area I there will not be cross-over trade because only one good will be exported, and only one region of the country will export it. Of course, these results for the north-west portion of the Box are duplicated in the south-east, where exactly symmetric results obtain.

Thus, for the special case considered so far of WFPE prices and zero net factor-content trade when factors are interregionally immobile, lumpiness of factors can indeed lead to trade. If factors are sufficiently lumpy – that is, if they are sufficiently unevenly allocated across regions – and if both regions remain sufficiently large that they may need to trade with the outside world, then the phenomenon of cross-over trade arises quite naturally.

I would also note that this trade, caused by lumpiness, is trade in goods, and need not involve any net trade in factor content. In area II of Figure 5.2, for example, the factor content of production is equal to the factor content of consumption, and the net factor content of trade is therefore still zero. Thus lumpiness may lead to trade in goods that is contrary to the Heckscher–Ohlin model in another sense: it is not detectable by a Leontief-like factor-content test of trade patterns.[10] Likewise, outside of areas I and II, where at least one region of the country completely specializes, the factor content of trade may well be nonzero, though since different techniques of production are then optimal within different regions, this will depend in part on how one chooses to measure factor content.[11]

Nonzero net factor-content trade

Now consider briefly how results may change in the more general case in which the country would not be able to produce its consumption bundle under free trade if factors were mobile. Such a case is shown in Figure 5.4. Here the three vectors indicating the factor requirements of consumption, $\tilde{v}_1, \tilde{v}_2$, and $\tilde{v}_3$, add up to point C that is different from the endowment point, E. With balanced trade, the value of consumption must equal the value of income, and therefore point C must lie on the same isocost line as point E, valued at the world factor prices shown in Figure 5.1. With a nonzero factor content of trade, however, C could lie either to the right or to the left of point E, depending on the nature of the goods demanded and hence on the factor content of consumption.

As drawn, point C lies to the right of E, so that the country (with free trade and mobile factors) is a net importer of labor and a net exporter of capital in factor content terms. One therefore expects a certain bias in favor of the country exporting the more capital-intensive good. Of interest is whether lumpiness can nonetheless cause one of the regions of the country to export the labor-intensive good.

Areas of the box that delineate various trade patterns are somewhat more complex than before, and I will therefore concentrate only on the top half of the box, above its (undrawn) diagonal. Symmetric remarks apply below.

The path $O\tilde{v}_3\tilde{v}_2\tilde{v}_1$ from O to C now yields information about production and specialization only in Region A. To determine analogous information about Region B, a parallel path, $E\tilde{v}_1\tilde{v}_2\tilde{v}_3$, needs to be drawn downward and to the left from the country's endowment point, E, which also is the origin

---

[10] See Deardorff (1984) for a discussion of such tests.

[11] In Deardorff (1982) a version of the Heckscher–Ohlin Theorem is derived measuring factor content (and factor intensity) in terms of techniques actually used to produce each unit of a good, wherever that production may occur. That theorem continues to be valid here, though its usefulness is clouded by the variety of techniques that may be in use in different locations.

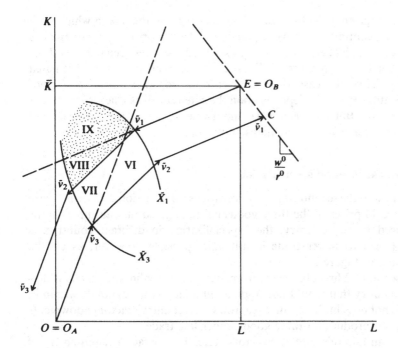

Figure 5.4

for measuring Region B's factor endowments. Inserting also the $\tilde{X}_3$ and $\tilde{X}_1$ isoquants relative to O and E respectively, one can identify additional areas of the box that bear discussing.

Consider area VI, for example. Here Region A is again in the situation of Figure 5.3, where it must produce more than $\tilde{X}_3$ of good 3 and must export it. However Region B is now not in that situation with respect to good 1, and in fact one cannot place any useful restrictions on Region B's outputs of the three goods in area VI. Thus while it is possible that cross-over trade may occur here, it is by no means assured. And this continues to be the case even in area VII of the box, where Region A now completely specializes in good 3 in excess of $\tilde{X}_3$.

In areas VIII and IX, on the other hand, cross-over trade is assured. In area VIII, Region B is in the situation of Figure 5.3, not specialized but producing more than $\tilde{X}_1$ of good 1. In area IX, it is specialized in good 1, again in excess of $\tilde{X}_1$. In either case, since Region A is also producing more than $\tilde{X}_3$ of good 3 in both areas, cross-over trade must occur. Thus cross-over trade once again occurs in the shaded area of Figure 5.4.

Note that the interesting case of area II from Figure 5.2 has now been diminished in importance, and could be eliminated entirely if net factor trade is large enough. In Figure 5.4 the portion of the box in which both countries continue to have equal world factor prices but nonetheless produce enough of goods 1 and 3 to export has been reduced to a tiny sliver at the north-east tip of area VIII. And it could easily have been eliminated entirely. Thus the case of cross-over trade together with factor price equalization evidently depends upon the extent of Heckscher–Ohlin trade being weak. But as areas VIII and IX make clear, the possibility of cross-over trade by itself remains substantial.

4. The case of world specialization

I turn now to the second configuration discussed in section 2. If, as in Figure 5.1B, world prices of the three goods fail to align so that all three can be produced in any country, then specialization in different countries is inevitable. Cross-over trade is still quite possible, however, as will be indicated in Figure 5.5.

In section 3 I first abstracted from Heckscher–Ohlin trade by considering a country that would not trade at all if factors were mobile within it. That is not possible here, since regardless of a country's factor endowments it will not produce all three goods under free trade.

Nor can I, in this case, use vectors indicating the factor requirements of consumption to map out the Edgeworth Box of a country, since the factors used to produce a good at world prices are not unique, at least in the case of good 2. Therefore the geometric techniques employed in section 3 will not work here. However, these difficulties are compensated for by the fact that outputs are no longer indeterminate.

Consider, then, a country whose factor endowments would lead it to specialize in the good of intermediate factor intensity, good 2, if factors were internally mobile. Thus its factor endowment lies between the rays k_2^1 and k_2^2 of Figure 5.1B. Figure 5.5 shows an Edgeworth Box for the two regions of such a country, with the various factor rays of Figure 5.1B drawn from both the lower-left-hand corner origin for Region A and from the upper-right-hand corner origin for Region B. These rays divide the box into a large number of areas within which the pattern of production, and sometimes trade, can be observed.

Looking again only at the upper portion of the box, above the (undrawn) diagonal, nine areas are identified by Roman numerals. The pattern of production in these areas for the two regions is as shown in the table opposite. Only in area I does the country produce as it would if factors were internally mobile. Everywhere else in the box goods 1 and/or 3 are produced in some region of the country, and in one area, IX, those are the only goods produced.

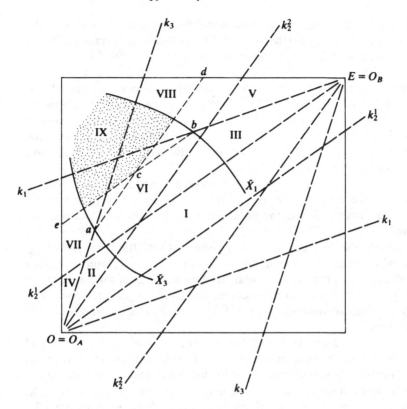

Figure 5.5

Area of Fig. 5.5	Region A	Region B
I	2	2
II	2,3	2
III	2	1,2
IV	3	2
V	2	1
VI	2,3	1,2
VII	3	1,2
VIII	2,3	1
IX	3	1

Especially in this latter area, IX, the pattern of production is strongly suggestive of cross-over trade, though there is no guarantee throughout that area that both regions produce enough of their respective outputs to be able to export them out of the country.[12] To further identify trade patterns it is necessary, as before, to enter certain isoquants into the figure.

Thus the isoquants for $\tilde{X}_3$ in Region A and $\tilde{X}_1$ in Region B have been added to Figure 5.5 as well. These are the quantities of goods 3 and 1 that the country as a whole demands with free trade, assuming that it faces the prices illustrated in Figure 5.1B and that it has the income that would be earned at those prices if factors were mobile. Within area IX, then, any allocation of factors between these two isoquants must entail cross-over trade, just as was argued earlier.

In other areas of the figure these isoquants cannot be used quite so directly, since more than one good is being produced in at least one region. It is still possible to use the information that these isoquants provide, however.

Consider the intersection of the $\tilde{X}_3$ isoquant with the k_3 ray out of O_A, labelled point a. By drawing another straight line, acd, from this point parallel to the k_2^2 ray one can isolate the factor allocations within areas VI and VIII where Region A produces more than $\tilde{X}_3$ of good 3. This follows from the familiar construction of the Edgeworth Box for two goods, applied to Region A.

Similarly, one can construct the line bce, parallel to the k_2^1 ray and starting at point b, the intersection of the $\tilde{X}_1$ isoquant with the k_1 ray from O_B. Together these two lines define the locus ecd, above and to the left of which, between the two drawn isoquants, there must be cross-over trade. Thus cross-over trade arises throughout the shaded area in Figure 5.5.

Thus, while the mechanics of tracing out production and trade patterns are rather different here from the previous case, the conclusion is largely the same. There is a sizable area of the Edgeworth Box, and hence a sizable range of inter-regional factor allocations, for which the country will engage in cross-over trade. These factor allocations are essentially those for which the factors are sufficiently lumpy, in the sense of being unevenly allocated across regions, with at the same time the two regions remaining of roughly comparable size.

5. Conclusion

This paper has shown how lumpiness of factors of production can lead to the phenomenon of cross-over trade. That is, if factors of production within a country are allocated sufficiently unevenly across regions, then those regions will specialize in different products than the country as a whole

---

[12] At least one must do so, of course, to pay for the country's imports of good 2.

would produce if factors were mobile. As a result, one region may well produce more of a labor-intensive good than the country can absorb, and if so it will export the excess to more capital-abundant countries elsewhere in the world. At the same time, the other region may specialize in the capital-intensive good and export it to more labor-abundant trading partners. This is not a particularly surprising or subtle phenomenon, but it is worth understanding that lumpiness may have this effect. For it means that lumpiness can have a more distorting effect on behavior in the economy than may have been previously understood.

In Courant and Deardorff (1992) we showed that lumpiness could lead a country to trade somewhat differently than it would if factors were mobile. But we did not suggest, and I do not here, that lumpiness would lead to a major departure from the predictions of the Heckscher–Ohlin model regarding trade. However, it appears now that, while the country's overall trade in terms, say, of its factor content, may not be very much changed by lumpiness, a great deal else can be. Lumpiness can completely alter the economic landscape, in terms of what individual goods are produced and where, compared to what would be observed if factors were mobile.

This conclusion must to some extent be tentative, for it has only been derived in the context of a far too simple model. In a world of many goods, countries, and factors, it may be that the stark effects of lumpiness seen here would tend to blur. However the analysis at least suggests that the issue is worth investigating.

References

Courant, Paul N. and Alan V. Deardorff 1992 "International Trade with Lumpy Countries," *Journal of Political Economy* 100 (February), 198–210.

Deardorff, Alan V. 1982 "The General Validity of the Heckscher–Ohlin Theorem," *American Economic Review* 72 (September), 683–94.

   1984 "Testing Trade Theories and Predicting Trade Flows," in Ronald Jones and Peter Kenen (eds.), *Handbook of International Economics*, Amsterdam, North-Holland.

   1987 "The Directions of Developing Countries' Trade: Examples from Pure Theory," in Oli Havrylyshyn, ed., *Exports of Developing Countries: How Direction Affects Performance*, Washington, D.C., The World Bank, pp. 9–21.

   1991 "The Possibility of Factor Price Equalization, Revisited," in process.

Deardorff, Alan V. and Paul N. Courant 1990 "On the Likelihood of Factor Price Equalization with Nontraded Goods," *International Economic Review*, 31, August, 589–96.

Dixit, Avinash K. and Victor Norman 1980 *Theory of International Trade*, London, Cambridge University Press.

Heller, Peter S. 1976 "Factor Endowment Change and Comparative Advantage:

72   **Alan V. Deardorff**

The Case of Japan, 1956–1969," *Review of Economics and Statistics*, 58, August, 283–92.

Johnson, Harry G. 1967 "The Possibility of Factor Price Equalization When Commodities Outnumber Factors," *Economica*, 34, 282–88.

Jones, Ronald W. 1956 "Factor Proportions and the Heckscher–Ohlin Theorem," *Review of Economic Studies* (October), 1–10.

1974 "The Small Country in a Many-Commodity World," *Australian Economic Papers* (December), 225–36.

Khanna, Ashok 1982 "Testing for Directionality of Trade: India's Exports of Manufactures in the 1970s," Ph.D Dissertation, Stanford University.

Lancaster, Kelvin 1957 "The Heckscher–Ohlin Trade Model: A Geometric Treatment," *Economica*, 24 (February), 19–39.

Melvin, James 1968 "Production and Trade with Two Factors and Three Goods," *American Economic Review*, 58, 1249–68.

Tatemoto, Masahiro and Shinichi Ichimura 1959 "Factor Proportions and Foreign Trade," *Review of Economics and Statistics*, 41 (November), 442–46.

Urata, Shujiro 1983 "Factor Inputs and Japanese Manufacturing Trade Structure," *Review of Economics and Statistics*, 65, 678–84.

Vanek, J. and T. Bertrand 1971 "Trade and Factor Prices in a Multi-Commodity World," in J. N. Bhagwati, R. W. Jones, R. A. Mundell, and J. Vanek, eds., *Trade, Balance of Payments and Growth*, Amsterdam, North-Holland.

Part III

The structure of simple trade models

6 Job market preferences and international trade

ROY J. RUFFIN

The hallmark of Ronald W. Jones's pioneering contributions to trade theory has been his extraordinary ability to capture the essence of a problem in a simple, elegant fashion. From my graduate-student days I can recall the young Ron Jones on the circuit in the spring of 1965 promoting his classic paper (Jones, 1965) on "Simple General Equilibrium Models." We should remember that these were the days when the abstract school of general equilibrium ruled the world. The message I got from the talk is that something could be done with general equilibrium. Everything was not possible: dual magnification effects ruled Jones's world. The anything-could-happen school of general equilibrium theorists thought this was heresy, and that something had to be wrong – it was just too neat! Today, the abstract school of general equilibrium is in retreat, and simple general equilibrium models are found in macroeconomics, economic history, public finance, and industrial organization.

While Jones made his mark with Heckscher–Ohlin, his Ricardian credentials have been impeccable (Jones, 1961). In the present paper I try to apply a simple Ricardian model to bringing out the role of job-market preferences in international trade. One of the standard assumptions of trade theory has always been that labor is indifferent between equal-paying jobs. But workers have preferences for different jobs. Adam Smith succinctly summarized the theory of compensating wage differentials: "The wages of labour vary with the ease or hardship, the cleanliness or dirtiness, the honourableness or dishonourablenes of the employment." This theory has been disputed in recent years (Krueger and Summers, 1988), but it still has defenders (Rosen, 1986; Murphy and Topel, 1987, and Ruffin, 1990b).

The motivation for this paper is that labor is by far the most important productive factor in relative costs because land is a small component of costs and capital is an internationally mobile factor. Thus, job-market preferences may have an important but neglected impact on international trade. According to Michael Porter (1990, p. 91): "National passions

75

translate into internationally competitive industries with striking regularity." We shall see that with a Ricardian production structure within each country job-market preferences ("national passions") do not make the theory more complicated; trade theory is simply enriched to include an additional cause of international trade. I also discuss factor mobility, nontraded goods and economic rents.

Section 1 reviews the literature and motivates the study by comparing industry wage structures in the United States and Germany. We find German wages tend to be relatively lower in those industries in which Germany is a world leader. Sections 2 and 3 develop the basic model in which different worker types have Ricardian comparative advantages (Ruffin, 1988; Rosen, 1978) as well as job-market preferences. It is shown that job market preferences can easily cause efficient production points to be below the production-possibility frontier. The concept of reservation wages is used to modify the typical bilateral cost ratios. Section 4 shows how job-market preferences affect the pattern of international trade. Job-market preferences can affect national comparative advantages just as much as factor endowment differences or technology differences. It is shown that if job-market preferences differ between countries, world demand may become a crucial determinant of the pattern of international trade. Section 5 discusses factor price equalization in the presence of job-market preferences. I show that under the assumption of identical technologies, the world equilibrium is still the same as if there were an integrated world economy. Section 6 presents a mild case for using job-market preferences to explain some of the differences in the prices of nontraded goods across developed countries. Section 7 shows that explaining compensating differentials in the Ricardian structure is preferable to the Heckscher–Ohlin structure because the former generates economic rents at the industry level.

1. Literature review

Karl Forchheimer (1947) argued long ago that relative wages were likely to be an important determinant of comparative advantage in some industries. But his views have been eclipsed by the long shadow cast by the empirical work of Frank Taussig (1927) and Irving Kravis (1956). The fundamental empirical problem is the claim by Taussig that international differences in wage structure had little impact on trade patterns because the structure of wages is about the same from country to country. Table 6.1 presents 1984 data for Germany and the United States. The following regression shows the mean relationship between wages in the U.S. (W_{us}) for a particular industry and German wages (W_g) in the same industry:

Table 6.1. *German/United States Wages, 1984*

Industry (3-digit SIC)	German	U.S.	Residual
Tobacco Mfg. (314)	$5.23	$11.27	2.3
Textiles (321)	4.53	6.46	−0.7
Wearing Apparel (322)	3.95	5.55	−0.1
Leather products (323–24)	4.05	5.70	−0.2
Wood products (331)	5.05	8.03	−0.4
Non-metal furniture (332)	5.41	6.85	−2.5
Paper and paper products (341)	5.90	10.41	−0.2
Chemicals (351–52)	5.93	11.08	0.3
Printing and publishing (342)	6.06	9.40	−1.7
Petroleum refineries (353)	7.44	14.57	−0.1
Plastic products (356)	4.96	7.64	−0.6
Pottery, china, etc. (361)	4.64	8.13	0.7
Basic metal industries (371–72)	5.69	11.47	1.3
Fabricated metal products (381)	5.13	9.38	0.7
Nonelectrical machinery (382)	5.74	9.96	−0.3
Electrical machinery (383)	5.08	9.04	0.5
Transport equipment (384)	6.10	12.22	1.0
Professional and scientific equipment (385)	5.02	8.85	0.4

Source: *ILO Yearbook of Labour Statistics*. Exchange rate (1984): $1 = 2.83 D.M.

$$W_{us} = 4.4 + 2.56 W_g \quad R^2 = 0.79$$
$$(0.33)$$

The correlation between U.S. and German wage structures is high (0.79). After examining similar data between the United States and Japan, Kravis (1956) also concluded that the wage structure is unimportant. Kravis also found that export industries pay higher wages than import industries in the United States and concluded that productivity differences were more important in determining trade patterns.

The theory of comparative advantage, however, suggests that what matters are the relative differences not the similarities between countries. The last column of Table 6.1 shows the residuals from the above regression of U.S. wages on German wages. A positive residual means that U.S. wages in that industry are relatively high; a negative residual means German wages in that industry are relatively high. From these residuals alone one would conclude that Germany should have a competitive advantage over the U.S. in tobacco (314), chemicals (351–52), basic metals (371–72), fabricated metal products (381), electrical machinery (383), transport equipment (384), and professional equipment (385). Among these industries – except for the tobacco industry (in which the U.S. productivity advantage is enormous) – Germany has a strong presence in world markets. Germany is the world leader in chemicals, materials and metals, power generation equipment, and second only to Japan in transport equipment – all industries in which German wages are relatively low.[1] But the United States dominates Germany in plastics, where U.S. wages are relatively low. This way of looking at the data suggests that the structure of relative wages between countries may have some bearing on trade patterns.

2. The Ricardian factor endowment model

As the basis for my analysis, I will use the Ricardian factor endowment model (Ruffin, 1988; 1990a; 1992). Suppose an economy has two factors, labor type 1 and labor type 2. Each factor has a unique Ricardian comparative advantage. Let a_{ij} be the fixed amount of type i labor that can produce a unit of good j. The supply of type i factor is fixed at L_i. There are two goods, 1 and 2. We assume factor i has a comparative labor advantage in good i. The relative labor cost of producing good 1 by factor i is a_{i1}/a_{i2}. Thus:

$$a_{11}/a_{12} < a_{21}/a_{22}. \tag{1}$$

We let good 2 be the numeraire so that p is the (relative) price of good 1. If workers have no job-market preferences, they simply choose the job that maximizes their income.

$$w_i = \max(p/a_{i1}, 1/a_{i2}), \tag{2}$$

where w_i is the wage of factor i. If p is in between the relative production costs it follows that:

$$w_1 = p/a_{11} \quad \text{and} \quad w_2 = 1/a_{22}. \tag{3}$$

Relative factor prices w_1/w_2 are determined by the commodity price ratio p. Clearly, from (3),

$$w_1/w_2 = pa_{22}/a_{11}. \tag{4}$$

3. Job market-preferences

Job market preferences exist if preferences are defined over the workplace as well as the commodity space. Following Ruffin (1990b) I assume that the

---

[1] See Porter (1990), pp. 536–38 for data on the share of different countries in world exports of different industrial clusters.

utility function is homogeneous of degree one in the commodity space and that the workplace only affects total utility. Thus, neither the workplace nor income affects how workers spend a dollar. All workers are also assumed to have the same homothetic indifference curves in the commodity space. All type i workers have the same job-market preferences as well as productivities. A type i worker is representative of his or her entire class; and we can refer to a typical representative as "worker i." Thus, the (indirect) utility of a type i worker in industry j is

$$u_{ij} = b_{ij} w_{ij} v(p), \tag{5}$$

where w_{ij} is the wage of worker i working in industry j, b_{ij} reflects worker i's job preferences, and $v(p)$ shows the dependence of utility on relative prices.

Workers maximize utility instead of maximizing income. The analogue to (2) is

$$u_i = \max(u_{i1}, u_{i2}). \tag{6}$$

From equation (5) we can see that worker 1 will choose job 1 if and only if

$$b_{11} w_{11} > b_{12} w_{12}. \tag{7}$$

Worker i's possible earnings are

$$w_{i1} = p/a_{i1} \quad \text{or} \quad w_{i2} = 1/a_{i2}. \tag{8}$$

Combining (7) and (8) we see that worker 1 maximizes utility in job 1 if and only if

$$p > a_{11} b_{12}/a_{12} b_{11}. \tag{9}$$

Similarly, worker 2 will choose job 2 if and only if

$$p < a_{21} b_{22}/a_{22} b_{21}. \tag{10}$$

There are two fundamental ratios. Worker i's preference for working in industry 2 can be measured by

$$h_i = b_{i2}/b_{i1}. \tag{11}$$

If $h_i > (<) 1$, worker i prefers working in industry 2 (industry 1) with the same wages. Indeed, the ratio h_i measures the wage differential that exactly makes a worker indifferent. If $u_{i1} = u_{i2}$, it follows immediately from (5) that $h_i = w_{i1}/w_{i2}$. Clearly, h_i is worker i's rate of job preference for industry 2. It is a fundamental constant of our theory. The larger h_i, the larger the preference for working in industry 2 or the smaller the relative disagreeableness of working in industry 1.

Another fundamental constant is factor i's relative labor cost of producing good 1:

80   **Roy J. Ruffin**

$$c_i = a_{i1}/a_{i2}. \tag{12}$$

Combining (9) and (10) we have the fundamental law that factor 1 (factor 2) will maximize utility working in industry 1 (industry 2) if and only if:

$$c_1 h_1 < p < c_2 h_2. \tag{13}$$

Analogously, factor 1 (factor 2) will maximize utility working in industry 2 (industry 1) if and only if:

$$c_2 h_2 < p < c_1 h_1. \tag{14}$$

It follows that job-market preferences are just as important as Ricardian comparative advantages in determining the allocation of resources.

The term $c_i h_i$ may be interpreted as the relative utility cost of producing good 1 by factor i. Good 1 is not produced by factor i if $p < c_i h_i$; good 2 is not produced by factor i if $p > c_i h_i$. If p is outside the ranges indicated in (13) or (14) the economy will specialize in one of the goods. For example, if $p < c_1 h_1 < c_2 h_2$, both factors will specialize in good 2.

To understand the economics more clearly, let us consider the reservation wage of type i workers – the wage that must be paid to induce them to leave an industry. We assume the case in which $c_1 h_1 < c_2 h_2$. Let r_{ij} denote the reservation wage of factor i to move to industry j. For factor 1 it is defined by

$$b_{11} w_{11} v(p) = b_{12} r_{12} v(p). \tag{15}$$

Therefore, the wage that must be paid for factor 1 to be on the verge of leaving industry 1 is:

$$r_{12} = w_{11} b_{11}/b_{12} = w_{11}/h_1. \tag{16}$$

By similar reasoning the reservation wage for factor 2 is

$$r_{21} = h_2 w_{22}. \tag{17}$$

The relative utility cost of producing good 1 by factor 1 is $a_{11} w_{11}/a_{12} r_{12}$. Using (12) and (16), this reduces to $c_1 h_1$. Similarly, the relative utility cost of producing good 1 by factor 2 is $a_{21} r_{21}/a_{22} w_{22} = c_2 h_2$.

We still assume without loss of generality that labor type i has a comparative labor cost advantage in the production of good i, as implied by inequality (1). In the absence of job-market preferences, type i workers specialize in good i. If job-market preferences are not strong enough to change the pattern of specialization, then (13) would hold. If p is strictly in between the relative utility costs in (13), then the output ratio X_1/X_2 would be given by:

$$X_1/X_2 = L_1 a_{22}/L_2 a_{11}. \tag{18}$$

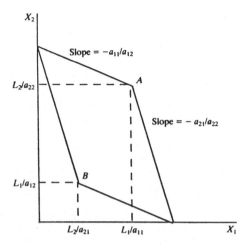

Figure 6.1

If job-market preferences are negatively correlated with comparative advantages, they may cause workers with a comparative advantage in industry i to work in industry j. If type 1 workers have a much larger preference for industry 2 than type 2 workers, so that $c_1 h_1 > c_2 h_2$, then it is possible to reverse the assignment of workers to jobs. If p is strictly in between the relative utility costs in (14), then

$$X_1/X_2 = L_2 a_{12}/L_1 a_{21}. \qquad (19)$$

Since output is maximized when each worker is assigned to the job that maximizes her labor income, we know that when (1) and (14) hold production is below the production-possibility curve.

Figure 6.1 shows the production-possibility curve. When job-market preferences do not outweigh comparative advantages, the economy produces at point A. If job-market preferences are stronger than comparative advantages, the economy produces at point B, below the production-possibility curve.

Figures 6.2 and 6.3 show how the autarkic relative price is determined in the present model. The relative supply curve is $S = X_1/X_2$; and the relative demand curve is $D = D_1/D_2$. Figure 6.2 assumes condition (13) holds so that factor 1 (factor 2) maximizes utility in industry 1 (industry 2). The vertical section reflects the output ratio $X_1/X_2 = L_1 a_{22}/L_2 a_{11}$. If L_1/L_2 rises, the relative price of good 1, p, falls. Figure 6.3 assumes condition (14)

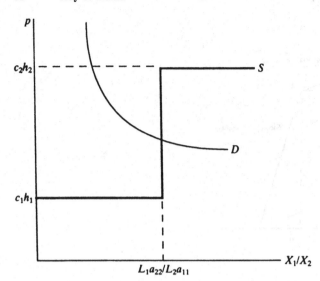

Figure 6.2

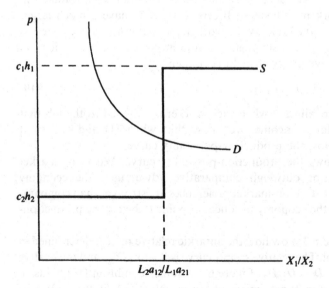

Figure 6.3

holds so that factor 1 (factor 2) maximizes utility in industry 2 (industry 1). Now the vertical section reflects $X_1/X_2 = L_2 a_{12}/L_1 a_{21}$. Now, if L_1/L_2 increases, the relative price p will rise. This only makes sense because type 2 labor specializes in good 1. Factor prices are now determined by:

$$w_{12} = 1/a_{12} \quad \text{and} \quad w_{21} = p/a_{21}. \tag{20}$$

4. Job-market preferences and international trade

This section examines the consequences of job-market preferences as a separate cause of international trade. Throughout we assume two countries, the home and the foreign. Starred variables are foreign values. The workforces of both countries face the same Ricardian production functions, so that $a_{ij} = a_{ij}*$ and, therefore, $c_i = c_i*$.[2] However, job-market preferences and factor endowments may differ between the countries.

If job-market preferences are the same between countries, international trade is determined by factor endowments alone. All of the properties of the factor endowment theory hold. The only amendment to the usual factor endowment theory is that we can no longer say that a country exports the good in which its abundant factor has a comparative advantage. Instead, we must say that the country exports the good in which its abundant factor maximizes its utility. This is important because it shows that the factor endowment theory of trade generalizes to the case in which workers maximize utility rather than maximize money income.

The point of this paper is that the assumption of identical job-market preferences between countries is suspect. Porter (1990) has argued that "nations tend to be competitive in activities that are admired or depended upon." For example, the chemical sector in Germany or steel and consumer electronics in Japan are prestigious occupations. Porter gives other examples: "In Italy, it is fashion and furnishings, among others. In the United States, it is finance and anything to do with entertainment, including movies, popular music, professional sports, and related fields. In Israel, the highest callings have been defense-related endeavors and agriculture" (Porter, 1990, p. 115).

Figure 6.4 shows a situation in which the only difference between the two countries is in job-market preferences: technology, relative product demand, and factor endowments are the same. I assume that $h_i* < h_i$ ($i = 1, 2$) so that each labor type in the home country has a stronger rate of preference for working in industry 2 than the comparable labor type in the foreign country. Equivalently, labor in the foreign country prefers industry 1 compared to the home country. Because of job-market preferences, the

[2] In Ruffin (1992) I examine the role of different technologies in international trade.

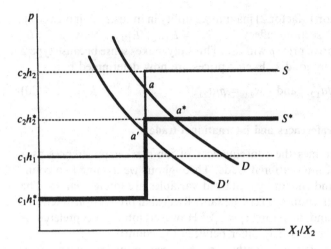

Figure 6.4

relative supply curve for the foreign country, S^*, has lower horizontal portions than the home country's supply curve, S; but the two curves partially overlap in their vertical sections.

In this case, there need not be international trade. The relative demand curve D' intersects both relative supply curves at the same point a'. Thus, there would be no international trade because each country would have the same autarkic price. Workers in each country are involved only in the industry in which they have a Ricardian comparative advantage. The workers are happily maximizing their utility with price-determined economic rents that simply reflect their job market preferences. The price at point a' is determined by the combination of demand and the positioning of the vertical section of the relative supply curve (which depends only on factor endowments and productivities).

International trade requires that job-market preferences affect prices. When the relative demand curve is D, autarky prices are at points a and a^*. In this case, each country would export the good in which its labor force had a job-market preference: the home country would export good 2 and the foreign country good 1. With the demand curve D the demand for good 1 is so high that in autarky some of the foreign country's type 2 labor must work in the production of good 1. Thus, at point a, type 2 labor in the foreign country is receiving an exact compensating wage differential between the two industries. Since foreign workers have a relative preference for working in industry 1 (compared to the home country), the foreign country has a lower autarkic price for good 1 compared to the home country.

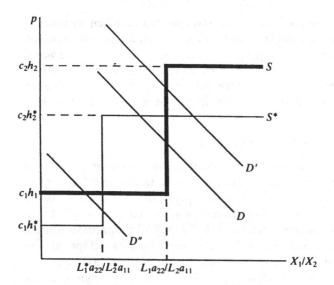

Figure 6.5

In the standard Heckscher–Ohlin model, with homothetic preferences, world demand has no impact on trade patterns. As Jones (1976) has stated, "in the two-by-two case each country has only one commodity it can ever export (excluding technological progress)." This would also be true in Figure 6.4. However, when job-market preferences interact with factor endowments to explain trade patterns, world demand becomes a crucial ingredient. Indeed, any time there are multiple supply-side causes of international trade world demand can affect the trade pattern (Ruffin, 1992).

In Figure 6.5, it is again assumed that workers in the foreign country have a stronger preference for working in industry 1 – or a smaller distaste for working in industry 1 – than those in the home country (i.e. $h_i^* < h_i$). However, suppose the home (foreign) country has a relatively larger endowment of type 1 (type 2) labor (since $L_1^*/L_2^* < L_1/L_2$). Thus, the foreign country's relative supply curve for good 1, S^*, is generally lower than the home country's relative supply curve S, but there is a range where the factor endowment effect dominates. When the relative demand curve is D', the foreign country will export good 1 because before trade the autarky price of good 1 for the home country exceeds that of the foreign country. In this case, the world demand for good 1 is relatively high. The foreign country, even though it has a smaller endowment of type 1 labor than the home country, exports good 1 because of the high demand for the good in which its factors have a (relative) job market preference. When the demand for good 1 is D, then the foreign country exports good 2 – the good in which its abundant factor has a comparative advantage. Finally, when the world demand for good 1 is very low, as with D'', or the world demand for good 2 is relatively high, then the home country will export good 2 because there is a high demand for the good in which its factors have a relative job-market preference.

5. Factor mobility and factor price equalization

It might appear that the factor price equalization theorem may fail when job-market preferences differ between countries. In Figure 6.5, if the free trade price is in the open interval $(c_1h_1, c_2h_2{}^*)$, then there will be factor price equalization because in both countries $w_{11} = p/a_{11}$ and $w_{22} = 1/a_{22}$. However, if p is in the open interval $(c_2h_2{}^*, c_2h_2)$, all factor prices will not be equalized. In this case, everybody in the foreign country will specialize in good 1 production. But in the home country only those with a comparative advantage in good 1 produce good 1. So in the foreign country, $w_{21}{}^* = p/a_{21}$ and $w_{11}{}^* = 1/a_{11}$; and in the home country, $w_{11} = p/a_{11}$ and $w_{22} = 1/a_{22}$. Factor 1's wages are equalized, but factor 2's wages are not equalized.

The breakdown of factor price equalization is only apparent, not real. If some factor 2 left the foreign country and moved to the home country, holding job-market preferences constant, all that would happen is that they would take their foreign wages with them! It is more accurate to say that there is virtual factor price equalization. The same opportunities are present. For example, in the above case, factor 2 earns p/a_{21} in the foreign country and $1/a_{22}$ in the home country. But the reason is because foreigners prefer industry 1 at those wage rates. There is no incentive for workers to move.

This proposition is really quite apparent. As long as the a_{ij} coefficients are the same the world over and as long as the utility function is independent of his or her location, moving a worker from one country to the next can have no impact on the world free trade equilibrium. Let p be the free trade equilibrium corresponding to a set of workers along with their preferences. A worker chooses a job that maximizes his or her utility given that p. If this is part of a world free trade equilibrium, the utility-maximizing choices of each worker just happen to produce the amounts of each good that are demanded on the world market. If the a_{ij}s are the same everywhere, a worker can be moved from one country to the next without affecting anything but the pattern of international trade.

To explain the movement of labor with the above model it is essential to assume different technologies, tariffs, nontraded goods, or some combination of these factors. Under any of these circumstances, workers could improve their utility moving from one country to the next.

6. Nontraded goods

Traditionally, there are two reasons for the relative price of nontraded goods to differ across nations: differences in factor endowments and technology (Kravis et al., 1983). It has been hypothesized that the developing countries have lower nontraded goods prices because they involve services. Since services are labor-intensive, nontraded goods will be cheaper in the labor-abundant countries. Since productivity differentials are smaller for services than for manufactured goods, services will be relatively cheaper in the developing countries.

But job-market preferences can also provide a reason for the prices of nontraded goods to differ among countries. Just as Figure 6.4 explained trade as a consequence of different job-market preferences, the same figure can explain different prices of nontraded goods. The "national passions" explanation has some desirable features. The traditional explanation applies only to the case of comparing developed with developing countries. But nontraded goods prices differ between developed countries among particular categories. The traditional explanations break down because it is more difficult to rely on the factor intensity or productivity differential hypothesis. A classic example would be the French job-market preference for cooking. There are many delightful and relatively cheap restaurants in Paris that prepare dishes that would cost much more in New York for a comparable quality (if indeed that is even possible). Historically, personal services (maids, butlers, barbers, etc.) have been relatively cheaper in England than in, say, the United States. In Germany, the mechanical trades have much more prestige than similar jobs in the United States.

7. Economic rents and the Heckscher–Ohlin model

The Ricardian structure of the present model has the distinct advantage that at least one of the types of labor must be specialized. When the relative price of a commodity exceeds its relative utility cost to a particular labor type, that labor type earns an economic rent at the industry level. Let us assume that $c_1 h_1 < c_2 h_2$, so that labor type 1 (type 2) maximizes utility working in industry 1 (industry 2). The economic rent of any worker in a particular industry is the excess of his or her reservation wage for working in another industry over his or her current wage. The economic rent of a type 1 worker is

$$e_1 = r_{12} - w_{12}, \tag{21}$$

because r_{12} is the reservation wage you must pay factor 1 to work in industry 2 given their wage in industry 1. From (16) we know that $r_{12} = w_{11}/h_1$. The economic rent of a type 2 worker is

$$e_2 = r_{21} - w_{21}, \tag{22}$$

where from (17) $r_{21} = h_2 w_{22}$. Since $w_{11} = p/a_{11}$ and $w_{22} = 1/a_{22}$, their economic rents are

$$e_1 = (1/a_{11})(p/h_1 - a_{11}/a_{12}) \tag{23}$$

$$e_2 = (1/a_{22})(h_2 - pa_{22}/a_{21}). \tag{24}$$

Suppose industry 1 is disagreeable ($h_i > 1$). If the demand for good 1 is sufficiently low, so that some type 1 workers must work in industry 2, then $p = c_1 h_1$ and compensating differentials for type 1 workers will exactly offset the wage differential. Type 2 workers will earn an economic rent. If p is in the open interval $(c_1 h_1, c_2 h_2)$, then both factors will earn economic rents.

If a Heckscher–Ohlin production structure is used, economic rents for workers in a particular industry disappear. For example, let l_{ij} denote the amount of type i labor used in a unit of good j. Then workers will maximize their utility and each industry will earn zero profits when

$$p = l_{11}w_{11} + l_{21}w_{21} \tag{25}$$

$$1 = l_{12}w_{12} + l_{22}w_{22} \tag{26}$$

$$b_{11}w_{11} = b_{12}w_{12} \tag{27}$$

$$b_{22}w_{22} = b_{21}w_{21}. \tag{28}$$

There are no economic rents at the level of the industry because of (27) and (28): compensating differentials are exact. Equations similar to (25) through (28) have, of course, been used in the theory of factor market distortions (Jones, 1971). However, in the present context, the allocation of resources is Pareto efficient.

The Ricardian structure of the present model is not just a convenient simplification. Economic rents are a feature of the real world. For example, it has been frequently observed in the labor economics literature that differential economic rents may explain why some industries experience lower labor quit rates than other industries (Krueger and Summers, 1988). This fact is presumably inconsistent with the Heckscher–Ohlin model. As has been pointed out before, the Stolper–Samuelson theorem has the unappealing empirical implication that workers in the capital-intensive industry would be made better off by a tax on that industry or a subsidy to the labor-intensive industry.

8. Conclusion

We have shown that in a simple Ricardian factor endowment model job-market preferences do not make the theory of international trade any more difficult. It is my hope that this paper will suggest to international economists the importance of integrating labor economics with international trade. The crucial issue is whether the detailed differences in the structure of wages resulting from job-market preferences between countries help explain trade patterns, immigration flows, or the prices of nontraded goods. The rough calculations in the first section of this paper show they might be important, but far more sophisticated techniques should be used.

References

Forchheimer, Karl 1947 "The Role of Relative Wage Differences in International Trade, *Quarterly Journal of Economics*, 62, (November), 1–30.

Jones, Ronald W. 1961 "Comparative Advantage and the Theory of Tariffs: A Multi-Country, Multi-Country Model," *Review of Economic Studies* (June), 161–75.

1965 "The Structure of Simple General Equilibrium Models," *Journal of Political Economy*, 73 (December), 557–72.

1971 "Distortions in Factor Markets and the General Equilibrium Model of Production," *Journal of Political Economy* (May/June), 437–59.

1976 *"Two-Ness" in Trade Theory: Costs and Benefits*, Special Papers in International Economics, No. 12, Princeton University.

Kravis, Irving 1956 "Wages and Foreign Trade," *Review of Economics and Statistics*, 38 (February), 14–30.

Kravis, Irving, A. Heston, and R. Summers 1983 "The Share of Services in Economic Growth," in F. G. Adams and B. G. Hickman (eds.), *Global Econometrics: Essays in Honor of Lawrence R. Klein*, Cambridge, Mass.: MIT Press.

Krueger, Alan B. and Larry H. Summers 1988 "Efficiency Wages and the Inter-Industry Wage Structure," *Econometrica*, 56 (March), 259–93.

Murphy, Kevin M. and Robert H. Topel 1987 "Unemployment, Risk, and Earnings: Testing for Equalizing Differences in the Labor Market," in Kevin Lang and Jonathan S. Leonard (eds.), *Unemployment and the Structure of Labor Markets*, Basil Blackwell, New York, 103–40.

Porter, Michael E. 1990 *The Competitive Advantages of Nations*, New York, The Free Press.

Rosen, Sherwin 1978 "Substitution and the Division of Labor," *Economica*, 45 (August), 235–50.

1986 "The Theory of Equalizing Differences," in Orley Ashenfelter and Richard Layard (eds.), *The Handbook of Labor Economics*, Vol. I, North-Holland, Amsterdam.

Ruffin, Roy J. 1988 "The Missing Link: The Ricardian Approach to the Factor Endowments Theory of Trade," *American Economic Review*, 78 (September), 759–72.

1990a "The Ricardian Factor Endowment Theory of Trade," *International Economics Journal* (Winter).

1990b "Comparative Advantage, Compensating Differentials, and Wages," Mimeo, University of Houston, September.

1992 "First and Second Best Factor Comparative Advantages and International Trade," *Economica*, 59 (November), 453–63.

Taussig, Frank W. 1927 *International Trade*, New York.

7 Production indivisibilities in a short-run trade model

WOLFGANG MAYER AND JUN LI[1]

1. Introduction

The reallocation of factors of production, triggered by changes in world prices, trade barriers, endowments, or technology, is generally not instantaneous. The major impediments to short-run adjustments are limited interindustry mobility of factors, rigidity of factor returns, and indivisibilities in production. The international trade literature has discussed the first two impediments quite thoroughly, with particular emphasis on their implications for resource allocations and the distribution of income.[1] The role of production indivisibilities, on the other hand, has not yet received such complete and systematic treatment.[2] To fill this void, we develop a short-run general equilibrium model with indivisibilities in production, which then is employed to explain the possibility of social welfare losses from the type of exogenous changes which under perfect divisibility and perfect competition would have led to welfare improvements.

Production indivisibilities exist when firms – based on economic, technological, or institutional constraints – cannot or will not adjust input use in a continuous manner. Although most real world production adjustments are discrete, theoretical analyses are quite justified in abstracting from this feature when discrete changes are relatively small. Not all real world production adjustments are small, however, especially not in the

[1] Comments by Eric Fisher were of great value in revising this paper.
[1] See Jones (1971, 1975), Mayer (1974), Mussa (1974), and Neary (1978) on specific factor models, and Brecher (1974), Bhagwati and Srinivasan (1974), and Srinivasan and Bhagwati (1975) on models with sticky factor prices.
[2] In contrast to the trade literature, microeconomic writings frequently hint at the importance of discontinuities in production as a real world phenomenon. For the most part, discontinuities are dealt with in the context of economies of scale, as in Hahn (1949), McLeod (1949), and Lerner (1949). Samuelson presents a treatment of optimal input choice when production functions are discontinuous. The most extensive analysis of indivisibilities in production at the firm level is provided by Frank (1969).

91

short run when a firm's actions are subject to rigid technological and institutional constraints. Frequently, feasible short-run adjustments are limited to changing the number of work shifts, the number of operating plants, or a combination of the two.

This essay focuses on adjustments through variations in work shifts, highlighting the short-run responses of overall social welfare and factor income distribution to exogenous changes. In some situations, exogenous shocks have no or only minor visible effects on the economy. In other situations, these shocks can be absorbed with great difficulty only. In the first case, there may be no output adjustments and only small welfare repercussions, while the second case is characterized by abrupt and large responses in industry output, factor returns, and social welfare. Not only may these responses be quite strong, but they may take rather unexpected directions. A small country's removal of a tariff may lower social welfare; technological advances or factor endowment growth may lead to immiserization; and immigration of labor may raise wage rates and lower returns on some industry-specific factors. Which of the two situations, minor effects or major repercussions, comes about depends on the number of firms in the industry with indivisibilities and their incentives to adjust the number of work shifts employed.

Sizeable production indivisibilities arise in both large and small firms. Since we are dealing with a small, open economy, all firms are always price takers in commodity markets. However, the same cannot be assumed about factor markets. One firm, such as a steel producer, may make up the entire industry and, therefore, have monopsony power in the factor market. Alternatively, an industry may consist of just a few or many small firms. This paper deals with both situations, showing how adjustments are gradually smoothed out as the number of firms in the industry rises.

2. Production indivisibilities and the firm's input choice

A firm is subject to production indivisibilities if it is either unable or unwilling to make continuous adjustments in input use. This type of adjustment impediment manifests itself especially in the short run when technological and institutional constraints interact to create indivisibilities in the employment of labor.[3] The *technological constraint* has its origin in

---

[3] Among the real world circumstances which are most likely to lead to indivisibilities in production, Frank (1969, p. 32) mentions that (a) a commodity cannot be physically divided in a meaningful sense; (b) fractional parts of a commodity cannot be combined meaningfully; (c) institutional restrictions prohibit the firm from buying fractional input parts; and (d) outputs cannot be sold in fractional parts.

the putty-clay nature of many production processes.[4] Assuming that labor services, L_x, and capital services, K_x, are required to produce commodity X and that the firm's capital *stock*, κ_x, is already installed in the short run, it takes a work team of fixed size, $L_0 = \alpha \kappa_x$, to operate the capital stock. The *institutional constraint*, on the other hand, specifies that workers, if employed at all, must be employed for a fixed duration, h, which for convenience sake we set equal to 1. While these technological and institutional features impose serious adjustment constraints, they do not imply complete fixity of input use. There exists the possibility to alter the capital stock–labor flow ratio, κ_x/L_x, by changing the number of work shifts, each of which is employed for a time period $h = 1$. The firm can adjust labor use in increments of L_0, the amount of labor services required to staff one shift of workers.

The firm's production function is written as:

$$x = f(L_x, K_x), \tag{1}$$

where x is the firm's output, and L_x and K_x are the *flows* of labor and capital services respectively. It is assumed that both inputs are required to produce a positive amount of output, that $f(\cdot)$ is homogeneous of degree one, $f_L > 0$, $f_K > 0$, and $f_{KK} < 0$ for all $L \geq 0$ and $K \geq 0$.

Concerning the input variables, the assumption that a fixed number of workers must be employed to operate the capital stock for one work shift, L_0, implies that total employment to operate n work shifts is:

$$L_x(n) = nL_0 = {}^n\alpha\kappa_x, \tag{2a}$$

where α and κ_x are fixed while n is an adjustable integer. The capital flow, K_x, on the other hand, is related to the capital stock, κ_x, through:

$$K_x = n\beta(n)\kappa_x, \tag{2b}$$

where $\beta(n)$, the flow of capital services per unit of time, is assumed to decline at an increasing rate with the length of time the capital stock is in operation;[5] that is, $\beta' < 0$ and $\beta'' < 0$.

Substitution of (2a) and (2b) in (1) yields:

$$x(n) = f[n\alpha\kappa_x, n\beta(n)\kappa_x] = n\alpha\kappa_x f[1, \beta(n)/\alpha] \tag{1'}$$

which expresses output of good X when n shifts are employed and for which

[4] Substitutions between inputs can be made ex ante, but not ex post; that is, the amount of labor employed per machine is flexible before the machine has been chosen and installed, but it becomes constant once the machines are built and put in operation. For early work on the putty-clay model, see Johansen (1959) and Phelps (1963).

[5] All machinery requires regular maintenance to avoid breakdowns. Performing this maintenance is less disruptive to production when operation of the machinery is stopped at regular intervals than when it is continuous. Also, wear and tear of the machinery itself may be greater under continuous operations than under operations with rest periods.

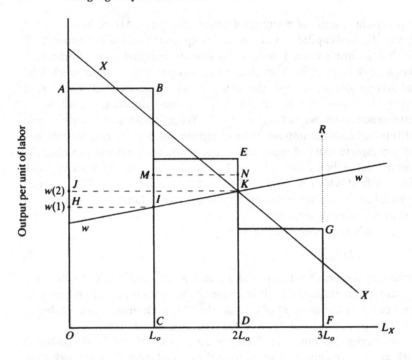

Figure 7.1

$\partial x/\partial n > 0$ for sufficiently small values of n and $\partial^2 x/\partial n^2 < 0$, as reflected by the XX curve in Figure 7.1.

A firm employs n work shifts to uniquely maximize profits, given the work shift choices by other firms in the industry, if:

$$\begin{aligned}[x(n) - x(n-1)]/L_0 &> \{w(n) + [n-1][w(n) - w(n-1)]\} \\ [x(n+1) - x(n)]/L_0 &< \{w(n+1) + n[w(n+1) - w(n)]\}\end{aligned}, \quad (3)$$

where $x(n)$ is output of the firm and $w(n)$ is the wage rate per work period in terms of X when n work shifts are employed. n is the optimal number of work shifts if the incremental output per work hour of the nth shift, $[x(n) - x(n-1)]/L_0$, exceeds the incremental cost, $\{nw(n) - [n-1]w(n-1)\} = \{w(n) + [n-1][w(n) - w(n-1)]\}$, while the reverse is the case for the incremental output of the $(n+1)$st shift of labor. The choice of n shifts is unique since strong inequalities are stated in (3). If, on the other hand, an equality held in either the first or the second relation of (3), the firm would be indifferent between employing n and $(n-1)$ shifts in the first case and between n and $(n+1)$ shifts in the second case.

Figure 7.1 illustrates the firm's optimal choice of the number of work shifts. The XX curve would be the usual marginal product of labor curve if labor were perfectly divisible, such as when shifts can be assigned arbitrarily short working hours. The XX curve is used to obtain incremental output for different numbers of shifts of workers when the length of the work shift cannot be altered. When one shift of workers is employed, L_0, the area under the XX curve between the origin, O, and L_0 measures the total output produced by the first shift. Drawing a block of equal size and base L_0, namely $OABC$, allows us to interpret the distance CB as the incremental output of the first shift. Similarly, distance DE indicates the incremental output of the second shift, while FG does the same for the third shift.

The WW curve portrays the labor supply curve as faced by the firm under consideration. Its position, to be examined in the next section, depends on the country's overall labor endowment and demand for labor by firms in both their own and other industries. Holding demand by other firms constant, one obtains the nth shift's incremental cost of labor, $IC(n) = \{nw(n) - [n - 1]w(n - 1)\}$, as follows. When $n = 1$, the wage rate is $w(1)$, total wage cost is given by the area $OHIC$ and $IC\{1\} = CI$. When $n = 2$, the wage rate is $w(2)$, the total wage cost is $OJKD$, total incremental cost of the second shift is $CMND$, and $IC(2) = DN$. Similarly, $IC(3) = FR$. As drawn, the firm's optimal employment is two shifts, since $DE > DN$ but $FG < FR$.

3. Short-run equilibrium of the economy

We are describing a small, open economy in which two industries, X and Y, produce an import-competing good X and an export good Y, respectively. Firms in these industries employ labor and capital, whose endowments are fixed and fully employed. Short-run features are introduced by assuming that only labor is intersectorally mobile, while capital is firm specific, and that production indivisibilities exist in industry X, but not in industry Y.

Industry X consists of $m \geq 1$ identical firms. A given firm j faces wage rate $w(n_j)$ when it employs n_j shifts. In industry Y there are no production indivisibilities and the industry production function is given by:

$$Y = g(L_y, K_y), \tag{4}$$

where Y is output, L_y and K_y are labor and industry-specific capital employed by sector Y, $g(\cdot)$ is homogeneous of degree one, $g_L > 0$, $g_K > 0$, and $g_{LL} < 0$ for all $L_y \geq 0$ and $K_y \geq 0$. Cost-minimizing firms employ labor such that:

$$pg_L(L_y, K_y) = w, \tag{5}$$

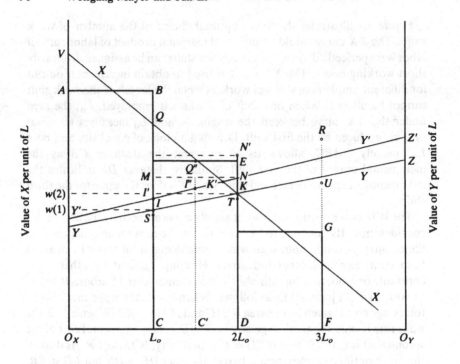

Figure 7.2

where p is the price of good Y in terms of good X. Given the economy's labor endowment, L, and the full employment constraint, the wage rate faced by firm j when it employs n_j work shifts can be expressed as:

$$w(n_j) = pg_L\left[\bar{L} - n_j L_0 - \sum_{i \neq j}^{m} n_i L_0, K_y \right], \tag{6}$$

where n_i refers to the number of work shifts employed by the ith other firm in industry X.

Industry X may consist of one or more firms, all of which are assumed to possess the same stock of specific capital. If there is only one firm in industry X, then (6) reduces to:

$$w(n) = pg_L[\bar{L} - nL_0, K_y] \tag{6'}$$

which, together with (3), describes how many work shifts are employed by the single firm in industry X and which wage rate prevails in equilibrium. This is illustrated in Figure 7.2, where the distance between O_X and O_Y measures the country's labor endowment, YY is industry Y's value of marginal product curve, and, as in Figure 7.1, CB (CI), DE (DN), and FG (FR) are the incremental product (cost) for the first, second, and third shift, respectively. As drawn, the single firm of industry X chooses to employ two work shifts, since $DE > DN$ but $FG < FR$, and the economy-wide wage rate is $w(2)$.

When there is more than one firm in industry X, an equilibrium may not exist. This can be seen by substituting (6) in (3). If all m identical firms acted in exactly the same way such that each of them always employs the same number of work shifts, may it be n, $n - 1$, or $n + 1$, then (3) would be rewritten as:

$$[x(n) - x(n-1)]/L_0 > w[mn] + [n-1]\{w[mn] - w[m(n-1)]\}$$
$$[x(n+1) - x(n)]/L_0 < w[m(n+1)] + n\{w[m(n+1)] - w[mn]\}$$

$$(3')$$

where $w[mn]$ stands for $pg_L[\bar{L} - mnL_0, K_y]$. This condition states that, if each firm had to employ exactly the same number of shifts, it would be profitable for them to employ n rather than $(n + 1)$ shifts. Condition (3'), however, does not describe an equilibrium unless there is a labor market adjustment mechanism in place which assures that either all firms or none of them adjust the number of work shifts at the same time. In the absence of such a mechanism, each individual firm may still be able to raise its profits by adding another work shift, given the choice of shifts by others. That is, the second equation of (3') does not preclude the possibility that for firm j:

$$[x(n_j + 1) - x(n_j)]/L_0 > w(mn + 1)] + n_j\{w[(mn + 1)] - w[mn]\}.$$

$$(7)$$

Consequently, while it is not profitable for all firms together to add another shift, it may be very profitable to do so for at least one of the firms.

To assure existence of equilibrium in the labor market with many firms, a mechanism must be designed to allocate the addition of production shifts to some but not all firms of the industry. As recently suggested by Rogerson (1988) for the case of indivisible labor, this mechanism can be based on randomizing the allocation of work shifts through a lottery. In order to describe this randomized process, we assume that initially all firms employ n shifts and that at least one firm can raise its profits by expanding to $(n + 1)$ shifts, if the others do not adjust, a condition stated in (7). These m firms participate in a lottery which assigns the right to employ n shifts to m_1 firms and the right to employ $(n + 1)$ shifts to $m_2 = (m - m_1)$ firms. The equilibrium allocation of m_1 is chosen by maximizing expected profits of each of the identical firms, whereby expected profits (payments to capital owners) are given by

$$E[\pi(m_1)] = [m_1/m][x(n) - L_0 nw(N)]$$
$$+ [(m - m_1)/m]\{x(n + 1) - L_0[n + 1]w(N)\}. \quad (8)$$

In (8), (m_1/m) is the probability of getting no increase in the number of work shifts, $N = [m_1 n + m_2(n + 1)]$ is the total number of work shifts employed by all firms, those that use n and those that use $(n + 1)$ shifts, and $[x(n) - L_0 nw(N)]$ are profits to the firm when it employs n shifts while the whole sector employs N shifts. The allocation m_1^* is uniquely optimal if $E[\pi(m_1^*)] > E[\pi(m_1)]$ for all m_1. Adding or subtracting one firm from the optimal number m_1^* and comparing the corresponding expected profits implies that:

$$w(N) + [N - 1][w(N) - w(N - 1)] < [x(n + 1) - x(n)]/L_0$$
$$< w(N + 1)$$
$$+ N[w(N + 1) - w(N)].$$

This condition states that the number of firms allowed to employ $(n + 1)$ shifts should be increased until the wage rate has risen sufficiently that the additional benefit to the firm (and industry), $x(n + 1) - x(n)$, falls short of the additional cost to the entire industry, $\{w(N + 1) + N[w(N + 1) - w(N)]\}L_0$.

What is special about this allocation is that it coincides with the optimal choice of the number of work shifts if all plants in the industry were owned by one firm which tried to maximize its own profit. Hence, a single firm would make the same shift allocation decision as comes about through the lottery in an industry with many firms. This interpretation is useful in evaluating social welfare and distribution of income results in the presence of more than one firm.

4. Welfare-reducing improvements of the economy

The objective of this section is to demonstrate that such "positive developments" as technological advances, specific factor growth, tariff removals, and improved terms of trade do not necessarily yield gains in social welfare even in a small economy. These detrimental effects occur because private and social optima are not necessarily the same, resulting in possible private underproduction of good X.

4.1. Private versus social optima

When there is only one firm in industry X, the allocation of labor between sectors and the wage rate are determined by (3) and (6'). In Figure 7.2 such an equilibrium was illustrated at $n = 2$ and $w = w(2)$. The socially optimal number of work shifts, $\tilde{n}$, on the other hand, is employed if national income, $X + pY$, cannot be raised by any further adjustment in the number of work shifts in sector X; that is, if:

$$[X(\tilde{n}) - X(\tilde{n} - 1)] > p[Y(\tilde{n} - 1) - Y(\tilde{n})]$$
$$[X(\tilde{n} + 1) - X(\tilde{n})] < p[Y(\tilde{n}) - Y(\tilde{n} + 1)] \tag{9}$$

where $Y(\tilde{n}) = g[L - \tilde{n}L_0, K_y]$ denotes output of industry Y when $\tilde{n}$ work shifts are employed by the single firm of industry X. The right-hand sides of (9) indicate the incremental social cost of employing another shift in sector X. In Figure 7.2, these incremental social costs per work shift are measured by distances CS for one shift, DT for two shifts, and FU for three shifts. These measures are obtained by considering the area under the YY curve for a given work shift, such as $CIKD$ for adding the second shift, drawing a block of the same size and base L_0, and measuring the block's height, DT.

Figure 7.2 reveals that

$$p[Y(n) - Y(n - 1)]/L_0 < \{w(n) + [n - 1][w(n) - w(n - 1)]\}$$

for all $n \geq 1$. Considering (3) and (9), this implies that, at a given commodity price, socially optimal production of X is at least as large as production under monopsony. Note that we say "at least" as large, since it is possible that the number of work shifts chosen by the single firms is the same as the socially optimal number of shifts, a situation depicted in Figure 7.2.

An appropriately chosen wage subsidy to industry X can induce the firm to always choose the socially optimal number of work shifts. This subsidy rate's value, s_x, depends on the number of work shifts to be employed. If only one shift is to be employed, a subsidy must be granted such that private cost, $w(1)[1 - s_x(1)]$, equals social cost, $p[Y(0) - Y(1)]/L_0$, per work shift, yielding a subsidy rate of $s_x(1) = 1 - p[Y(0) - Y(1)]/[w(1)L_0]$. It can be shown that for the nth shift, the optimal subsidy is:

$$s_x(n) = 1 - p[Y(0) - Y(n)]/[L_0 nw(n)]. \tag{10}$$

4.2. The welfare effects of exogenous changes

The "improvements" to the economy we are discussing here, namely technological advances and specific factor growth in industry Y, tariff removals, and improved terms of trade, have in common that they shift the value of marginal product curve of industry Y upward, say from YY to $Y'Y'$ in Figure 7.2. Such an upward shift either leaves industry X's number of work shifts unchanged or lowers it.

When the number of work shifts changes, the adjustment in national income is discontinuous, as can be seen from Figure 7.2. A small upward shift of the YY schedule to $Y'Y'$ raises incremental cost of the second shift from DN to DN' such that $DN' > DE$. The single firm of industry X has an incentive to cut back to one shift and national income at domestic prices changes from $O_X VKZO_Y$ to $O_X VQI'Z'O_Y$.

When the number of work shifts adjusts, a small, continuous upward movement of the YY schedule results in large, discontinuous adjustments in national income. To account for these discontinuities in assessing the direction of welfare changes, we apply a variant of Ohyama's (1972) approach, as presented in Caves and Jones (1985, 527–30). Compared are two situations of the economy: the initial one, marked by superscript 0, and the new one, marked by superscript 1, where "new" means alternatively that industry Y has more industry-specific capital, employs better technology, or faces a higher relative price due to better terms of trade or the removal of import tariffs on good X. In all instances it is assumed that free trade prevails in situation 1.

The country in question is better off in the initial situation than after these "improvements" if society could initially also have afforded the consumption bundle available in the "improved" situation but did not choose it. In other words, society is better off before the "improvement" if:

$$D_x^0 + p^0 D_y^0 > D_x^1 + p^0 D_y^1, \tag{11}$$

where D_j^i indicates society's consumption of commodity $j = X, Y$ in situation $i = 0, 1, p^0 = \pi^0/(1 + t^0), \pi^0$ denotes the initial world price of Y in terms of X, and t^0 is the country's initial ad valorem tariff rate on import good X.

Adding and subtracting $\pi^0 D_y^0$ on the left side and $\pi^1 D_y^1$ on the right side of (11) yields:

$$D_x^0 + \pi^0 D_y^0 + (p^0 - \pi^0)D_y^0 > D_x^1 + \pi^1 D_y^1 + (p^0 - \pi^1)D_y^1. \tag{11'}$$

Making use of the balance of payments constraint for a given period i,

$$D_x^i + \pi^i D_y^i = X^i + \pi^i Y^i, \tag{12}$$

and adding and subtracting $p^0 Y^0$ on the left side, allows us to restate (11) as:

$$X^0 + p^0 Y^0 > X^1 + \pi^1 Y^1 + (p^0 - \pi^1)D_y^1 - (p^0 - \pi^0)(D_y^0 - Y^0). \tag{11''}$$

Since $p^0 = \pi^0/(1 + t^0) \leq \pi^1$ for $\pi^0 \leq \pi^1$ and $t^0 \geq 0, (p^0 - \pi^0) = -\pi^0 t^0/(1 + t^0) \leq 0$, and $(D_y^0 - Y^0) < 0$ as good Y is exported, it follows that a sufficient condition for welfare-reducing "improvements" of the economy is that:

$$X^0 + p^0 Y^0 > X^1 + \pi^1 Y^1. \tag{13}$$

The economy must be worse off after the "improvement" if national income at domestic prices before the change was greater than national income at world (and domestic) prices after the change.

Let us now describe the initial and new values of output more precisely. It is assumed that the initial position of industry Y's value of marginal product function, in terms of domestic prices, is determined by parameter α^0, whereby in equilibrium the single firm of industry X employs n shifts of workers. The relevant values of industry output are:

$$X^0 = X(n) \quad \text{and} \quad p^0 Y^0 = y(n, \alpha^0). \tag{14}$$

In the new situation, an "improvement" has taken place and α has risen from α^0 to α^1, as either p, due to a terms of trade rise or tariff removal, or Y, due to specific factor endowment or technology growth, increases. This shifts industry Y's value of marginal product curve upward. If this rise in α does not affect industry X's number of work shifts, then:

$$X^1 = X(n) = X^0 \quad \text{and} \quad \pi^1 Y^1 = y(n, \alpha^1) > p^0 Y^0 = y(n, \alpha^0). \tag{15}$$

Clearly, with no change in the number of work shifts, (13) cannot be satisfied. In fact, one can show that the country must be at least as well off under the new situation.

If, on the other hand, the increase in the value of α is of sufficient magnitude that industry X's firm cuts back employment to $(n-1)$ shifts, while industry Y picks up the released labor, then:

$$X^1 = X(n-1) < X^0 \quad \text{and} \quad \pi^1 Y^1 = y(n-1, \alpha^1) > p^0 Y^0$$
$$= y(n, \alpha^0). \tag{16}$$

In order to interpret the sufficient condition for immiserization, (13), in situations when a switch in the number of work shifts occurs, we substitute (16) in (13) and restate the latter as:

$$[X(n) - X(n-1)] - [y(n-1, \alpha^1) - y(n, \alpha^0)] < 0, \tag{17}$$

where the first bracketed term is depicted in Figure 7.2 by area $CQKD$ and the second bracketed term is described by area $CI'Z'ZKD$. There is a loss in welfare from the "improvement" if area $I'QK'$ exceeds area $K'KZZ'$. Such an immiserizing "improvement" is most likely if, as in Figure 7.2, the "improvement" is small in magnitude and the indivisibility, as measured by the size of one work shift in industry X, is large relative to total employment in industry Y; that is, CD is large relative to $O_Y D$.

The occurrence of social welfare-reducing "improvements" is quite likely when there is just one firm in industry X and the indivisibility is large. If more firms operated in industry X and the distances $O_X C$, CD, etc. measured the sum of all firms' labor to staff one shift, the welfare losses from the firms' tendency to underproduce would be lower than is the case for just one firm. For example, if there were two firms in industry X, a small upward shift of the YY schedule would lead to a cutback in labor use by industry X to C' where one firm employs one shift and the other one uses two shifts. There still is a discontinuous adjustment in national income, but the loss from the cutback in the number of work shifts is now reduced from $[I'QK' - KK'Z'Z]$ to $[I''Q''K' - KK'Z'Z]$. As drawn in the diagram, there may be no net loss in national income for a nonnegligible upward shift of YY.

Finally, it should be noted that no such impoverishing "improvements" would occur if the government subsidized the indivisibility-ridden industry X according to the rule established in (10). The wage subsidy to industry X guarantees that firms will not cut back workshifts to $(n-1)$ until $[X(n) - X(n-1)] < p[Y(n-1) - Y(n)]$ *which, in turn, implies that the country must be better off in the new situation.*

5. Income distribution effects

This section examines the responses of wage rates and specific factor returns in the indivisibility-ridden industry to price increases of commodity Y and immigration of labor. The objective is to point out that, in the presence of indivisibilities, the direction of these responses is crucially affected by adjustments in the number of work shifts. If a *small* change in the exogenous variable is accompanied by a switch in the number of work shifts, "paradoxical" effects take place[6]: a price rise of commodity Y causes the wage rate to fall drastically and the return on industry Y's specific factor to make a big jump; immigration results in an abrupt increase of the wage rate and a sharp decline in Y's specific factor return. All these results were obtained for one firm in industry X, but we also indicate what these effects would be if there were more than one firm.

First, let us consider the *relationships between factor returns and commodity Y's price.* Recalling (6') one can define the wage rate as:

$$w[n(p, L), p, L] = pg_L(L - nL_0, K_y],\qquad(18)$$

[6] In the specific factor model with perfect divisibility, a price increase raises the wage rate and its own sector's specific factor return, but lowers the other sector's specific factor return. Immigration lowers the wage rate and raises both specific factor returns.

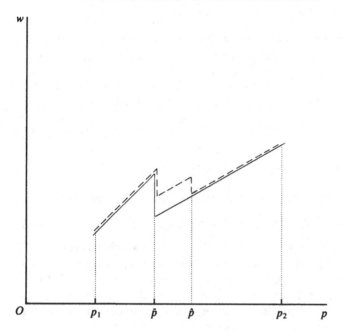

Figure 7.3

where $n(p, L)$ indicates that, according to the equilibrium conditions of (3) and (6'), the number of work shifts depends on the prevailing price and labor endowment. Assuming that n work shifts are initially in place and that the change in price is too small to affect n, the wage rate must rise as p alone is increased. However, as p is raised further and further, the accompanying rise in the wage rate, as well as in the firm's incremental cost of operating the nth shift, will eventually lead to a situation where the single firm in industry X becomes indifferent between employing n and $(n-1)$ work shifts. At this price, denoted by $\tilde{p}$:

$$[x(n) - x(n-1)]/L_0 = w(n, \tilde{p}, L)$$
$$+ [n-1][w(n, \tilde{p}, L) - w(n-1, \tilde{p}, L)], \tag{19}$$

as follows from (3). If, at price $\tilde{p}$, the firm employed n work shifts, the wage rate would be higher than if employed only $(n-1)$ shifts, as the released labor moves to industry Y. That is:

$$w(n, \tilde{p}, L) > w(n-1, \tilde{p}, L).$$

There occurs a drop in the wage rate when the number of work shifts is cut in industry X.

The relationship between the wage rate and commodity price is summarized in Figure 7.3. The wage rate rises as p goes up from p_1 to $\tilde{p}$, then takes a plunge before rising again from $\tilde{p}$ to p_2. The dashed line shows the adjustment in the case when there are two firms, each with half the shift size of a single firm, and a lottery is used to allocate work shifts. There are still drops in the wage rate at the price where one of the two firms releases a work shift, but the drops are less. The more firms there are the smoother the adjustment in wage rates, which eventually leads to a flat segment in the wage–price relationship between $\tilde{p}$ and $\hat{p}$ as the number of firms becomes very large.

The return on industry X's specific factor can be expressed as:

$$r_x[n(p,L), p, L] = \{x[n] - w[n(p,L), p, L]L_0 n\}/K_x. \tag{20}$$

Again we consider first the range of price increases in which n is not affected. The price increase raises w, as mentioned before, and $r_x(n)$, therefore, must decline. Once p reaches $\tilde{p}$, however, and the wage rate is such that (19) prevails, the number of work shifts will adjust. At $\tilde{p}$ the firm of industry X is indifferent between employing n and $(n-1)$ shifts, and the return of the specific factor with $(n-1)$ shifts employed becomes:

$$r_x(n-1, \tilde{p}, L) = \{x(n-1) - w(n-1, \tilde{p}, L) L_0[n-1]\}/K_x$$
$$= \{x(n) - w(n, \tilde{p}, L)L_0 n\}/K_x = r_x(n, \tilde{p}, L), \tag{21}$$

where we used (19) and (20). Hence, there is no jump in the return on capital in industry X similar to the jump in the wage rate when the number of work shifts in the single firm is reduced. There is, however, a positive jump in the return on capital in industry Y, r_y, when work shifts are switched in industry X from n to $(n-1)$ since:

$$r_y(n, \tilde{p}, L) = \tilde{p}g_K[L - L_0 n, K_y] < \tilde{p}g_K[L - L_0(n-1), K_y]$$
$$= r_y(n-1, \tilde{p}, L). \tag{22}$$

The *relationship between immigration of labor and factor returns* is subject to similar discontinuities. Returning to (18), one can see immediately that an increase in L, holding n and p constant, reduces the wage rate. However, as labor endowment expands further, it eventually reaches a level, $\tilde{L}$, where the wage rate and the firm's incremental cost of adding another shift have dropped sufficiently that the firm in industry X becomes indifferent between employing n and $(n+1)$ work shifts; that is:

$$[x(n+1) - x(n)]/L_0 = w[n+1, p, \tilde{L}]$$
$$+ n[w(n+1, p, \tilde{L}) - w(n, p, \tilde{L})]. \tag{23}$$

One can see from (18) that an increase in work shifts at $\tilde{L}$ implies that $w(n + 1, p, \tilde{L}) > w(n, p, \tilde{L})$, since the aggregate demand for labor rises suddenly much more than labor's endowment. Hence, at the labor supply level where industry X's firm adds another shift, the increase in labor endowment raises the wage rate. Apart from this discontinuous jump, however, the wage rate falls continuously as labor endowment expands. If there were more than one firm, similar increases in the wage rate would occur when work shifts are added, but the jumps would be smaller.

Concerning the responses of specific factors' returns, r_x and r_y, to labor endowment changes, the story corresponds to the one told for the change in commodity price. In the absence of work shift changes, a rise in L raises both r_x and r_y, but at the value of $\tilde{L}$, where the single firm X adds another shift, $r_x(n, p, \tilde{L}) = r_x(n - 1, p, \tilde{L})$ as follows from (20) and (23). In industry Y, however, the increase in labor employment by firm X draws so much labor away from industry Y that the return of the latter's specific factor abruptly declines; that is, at $\tilde{L}$:

$$r_y(n, p, \tilde{L}) = pg_K[\tilde{L} - nL_0, K_y] > pg_K[\tilde{L} - (n + 1)L_0, K_y]$$
$$= r_y(n + 1, p, \tilde{L}). \tag{24}$$

6. Concluding remarks

Indivisibilities in the use of labor are frequently encountered in many different industries. Although the reported news on adding or cutting of work shifts refers mostly to large firms, such as steel or automobile producers, adjustments of the number of work shifts are quite pervasive even among many smaller firms. This paper deals mostly with a large firm which is the only producer in the industry. However, it also suggests that similar discontinuities and paradoxical comparative statics results are possible when there are many smaller firms. Hence, the existence of indivisibilities in production offers one possible explanation why tariff cuts, terms of trade improvements, and factor growth may not only be detrimental to individual factor owners but also to society as a whole.

References

Bhagwati, J. N. and T. N. Srinivasan 1974 "On Reanalyzing the Harris–Todaro Model: Policy Ranking in The Case of Sector-Specific Sticky Wages," *American Economic Review* 66, 502–14.

Brecher, R. 1974 "Minimum Wage Rates and the Pure Theory of International Trade," *Quarterly Journal of Economics* 88, 98–116.

Caves, R. E. and R. W. Jones 1985 *World Trade and Payments*, Fourth Edition, Boston: Little Brown and Co.

106   Wolfgang Mayer and Jun Li

Frank, C. R. 1969 *Production Theory and Indivisible Commodities*, Princeton; Princeton University Press.

Hahn, F. 1949 "Proportionality, Divisibility and Economies of Scale: [one of] two Comments," *Quarterly Journal of Economics* 63, 131.

Johansen, L. 1959 "Substitution vs. Fixed Production Coefficients in the Theory of Economic Growth: A Synthesis," *Econometrica* 27, 157–75.

Jones, R. W. 1970 "The Role of Technology in the Theory of International Trade," in R. Vernon, ed., *The Technology Factor in International Trade* (New York: NBER), 73–92.

1971 "A Three-Factor Model in Theory, Trade, and History," in J. N. Bhagwati et al., eds., *Trade, Balance of Payments and Growth: Papers in International Economics in Honor of Charles P. Kindleberger*, North-Holland, Amsterdam.

1975 "Income Distribution and Effective Protection in a Multicommodity Trade Model," *Journal of Economic Theory* 11, 1–15.

Lerner, A. P. 1949. "Constant Proportions, Fixed Plant and Optimum Conditions of Production," *Quarterly Journal of Economics* 63, 215.

Mayer, W. 1974 "Short-Run and Long-Run Equilibrium for a Small Open Economy," *Journal of Political Economy* 82, 955–68.

McLeod, A. N. 1949 "Proportionality, Divisibility and Economies of Scale: [one of] Two Comments," *Quarterly Journal of Economics* 63, 128.

Mussa, M. 1974 "Tariffs and the Distribution of Income: The Importance of Factor Specificity, Substitutability, and Intensity in the Short-Run and Long-Run," *Journal of Political Economy* 82, 1191–204.

Neary, J. P. 1978 "Short-Run Capital Specificity and the Pure Theory of International Trade," *The Economic Journal* 88, 488–510.

Ohyama, M. 1972 "Trade and Welfare in General Equilibrium," *Keio Economic Studies* 9, 37–73.

Phelps, E. S. 1963 "Substitution, Fixed Proportions, Growth and Distribution," *International Economic Review* 4, 265–88.

Rogerson, R. 1988 "Indivisible Labor, Lotteries and Equilibrium," *Journal of Monetary Economics* 21, 3–16.

Samuelson, P. A. 1947 *Foundations of Economic Analysis* (Cambridge, MA: Harvard University Press), 70–81.

Srinivasan, T. N. and J. N. Bhagwati 1975 "Alternative Policy Rankings in a Large Open Economy with Sector-Specific Minimum Wages," *Journal of Economic Theory* 11, 356–71.

8 Firms, entry and hysteresis in the Heckscher–Ohlin–Samuelson model of production and trade

MICHIHIRO OHYAMA

1. Introduction

Simple general equilibrium models of production have been used extensively in the theory of international trade to study the determinants of comparative advantage and to explore the effects of various disturbances such as technological changes, factor growth and policy rearrangements on the structure of international trade and the distribution of income. The standard Heckscher–Ohlin–Samuelson model of two factors is the most popular of all although there are different possibilities such as the Ricardian model of a single factor and that of three or more factors. They commonly assume that technology of each sector exhibits constant returns to scale and that perfect competition prevails in all markets with the profits of firms being driven to zero in equilibrium.[1] An extremely useful method to analyze these models was developed by Jones (1965, 1971) and has been applied to a wide range of problems.

The common assumptions of the models are, however, rather restrictive. The assumption of constant-returns-to-scale technology, together with the assumption of perfect competition, implies that the size of firms in each industry is indeterminate. It obscures the identity of firms since they could be infinitesimally small. Admittedly, it agrees completely well with perfectly competitive markets, but it is often at variance with monopolistic or oligopolistic markets. The recently developed models of international trade under imperfect competition usually specify the identity of firms by introducing product differentiation and/or increasing returns to scale in technology (see Helpman 1983, Helpman and Krugman 1985, 1989 for instance). The assumption of zero profits is equally restrictive. It implicitly assumes away interindustry differentials in mark-up ratios, a possibly

---

[1] I am indebted to P. A. Samuelson, Koji Shimomura and an anonymous referee for valuable comments and discussions.
[1] Jones (1979) contains the analysis of various traditional models of production with these properties. See also Kemp (1969) for a survey of such models.

important source of domestic distortions. It also rules out hysteresis in production attributable to the positive costs of entry that firms incur once and for all when they enter an industry.

The present paper is an attempt to modify these restrictive assumptions of standard production models by introducing variable returns to scale into the technology of firms and allowing for the possibility of imperfectly competitive commodity markets. We shall explore the implications of this modification within the framework of the Heckscher–Ohlin–Samuelson model of two factors. The plan of the paper is as follows. In section 2, we describe the model of an industry in which identical firms operate with technology exhibiting variable returns to scale and analyze the property of its equilibrium. In section 3, we use the method of analysis developed by Jones (1965) to elucidate the structure of the modified 2×2 model of production in light of the results of the foregoing section. The Stolper–Samuelson theorem, as well as the Rybczynski theorem, is shown to carry over to the present model. In addition, we analyze the effects of a change in the mark-up ratio of an industry. In Section 4, we investigate the implications of positive markups for efficiency and hysteresis in production. In particular, we show that the restriction of free entry may bring about an outward or an inward shift of the economy's production frontier. We also reveal that a deterioration of the terms of trade may improve or deteriorate the productive efficiency of the import-competing industry through a reduction of its mark-up ratio, a point largely neglected in the literature on the gains from trade and protection. The concluding section summarizes the results of the paper and considers possible extensions of the present analysis.

2. Firms in an industry

Consider an industry in which firms, potential or actual, are able to produce a commodity using labor and land, with identical technology. Given managerial capacity and capital equipment, the production function, common to all firms, may be written as

$$Y = F(L, N), \tag{1}$$

where Y denotes the output, L labor and N land. This function is assumed to be twice continuously differentiable with positive first-order derivatives (i.e., positive marginal productivities of labor and capital). It is also assumed to be homogeneous in labor and land in the sense that the implied expansion path is a straight line from the origin. We depart from the conventional H.O.S. model, however, in allowing the function to exhibit variable returns to scale with the implied average cost curve being

U-shaped. This assumption is an extension of the usual assumption of a linear homogeneous production function. It suits the present context where an individual firm is clearly defined and implicitly associated with limited managerial capacity and capital equipment.

Each firm in the industry is assumed to determine its output so as to maximize its profit, taking prices in factor markets. The firm may be, however, monopolistic in the commodity market. The first-order conditions for profit maximization are:

$$(1 - \mu)pF_L = w, \tag{2}$$

$$(1 - \mu)pF_N = r, \tag{3}$$

where p denotes the price of the commodity, w the wage, r the rental of land, F_j ($j = L, N$) the partial derivative of F with respect to j, and μ the degree of monopoly of the industry. For simplicity assume that μ is an exogenously given parameter[2] and that the second-order conditions are satisfied.

The number of firms in the industry is given in the short run but it may change over time by entry or exit of firms. The mark-up ratio of firms, defined as the rate of excess of sales over running costs per unit of output, may be positive or negative both in the short run and in the long run. A positive mark-up ratio is likely to exist even in the long run since potential firms must bear positive entry costs, for example, to purchase and install capital equipment, recruit and train personnel, advertise their entry and to overcome various other entry barriers. The existence of a non-zero mark-up ratio may also result from governmental restriction or promotion of the industry by direct or indirect measures.[3] The mark-up ratio of a firm, π, is defined by

$$(1 + \pi)(wL + rN) = pY. \tag{4}$$

From (1)–(4), we obtain

$$F_L(L, N) = \omega F_N(L, N), \tag{5}$$

$$\rho[F_L(L, N)L + F_N(L, N)N] = F(L, N), \tag{6}$$

where $\omega(= w/r)$ is the wage/rental ratio and $\rho = (1 + \pi)(1 - \mu)$. Since $\rho = F/(F_L L + F_N N)$ from (6), ρ may be interpreted as an inverse measure of the degree of local scale economies.[4] For the time being, assume that ρ is a

---

[2] The degree of monopoly in an industry generally depends on the number of firms as well as on the level of demand for the product. It may be regarded, however, as a constant in the special case where all firms collude to maximize their joint profit and the representative consumer possesses a CES utility function (see Section 3 below).

[3] For instance, a production tax or a restriction of the number of firms gives rise to a positive markup.

[4] See Helpman and Krugman (1985), p. 33 for this point.

parameter. Given ω and ρ, equations (5) and (6) may be taken to determine the firm's "equilibrium" values of L and N.

In view of (1), the equilibrium output of the firm is also determined as a function of ω and ρ in the present model. The scale may be viewed as reflecting the indivisibility of managerial or organizational capacity associated with the production technology of the industry. To examine the properties of this equilibrium, differentiate (5) and (6) totally to obtain

$$(LdN - NdL)(F_{NL} - \omega F_{NN}) = F_N d\omega, \tag{7}$$

$$(F_N dN + F_L dL)[F_N - \rho(F_N + F_{NL}L + F_{NN}N)] = (F_N Y/\rho)d\rho. \tag{8}$$

where F_{ij} $(i, j = L, N)$ denotes the partial derivative of F_i with respect to j. To derive (7) and (8), we have employed the relationship

$$(F_{LL}L + F_{LN}N)F_N = (F_{NL}L + F_{NN}N)F_L, \tag{9}$$

implied by the homogeneity of the production function, $F(L, N)$. Note that the homogeneity of $F(L, N)$ entails

$$F_{NL} - \omega F_{NN} > 0. \tag{10}$$

Let us assume

$$F_N - \rho(F_N + F_{NL}L + F_{NN}N) > 0. \tag{11}$$

This assumption is satisfied if $F_N + F_{NL}L + F_{NN}N \leq 0$ or if ρ is sufficiently close to unity and the marginal cost of the firm is increasing.[5]

Figure 8.1 illustrates this equilibrium. The straight line OR from the origin shows the combinations of L and N that satisfy (5). The curve IQ illustrates the combinations of L and N that satisfy (6). Note that the IQ coincides with an isoquant of the firm. Clearly, the equilibrium exists uniquely as shown by the intersection, E, of PR and IQ. A rise in the wage/rental ratio shifts OR counterclockwise to OR', say, without affecting the IQ curve. The new equilibrium, E', is associated with a higher value of N and a lower value of L. Since E and E' are on the same isoquant, the equilibrium output is not affected by this disturbance. In contrast, a rise in ρ shifts IQ upward to $I'Q'$. As a result of this change, the equilibrium moves from E to E'', and the inputs of labor and land increase by the same proportion thereby increasing the equilibrium output. Let us write $Y(\rho)$ to indicate that Y is a function only of ρ..

Now define the two input coefficients by

$$a_L = \frac{L}{F(L, N)}, \quad a_N = \frac{N}{F(L, N)}. \tag{12}$$

[5] For example, the condition $F_N + F_{NL}L + F_{NN}N \leq 0$ is fulfilled with equality if
$$F(L, N) = \alpha \log L + \beta \log N + \gamma.$$

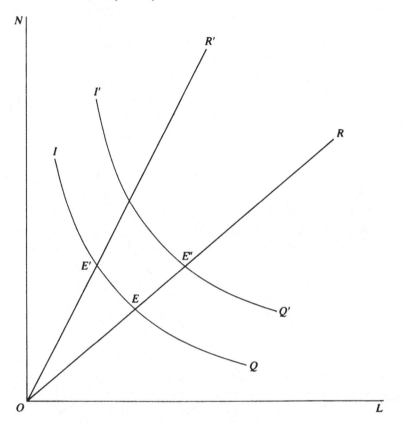

Figure 8.1 Firm's equilibrium and its comparative statics

Clearly, the coefficients are also functions of ω and ρ, via L and N. We are interested in the properties of these functions for later reference. Differentiate (12) and employ (7)–(9) to obtain

$$\frac{\partial a_L}{\partial \omega} = -\frac{\rho F_N^{\,2}}{(F_{NL} - \omega F_{NN})Y^2} < 0, \tag{13}$$

$$\frac{\partial a_N}{\partial \omega} = \frac{\rho \omega F_N^{\,2}}{(F_{NL} - \omega F_{NN})Y^2} > 0, \tag{14}$$

$$\frac{\partial a_L}{\partial \rho} = \frac{a_L F_N(\rho - 1)}{[F_N - \rho(F_N + F_{NL}L + F_{NN}N)]\rho}, \tag{15}$$

$$\frac{\partial a_N}{\partial \rho} = \frac{a_N F_N(\rho - 1)}{[F_N - \rho(F_N + F_{NL}L + F_{NN}N)]\rho}. \tag{16}$$

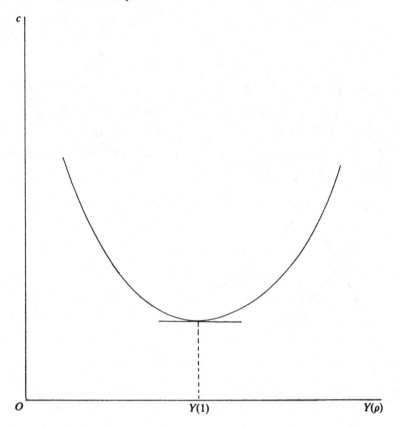

Figure 8.2   Average cost curve

From (15) and (16), we find

$$\frac{1}{a_L}\frac{\partial a_L}{\partial \rho} = \frac{1}{a_N}\frac{\partial a_N}{\partial \rho} \gtreqless 0 \quad \text{according as} \quad \rho \gtreqless 1. \tag{17}$$

Thus a rise in ω decreases a_L and increases a_N unambiguously, whereas a rise in ρ increases or decreases both a_L and a_N equiproportionately, depending upon whether it is greater than or less than unity. The unit cost, c, of the firm's product is defined by

$$c = wa_L + ra_N. \tag{18}$$

In view of (13) and (14) we obtain

$$\omega\frac{\partial a_L}{\partial \omega} + \frac{\partial a_N}{\partial \omega} = 0. \tag{19}$$

This means that the equilibrium marginal rate of substitution between labor and land is equal to the wage/rental ratio. From (18),

$$\frac{\partial c}{\partial \rho} = w\frac{\partial a_L}{\partial \rho} + r\frac{\partial a_N}{\partial \rho} \gtreqless 0 \text{ according as } \rho \gtreqless 1. \tag{20}$$

A rise in ρ lowers or raises productivity of both factors and, therefore, increases or decreases the unit cost of the firm's product, depending upon whether ρ is greater or less than unity. We have shown above that the equilibrium output of the firm is an increasing function of ρ and that it is independent of ω. Thus we may conclude that the average cost curve of the firm declines first (when $\rho < 1$) and rises later (when $\rho > 1$) as the firm's equilibrium output increases. Figure 8.2 depicts this relationship.

As noted above, there are alternative stories that justify the positive (or negative) mark-up ratios prevailing in the long run. It may be attributable to the entry cost the firm must pay to enter the industry or to government intervention. In the former case, new firms enter the industry as long as the present value of future profits exceeds the entry cost, E, or assuming static expectations,

$$pY - (wL + rN) > \iota E,$$

where ι denotes the real rate of interest (reflecting the social rate of time preference). If the entry cost is given in terms of the industry's product and thus proportional to the unit factor cost of the product, or if $E = k(wa_L + ra_L)$, the maximum possible value of π prevailing in the long-run industry equilibrium is implicitly given by

$$\bar{\pi} = \iota k/Y((1 - \mu)(1 + \bar{\pi})). \tag{21}$$

The incumbent firms will remain in the industry, however, as long as $\pi > 0$ since they have already sunk the entry cost. The number of firms in the industry becomes stationary when $0 < \pi < \bar{\pi}$ and it decreases over time if $\pi < 0$ as the incumbent firms quit the industry. Thus the range of π compatible with the long-run industry equilibrium is

$$0 \leq \pi \leq \bar{\pi}$$

in this case. Alternatively, we may suppose that the government imposes a production tax at the rate of t. Then

$$\pi = t \tag{22}$$

in the long-run industry equilibrium in the absence of entry costs. The foregoing discussion of the firm's equilibrium is readily applicable to the analysis of the industry equilibrium of either kind.

3. The structure of a simple general equilibrium

In this section we develop the analysis of a simple general equilibrium model by employing the basic concepts and relationships discussed in the preceding section. Suppose that there are two industries, labelled 1 and 2, using labor and land as common factors of production. Each industry is assumed to be in the industry equilibrium as defined above. The model may be interpreted as an extended version of the familiar Heckscher–Ohlin–Samuelson model (the H.O.S. model for short) of production and trade in the form considered by Jones (1965). As will be seen below, it virtually coincides with the H.O.S. model when all firms are price takers and their mark-up ratios are zero in both industries. We apply the method of analysis developed by Jones (1965) and explore the implications of non-zero markup ratios and positive degrees of monopoly for its workings.

Let us first lay out the basic relationships of the model. By the definition of markup ratios we have

$$a_{L1}(\omega, \rho_1)w + a_{N1}(\omega, \rho_1)r = p_1/(1 + \pi_1), \tag{23}$$

and

$$a_{L2}(\omega, \rho_2)w + a_{N2}(\omega, \rho_2)r = p_2/(1 + \pi_2), \tag{24}$$

where a_{ij} ($i = L, N; j = 1, 2$) denotes the coefficient of factor i in industry j, π_j the markup ratio prevailing in industry j and p_j the price of commodity j. Note that a_{ij} is a function of ω and ρ_j. Assuming that both labor and land are fully employed, we have

$$a_{L1}(\omega, \rho_1)Z_1 + a_{L2}(\omega, \rho_2)Z_2 = L, \tag{25}$$

$$a_{N1}(\omega, \rho_1)Z_1 + a_{N2}(\omega, \rho_2)Z_2 = N, \tag{26}$$

where L and N denote the total endowment of labor and land and Z_j ($j = 1, 2$) signifies the total output of commodity j. Let n_j be the number of identical firms in industry j and Y_j be the output of a single firm in the industry equilibrium. We may then write

$$Z_j = n_j Y_j(\rho_j) \quad (j = 1, 2) \tag{27}$$

which completes the description of the supply side of the economy. As shown in the preceding section, Y_j is an increasing function of ρ_j.

Turning to the demand side, we introduce the simplifying assumption that consumers possess a common utility function of the form

$$u = [\alpha_1 C_1^{-\beta_1} + \alpha_2 C_2^{-\beta_2}]^{-1/\beta} \tag{28}$$

where C_1 and C_2 represent his consumption of commodities 1 and 2. To simplify notation, let us regard C_1 and C_2 as the aggregate social consumption of commodities 1 and 2.[6] The elasticity of demand for each commodity is equal to $1/(1 + \beta_j)$ in this case. For simplicity suppose that all firms in this industry behave either as price takers or as tacit colluders to maximize the aggregate profits of the industry. Then, the degree of monopoly in industry j is either zero or $1 + \beta_j$, i.e.

$$\mu_j = 0, \quad \text{or} \quad 1 + \beta_j \quad (j = 1, 2) \tag{29}$$

in conformity with our assumption of constant degrees of monopoly.

The first-order conditions for utility maximization and the market equilibrium conditions $(Z_j = C_j, j = 1, 2)$ imply

$$\frac{Z_2^{1+\beta_2}}{Z_1^{1+\beta_1}} = \frac{\alpha_2 \beta_2}{\alpha_1 \beta_1} \frac{p_1}{p_2}. \tag{30}$$

The model consists of 7 equations, (23)–(27) and (30) in 10 variables, p_1, p_2, $w, r, n_1, n_2, \pi_1, \pi_2, Z_1$ and Z_2. We may set $p_2 = 1$ by taking commodity 2 as the numeraire of the system. Furthermore, any pair of the variables, n_1, n_2, π_1 and π_2, may be regarded as the exogenous variables of the system. For instance, we may suppose that $\pi_1 = \bar{\pi}_1$ and $\pi_2 = \bar{\pi}_2$ in the long-run industry equilibrium. In this case, the system of seven equations determine 7 variables, p_2, w, r, n_1, n_2, Z_1 and Z_2 for the given values of π_1 and π_2. Alternatively, we may take n_1 and n_2 as given parameters either in the short-run industry equilibrium or in the long-run industry equilibrium where $0 < \pi_j < \bar{\pi}_j$ $(j = 1, 2)$. Then, π_1 and π_2 become endogenous variables.

Let us first consider the case where the mark-up ratio of each industry is given in the long-run industry equilibrium. If $\pi_j = \mu_j = 0$ $(j = 1, 2)$, then the present model becomes virtually identical to the standard H.O.S. model as developed by Jones (1965) except that the adjustment of industrial output is explicitly assumed here to take place through the adjustment of the number of firms in the industry. Given π_j and μ_j, the mere inspection of equations (26)–(29), in light of the properties of $a_{ij}(\omega, \rho_j)$ derived in the preceding section, reveals that all the standard theorems of the H.O.S. model such as the Stolper–Samuelson Theorem and the Rybczynski Theorem carry over to the present model.

For simplicity, we assume that $\beta_1 = \beta_2 = \beta$ or $\mu_1 = \mu_2 = \mu$ and that they are fixed throughout the following analysis. Differentiating (23) and (24) totally and taking account of (17) and (19), we obtain

$$\theta_{L1}\hat{w} + \theta_{N1}\hat{r} = \hat{p}_1 - (1 + \varepsilon_1)\hat{\rho}_1 \tag{31}$$

---

[6] See Flam and Helpman (1987) for the use of a similar assumption in a partial equilibrium model.

$$\theta_{L2}\hat{w} + \theta_{N2}\hat{r} = \hat{p}_2 - (1 + \varepsilon_2)\hat{p}_2, \tag{32}$$

where the circumflex ($\hat{\ }$) over a variable indicates its relative change, θ_{ij} ($i = L, N; j = 1, 2$) is the share of factor i in the unit cost of commodity j and

$$\varepsilon_j = \frac{\rho_j}{a_{Lj}}\frac{\partial a_{Lj}}{\partial \rho_j} = \frac{\rho_j}{a_{Nj}}\frac{\partial a_{Nj}}{\partial \rho_j} = \frac{\rho_j}{c_j}\frac{\partial c_j}{\partial \rho_j}.$$

By the constancy of μ_j, $\hat{p}_j$ is equal to the change in π_j relative to $1 + \pi_j$. By definition, θ_{Lj} and θ_{Kj} add up to unity. We assume that $1 + \varepsilon_j > 0$. Subtract (32) from (31) to get

$$|\theta|\hat{\omega} = \hat{p} + (1 + \varepsilon_2)\hat{p}_2 - (1 + \varepsilon_1)\hat{p}_1 \tag{33}$$

where $p = p_1/p_2$ and $|\theta| = \theta_{L1}\theta_{N2} - \theta_{L2}\theta_{N1}$. For definiteness, suppose that commodity 1 is more labor intensive (or less land intensive) than commodity 2. This means that $|\theta| > 0$.

The foregoing analysis implies that given π_1 and π_2, a rise in the relative price of a commodity is associated with a more-than-proportionate rise in the price of the factor used relatively intensively in the production of that commodity and with a decrease in the price of the other factor (the Stolper–Samuelson Theorem). Clearly, the effects of a change in the markup ratio of each industry are qualitatively opposite to the effects of a change in the relative price of its product. Thus, a rise in the markup ratio of industry 1, *ceteris paribus*, lowers the wage/rental ratio since it forces the unit cost of its labor intensive product to decrease.

Total differentiation of (25) and (26) yields

$$\lambda_{L1}\hat{Z}_1 + \lambda_{L2}\hat{Z}_2 = \hat{L} + \delta_L\hat{\omega} - \lambda_{L1}\varepsilon_1\hat{p}_1 - \lambda_{L2}\varepsilon_2\hat{p}_2, \tag{34}$$

$$\lambda_{N1}\hat{Z}_1 + \lambda_{N2}\hat{Z}_2 = \hat{N} - \delta_N\hat{\omega} - \lambda_{N1}\varepsilon_1\hat{p}_1 - \lambda_{N2}\varepsilon_2\hat{p}_2, \tag{35}$$

where λ_{ij} ($i = L, N; j = 1, 2$) is the fraction of factor i employed in industry j and

$$\delta_L = \lambda_{L1}\theta_{N1}\sigma_1 + \lambda_{L2}\theta_{N2}\sigma_2; \quad \delta_N = \lambda_{N1}\theta_{L1}\sigma_1 + \lambda_{N2}\theta_{L2}\sigma_2$$

with σ_j ($j = 1, 2$) denoting the elasticity of substitution defined to be positive by

$$\sigma_j = \frac{\hat{a}_{Nj} - \hat{a}_{Lj}}{\hat{\omega}}$$

(see Jones [1965]). Subtract (35) from (34) to get

$$|\lambda|(\hat{Z}_1 - \hat{Z}_2) = \hat{L} - \hat{N} + (\delta_L + \delta_N)\hat{\omega} - |\lambda|(\varepsilon_1\hat{p}_1 + \varepsilon_2\hat{p}_2) \tag{36}$$

where $|\lambda| = \lambda_{L1}\lambda_{N2} - \lambda_{L2}\lambda_{N1}$. Clearly, $|\lambda|$ is positive under the present assumption that commodity 1 is labor intensive relative to commodity 2. Substituting (33) into (36), we obtain

$$\hat{Z}_1 - \hat{Z}_2 = \sigma_s \hat{p} + \frac{1}{|\lambda|}(\hat{L} - \hat{N}) + [\sigma_s + (1 + \sigma_s)\varepsilon_2]\hat{\rho}_2$$

$$- [\sigma_s + (1 + \sigma_s)\varepsilon_1]\hat{\rho}_1 \tag{37}$$

where $\sigma_s = (\delta_L + \delta_N)/|\theta|\,|\lambda|$. This result tells us that given p, π_1 and π_2, an increase in the endowment of labor relative to that of capital increases more than proportionately the output of commodity 1 relative to commodity 2 (the Rybczynski Theorem). It also confirms the normal association of the relative output of commodities with their relative price. In addition, a rise in the markup ratio of industry j is seen to decrease the relative output of that industry if $\sigma_s/(1 + \sigma_s) > -\varepsilon_j$. We may assume that this condition is satisfied.

To incorporate the demand side of the economy, differentiate (30) to get

$$\hat{Z}_1 - \hat{Z}_2 = -\mu\hat{p}. \tag{38}$$

Substitution of (38) into (37) yields

$$(\mu + \sigma_s)\hat{p} = -\frac{1}{|\lambda|}(\hat{L} - \hat{N}) + [\sigma_s + (1 + \sigma_s)\varepsilon_1]\hat{\rho}_1$$

$$- [\sigma_s + (1 + \sigma_s)\varepsilon_2]\hat{\rho}_2. \tag{39}$$

Thus, an increase in the endowment of labor relative to land lowers the relative price of commodity 1, or the labor intensive commodity. In the context of international trade theory, this result implies that a country tends to have comparative advantage in a labor intensive commodity if it is labor-abundant *vis-à-vis* the rest of the world (the Heckscher–Ohlin Theorem). Furthermore, a rise in the markup ratio of industry j raises the relative price of its product if $\sigma_j/(1 + \sigma_j) > -\varepsilon_j$. Thus, with other things being equal, a country tends to have comparative advantage in the industry whose markup ratio is relatively small in comparison with the rest of the world.

By virtue of (33) and (39), we may rewrite (34) and (35) as

$$(\lambda_{L1} + \phi_L)\hat{Z}_1 + (\lambda_{L2} - \phi_L)\hat{Z}_2 = \hat{L} - \gamma_{L1}\hat{\rho}_1 + \gamma_{L2}\hat{\rho}_2, \tag{40}$$

$$(\lambda_{N1} - \phi_N)\hat{Z}_1 + (\lambda_{N2} - \phi_N)\hat{Z}_2 = \hat{N} + \gamma_{N1}\hat{\rho}_1 - \gamma_{N2}\hat{\rho}_2, \tag{41}$$

where

$$\phi_i = \frac{\delta_i}{\mu|\theta|} \quad (i = L, N),$$

$$\gamma_{L1} = \frac{\delta_L}{|\theta|}(1 + \varepsilon_1) + \lambda_{L1}\varepsilon_1, \quad \gamma_{L2} = \frac{\delta_L}{|\theta|}(1 + \varepsilon_2) - \lambda_{L2}\varepsilon_2,$$

$$\gamma_{N1} = \frac{\delta_N}{|\theta|}(1 + \varepsilon_1) - \lambda_{N1}\varepsilon_1, \quad \gamma_{N2} = \frac{\delta_N}{|\theta|}(1 + \varepsilon_2) + \lambda_{N2}\varepsilon_2.$$

We can solve (40) and (41) for the effects of various exogenous disturbances on the aggregate outputs of industries. In particular, subtracting (41) from (40) gives

$$(|\lambda| + \phi_L + \phi_N)(\hat{Z}_1 - \hat{Z}_2) = \hat{L} - \hat{N} - (\gamma_{L1} + \gamma_{N1})\hat{\rho}_1$$
$$+ (\gamma_{L2} + \gamma_{N2})\hat{\rho}_2. \tag{42}$$

Thus, a rise in the labor/land endowment ratio increases the relative output of the labor intensive commodity unambiguously, whereas a rise in the markup ratio of industry i decreases its relative output unless ε_i is negative and very large in absolute value.

To clarify the effects of disturbances on the number of firms, differentiate (27) to get

$$\hat{Z}_j = \hat{n}_j + \eta_j\hat{\rho}_j \quad (j = 1, 2) \tag{43}$$

where $\eta_j \ (= \rho_j/\gamma_j \, \partial\gamma_j/\partial\rho_j)$ is the elasticity of output in industry j. The assumption of the present paper ensures $\eta_j > 0$. Substituting (43) into (40) and (41), we obtain

$$(\lambda_{L1} + \phi_L)\hat{n}_1 + (\lambda_{L2} - \phi_L)\hat{n}_2 = \hat{L} - v_{L1}\hat{\rho}_1 + v_{L2}\hat{\rho}_2, \tag{44}$$

$$(\lambda_{N1} - \phi_N)\hat{n}_1 + (\lambda_{N2} + \phi_N)\hat{n}_2 = \hat{N} + v_{N1}\hat{\rho}_1 - v_{N2}\hat{\rho}_2, \tag{45}$$

where

$$v_{L1} = \gamma_{L1} + (\lambda_{L1} + \phi_L)\eta_1, \quad v_{L2} = \gamma_{L2} - (\lambda_{L2} - \phi_L)\eta_2,$$
$$v_{N1} = \gamma_{N1} - (\lambda_{N1} - \phi_N)\eta_1, \quad v_{N2} = \gamma_{N2} + (\lambda_{N2} + \phi_N)\eta_2.$$

Subtract (45) from (44) to get

$$(|\lambda| + \phi_L + \phi_N)(\hat{n}_1 - \hat{n}_2) = \hat{L} - \hat{N} - (v_{L1} + v_{N1})\hat{\rho}_1$$
$$+ (v_{L2} + v_{L2})\hat{\rho}_2 \tag{46}$$

where

$$v_{L1} + v_{N1} = \gamma_{L1} + \gamma_{N1} + (|\lambda| + \phi_L + \phi_N)\eta_1,$$
$$v_{L2} + v_{N2} = \gamma_{L2} + \gamma_{N2} + (|\lambda| + \phi_L + \phi_N)\eta_2.$$

Thus a rise in the labor/land endowment ratio increases the relative number of firms in the labor intensive industry, and a rise in the markup ratio of an industry decreases the relative number of firms in that industry. We can also ascertain the effects of disturbances on the absolute number of firms in each industry. For instance, an increase in the endowment of labor increases the number of firms in the labor intensive industry, but its effect on the number of firms in the capital intensive industry is unclear. On the other hand, a rise in the markup of an industry is most likely to decrease the number of firms in that industry, but it may also decrease the number of firms in the other industry.

So far we have treated π_1 and π_2 (or ρ_1 and ρ_2) as exogenous variables. There are, however, a number of alternative interpretations of the present model. For instance, consider the case where n_1 and n_2 are exogenous variables, with π_1 and π_2 becoming endogenous. This situation may be taken to represent either the short-run equilibrium defined at a given point of time or the long-run stationary equilibrium in which the number of firms is not affected by small disturbances because the prevailing positive markup ratios are sufficiently low to discourage the entry of new firms. In this case we have to change the role of variables in (44) and (45) to solve for $\hat{\rho}_1$ and $\hat{\rho}_2$ in terms of $\hat{L}$, $\hat{N}$, $\hat{n}_1$ and $\hat{n}_2$. For instance, it can be shown that an increase in the number of firms in an industry is likely to reduce the markup ratio in that industry, but its effect on the markup ratio of the other industry is ambiguous. An increase in the endowment of labor increases the markup ratio in the labor intensive industry, but it may reduce the markup ratio in the capital intensive industry. In this case, the simple relationships such as the Stolper–Samuelson Theorem and the Rybczynski Theorem are no longer valid.

4. Inefficiencies, hysteresis and gains from trade

In the preceding section we considered a simple general equilibrium economy in the long run where firms in all industries are explicitly defined and specified with their average-cost curves being U-shaped. In this section we investigate some welfare implications of the model. In the first place, we clarify how the presence of positive markups may affect efficiency in production. Secondly, we show that positive markups due to positive entry costs give rise to hysteresis in the production structure of the economy to the extent that once established incumbent firms are willing to lower their markup ratios to endure adverse times. We also consider the opening up of the economy to the outside world and discuss important implications of hysteresis for the gains from foreign trade.

Let us begin by elucidating the determinants of national income when production technologies and factor endowments are all given and unchanging. By the definition of the markup ratios we have

$$(1 + \pi_1)(L_1 w + N_1 r) = p_1 Z_1 \tag{47}$$

$$(1 + \pi_2)(L_2 w + N_2 r) = p_2 Z_2 \tag{48}$$

where L_j and N_j $(j = 1, 2)$ denote the aggregate employment of labor and land in industry j respectively. Differentiating (47) and (48) totally and combining the results gives

$$\sum p_j dZ_j = \sum (1 + \pi_j)(L_j dw + N_j dr + w dL_j + r dN_j) + \sum p_j Z_j \hat{\rho}_j$$
$$- \sum Z_j dp_j, \tag{49}$$

where summation runs over 1 and 2. On the other hand, differentiating (23) and (24) totally and multiplying the results by Z_1 and Z_2 respectively yields

$$\sum (1 + \pi_j)(L_j dw + N_j dr) + \sum (1 + \varepsilon_j) p_j Z_j \hat{\rho}_j - \sum Z_j dp_j \tag{50}$$

Since $\sum dL_j = 0$ and $\sum dN_j = 0$, (49) and (50) imply

$$\sum p_j dZ_j = (\pi_2 - \pi_1)(w dL_2 + r dN_2) - \sum \varepsilon_j p_j z_j \hat{\rho}_j. \tag{51}$$

Given production technologies, factor endowments *and* industrial markup ratios, the production frontier of the economy may be traced out by changing employment of factors in the two industries efficiently.

Here, positive markups affect the productive efficiency of the economy through two distinct channels. For one thing, a rise in the markup ratio of industry j lowers (resp. raises) the productivity of firms in industry j and thereby brings about an inward (resp. outward) shift of the production frontier if $\rho_j > 1$ (resp. $\rho_j < 1$).[7] Under the assumptions of the present chapter, it invariably increases the output of firms in the industry,[8] but its effect on factor productivity is negative (resp. positive) if they are operating to the right (resp. left) of the lowest point of their average cost curve. For another thing, an increase in the output of commodity 2 and a corresponding decrease in the output of commodity 1 *along* the given production frontier increases (resp. decreases) the national income evaluated at the initial prices if and only if $\pi_2 > \pi_1$ (resp. $\pi_1 < \pi_2$). This means that the relative price of commodity 2 exceeds (resp. falls short of) the corresponding marginal rate of transformation if industry 2 enjoys a greater (resp. smaller) markup ratio than industry 1. The deviation of the relative price, or the marginal rate of substitution from the marginal rate of transformation is solely attributable to the inter-industry differential in markup ratio. Contrary to the usual presumption, inter-industry differences in the degree of monopoly have nothing to do with the domestic distortion of this kind.

---

[7] Given L, N, ρ_1 and ρ_2 the production frontier is implicitly defined by the full employment condition of factors, or (25) and (26). It is the loci of Z_1 and Z_2 that satisfy (25) and (26) for different values of ω.

[8] As noted in the preceding section, a rise in π_1 may be presumed to decrease Z_1/Z_2 (see (42)).

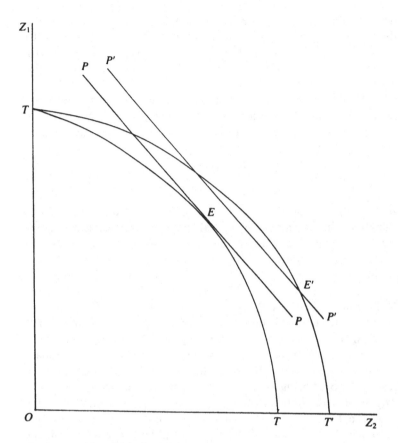

Figure 8.3　The effect of a fall in π_2

Figure 8.3 illustrates this point for the case where commodity prices are given, say, in the world markets and all domestic firms have no influence over them, or $\mu_j = 0$ $(j = 1, 2)$. The curve TT shows the production frontier where $\pi_1 = \pi_2 > 0$. The equilibrium production point under these circumstances is indicated by E where the line PP with the slope of p_2/p_1 is tangent to the production frontier. Starting from this situation, consider the effects of a fall in the markup ratio of commodity 2. The curve TT' is new production frontier where π_2 is now smaller than π_1. It lies uniformly above TT except for the point T where the economy specializes completely in commodity 1. The new equilibrium production point is E' where the given relative price of commodity 2 is smaller than the slope of the frontier. The output of commodity 2 increases and that of commodity 1 decreases as a result. Next consider the effects of a fall in the relative price of commodity 2 when the equilibrium is initially at E'. In view of the analysis given in the preceding section, this change causes the output of commodity 2 to decrease and that of commodity 1 to increase along the production frontier TT' (see (37)). The real national income of the economy evaluated at the initial prices increases in consequence.

In view of (51), one may wish to control π_1 and π_2 in order to improve productive efficiency. As a reference state, first consider the standard long-run industry equilibrium with no entry costs or no government intervention where $\pi_1 = \pi_2 = 0$. This state of the economy is efficient only if the commodity markets are perfectly competitive, or $\mu_1 = \mu_2 = 0$ so that $\rho_1 = \rho_2 = 1$, and therefore, $\varepsilon_1 = \varepsilon_2 = 0$. It would be inefficient if the commodity markets are monopolistic, i.e., if $\mu_1 > 0$ or $\mu_2 > 0$. In such a case, $\rho_1 = 1 - \mu_1 < 1$ or $\rho_2 = 1 - \mu_2 < 1$ implying $\varepsilon_1 < 0$ or $\varepsilon_2 < 0$. Thus, the real national income may be increased by slightly increasing π_1 or π_2. It means that there are too many firms in the industry at the zero profit equilibrium. This conclusion is known as the "excess entry thesis." Originating with Kahn (1935) and Meade (1937), it has been recently revived and elaborated by Von Weiszacker (1980), Perry (1984), Mankiw and Whinston (1986) and Suzumura and Kiyono (1987) within the framework of partial equilibrium models. The present analysis shows that the thesis carries over easily to our simple general equilibrium model.

In the presence of entry costs, however, markup ratios may remain positive even in the long run. Suppose that $\pi_1 = \pi_2 > 0$. In such a case, a decrease in π_j would bring about an increase in national income if $\rho_j > 1$. This implies that the number of firms in industry j is too small from the viewpoint of national economic welfare. Thus we obtain what may be called the "insufficient entry thesis."[9] This point has been overlooked in the literature on entry because of the prevailing zero-profit assumption. Generally speaking, the number of firms in any industry may be excessive or deficient depending upon whether they operate to the right or to the left of the lowest point of their average cost curve.

Let $\tilde{\pi}_j$ denote the optimal markup ratio in industry j. The expression for $\tilde{\pi}_j$ is generally complicated. If the degree of monopoly in industry 1 is greater than that in industry 2, or if $\mu_1 > \mu_2$, we can show

$$\frac{\mu_1}{1 - \mu_1} > \tilde{\pi}_1 > \tilde{\pi}_2 > \frac{\mu_2}{1 - \mu_2}. \tag{52}$$

Point M in Figure 8.4 shows the optimal markup ratios. The ovally shaped curves represent the combinations of π_1 and π_2 that keep the real national

[9] To evaluate the entry of a new firm rigorously, we must weigh the gain in national income against the once-and-for-all loss of resources in the form of entry costs. Here, entry costs are implicitly assumed to be unimportant in comparison with the gain in national income.

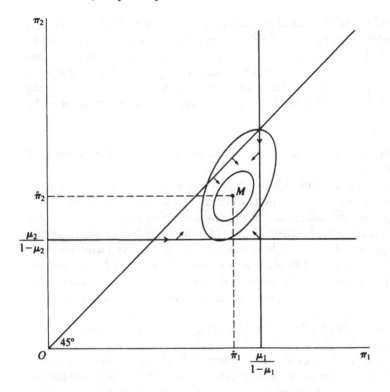

Figure 8.4   The optimal mark-up ratios

income at constant levels. Arrows indicate the changes in π_1 and π_2 that increase the national income. Thus the greater degree of monopoly implies the greater value of optimal markup ratio. Moreover, the optimal markup ratios are trapped between the price-cost margins of the two industries. In the special case where $\mu_1 = \mu_2 = \mu$, we have

$$\tilde{\pi}_1 = \tilde{\pi}_2 = \frac{\mu}{1 - \mu} \tag{53}$$

which implies that $\varepsilon_1 = \varepsilon_2 = 0$. In this case, the optimal markup ratio common to the two industries is zero only when the commodity markets are perfectly competitive and increases as the degree of monopoly, μ, increases. Generally speaking, entry of firms to industry j is excessive (resp. deficient) if $\pi_j < \min(\mu_1/(1 - \mu_1),\ \mu_2/(1 - \mu_2))$ (resp. $\pi_j > \max(\mu_1/(1 - \mu_1), \mu_2/(1 - \mu_2)))$ in the long-run.

Next, let us consider the effects of opening up the economy to the rest of the world in the absence of governmental intervention. Suppose that new firms enter industry j only if its markup ratio exceeds a critical value, $\bar{\pi}_j$, determined by the entry cost which a potential entrant must pay once and for all. The incumbent firms may be assumed to operate as long as they earn non-negative profits since they have alredy sunk the entry cost. As noted before, the range of π_j in the long-run equilibrium is, therefore, given by

$$0 \leqq \pi_j \leqq \bar{\pi}_j.$$

This situation gives rise to the so-called hysteresis in the response of industrial output to external disturbances.

In order to illustrate this point, consider a small country facing given commodity prices in the world markets and suppose that the upper limit of markup ratios prevail initially in all industries. Starting from this situation, consider the effects of a fall in the price of commodity 2. If the markup ratios were kept unchanged, then the number of firms of industry 1 would increase and that of industry 2 would decrease. Firms in industry 2, however, will actually continue their operation by allowing their markup ratio to decline. Thus n_2 is now to be regarded as an exogenous variable and π_2 as an endogenous variable.

In view of (33), (34), (35) and (43), a fall in p_2 will cause π_2 to decrease when n_2, π_1 and p_1 are given. From (17), this will bring about an equiproportionate fall in a_{L2} and a_{K2} or an improvement in the efficiency of the production of commodity p. Figure 8.5 illustrates the effects of this change on industrial outputs. The curve TT is the production frontier corresponding to the initial situation and E is the equilibrium production point on the assumption that $\pi_1 = \pi_2 = \bar{\pi}_1 = \bar{\pi}_2 > 0$ initially. The line PP has the slope of the initial relative price of commodity 2 and is tangent to the production frontier at E. With a fall in p_2, the production frontier would shift outward to TT'. The new equilibrium is indicated by E' where the new production frontier TT' has a slope greater than that of the new price line $P'P'$.

If the initial markup ratios were unchanged, a fall in p_2 would lead to a different production equilibrium, E'', where the new price line $P''P''$ is tangent to the old production frontier TT. Comparing E' with E'', we may conclude that the actual decrease in the output of commodity 2 in response to the price change is smaller than expected for the case in which the markup ratio of the industry is kept at the initial level. In fact, the number of firms in industry 2 remains unchanged and the markup ratio of the industry falls alleviating the response of output to the price change. This phenomenon is referred to as *hysteresis* in the literature.[10]

---

[10] Hysteresis is taken here to mean the failure of a certain variable disturbed by an external agent to return to its original value when the cause of the change is removed. This concept originates in physics, and its relevance to Economics was emphasized and illustrated by

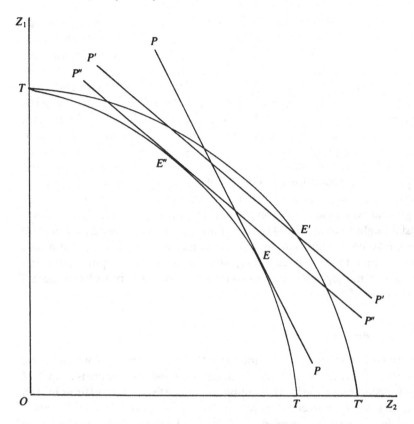

Figure 8.5   The effect of a fall in p_2

It is important to understand the implications of hysteresis for the gains from trade. Referring back to Figure 8.5, suppose that E is the autarkic equilibrium of the country and that E' is the free-trade production point after opening up the country. With no change in markup ratios, production equilibrium would shift from E' to E'' bringing about a production gain through specialization. The exposure of firms in industry 2 to competitive pressure in the world market, however, reduces the markup ratio of the industry enhancing its productivity. It brings about an additional gain in production represented by the shift from E'' to E'. This possible gain due to increased efficiency of the import-competing industry is seldom discussed in the standard literature on gains from trade but it may occasionally be more important than the much publicized gains through specialization.

Kemp and Wan (1974). Recently, it has been evoked to explain the persistent real effects of large exchange shocks when market entry costs are sunk. For instance, see Baldwin (1988), Baldwin and Krugman (1989) and Dixit (1989).

In the above illustration, the country in question is assumed to take prices so that $\rho_j \, (= 1 + \bar{\pi}_j) > 1$ in the initial situation. When firms are price-setters, however, $\rho_j \, (= (1 + \pi_j)(1 - \mu_j))$ may be smaller than unity initially. Suppose now that this is the case in the autarkic equilibrium of the country and suppose that the opening up of the economy to the rest of the world results in a fall in the markup ratio of industry 2 and an increase in the number of firms in industry 1. In such a case, the productivity of industry 2 declines as a result of the external trade and brings about an inward shift of the economy's production frontier. The loss arising from this shift of the production frontier may outweigh the gain from specialization. The argument for protection on account of increasing returns in the import-competing industry goes back to the seminal work by Graham (1923). His argument was based, however, on the assumption of perfect competition and thought to be applicable only to the case where increasing returns arise from external rather than internal economies of scale. The present model implies that there is a case for protection when the import-competing industry is monopolistic and enjoys increasing returns arising from internal economies of scale.

5. Concluding remarks

There are two restrictive assumptions in the standard models of production widely used in the theory of international trade and in other areas of applied microeconomics. One is the assumption that the technology of firms in each industry is subject to constant returns to scale. The other is the assumption of perfect competition in product markets with the profits of firms declining to zero in the long-run industry equilibrium. In this paper we have replaced the former by the assumption of intra-firm variable-returns-to-scale technologies so that we may be able to identify firms and discuss their operating scale in equilibrium. This modification is desirable, especially if one is to consider the decision problems of firms in imperfectly competitive markets. We have also relaxed the latter assumption and allowed positive profits in the industry equilibrium. In fact, positive profits may prevail even in the long run because of governmental regulations on entry or due to the costs of entry that firms must bear once and for all when they enter the industry.

The implications of the modification are considerable. We have analyzed them within the framework of a simple 2×2 model of production. The celebrated Samuelson–Stolper and Rybczynski Theorems are all valid in the present model provided that industrial markup ratios are exogenously given. In addition, the effects of changes in industrial markups are investigated. For instance, a rise in the markup ratio of an industry is shown to decrease the relative output of that industry under a plausible assumption. The model may also be applied to an economy where the number of firms in an industry is fixed and its markup ratio is endogenous. The implications of the present model for the efficiency of production is even more interesting. A rise in the markup ratio of an industry deteriorates (resp. improves) the productive efficiency of the economy if its representative firm is operating under increasing (resp. decreasing) average cost. This fact implies the well-known proposition that the number of firms tends to be excessive in an imperfectly competitive industry with zero profits in the long-run industry equilibrium. It also implies the converse of this proposition once the markup ratio of the industry is allowed to remain positive. The positive costs of entry to an industry leads to hysteresis in production because incumbent firms continue to operate as long as their profits are non-negative whereas potential entrants do not actually enter the industry unless they expect to obtain positive profits sufficient to cover the entry cost. Thus the response of the industrial output to external disturbances depends upon the number of incumbent firms. This hysteresis in production has important implications for gains from trade and protection of import-competing industries enjoying increasing returns to scale.

The use of the 2×2 model to illustrate these implications is convenient but not necessary. It should be clear that our method of analysis is applicable to the model of production with any number of commodities and factors. Throughout the chapter we have assumed that the degree of monopoly in each industry is constant independent of the outputs of industries. This assumption is introduced for the sake of simplicity, but it is justifiable only if the utility function of the representative consumers is of the CES form and all firms in the industry collude to maximize their joint profits. In the case of a Cournot–Nash symmetric equilibrium, the degree of monopoly depends on the number of firms even when the elasticity of aggregate demand for the product perceived by firms is constant.[11] It may be worthwhile to extend the analysis of this paper to this and more general cases. We have considered the implications of the present model for comparative advantage and gains from trade. It is also suitable to the analysis of multinational firms. The task is, however, beyond the scope of the present chapter.

---

[11] Let n denote the number of firms and ξ the elasticity of demand for their product. Then the degree of monopoly in the symmetric Cournot-Nash equilibrium becomes ξ/n. See Helpman and Krugman (1985), p. 129.

128   Michihiro Ohyama

References

Baldwin, R. 1988 "Hysteresis in Import Prices: The Beach-head Effect," *American Economic Review*, 78, 773–85.
Baldwin, R. and P. R. Krugman 1989 "Persistent Trade Effects of Large Exchange Rate Shocks," *Quarterly Journal of Economics*, 104, 635–54.
Dixit, A. 1989 "Hysteresis, Import Penetration, and Exchange Rate Pass-Through," *Quarterly Journal of Economics*, 104, 205–28.
Flam, H. and E. Helpman 1987 "Industrial Policy under Monopolistic Competition," *Journal of International Economics*, 22, 79–102.
Graham, F. D. 1923 "Some Aspects of Protection Further Considered," *Quarterly Journal of Economics*, 37, 199–227.
Helpman, E. 1983 "Increasing Returns, Imperfect Markets, and Trade Theory," in R. W. Jones and P. B. Kenen (eds.), *Handbook of International Economics*, 1, North-Holland, Amsterdam.
Helpman E. and P. R. Krugman 1985 *Market Structure and Foreign Trade*. MIT Press, Cambridge, MA.
1989 *Trade Policy and Market Structure*. MIT Press, Cambridge, MA.
Jones, R. W. 1965 "The Structure of Simple General Equilibrium Models," *Journal of Political Economy*, 73, 557–72.
1971 "Three-Factor Model in Theory, Trade and History," in J. Bhagwati *et al.* (eds.), *Trade, Balance of Payments, and Growth*. North-Holland, Amsterdam.
1979 *International Trade: Essays in Theory*. North-Holland, Amsterdam.
Kemp, M. C. 1969 *The Pure Theory of International Trade and Investment*. Prentice-Hall, Englewood Cliffs, N.J.
Kemp, M. C. and H. Wan 1974 "Hysteresis of Long-run Equilibrium from Realistic Adjustment Costs," in G. Horwich and P. A. Samuelson (eds.), *Trade, Stability, and Macro-economics*, Academic Press, New York.
Mankiw, N. G. and M. D. Whinston 1986 "Free Entry and Social Inefficiency," *Rand Journal of Economics*, 17, 48–58.
Perry, M. K. 1984 "Scale Economies, Imperfect Competition and Public Policy," *Journal of Industrial Economics*, 13, 197–205.
Suzumura, K. and K. Kiyono 1987 "Entry Barriers and Economic Welfare," *Review of Economic Studies*, 177, 157–67.
Von Weizsacker, C. C. 1980 "A Welfare Analysis of Barriers to Entry," *Bell Journal of Economics*, 11, 399–420.

Part IV

Policy towards international trade

9 Welfare effects of tariffs and investment taxes

J. PETER NEARY

1. Introduction

In a world with internationally mobile factors of production, commercial policy is intimately bound up with the questions of whether and to what extent factor flows should be restricted. This is true even in a small open economy which cannot influence the world prices at which goods and factors are traded: non-interference with all international transactions is the first-best policy but constraints on the implementation of this policy on one category of transactions will in general imply non-zero levels of optimal second-best regulation of the other category. In a large economy which can influence its terms of goods and factor trade, the interdependence between restrictions on trade and international factor flows is even more pronounced. The first-best policy package may now call for a *subsidy* to some transactions rather than a tax; and constraints on policy choice may have surprising implications for the optimal values of those instruments whose values may be altered.

All these issues have been extensively considered in the literature and especially in the writings of Ronald Jones.[1] However, the general principles underlying optimal policy choice when both goods and factors are internationally mobile seem to defy convenient synthesis. A major reason for this must be the concentration in much of the literature on the Heckscher–Ohlin case. As is well known, this framework introduces an

Earlier versions of this chapter were presented to the Canadian Economic Theory Conference, Université de Montreal, to the NBER Summer Institute, to the Mid-West International Economics Meetings, Ann Arbor, to the Canadian Macroeconomic Study Group Conference, Banff, and to seminars at Boston College and at the University of Cincinnati. I am grateful to participants at these meetings and to Rick Brecher, Avinash Dixit, Lorraine Eden, Rob Feenstra, Ray Riezman, Frances Ruane, Lars Svensson and Scott Taylor for helpful comments.
[1] Jones (1967, 1979, 1987), Jones and Ruffin (1975) and Jones, Coelho and Easton (1986). See also MacDougall (1960), Pearce and Rowan (1966), Kemp (1966), Chipman (1972) and Brecher and Feenstra (1983).

indeterminacy in the pattern of specialization and the results obtained appear to be very sensitive to detailed assumptions about the structure of production. Two exceptions to the general concentration on the Heckscher–Ohlin case may be mentioned. Gehrels (1971) gives a full analysis of optimal restrictions on trade and foreign investment in the case where aggregate supply functions are assumed to be differentiable; and Jones (1979) discusses these issues in the specific-factors model. Despite the insights obtained from these papers, it seems fair to say that they do not lead to any simple general conclusions about the relationship between the two types of restrictions.

The objective of this paper is to reexamine these issues and to show that the essential features of the interaction between optimal restrictions on trade and factor flows may be summarized in terms of a few simple principles. In particular, provided we concentrate on the differentiable case, so that changes in the pattern of specialization are ignored, it turns out that many of the results hinge on whether importables use internationally traded factors intensively or not.

In order to derive the results in an easily interpretable way, it is desirable to specify appropriately the underlying behavioral relationships of the model. In particular, considerable insight is obtained by treating goods and internationally mobile factors *symmetrically* but the home and the foreign countries *asymmetrically*. Specifically, I model domestic behavior as depending on the prices of both goods and factors but foreign behavior as depending on the volume of net trades in goods and factors.[2] The fact that the home and foreign countries are specified differently simply reflects the asymmetric nature of the assumptions made about them: the home country is relatively free to choose the values of trade and international capital restrictions, whereas the foreign country responds passively without any retaliation. An additional technical contribution of the paper is to introduce some new functions which facilitate this asymmetric specification.

The plan of the paper is as follows. Section 2 introduces the specification of the home country and Section 3 considers the relationship between domestic welfare and the values of the two sets of policy instruments when the terms of goods and factor trade cannot be influenced by the home country. Section 4 then turns to the large country case and shows how the pattern of first-best and second-best intervention is identified. Finally, the concluding section presents some general principles which the analysis implies.

[2] By contrast, Kemp and Jones treat goods and factors asymmetrically (expressing welfare as a function of the relative price of imports and the quantity of capital imported or exported); but they treat the home and foreign countries symmetrically (since the same specification is adopted for both countries).

2. Equilibrium in the domestic economy

Throughout the chapter, the setting is that of a competitive economy trading m factors and $n + 1$ final commodities with the rest of the world. One of the final commodities is chosen as numeraire, and its price is suppressed throughout.[3] The traded factors are collectively referred to as "capital," whereas non-traded factors are not considered explicitly, since they play no role in the analysis. World prices are denoted by vectors r^* and p^* and the only departures from Pareto efficiency considered are restrictions on trade and foreign investment by the home country. In particular, undistorted competition is assumed to prevail at home and abroad and the foreign country is assumed not to retaliate against home policies. The home country is thus free to choose the deviations between the domestic and foreign prices of factors and commodities, denoted by an m-by-one vector of investment taxes ρ and an n-by-one vector of trade taxes τ respectively:[4]

$$r = r^* + \rho, \quad p = p^* + \tau. \tag{2.1}$$

The specification of household behavior in the home country is conventional. Since I am concerned only with efficiency, I assume that aggregate welfare can be represented by a scalar utility measure.[5] The minimum outlay needed to attain a given utility level facing given prices can therefore be represented by an expenditure function, $e(p, u)$, which is a concave function of prices. A key feature of the model is that factors of production do not yield utility directly.

To model producer behavior, I adopt a slightly less orthodox specification. Assume that the vector $\bar{k}$ denotes home *ownership* of capital and that the vector k denotes *net imports* of capital. The vector $\bar{k} + k$ therefore denotes the amounts of capital used in production at home. For a given level of foreign investment, competition maximizes the value of production in the home country, and the maximized value may be denoted by a GDP function $g(p, \bar{k} + k)$, which is convex in p and concave in k.[6] However, the

[3] The choice of numeraire does not affect the ranking of commodities by the deviation between their domestic and foreign prices at the optimum. However, it does affect the sign of the optimal restriction. See Bond (1990) for further discussion. The algebraic results in the paper hold whether the numeraire good is imported or exported, but in the diagrams, for concreteness, it is assumed to be exported.

[4] The numeraire is untaxed. Note that the elements of ρ and τ need not be positive. As we shall see, some of these values may be negative even in the first-best optimum. If good i is imported then a positive value for τ_i represents a tariff and a negative value an import subsidy; whereas if good i is exported a positive value for τ_i represents an export subsidy and a negative value an export tax.

[5] See Diewert, Turunen and Woodland (1989) and Dixit (1987) for discussion of the many-person case in models with trade in goods only.

[6] As explained in the introduction, I wish to exclude the possibility of changes in the pattern of specialization. Hence I assume that the function $g(p, k)$ is strictly concave in k so that the

level of foreign investment is not exogenous. Instead, it is carried out to the point where the vector of domestic rentals equals the vector of world rentals plus domestic capital taxes, ρ, as indicated by (2.1). The domestic rentals in turn are equated by competition to the marginal products of the capital factors in every domestic use, which, from a standard property of the function $g(p, \bar{k} + k)$, may be written as:[7]

$$g_k(p, \bar{k} + k) = r. \tag{2.2}$$

With capital internationally mobile, it proves to be convenient to specify producer behavior as depending on the variables p and r which are exogenous to the domestic production sector. This is achieved by working with the mobile-capital GNP function, which equals the maximum value of gross domestic product less the gross returns to foreign-owned factors:

$$\tilde{g}(p, r, \bar{k}) = \max_k [g(p, \bar{k} + k) - k'r]. \tag{2.3}$$

This function was introduced in Neary (1985), where its properties were considered in detail. In particular, its derivatives were shown to be related to those of the GDP function at the same initial capital endowment, $\bar{k} + k$, as follows:

$$\tilde{g}_p = g_p, \qquad\qquad \tilde{g}_r = -k, \tag{2.4}$$

$$\tilde{g}_{pp} = g_{pp} - g_{pk} g_{kk}^{-1} g_{kp}, \quad \tilde{g}_{rr} = -g_{kk}^{-1}, \tag{2.5}$$

$$\tilde{g}_{pr} = g_{pk} g_{kk}^{-1}. \tag{2.6}$$

Following Dixit and Norman (1980), the cross derivatives of the GDP function, the elements of the matrix g_{pk}, may be interpreted as general equilibrium measures of factor intensity.[8] In the mobile-capital case, a similar interpretation applies to the elements of the matrix $-\tilde{g}_{pr}$, which may be defined as general equilibrium measures of *inverse* factor intensity. Thus, the typical element of $-\tilde{g}_{pr}$ is positive if the output of a given sector increases following a fall in the price of a given factor, whereas the corresponding element of g_{pk} is positive if the sector's output increases following a rise in the endowment of the factor. The negative sign before $\tilde{g}_{pk}$ ensures that the two senses of factor intensity are closely related (since g_{kk} is

---

matrix g_{kk} is non-singular. From (2.5) below, this implies that the aggregate supply functions are differentiable in output prices.

[7] Throughout the chapter, subscripts denote partial derivatives and a prime denotes the transpose of a vector.

[8] It is possible for all the elements of any row of g_{pk} to be positive. Hence, if any sector uses a particular factor intensively, it need not follow that it must use any other factor unintensively. An example is the simple specific-factors model, where both sectors use the mobile factor intensively in the Dixit–Norman sense.

negative semi-definite), although they correspond exactly only in simple cases.[9]

The final function to be introduced brings together the consumer and producer sectors. Since I wish to work with net imports of the home country, the model is most easily specified in terms of the *mobile-capital trade expenditure function*, which equals the excess of domestic expenditure over GNP as defined in (2.3), all at domestic prices:[10]

$$E(p, r, \bar{k}, u) \equiv e(p, u) - \tilde{g}(p, r, \bar{k}). \tag{2.7}$$

The properties of E follow directly from those of the e and $\tilde{g}$ functions. In particular, it is homogeneous of degree zero in all commodity prices,[11] it is concave in *both* p and r and its partial derivatives with respect to these two arguments equal the Hicksian net import demand functions and the excess demand functions for foreign investment respectively:

$$E_p = e_p - \tilde{g}_p = m(p, r, \bar{k}, u), \tag{2.8}$$

$$E_r = -\tilde{g}_r = k(p, r, \bar{k}). \tag{2.9}$$

Capital does not yield utility directly, so the demand functions for foreign investment in (2.9) are independent of u. Strict concavity of E implies that the sub-matrices of own-price derivatives are negative semi-definite:

$$E_{pp} = e_{pp} - \tilde{g}_{pp} \quad \text{and} \quad E_{rr} = -\tilde{g}_{rr} = g_{kk}^{-1}. \tag{2.10}$$

The cross derivatives of E also have a useful interpretation. From (2.8) and (2.6):

$$E_{pr} = -\tilde{g}_{pr} = -g_{pk}g_{kk}^{-1}. \tag{2.11}$$

Thus the cross derivatives are measures of inverse factor intensities.[12]

---

[9] For example, in the two-good one-mobile factor case, $-\tilde{g}_{pr}$ and g_{pk} are both scalars and are positive if and only if importables are capital-intensive in home production. Since I have assumed that the matrix g_{kk} is invertible, the two-factor two-good Heckscher–Ohlin model with mobile capital is not subsumed under the two-good, one-mobile-factor case. However, many other interesting models are, including the specific-factors model of Jones (1971) and the three-factor two-good model of Jones and Easton (1983) with international mobility of capital.

[10] The trade expenditure function when factors are internationally immobile has been considered under a variety of names by many authors. Textbook expositions are given in Dixit and Norman (1980) and Woodland (1982). To the best of my knowledge the extension to the case of international factor mobility is new.

[11] Commodity prices here include p, r and the price of the numeraire good. Following standard practice, I assume that there is some substitutability in excess demand between the numeraire and other goods, so that the Hessian of E is non-singular. This also ensures that E is *strictly* concave in p and r.

[12] This shows that the difference between direct and inverse measures of factor intensity is similar to that between q- and p-measures of complementarity and substitutability in consumer theory. See Bond (1989).

Since the function E is the excess of private-sector spending over GNP at domestic prices, it differs from zero in general when international transactions are distorted. Throughout the paper, I assume that any net revenue from tariffs or foreign-investment taxes is returned to the household sector as a lump-sum subsidy (and, conversely, if trade and capital flows are subsidized on average, the net disbursements are financed by a lump-sum tax). The household's budget constraint, which is also the condition for balance of payments equilibrium, may therefore be written in the following form:[13]

$$E(p, r, \overline{k}, u) = \tau' m + \rho' k. \tag{2.12}$$

This equation, when combined with (2.8) and (2.9), gives $m + n + 1$ equations which may be solved for the values of the $m + n + 1$ endogenous variables, k, m and u, as functions of world prices, r^* and p^*, and policy variables ρ and τ.

Finally, it will be convenient at times to reexpress the model in a more compact fashion, which draws attention to the symmetry between trade in goods and factors. I do this by introducing the vector M to denote the net imports of all commodities, both goods and factors, with q, q^* and t denoting corresponding vectors of home prices, world prices and trade taxes:

$$M \equiv \begin{bmatrix} m \\ k \end{bmatrix}; \quad q \equiv \begin{bmatrix} p \\ r \end{bmatrix}; \quad q^* \equiv \begin{bmatrix} p^* \\ r^* \end{bmatrix}; \quad t \equiv \begin{bmatrix} \tau \\ \rho \end{bmatrix}. \tag{2.13}$$

The equilibrium conditions, equations (2.8), (2.9) and (2.12), may now be expressed in more compact form as follows:

$$E_q(q, \overline{k}, u) = M, \tag{2.14}$$

$$E(q, \overline{k}, u) = t'M. \tag{2.15}$$

3. Welfare effects of intervention in a small open economy

It is immediately clear that the first-best policy for an economy which cannot influence the prices of any traded commodities is to avoid any restrictions on goods or factor trade. However, this does not exhaust the range of questions which can be considered in the small open economy case. On the contrary, an extensive literature has developed concerned with questions of "second-best" intervention in this context[14] and the frame-

---

[13] This is more easily seen to be a budget constraint if it is rewritten, using (2.1), (2.3) and (2.7), as equating expenditure to GDP plus tariff revenue less *net* payments to foreign-owned capital:

$$e(p, u) = g(p, \overline{k} + k) + \tau' m - k' r^*. \tag{2.12a}$$

[14] Naturally, the term "second-best" is to be interpreted throughout with respect only to the

work introduced in the last section allows us to synthesize and extend this literature. In any case, since the same considerations continue to influence policy choice in the large open economy case, it is convenient to consider them first in the simplifying context of fixed world prices.

I begin by differentiating (2.15). With fixed world prices (so that $dp = d\tau$ and $dr = d\rho$), this simplifies to give the following:

$$dy = \tau'dm + \rho'dk. \tag{3.1}$$

Here I have used dy as a shorthand for $e_u du$, the change in utility or real income measured in expenditure units. Equation (3.1) thus gives the familiar result that welfare is positively related to the volume of imports (in this case, of either goods or traded factors) when the latter are restricted by trade taxes. Since m and k are themselves endogenous the next step is to differentiate (2.14) and substitute into (3.1). Collecting terms, this yields:

$$(1 - t'X_I)dy = t'E_{qq}dt. \tag{3.2}$$

Following Jones (1969), the coefficient of dy on the left-hand side is the inverse of the "tariff multiplier," which arises from the spending effects induced by changes in tariff revenue. In the literature on project appraisal the tariff multiplier is often called the "shadow price of foreign exchange," since it measures the marginal effect on welfare of a unit transfer from abroad of the numeraire good. The term X_I is the vector of income effects on domestic demand, but since capital does not yield utility directly this can be written as:

$$X_I = \begin{bmatrix} x_I \\ k_I \end{bmatrix} = \begin{bmatrix} E_u^{-1}E_{pu} \\ 0 \end{bmatrix}. \tag{3.3}$$

Hence the tariff multiplier can alternatively be written as $1 - \tau'x_I$. I will assume throughout that this term is positive. A *sufficient* condition for this is that all goods are non-inferior in demand. It has also been noted in both the public finance and international trade literatures that a positive value of this multiplier is necessary for local stability of equilibrium.[15] In order to justify the diagrams which I draw below, it is necessary to assume that this restriction holds globally, since otherwise welfare is not a unique function of a given vector of tax and tariff rates.

Turning to the right-hand side of (3.2), setting dt equal to $td\alpha$, where α is a scalar measure of the average height of both tariffs and capital taxes, implies

set of instruments considered. It goes without saying that allowing for other instruments such as consumption or production taxes could make my "second-best optimal tariffs and capital taxes" third-best or worse.

[15] See Dixit (1975), Hatta (1977) and Smith (1980). Vanek (1965) appears to have been the first to point out the association between paradoxical outcomes (such as an increase in a tariff raising welfare in a small open economy) and negative values of this term.

the following result (which generalizes results by Foster and Sonnenschein 1970, Bruno 1972, Dixit 1975, Hatta 1977 and others on radial reductions in models with trade in final goods only):

Proposition 1: A uniform reduction in both tariff and capital tax rates must raise welfare.

Algebraically, this result follows from the concavity of E in q (i.e., in p and r together), so that the quadratic form $t'E_{qq}t$ is negative semi-definite. The economic interpretation is that a uniform reduction in all distortions permits us to treat total net imports of all tariff and tax-ridden commodities as a Hicksian composite commodity.

Suppose next that tariffs and capital taxes cannot be chosen simultaneously. Rewrite (3.2) in a form which relates welfare changes to changes in the levels of tariffs and investment taxes separately:

$$(1 - \tau'x_I)dy = (\tau'E_{pp} + \rho'E_{rp})d\tau + (\tau'E_{pr} + \rho'E_{rr})d\rho. \qquad (3.4)$$

Here, the terms E_{ij} are the appropriate sub-matrices of the matrix E_{qq}. Now, for given values of either set of instruments, $\bar{p}$ or $\bar{\tau}$, we can solve explicitly for the optimal second-best values of the other instruments, τ^o or ρ^o, by setting the coefficients of $d\tau$ and $d\rho$ equal to zero in turn:

$$(\tau^o)' = -\bar{\rho}'E_{rp}E_{pp}^{-1}, \qquad (3.5)$$

$$(\rho^o)' = -\bar{\tau}E_{pr}E_{rr}^{-1}. \qquad (3.6)$$

Because capital does not yield utility directly, (3.6) may be written in terms of production parameters only, using (2.10) and (2.11):

$$(\rho^o)' = \bar{\tau}'g_{pk}. \qquad (3.7)$$

The right-hand side of (3.7) equals the difference between the market and shadow prices of capital,[16] and the right-hand side of equation (3.5) may be interpreted as the difference between the market and shadow prices of importables.[17] This allows us to state the following:

---

[16] The proof is straightforward (see Neary and Ruane (1988) for further details). Write $\bar{E}(p, \bar{k} + k, u) \equiv e(p, u) - g(p, \bar{k} + k)$ for the trade expenditure function when capital is internationally immobile, set it equal to $\tau'm$ and differentiate to obtain:

$$(1 - t'x_I)dy = (r' - \tau'g_{pk})dk. \qquad (3.8)$$

[17] This is most easily shown by specifying a new trade expenditure function corresponding to the case where importables are quota-constrained but capital is freely mobile internationally:

$$E(m, r, u) \equiv \min_p[E(p, r, u) - m'p]. \qquad (3.9)$$

This function has derivative properties analogous to those of E as set out in equations (2.8) to (2.11):

$$E_m = -p, \quad E_r = E_r = k \quad \text{and} \quad E_{rm} = E_{rp}E_{pp}^{-1}.$$

Proposition 2: If the levels of restriction on one category of international transactions cannot be altered, second-best optimal intervention requires that the domestic shadow prices (and *not* the domestic market prices) of the other category of traded commodities be set equal to their world prices.

A different route to interpreting (3.5) and (3.6) is to note that they imply that the relationship between the fixed values of one set of instruments and the second-best values of the other set hinges on factor intensities. Equation (3.7) permits a particularly simple interpretation along these lines:

Proposition 3: In the presence of irremovable trade restrictions, the optimal second-best tax on any mobile factor is positive if and only if on average that factor is used intensively in sectors subject to higher tariff rates.[18]

The implications of (3.5) and (3.7) may be seen most clearly in the two-good one-mobile-factor special case:

Corollary: With only two traded goods and one traded factor, the fixed policy instrument and the second-best optimal instrument have the same sign if and only if importables are capital-intensive.

To see intuitively why this is so, consider the effect of a fixed tax on capital imports. This lowers welfare by reducing capital imports below their optimal level. From (3.1), any policy which offsets this reduction will raise welfare. If importables are capital-intensive, a tariff has such an effect, since it raises the home demand for capital and so encourages a capital inflow. Of course, a tariff also tends to reduce welfare directly by restricting imports of goods, but for a small tariff this effect can be ignored, and so the optimal second-best tariff is positive when imports are capital-intensive.

Returning to (3.4), equations (3.5) and (3.6) can now be used to rewrite it in an illuminating way:

$$(1 - \tau'x_I)dy = (\tau - \tau^o)'E_{pp}d\tau + (\rho - \rho^o)'E_{rr}d\rho. \tag{3.11}$$

This suggests that another radical reduction result can be obtained by writing $d\tau$ as $(\tau - \tau^o)d\beta$ and $d\rho$ as $(\rho - \rho^o)d\gamma$, where β and γ are scalars. However, this must be interpreted with care, since for such a result to hold the second-best optimal instruments τ^o and ρ^o must be evaluated at the

---

By making use of these properties, setting $\mathbf{E}(p, r, u)$ equal to $\rho'k$ and totally differentiating, the following expression for the shadow price of importables may be derived:

$$dy = (p + E_{mr}\rho)'dm = (p' + \rho'E_{rp}E_{pp}{}^{-1})dm. \tag{3.10}$$

[18] This proposition follows by rewriting (3.7) to link the optimal capital tax *rate* on factor i to the tariff rates on all goods (including the numeraire):

$$\rho_i^o/r_i = \sum_j (p_j g_{ij}/r_j)(\bar\tau_j/p_j). \tag{3.7'}$$

This is a true weighted average, since the first term in parentheses sums to unity from homogeneity.

same points as the matrices E_{pp} and E_{rr}. To see this, I rewrite (3.11) with ρ held constant, using $\psi(\tau,\rho)$ to denote the function implied by (3.5) (i.e., $\tau^o = \psi(\tau^o,\bar{\rho})$):

$$(1 - \tau'x_I)dy = [\{\tau - \psi(\tau^o,\bar{\rho})\} + \{\psi(\tau^o,\bar{\rho}) - \psi(\tau,\bar{\rho})\}]'E_{pp}(\tau,\bar{\rho})d\tau.$$

$$(3.12)$$

Thus a welfare improvement following a radical reduction in the gap between τ and τ^o is only guaranteed if the term $\psi(\tau^o,\bar{\rho}) - \psi(\tau,\bar{\rho})$ can be ignored. This will be the case if the starting point is close to the optimum or if third and higher derivatives of E vanish (so that ψ is independent of τ). Alternatively, (3.11) may be interpreted as an exact result if τ^o is evaluated at the initial value of τ and ρ^o at the initial value of ρ; this approach guarantees a welfare improvement and can be viewed as an algorithm for approaching the optimum provided ψ is recalculated at each step. Summarizing:

Proposition 4: If the values of one set of instruments cannot be altered, then for small deviations from the optimum or if the third and higher derivatives of E vanish, welfare will be increased by a uniform proportionate reduction in the distance between the values of the other instruments and their optimal second-best levels.

Note that this implies that there are many circumstances in which welfare is an *increasing* function of the instruments which policy-makers are free to alter. Note also that a uniform proportionate reduction in the gaps between either τ or ρ and their optimal second-best values need not raise welfare. Hence the composite commodity interpretation given to Proposition 1 cannot be applied here.

A different set of results may be obtained by expressing each of the coefficients on the right-hand side of (3.4) in terms of deviations of the *other* instrument from its second-best optimal levels. Straightforward derivations yield:

$$(1 - \tau'x_I)dy = [\tau'(E_{pp} - E_{pr}E_{rr}^{-1}E_{rp}) + (\rho - \rho^o)'E_{rp}]d\tau$$
$$+ [\rho'(E_{rr} - E_{rp}E_{pp}^{-1}E_{pr}) + (\tau - \tau^o)'E_{pr}]d\rho.$$

$$(3.13)$$

It can now be shown that the first expression in parentheses in each of the terms on the right-hand side of (3.13) is negative semi-definite.[19] Consider the first term in the coefficient of $d\tau$ in (3.13). From the properties of E and $\tilde{g}$ noted in Section 2, this may be simplified as follows:

---

[19] The fact that these expressions are negative semi-definite may be deduced immediately by making use of a standard property of partitioned inverses. Since E_{qq} is negative semi-definite, so is its inverse; but the two expressions in (3.13) are the inverses of the diagonal sub-matrices in the inverse and so are themselves negative semi-definite.

$$E_{pp} - E_{pr}E_{rr}{}^{-1}E_{rp} = e_{pp} - g_{pp} + g_{pk}g_{kk}{}^{-1}g_{kp}$$

$$- g_{pk}g_{kk}{}^{-1}g_{kk}g_{kk}{}^{-1}g_{kp} \equiv \bar{E}_{pp}. \tag{3.14}$$

Here I have used $\bar{E}_{pp}$ to denote $e_{pp} - g_{pp}$, the matrix of price derivatives of the *immobile capital* trade expenditure function.[20] As required, it is negative semi-definite. A similar series of substitutions shows that the first expression in parentheses in the coefficient of $d\rho$ in (3.13) is the inverse of the sum of two negative semi-definite matrices:

$$E_{rr} - E_{rp}E_{pp}{}^{-1}E_{pr} = (g_{kk} + g_{kp}\bar{E}_{pp}{}^{-1}g_{pk})^{-1}. \tag{3.15}$$

After these changes, (3.13) may be rewritten in the following form:

$$(1 - \tau'x_I)dy = [\tau'\bar{E}_{pp} + (\rho - \rho^o)'E_{rp}]d\tau$$

$$+ [\rho'(g_{kk} + g_{kp}\bar{E}_{pp}{}^{-1}g_{pk})^{-1} + (\tau - \tau^o)'E_{pr}]d\rho. \tag{3.16}$$

This yields a number of new results. Considering first the coefficient of $d\tau$ in (3.16), note that the matrix E_{pp} differs from $\bar{E}_{pp}$ by a negative semi-definite matrix: heuristically, international capital mobility increases the price-output responsiveness of the economy.[21] In Neary and Ruane (1988) this result was applied to the measurement of the cost of tariff protection: with no capital taxes in operation ($\rho = 0$), it was shown that international capital mobility *raises* the cost of protection. (The welfare cost of a uniform increase in tariffs is $\tau'\bar{E}_{pp}\tau$ when capital is internationally immobile and, from (3.16), $[\tau'\bar{E}_{pp} - (\rho^o)'E_{rp}]\tau$, which, from (3.6) and (3.14), equals $\tau'E_{pp}\tau$, when it is internationally mobile but untaxed.) Equation (3.16) allows us to generalize this result to the case where capital taxation is in force, in which case the crucial term is $(\rho - \rho^o)'E_{rp}\tau$:

Proposition 5: International capital mobility raises the cost of tariff protection if and only if, on average, protected goods use intensively (in the *inverse* sense) internationally mobile factors which are subject to taxes *below* their optimal second-best levels.

A similar interpretation may be applied to the coefficient of $d\rho$ in (3.16). Just as the term $\bar{E}_{pp}$ may be interpreted as the price responsiveness of import demand when foreign investment is quota-constrained, so also the term $(g_{kk} + g_{kp}\bar{E}_{pp}{}^{-1}g_{pk})^{-1}$ in the coefficient of $d\rho$ equals the rental responsiveness of home demand for foreign investment when imports are quota-constrained (see Neary 1988). This yields a result symmetric to Proposition 5, hinging on the sign of the term $(\tau - \tau^o)'E_{pr}\rho$:

[20] This function was defined in footnote 16.
[21] As with Proposition 4, this result is exact only if the two matrices are evaluated at the same point (see Neary 1985).

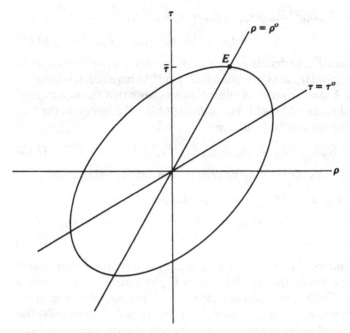

Figure 9.1   Iso-welfare contour in the small open economy case when importables are relatively capital-intensive

Proposition 6: The welfare cost of a tax on international capital movements is greater when imports of goods are tariff-restricted than when they are quota-constrained if and only if, on average, the taxed factors are used intensively (in the *inverse* sense) in sectors which are subject to tariffs *below* their optimal second-best levels.

Equation (3.16) can also be interpreted as implying a number of envelope-type results. Thus, the coefficient of $d\tau$ shows that if capital is always optimally taxed (so that ρ equals ρ^o), then the relationship between welfare and the tariff rate is exactly the same as when capital is internationally immobile (at the same initial endowments as in the mobile-capital case). Similarly, from the coefficient of $d\rho$, the relationship between welfare and the rate of capital taxation is the same whether imports are quota-constrained or subject to the second-best optimal tariff.

These results have a particularly illuminating representation in the one-importable one-mobile-factor case, as Figures 9.1 and 9.2 illustrate.[22]

---

[22] Similar diagrams have been considered by Foster and Sonnenschein (1970), though they did not examine their properties in detail, and by Das (1983) in a model with a traded intermediate good. Bond (1989) also presents similar diagrams in his discussion of the one-good, two-mobile-factor model of Jones, Coelho and Easton (1986), though his are drawn in the space of factor trades rather than (as here) in instrument space.

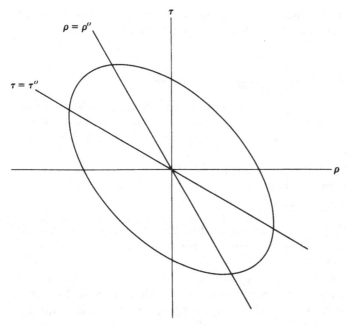

Figure 9.2   Iso-welfare contour in the small open economy case when importables are relatively labor-intensive

Each of these diagrams shows illustrative iso-welfare contours in the space of the policy instruments. Since E is concave in p and r (provided the tariff multiplier is positive, as I assume), we would expect these contours to enclose convex sets and this is approximately true in general.[23] The key difference between the two diagrams is the assumption about factor intensities. In Figure 9.1, importables are capital-intensive and as a result the contours have an upward tilt. Capital and importables are substitutes in the trade expenditure function in this case (E_{pr} is positive) and this property underlies a number of recent results in the literature.[24] Note one important implication in particular: if tariffs cannot be removed, then welfare will be increased by a tax on capital imports (e.g., if the tariff rate $\bar{\tau}$ in the diagram cannot be removed, then welfare is maximized by imposing a capital import

---

[23] The assumption that the second-best instruments defined by (3.5) and (3.6) exist ensures that the contours are concave towards the origin in the neighborhood of the loci τ^o and ρ^o. It may be checked that the contours are concave everywhere in the case of import demands which are linear in prices (i.e., provided terms in third and higher-order derivatives of E are ignored).

[24] See, for example, Brecher and Findlay (1983) and Casas (1985). These papers consider the specific-factors model with internationally mobile capital used only in one sector, which implies that that sector is capital-intensive in the general equilibrium sense.

tax to move the economy to point E). By contrast, in Figure 9.2 the contours have a downward tilt because importables are not intensive in the use of capital.

4. Optimal intervention in a large open economy

Naturally, the conclusions of the last section require considerable qualification if the domestic economy is able to influence relative prices in the world economy. To see how this alters the analysis, once again totally differentiate (2.14) but without holding world prices constant. Making use of the fact that $dq = dq^* + dt$, this allows me to relate home welfare to changes in the volume and terms of trade:

$$dy = t'dM - M'dq^*. \tag{4.1}$$

So far, this derivation is standard. However, it turns out to be most convenient to diverge from common practice at this point by expressing foreign demands not in terms of import demand functions but rather in terms of *inverse import demand functions*.[25] These express the world price vector, q^*, as a function of the net import vector offered for trade by the rest of the world, M^*. As we shall see, this approach has the great advantage that the results of Section 3 for the small open economy emerge as special cases of those for the large open economy.[26] Assuming that the inverse import demand functions are differentiable, their differentials may be written as:

$$dq^* = q_M^*dM^*. \tag{4.2}$$

I shall refer to the matrix of inverse demand responses, q_M^*, as the *Antonelli matrix*. Since foreign net imports M^* plus home net imports M must sum to zero in balanced trade, (4.1) and (4.2) combine to give:

$$dy = (t' + M'q_M^*)dM. \tag{4.3}$$

This immediately gives standard expressions for first-best optimal restrictions on trade:

$$(t^{oo})' = -M'q_M^*, \tag{4.4}$$

which in turn may be disaggregated to give the first-best optimal tariffs and capital taxes:

$$(\tau^{oo})' = -m'p_m^* - k'r_m^*, \quad \text{and} \quad (\rho^{oo})' = -m'p_k^* - k'r_k^*. \tag{4.5}$$

It is clear that the pattern of optimal tariffs and capital taxes depends

[25] Dixit (1986) also adopts this approach.
[26] By contrast, the usual treatment proceeds in two different directions from (4.1) depending on whether the small or large open economy case is being considered.

crucially on the derivatives of the inverse import demand functions. General expressions for these are derived in Appendix 1, whose results are summarized in the following lemma. (To allow intuitive explanations for the results, I concentrate in the text henceforward on the case of a single imported good and a single imported factor. The formulae throughout refer to the general case.)

> *Lemma*: Substitution effects in the foreign country imply downward-sloping inverse excess demand functions for both home imports and traded capital ($p_m{}^*$ and $r_k{}^* < 0$), while the cross effects $r_m{}^*$ and $p_k{}^*$ are negative if and only if foreign exportables are capital-intensive in foreign production. However, income effects in the foreign country could offset all these effects.

This suggests that the optimal values of both instruments are more likely to be positive the more capital-intensive are foreign exports. Consider first the optimal tariff (combining (4.5) with (A.9)):

$$(\tau^{oo})' = -(m' + k'g_{kp}{}^*)p_m{}^*. \tag{4.6}$$

Evidently, provided $p_m{}^*$ is negative, the optimal tariff is positive if foreign exports are capital-intensive. If they are not (so that $g_{kp}{}^*$ is negative), then a subsidy to imports may (but need not) be optimal because the worsening of the goods terms of trade (due to the rise in import prices) may be offset by an improvement in the capital terms of trade. An optimal subsidy is more likely the smaller are goods imports, m, and the larger are capital imports, k, since it is the indirect effect working through the latter which makes perverse outcomes possible. Similar conclusions hold for the optimal tax on capital imports. From (4.5), (A.11) and (A.13):

$$(\rho^{oo})' = -k'g_{kk}{}^* - (m' + k'g_{kp}{}^*)p_m{}^*(g_{pk}{}^* - x_I{}^*k'g_{kk}{}^*). \tag{4.7}$$

Once again the direct effect of restricting capital imports is to lower the rental abroad and so to improve the terms of capital trade. However, if foreign exports are produced in a non-capital-intensive manner, then a subsidy to capital *raises* the foreign output of exportables and so encourages an improvement in the goods terms of trade.

Finally, we may ask if the optimal level of restrictions must be positive on average, in the sense of a positive value of total revenue from tariffs and taxes. Inspection of the expression for this shows that it must be positive if *either* foreign exports are capital-intensive (assuming normality and p_m^* negative) *or* foreign income effects are negligible:[27]

[27] With no income effects abroad, it follows directly from (4.4) that $(t^{oo})'M$, which equals $-M'q_M{}^*M$, is minus a quadratic form in a negative definite matrix. Feenstra (1986) and Bond (1990) derive this result for the multi-commodity optimal tariff case (in the absence of international capital mobility).

$$(\tau^{oo})'m + (\rho^{oo})'k = -k'g_{kk}*k$$
$$- (m' + k'g_{kp}*)p_m*(m + g_{pk}*k - x_I*k'g_{kk}*k).$$
$$(4.8)$$

To summarize these results:

Proposition 7: A downward-sloping foreign inverse demand function for home imports and capital-intensive production of foreign exports are together sufficient for the home optimal tariff and capital tax to be positive.

So much for the first-best optimum. What if tariffs and capital taxes are not at optimal levels? Note first that (4.3) may be rewritten as:

$$dy = \hat{t}'dM,   (4.9)$$

where:

$$\hat{t} \equiv t - t^{oo},   (4.10)$$

the vector of deviations of actual instruments from their "quasi-optimal" levels, calculated by evaluating (4.4) at the initial equilibrium. (The latter may differ even in sign from the values at the optimum.) Equation (4.9) is clearly an extension of (3.1) to the large open economy, and it has a similar interpretation: if tariffs and investment taxes are above their optimal levels, any policy which increases import volumes will raise welfare.

The next step, as in the small open economy case, is to eliminate dM from (4.9). Differentiating (2.14) and making use of (4.2) yields the following general equilibrium import demand equation:

$$dM = M_t dt + M_I dy,   (4.11)$$

where:

$$M_t = (I_{mn} + E_{qq}q_M*)^{-1}E_{qq},   (4.12)$$

and:

$$M_I = (I_{mn} + E_{qq}q_M*)^{-1}X_I.   (4.13)$$

(Here I_{mn} is the identity matrix of order $(m + n)$.) Finally, substituting from (4.11) into (4.9) and collecting terms yields:

$$(1 - \hat{t}'M_I)dy = \hat{t}'M_t dt.   (4.14)$$

The formal resemblance between (4.14) and equation (3.2) in the last section is striking and it would be very desirable to interpret (4.14) in the same manner. To investigate whether this is possible, I consider the individual terms in (4.14) in turn.

Considering first the coefficient of dy, it is a generalization to the large open economy of the tariff multiplier introduced in Section 3 (the coefficient of dy in (3.2)) and it clearly reduces to the latter when world prices are fixed, so that the elements of $q_M{}^*$ are zero. It is also clear that it reduces to unity when the home country imposes optimal tariffs and investment taxes ($\hat{t} = 0$). This accords with the interpretation of $(1 - \hat{t}'M_I)^{-1}$ as the shadow price of foreign exchange: when optimal policies are in effect, a unit transfer of the numeraire good raises real income in terms of the numeraire by exactly one unit. When policies are not at their optimal levels, the sign of this term is indeterminate but, as in the small open economy case, a heuristic stability argument can be used to justify a positive sign. In particular, if prices are assumed to adjust instantaneously and equilibrium is attained by a redistribution of lump-sum income between the two countries until trade is balanced, it can be shown that a positive value for $(1 - \hat{t}'M_I)^{-1}$ is necessary and sufficient for local stability.[28] As in Section 3, in order to justify diagrammatic analysis, it is necessary to assume in addition that this term is globally as well as locally positive, and I make this assumption from now on.

Turning next to the term M_t, it represents the responsiveness of home import demand to changes in home tariffs at a given level of home utility, but allowing for the effects of the tariff changes on foreign income. Explicit expressions for the sub-matrices of M_t are presented in Appendix 2, where they are shown to depend on income effects in the foreign country as well as on differences in substitution effects between the two countries. As a result, there is no guarantee that this matrix need be symmetric, far less that it be negative semi-definite. Hence, it is not possible in general to state propositions corresponding to those in Section 3. However, we can proceed as before to derive second-best optimal levels of intervention. Thus, rewriting (4.14) in a form similar to (3.4):

$$(1 - \hat{t}'M_I)dy = (\hat{\tau}'m_\tau + \hat{\rho}'k_\tau)d\tau + (\hat{\tau}'m_\rho + \hat{\rho}'k_\rho)d\rho, \qquad (4.15)$$

where the new terms in the expression are the appropriate sub-matrices of the matrix M_t (given explicitly in Appendix 2). As before, this yields:

$$(\hat{\tau}^o)' = -\bar{\rho}'k_\tau m_\tau^{-1}. \qquad (4.16)$$

$$(\hat{\rho}^o)' = -\bar{\tau}m_\rho k_\rho^{-1}, \qquad (4.17)$$

where $\bar{\rho}$ and $\bar{\tau}$ are the fixed values of the other instrument, expressed as

[28] If instead, equilibrium is assumed to be brought about by the adjustment of international prices, the stability condition involves restrictions on a matrix which is a multi-market generalization of the Marshall–Lerner condition. If stability is required for all possible adjustment speeds of prices and lump-sum incomes, then once again a positive value for $(1 - \hat{t}'M_I)^{-1}$ is implied at stable equilibria.

deviations from the first-best optimum value. These equations not only give the optimal second-best value of each instrument, they also define the loci of horizontal and vertical points along the iso-welfare contours defined by (4.14). Thus a geometric interpretation similar to that given in Section 3 is possible, with the principal difference that the first-best optimal intervention point around which the contours are centered is now the vector t^{oo} rather than the origin. This allows a particularly interesting interpretation, since, from (4.4), the values of the first-best instruments depend directly *only* on parameters relating to the foreign country, whereas the shape of the iso-welfare contours themselves depends on *both* home and foreign parameters. To see the implications of this, we consider two interesting special cases.[29]

Case 1: No Foreign Income Effects. Identical Substitution Effects. Factor intensities are now the same at home and abroad, and so from (A.3) the matrix $q_M{}^*$ equals $E_{qq}{}^{-1}$ and M_t reduces to $E_{qq}/2$. In this case, *all* of Propositions 3 to 6 apply without any qualification whatsoever to the large open economy case. Some of the possibilities which now arise when only one imported good and one imported factor are subject to trade restrictions are illustrated in panels (a) to (c) of Figure 9.3. In panel (a), home importables are capital-intensive in both countries so (from Proposition 7) the optimal tariff and investment tax are positive, and, as in Figure 9.1, iso-welfare contours are upward-sloping. Starting from free trade, a rise in either type of intervention must raise welfare. The same is true in panel (b), where home importables are labor-intensive at home and abroad (so the iso-welfare contours have a downward tilt) but not sufficiently to reverse the sign of either instrument at the first-best optimum. However, one difference is that now the optimal second-best tariff when capital cannot be taxed lies above the first-best optimal level(i.e., point A lies above point F in panel (b) whereas it lies below it in panel (a)). Finally, in panel (c), commodity imports are sufficiently large relative to capital imports that (from (4.7)) the latter should be subsidized at the optimum. Moreover, in the case drawn, the locus of second-best optimal tariffs, $\hat{\tau}^o$, now passes below rather than above the origin. It follows that the second-best optimal trade intervention if capital cannot be taxed is an import *subsidy* rather than a tariff.

Case 2: No foreign income effects, opposing substitution effects. Suppose now that all the assumptions of Case 1 are retained except that factor intensities abroad are assumed to be the opposite to those at home. Appendix 2 shows that in this case the matrix M_t is diagonal and negative

[29] Of course, the restrictions required for either of these cases to hold globally are extremely stringent.

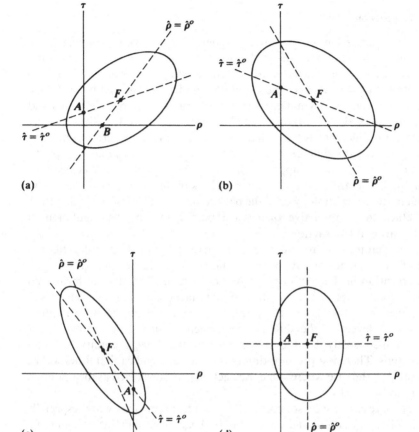

Figure 9.3   Iso-welfare contours in the large open economy case

definite. Thus the second-best problem vanishes in this case and the values
of the two instruments can be set independently of each other. Intuitively, a
rise in the tariff leads to exactly opposing changes in the demand for capital
in the two countries. Hence there is no indirect effect to offset the direct
effect of moving the tariff towards or away from its first-best value. Panel
(d) illustrates the case where home importables are capital-intensive
abroad, so that both instruments are positive at the first-best optimum, but
capital-unintensive at home, so that the $\hat{\tau}^o$ and $\hat{\rho}^o$ loci are horizontal and
vertical respectively.

5. Conclusion

In this chapter I have presented a general framework for analyzing the simultaneous choice of optimal restrictions on trade and international factor flows. My approach contrasts with existing studies of this issue in its treatment of the two asymmetries in the model. On the one hand, I have deemphasized the asymmetry between internationally mobile goods and factors. Since there is no difference between them in tradeability, the only important difference is that goods yield utility directly whereas factors do not; and even this difference is of secondary importance for many purposes. On the other hand, my approach has adopted very different specifications for the home and foreign countries. The key distinction arises not from differences in technology or in the pattern of specialization but rather from whether they are active or passive participants in the regulation of international transactions.

The chapter has presented a novel derivation of the first-best pattern of optimal intervention. As is well known from earlier work, first-best intervention in the small open economy case requires that all tariffs and investment taxes be zero. If the economy faces less than infinitely elastic supplies from the rest of the world, then first-best intervention requires non-zero levels of the different instruments, with their optimal levels determined solely by the parameters of the *foreign* country's excess demands. There is a presumption that both trade and capital flows will be taxed, but the case where some transactions are subsidized at the optimum cannot be ruled out.

These results are reasonably well known from previous work, especially that of Kemp (1966) and Jones (1967). Apart from illustrating them in a novel way, the principal contribution of this chapter is to demonstrate what can be said about the relationship between welfare and the available policy instruments when the values of some of the latter are constrained. In particular, it has been shown that the pattern of optimal second-best tariffs and investment taxes in a small open economy hinges on whether or not importables are capital-intensive, in the general equilibrium sense of whether or not a fall in the rental elicits an increase in the output of importables. If importables are capital-intensive, then contours of constant welfare are upward-tilted in the space of the tariff and the investment tax; the implication is that restrictions on either type of international transaction have counteracting effects on welfare. Thus, if an exogenous constraint sets the rate of capital taxation at a positive level, the optimal second-best restriction on trade is a tariff. The reverse holds if importables are labor-intensive: constant-welfare loci are now downward-tilted and (for example) exogenously set levels of capital taxation imply that imports should be subsidized at the second-best optimum. In the large open economy, the range of possibilities is considerably greater and the shape of the iso-welfare contours depends on the degree of capital-intensity of imports in both countries. A further difference is that, in the small open economy case, the iso-welfare contours center around the point of zero intervention, whereas in the large open economy case they center around the point corresponding to the first-best tariffs and investment taxes.

It was noted in the introduction that this paper differs from most earlier treatments of the choice of optimal tariffs and investment taxes in not dealing with the Heckscher–Ohlin model. A disadvantage of this is that I have had to assume that a particular pattern of production and trade prevails for all values of the policy instruments considered. However, this drawback necessarily arises in any study which uses calculus tools to determine the optimal values of policy instruments. In the classic papers of Kemp (1966) and Jones (1967), for example, a detailed consideration was required of the circumstances in which one or other country specialized in production, and different rules for optimal intervention were calculated in each case. Assuming a particular pattern of specialization, as I have done here, is therefore no less general an approach. Presumably a full analysis of optimal intervention which takes account of policy-induced changes in the pattern of specialization will require simulations of computable models.

Finally, the fact that I have treated traded goods and factors in a totally symmetric fashion throughout suggests that the techniques introduced in this paper could be applied to the analysis of policy choice in models where factors are internationally immobile but more than one category of imports is distinguished. This application can indeed be carried out,[30] which links the results of the present chapter with the recent work on optimal tariffs in multi-good models by Feenstra (1986), Itoh and Kiyono (1987) and Bond (1990).

Appendix 1: Properties of the foreign Antonelli matrix

The home and foreign countries have similar structures, the only difference being that the foreign country does not impose any tariffs or investment taxes. Changes in net imports of (non-numeraire) goods and (traded) factors by the foreign country are determined as follows:

$$dM^* = E_{qq}^* dq^* + X_I^* dy^*. \tag{A.1}$$

From (4.1), since t^* is zero, the change in foreign income is simply:

---

[30] See Neary (1989).

$$dy^* = -M^{*\prime}dq^* = M'dq^*,$$ (A.2)

where the last equality holds since home and foreign net imports must add to zero $(M + M^* = 0)$. Combining (A.1) and (A.2) and inverting yields an inverted Slutsky-type expression for the Antonelli matrix of derivatives of the foreign inverse demand functions:

$$q_M^* = (E_{qq}^* + X_I^*M')^{-1}.$$ (A.3)

Recalling the absence of income effects on the demand for capital from (3.3), (A.3) may be rewritten as follows:

$$q_M^* \equiv \begin{bmatrix} p_m^* & p_k^* \\ r_m^* & r_k^* \end{bmatrix} = \begin{bmatrix} m_p^* & m_r^* \\ E_{rp}^* & E_{rr}^* \end{bmatrix}^{-1}$$ (A.4)

where I have used $m_p^* \equiv E_{pp}^* + x_I^*m'$ and $m_r^* \equiv E_{pr}^* + x_I^*k'$.

The sub-matrices of q_M^* may now be evaluated using standard properties of partitioned inverse matrices and some of the results in Sections 2 and 3. Consider first p_m^*, which gives the effects of additional net imports of non-numeraire goods on their demand prices (or marginal valuations) in the foreign country:

$$p_m^* = [m_p^* - m_r^*(E_{rr}^*)^{-1}E_{rp}^*]^{-1}$$ (A.5)

$$= [\bar{E}_{pp}^* + x_I^*m' - x_I^*k'(E_{rr}^*)^{-1}E_{rp}^*]^{-1} \quad \text{(from (3.14))}$$ (A.6)

$$= (\bar{E}_{pp}^* + x_I^*m' + x_I^*k'g_{kp}^*)^{-1} \quad \text{(from (2.10) and (2.11))}$$ (A.7)

Evidently, in the absence of foreign income effects $(x_I^* = 0)$, the matrix p_m^* is negative definite and so the inverse demand functions must be downward-sloping. Assuming normality, income effects could offset the substitution effect if the foreign country exports goods which are subject to tariffs by the home country $(m > 0)$ or if it exports capital which is used intensively by its export industries $(k > 0$ and $g_{kp}^* > 0)$.

Consider next the off-diagonal sub-matrices of q_M^*. That giving the effect of extra goods imports on capital rentals takes a particularly simple form:

$$r_m^* = -(E_{rr}^*)^{-1}E_{rp}^*p_m^*$$ (A.8)

$$= g_{kp}^*p_m^*,$$ (A.9)

(using the same substitutions which led to (A.7)). Thus, a rise in net imports of non-numeraire goods by the foreign country lowers their prices there (assuming income effects do not dominate p_m^*) which, if they are capital-intensive $(g_{kp}^* > 0)$, leads to a fall in rentals. The other off-diagonal matrix, $p_k{}^*$, is simply the transpose of (A.9) in the absence of income effects. The full expression for it is:

$$p_k{}^* = -p_m{}^*m_r{}^*(E_{rr}{}^*)^{-1} \tag{A.10}$$

$$= p_m{}^*(g_{pk}{}^* - x_I{}^*k^*g_{kk}{}^*). \tag{A.11}$$

Finally, the effect of additional capital imports on foreign rentals is given by the following:

$$r_k{}^* = (E_{rr}{}^*)^{-1} + (E_{rr}{}^*)^{-1}E_{rp}{}^*p_m{}^*m_r{}^*(E_{rr}{}^*)^{-1} \tag{A.12}$$

$$= g_{kk}{}^* + g_{kp}{}^*p_m{}^*g_{pk}{}^* - g_{kp}{}^*p_m{}^*x_I{}^*k'g_{kk}{}^*. \tag{A.13}$$

Once again, the own-market substitution effects encourage a downward-sloping inverse demand curve but this could conceivably be offset by the income effect in the final term.

Appendix 2: Properties of the M_t matrix

The key feature of the expression for M_t, given in (4.12), is the product of two matrices of derivatives: the Slutsky matrix of price derivatives of the home compensated direct demand functions, E_{qq}, and the Antonelli matrix of quantity derivatives of the foreign uncompensated indirect demand functions, $q_M{}^*$. Direct calculation, using results from Appendix 1, yields:

$$E_{qq}q_M{}^* = \begin{bmatrix} A_{11} & A_{12} \\ A_{21} & A_{22} \end{bmatrix} \tag{A.14}$$

where:

$$A_{11} = [\bar{E}_{pp} + g_{pk}g_{kk}{}^{-1}(g_{kp} - g_{kp}{}^*)]p_m{}^* \tag{A.15}$$

$$A_{12} = -g_{pk}g_{kk}{}^{-1}g_{kk}{}^* + A_{11}(g_{pk}{}^* - x_I{}^*k'g_{kk}{}^*) \tag{A.16}$$

$$A_{21} = -g_{kk}{}^{-1}(g_{kp} - g_{kp}{}^*)p_m{}^* \tag{A.17}$$

$$A_{22} = g_{kk}{}^{-1}g_{kk}{}^* + A_{21}(g_{pk}{}^* - x_I{}^*k'g_{kk}{}^*). \tag{A.18}$$

Clearly, the deviations of A_{11} and A_{22} from identity matrices and the deviations of A_{12} and A_{21} from zero matrices depend on the *differences* between the two countries, both in factor intensities (measured by $g_{kp} - g_{kp}{}^*$) and in the slopes of the inverse demand functions for net imports of goods and capital (measured by $\bar{E}_{pp}(\bar{E}_{pp}{}^*)^{-1}$ and $g_{kk}{}^{-1}g_{kk}{}^*$), as well as on the strength of the foreign income effect for foreign exportables, $x_I{}^*$.

Direct calculation of the sub-matrices of M_t now yields:

$$m_\tau = \Delta[E_{pp} - A_{12}(I_m + A_{22})^{-1}E_{rp}] \tag{A.19}$$

$$m_\rho = \Delta[E_{pr} - A_{12}(I_m + A_{22})^{-1}E_{rr}] \tag{A.20}$$

$$k_\tau = (I_m + A_{22})^{-1}[E_{rp} - A_{21}m_\tau] \tag{A.21}$$

$$k_\rho = (I_m + A_{22})^{-1}[E_{rr} - A_{21}m_\rho] \tag{A.22}$$

where:

$$\Delta \equiv [I_n + A_{11} - A_{12}(I_m + A_{22})^{-1}A_{21}]^{-1} \tag{A.23}$$

where I_m and I_n are m-by-m and n-by-n identity matrices respectively.

Finally, in special case 2 in the text, $x_I^* = 0$, $\bar{E}_{pp} = \bar{E}_{pp}^*$, $g_{kk} = g_{kk}^*$ and $g_{kp} = -g_{kp}^*$. In the scalar case ($m = n = 1$), it may now be checked that $\Delta = \frac{1}{2}$ and so:

$$M_t = \begin{bmatrix} \frac{1}{2}E_{pp} & 0 \\ 0 & \frac{1}{2}(1 + g_{pk}g_{kk}^{-1}g_{kp}p_m^*)^{-1}g_{kk}^{-1} \end{bmatrix}. \tag{A.24}$$

References

Bond, E. W. 1989 "Optimal Policy toward International Factor Movements with a Country-Specific Factor," *European Economic Review*, 33, 1329–344.

 1990 "The Optimal Tariff Structure in Higher Dimensions," *International Economic Review*, 31, 103–16.

Brecher, R. A. and R. C. Feenstra 1983 "International Trade and Capital Mobility between Diversified Economies," *Journal of International Economics*, 14, 321–40.

Brecher, R. A. and R. Findlay 1983 "Tariffs, Foreign Capital and National Welfare with Sector-Specific Factors," *Journal of International Economics*, 14, 277–88.

Bruno, M. 1972 "Market Distortions and Gradual Reform," *Review of Economic Studies*, 39, 373–83.

Casas, F. R. 1985 "Tariff Protection and Taxation of Foreign Capital: The Welfare Implications for a Small Country," *Journal of International Economics*, 19, 181–88.

Chipman, J. S. 1972 "The Theory of Exploitative Trade and Investment Policies: A Reformulation and Synthesis," in L. E. Di Marco (ed.), *International Economics and Development: Essays in Honour of Raul Prebisch*, New York, Academic Press, 881–916.

Das, S. 1983 "Optimal Tariffs on Final and Intermediate Goods," *International Economic Review*, 24, 493–508.

Diewert, W. E., A. H. Turunen-Red and A. D. Woodland 1989 "Productivity- and Pareto-Improving Changes in Taxes and Tariffs," *Review of Economic Studies*, 56, 199–216.

Dixit, A. K. 1975 "Welfare Effects of Tax and Price Changes," *Journal of Public Economics*, 4, 103–23.

1986 "Tax Policy in Open Economies," in A. Auerbach and M. Feldstein (eds.), *Handbook of Public Economics, Vol. 1*, Amsterdam, North-Holland, 313–74.

1987 "On Pareto-Improving Redistributions of Aggregate Economic Gains," *Journal of Economic Theory*, 41, 133–53.

Dixit, A. K. and V. Norman 1980 *The Theory of International Trade: A Dual General Equilibrium Approach*. Welwyn, James Nisbet and Cambridge, Cambridge University Press.

Feenstra, R. C. 1986 "Trade Policy with Several Goods and Market Linkages," *Journal of International Economics*, 20, 249–67.

Foster, E. and H. Sonnenschein 1970 "Price Distortion and Economic Welfare," *Econometrica*, 38, 281–97.

Gehrels, F. 1971 "Optimal Restrictions on Foreign Trade and Investment," *American Economic Review*, 61, 147–59.

Hatta, T. 1977 "A Theory of Piecemeal Policy Recommendations," *Review of Economic Studies*, 44, 1–21.

Itoh, M. and K. Kiyono 1987 "Welfare-Enhancing Export Subsidies," *Journal of Political Economy*, 95, 115–37.

Jones, R. W. 1967 "International Capital Movements and the Theory of Tariffs and Trade," *Quarterly Journal of Economics*, 81, 1–38.

1969 "Tariffs and Trade in General Equilibrium: Comment," *American Economic Review*, 59, 418–24.

1971 "A Three-Factor Model in Theory, Trade and History," in J. N. Bhagwati et al. (eds.), *Trade, Balance of Payments and Growth: Essays in Honor of Charles P. Kindleberger*, Amsterdam, North-Holland, 3–21.

1979 "Comment" on "Trade and Direct Investment," by R. McCullough, in R. Dornbusch and J. Frenkel (eds.), *International Economic Policy*, Baltimore, Johns Hopkins Press, 105–11.

1987 "Tax Wedges and Mobile Capital," *Scandinavian Journal of Economics*, 89, 335–46.

Jones, R. W., I. Coelho and S. Easton 1986 "The Theory of International Factor Flows: The Basic Model," *Journal of International Economics*, 20, 313–27.

Jones, R. W. and S. Easton 1983 "Factor Intensities and Factor Substitution in General Equilibrium," *Journal of International Economics*, 15, 65–99.

Jones, R. W. and R. Ruffin 1975 "Trade Patterns with Capital Mobility," in M. Parkin and A. R. Nobay (eds.), *Current Economic Problems*, Cambridge, Cambridge University Press, 307–32.

Kemp, M. C. 1962 "Foreign Investment and the National Advantage," *Economic Record*, 38, 56–62.

1966 "The Gain from International Trade and Investment: A Neo–Heckscher–Ohlin Approach," *American Economic Review*, 56, 788–809.

MacDougall, G. D. A. 1960 "The Benefits and Costs of Private Investment from Abroad: A Theoretical Approach," *Economic Record*, 36, 13–35.

Neary, J. P. 1985 "International Factor Mobility, Minimum Wage Rates, and Factor-Price Equalization: A Synthesis," *Quarterly Journal of Economics*, 100, 551–70.

1988 "Tariffs, Quotas and Voluntary Export Restraints with and without

156   **J. Peter Neary**

International Capital Mobility," *Canadian Journal of Economics*, 21, 714–35.
1989 "Trade Liberalisation and Shadow Prices in the Presence of Tariffs and Quotas," Working Paper No. 89-4, Centre for Economic Research, University College Dublin.

Neary, J. P. and F. P. Ruane 1988 "International Capital Mobility, Shadow Prices and the Cost of Protection," *International Economic Review*, 29, 571–85.

Pearce, I. F. and D. C. Rowan 1966 "A Framework for Research into the Real Effects of International Capital Movements," in T. Bagiotti (ed.), *Essays in Honor of Marco Fanno*, Padua: Cedam, 505–35; reprinted in J. H. Dunning (ed.), *International Investment*, London, Penguin Books.

Ramaswami, V. K. 1968 "International Factor Movement and the National Advantage," *Economica*, 35, 309–10.

Smith, A. 1980 "Optimal Public Policy in Open Economies," Economic Research Paper No. 176, University of Warwick.

Vanek, J. 1965 *General Equilibrium of International Discrimination*, Cambridge, Mass., Harvard University Press.

Woodland, A. D. 1982 *International Trade and Resource Allocation*, Amsterdam, North-Holland.

10 The case of the vanishing revenues: auction quotas with oligopoly

KALA KRISHNA

1. Introduction

One of the most common criticisms of voluntary export restrictions (VERs) and the way that quotas are currently allocated is that they allow foreigners to reap the rents associated with the quantitative constraints. It has been suggested that auctioning import quotas would remedy this. However, it is by now well understood that this policy may not raise significant revenues in the presence of market power on the part of producers. The reason is that in such environments, prices are chosen by producers, i.e. there is no supply curve and the response of producers to the constraint must be taken into account when determining the price of an auctioned license. For example, foreign producers can reduce the value of a license by raising their own price. Since this allows them to appropriate potential rents, they do so. This leads to low prices for licenses in equilibrium.

Krishna (1990a), Takacs (1987), and Helpman and Krugman (1989) analyze the response of producers to quotas, and the effects of this on license prices. Krishna considers a foreign monopolist who has other markets, while Takacs focuses on a single market. Helpman and Krugman look at foreign oligopoly. They use perceived marginal revenue and marginal cost tools applied to a model of price competition to argue that the license price is zero unless the quota is quite restrictive. They then work out a linear demand, foreign duopoly model with price competition and differentiated products. For this model they show that welfare, even when

I am grateful to the National Science Foundation (Grant No. SES8822204) and to the MacNamara Fellowships Program of The World Bank for research support, to Vijay Krishna for asking the question, to Susan Collins for the title, to Kathleen Hogan, Phillip Swagel, and Ling Hui Tan for able research assistance, and to Paul Krugman and Elhanan Helpman for early access to Chapter 4 of *Trade Policy and Market Structure*. I am also grateful to Lael Brainard for comments.

the quota is set optimally and licenses are auctioned, is below that under free trade.

The contribution of this chapter, over and above that of Helpman and Krugman (1989), is threefold. First, in contrast to their approach, I illustrate the response of producers with foreign duopoly using best response functions. I show how these change with a quota and how the restrictions of the quota affect the equilibrium. This provides an alternative way of illustrating producer response to quotas and this is the subject of Section 2.

Second, in Section 3, I provide an oligopoly example which allows parametrization of several important factors such as the degree of substitutability between foreign products, their own demand elasticity, and the number of foreign firms. In this example also, welfare cannot rise above free trade even when quotas are optimally set. Third, intuition for this result in general is provided, and other market structures are briefly discussed. Section 4 discusses the importance of the assumption of competitive markets, the implementation procedure, and directions for future research in this area.

2. Foreign duopoly

In order to develop some instuition, I first analyze a model of foreign duopoly. For simplicity, assume that the foreign firms are identical, i.e., impose symmetry. Let $x^1(p^1, p^2)$ and $x^2(p^1, p^2)$ be the demand functions facing the two foreign firms. The existence of domestic competitive supply can easily be incorporated here.[1] As usual, we will let subscripts denote partial derivatives and assume that $x_j^i > 0$ for $i \neq j$ and $x_j^i < 0$ for $i = j$ so that demand is downward sloping and foreign goods are substitutes for each other. Marginal costs of production are assumed to be constant at c for all firms.

In the absence of any quotas, each firm maximizes its profits, $\pi^i(p^1, p^2) = (p^i - c)x^i(p^1, p^2)$ taking p^j, $i \neq j$ as given. In other words, they are Bertrand competitors. The resulting first order condition, $\pi_i^i(p^1, p^2) = 0$, defines the best response of each firm for any price by its competitors. $B^1(p^2)$ and $B^2(p^1)$ denote these best responses for the two firms. They are depicted in Figure 10.1. Their intersection gives the Nash

---

[1] This is done by adding a third good which is competitively supplied and is a substitute for both goods. Its demand is $d^3(p^1, p^2, p^3)$. This is equated to $s^3(p^3)$, competitive supply. The equilibrium level of p^3 depends on p^2 and p^1 and is denoted by $p^3(p^1, p^2)$. Let $d^1(p^1, p^2, p^3)$ and $d^2(p^1, p^2, p^3)$ be the demands for good 1 and 2 respectively. Now let $x^1(p^1, p^2) \equiv d^1(p^1, p^2, p^3(p^1, p^2))$ and $x^2(p^1, p^2) \equiv d^2(p^1, p^2, p^3(p^1, p^2))$ to get the given specification. Of course, the interpretation of the partial derivatives of $x^1(\cdot)$, $x^2(\cdot)$ changes in an obvious way given this specification.

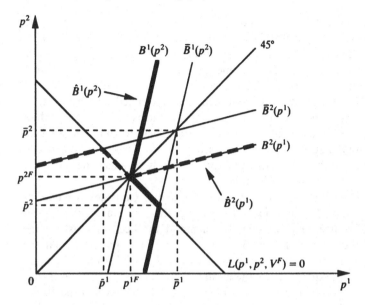

Figure 10.1. $V = V^F$

equilibrium prices under free trade, (p^{1F}, p^{2F}), which in turn give rise to the free trade level of imports denoted by V^F.

Now consider the effect of a quota at the free trade level, implemented by the sale of licenses. At this point it is important to be clear about exactly what constitutes a license, how licenses are sold, and what the timing of moves is. Throughout this paper a license is defined to be a piece of paper which entitles its owner to buy one unit of the product in question at the price charged by the seller.

The licenses are sold in a competitive market to either competitive domestic retailers with zero marginal costs of retailing or to consumers directly. I assume that the timing of moves is as follows. First, the government sets the quota. Then the firms set their prices. Finally, the market for licenses clears. This timing captures the idea that the market for licenses clears more frequently than the monopolist sets prices, and that the government sets the quota even less frequently than the producers set prices.

Note that while other assumptions about timing of moves can be made, there is much in favor of this assumption. Quota levels are changed infrequently, and as prices are set by producers, it is natural to think of them as being set at discrete intervals. However, as the market for licenses is competitive, it is natural to think of it as clearing practically continuously. Other assumptions about the allocation of licenses, and the market structure in the market for licenses could also be made. Changing the timing of moves complicates the model but should not change the flavor of the results.[2] The assumption that the firms are Bertrand competitors is made to allow strategic effects to emerge in the most natural way. Had I assumed firms chose their quantities, that is, played Cournot, the strategic variable itself would have to be assumed to be restricted by the quota, or some other way found of reconciling attempts by firms to export more than the total quota. This would correspond, in effect, to different ways of implementing the quota than the one used here, as well as to a difference in the strategic variable. Both these factors are likely to affect the outcome, and more work here would be useful.

The model is then solved backwards as usual. Consider the market for licenses first. If the prices charged by the firms are (p^1, p^2) and the price of a license is L, then the demand for licenses must be the same as the demand for imports at $(p^1 + L, p^2 + L)$, namely $x^1(p^1 + L, p^2 + L) + x^2(p^1 + L, p^2 + L)$. Note that while the products are differentiated, the quota limits their total imports treating them as if they were the same product. The supply of licenses is V, the level of the quota. Thus the equilibrium price of a license, when prices p^1 and p^2 are charged by the firms and V is the level of the quota, is given by $L(p^1, p^2, V)$ where $L(\cdot)$ is defined by the market for licenses clearing. Notice that if $x^1(p^1, p^2) + x^2(p^1, p^2) < V$, then $L(p^1, p^2, V) < 0$ as defined so far. However, since a quota is not binding if such prices are charged, $L(\cdot)$ is defined to be zero in this case.

Also, I assume that an increase in the price of all goods reduces the demand for any good, that is, that own price effects dominate cross price effects. This implies that $L(p^1, p^2, V)$ decreases as price charged by either firm rises. The license price also falls as the quota rises. This implies that the combinations of p^1 and p^2 such that the license price is just equal to zero is given by a downward sloping line in Figure 10.1. This is depicted by the line $L(p^1, p^2, V^F) = 0$ when the quota is set at the free trade level. Naturally, this line goes through the Nash equilibrium point (p^{1F}, p^{2F}). For prices above and to the right of this line, prices are so high that the quota is not binding and a license has no value. For prices below and to the left of this line, the quota is binding so that the price of a license is positive.

Moving to the second stage, each firm's profit function is also altered by the quota. Consider firm 1. For any price charged by firm 2, if it charges a

---

[2] See Krishna (1990a) for the analysis of a change in timing with monopoly. Changing the market structure in the license market leads to a model of auctions with endogenous valuations, see Krishna (1990b) and (1991b). Changing the allocation of licenses changes producer response, possibly undoing the incentive to increase prices as analyzed in Krishna (1991a) for the monopoly case and Tan (1991) for the oligopoly case.

price above the line $L(p^1, p^2, V^F) = 0$, its profits are unchanged by the quota. However, if it charges a price below this line, $L(\cdot)$ is positive so that its profits are given by:

$$\bar{\pi}^1(p^1, p^2, V^F) = (p^1 - c)x^1(p^1 + L(p^1, p^2, V^F), p^2 + L(p^1, p^2, V^F)).$$

Notice that along the line $L(p^1, p^2, V^F) = 0$, $\bar{\pi}^1(\cdot)$ equals $\pi^1(\cdot)$, and that $\bar{\pi}_1{}^1(\cdot) = \pi_1{}^1(\cdot) + (p^1 - c)[x_1{}^1(\cdot) + x_2{}^1(\cdot)]L_1(\cdot)$.

It is assumed that $x_1{}^1(\cdot) + x_2{}^1(\cdot) < 0$; that is, the effect of all prices rising equally is a reduction in demand; i.e., own price effects outweigh cross price effects. Hence, $\bar{\pi}_1{}^1(\cdot) > \pi_1{}^1(\cdot)$. This is a key aspect of the analysis. An increase in own price also reduces the license price. This effect reduces by the same amount the effective or license inclusive price of both goods in the presence of a binding quota. This additional factor makes the slope of the restricted profit function exceed that of the unrestricted one where they intersect along the $L(\cdot) = 0$ line as shown above.

Therefore only three possible cases exist when considering the derivatives $\bar{\pi}_1{}^1(\cdot)$ and $\pi_1{}^1(\cdot)$ along $L(\cdot) = 0$. Either:

(a) $\bar{\pi}_1{}^1(\cdot) > \pi_1{}^1(\cdot) \geq 0$,   or

(b) $\bar{\pi}_1{}^1(\cdot) > 0 > \pi_1{}^1(\cdot)$,   or

(c) $0 \geq \bar{\pi}_1{}^1(\cdot) > \pi_1{}^1(\cdot)$.

Recalling that profits are given by $\bar{\pi}^1(\cdot)$ below the line $L(p^1, p^2, V^F) = 0$, and by $\pi^1(\cdot)$ above the line, this means that the composite profit function facing firm 1 with a quota, denoted by $\hat{\pi}^1(\cdot)$, must look like that depicted in Figure 10.2(a), (b) and (c) in these three cases. Note that this composite profit function is concave in p^1 for given p^2 if both the component functions are concave. This prevents mixed strategy equilibria from arising due to a quota.

Assume that both $\bar{\pi}^1(\cdot)$ and $\pi^1(\cdot)$ are concave in p^1 given p^2. Let $\bar{B}^1(p^2)$ maximize $\bar{\pi}^1(\cdot)$ with respect to p^1. If we draw $\pi^1(\cdot)$ and $\bar{\pi}^1(\cdot)$, as in Figure 10.2, it is obvious that in case (a) it is best for firm 1 to choose $p^1 = B^1(p^2)$, in case (b) to choose the p^1 implicitly defined by $L(\cdot) = 0$, and in case (c) to choose $p^1 = \bar{B}^1(p^2)$.

Returning to Figure 10.1, the fact that $\bar{\pi}_1{}^1(\cdot) > \pi_1{}^1(\cdot)$ means that $\bar{B}^1(p^2)$ lies to the right of $B^1(p^2)$ at the point where $B^1(\cdot)$ crosses $L(\cdot) = 0$, as shown. Similarly, $\bar{B}^2(p^1)$ lies above $B^2(p^1)$ at the point where $B^2(\cdot)$ crosses $L(\cdot) = 0$.[3] Let the intersection of $\bar{B}^1(\cdot)$ and $\bar{B}^2(\cdot)$ be at $(\bar{p}^1, \bar{p}^2)$. The effect

---

[3] $\bar{B}^1(\cdot)$ and $\bar{B}^2(\cdot)$ are drawn everywhere above $B^1(\cdot)$ and $B^2(\cdot)$ respectively as this simplifies the diagram. This need not be the case in general. However, the arguments here about identifying the best response with a quota on the basis of the signs of $\bar{\pi}$ and π along $L(\cdot) = 0$ hold irrespective of this.

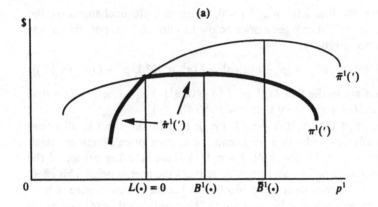

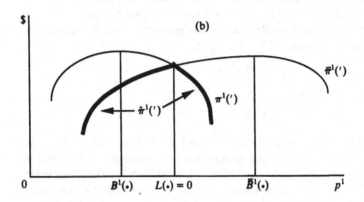

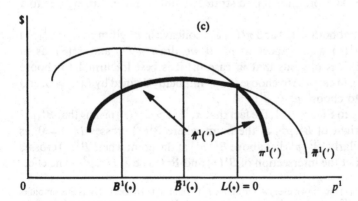

Figure 10.2

of the quota system on the best response of firm 1 is now apparent. Let $\bar{B}^1(p^2)$ intersect the $L(\cdot) = 0$ line when $p^2 = \tilde{p}^2$ and $\bar{B}^2(p^1)$ intersect the $L(\cdot) = 0$ when $p^1 = \tilde{p}^1$ as depicted. If p^2 exceeds p^{2F} then both $B^1(\cdot)$ and $\bar{B}^1(\cdot)$ lie above $L(\cdot) = 0$, so that $\pi_1{}^1(\cdot)$ and $\bar{\pi}_1{}^1(\cdot)$ are both positive along $L(\cdot) = 0$. Hence, we are in case (a). When p^2 lies between $\tilde{p}^2$ and p^{2F}, we are in case (b), and when p^2 lies below $\tilde{p}^2$ we are in case (c). Therefore, the best response function for firm 1 given the quota is $\hat{B}^1(p^2)$ which is drawn as a dark line in Figure 10.1.[4]

Analogous arguments show that for firm 2 the best response function is given by $\hat{B}^2(p^1)$ depicted by the dark shaded line in Figure 10.1. Notice that the equilibrium is not affected when a quota at the free trade level is imposed. Since the equilibrium lies along $L(\cdot) = 0$ selling licenses does not raise revenues.

Another way of understanding why the free trade equilibrium remains the equilibrium is to note that given the price of the other firm, the quota makes the demand curve facing a firm more inelastic whenever the quota binds, and leaves it unaffected otherwise. However if $p^2 = p^{2F}$, the quota binds only if $p^1 < p^{1F}$ so that demand is more inelastic for price decreases but not for price increases. Thus, there is no incentive to change price from p^{1F}. Similarly, firm 2 also has no incentive to change its price from p^{2F} so that these original prices constitute a Nash equilibrium even with the imposition of the quota at the free trade level.

Now consider the effect of reducing the quota. This shifts $L(\cdot) = 0$ outward. Corresponding to this quota are $\bar{B}^1(\cdot)$ and $\bar{B}^2(\cdot)$ analogous to those drawn in Figure 10.1. Figure 10.3 shows the effect of the lower quota on firms' reaction functions. It is easy to verify that this quota does affect the equilibrium.[5] In fact, there is a continuum of equilibria along the segment EF of $L(\cdot) = 0$ in Figure 10.3. However, all the equilibria correspond to $L(\cdot) = 0$ so that even if the quota is slightly restrictive, the license has no value in equilibrium.

Finally, if V is so small that the $L(\cdot) = 0$ line lies above the intersection of the $\bar{B}^1(\cdot)$ and $\bar{B}^2(\cdot)$ lines defined by that V, then the equilibrium is unique, and is given by the intersection of $\bar{B}^1(\cdot)$ and $\bar{B}^2(\cdot)$.[6] Again this comes from deriving $\hat{B}^1(\cdot)$ and $\hat{B}^2(\cdot)$ by comparing the derivatives of $\pi(\cdot)$ and $\bar{\pi}(\cdot)$ along $L(\cdot) = 0$. In this case, as prices are such that the quota binds in equilibrium, the licenses raise positive revenues. However, this occurs only when the quota is quite restrictive. Thus welfare first falls as the quota falls

---

[4] Although, for convenience, the Figures 10.1 and 10.3 depict the linear demand case, the arguments do *not* rely on linearity, only on uniqueness and stability of the equilibria.

[5] Note that $\bar{B}^1(\cdot)$ is defined by looking at $\bar{\pi}_1{}^1(\cdot)$ and $\pi_1{}^1(\cdot)$ along $L(\cdot) = 0$ to determine whether case (a), (b), or (c) is the relevant one. The same procedure applies for $\bar{B}^2(\cdot)$.

[6] I am assuming that $\bar{B}^1(\cdot)$ and $\bar{B}^2(\cdot)$ have a unique intersection, as do $B^1(\cdot)$ and $B^2(\cdot)$.

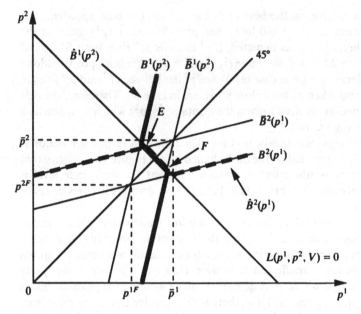

Figure 10.3

because prices rise so consumer surplus falls while there is no revenue raised. Only later when license revenues become positive can welfare rise as the quota falls.[7] Helpman and Krugman (1989), show that for an example with linear demand, foreign duopoly, and price competition it is never optimal to set a restrictive quota.

A simple example is developed in the next section in order to better understand how market structure and demand conditions affect the welfare consequences of such quotas.

3. An illustrative example and extensions

The effects of the quota system as described in the previous section depend on substitutability between products, demand elasticity for the product group, and the number of firms in the market. The following example illustrates the influence of these parameters.

Demand arises from utility maximization with the utility function given by:

$$u(X,N) = X^\alpha + N \quad \text{with} \quad \alpha \in (0,1)$$

---

[7] Although Figures 10.1 and 10.3 depict upward sloping best response functions, the same results are obtained if they are downward sloping. The symmetry assumption is likewise made for convenience but is not crucial to the results.

where X is a composite good or the services provided by the various products consumed and N is the consumption of a numeraire good. Also, $X = F(x^1, \ldots, x^n)$, where $F(\cdot)$ takes the standard constant elasticity of substitution form. $(x^1, \ldots, x^n)$ are the quantities of the n differentiated products consumed. Thus, $X = [\sum (x^i)^\gamma]^{1/\gamma}$ where $\gamma \in (-\infty, 1)$. Recall that the elasticity of substitution is $\sigma = 1/(1 - \gamma)$ and $\sigma \in (0, \infty)$.

Demand for a particular variety of the good is a derived demand, derived from the demand for the composite good. Because the composite good is in essence produced by the consumer, its price, P, equals the cost of production. Hence:

$$P = \phi(p^1, \ldots, p^n) = \left[\sum_{i=1}^{n} (p^i)^r \right]^{1/r}$$

where

$$r = \frac{\gamma}{\gamma - 1}, \quad \text{with } 1 - r = \sigma.$$

The demand for a particular variety is given by:

$$x^i(p^1, \ldots, p^n) = a^i(p^1, \ldots, p^n)X(\phi(p^1, \ldots, p^n)),$$

where $X(\cdot)$ is the demand for the composite good, and $a^i(\cdot)$ is the amount of variety i needed to make a unit of the composite good. The derivative of $\phi(\cdot)$ with respect to p^i is $a^i(\cdot)$ by Shephard's lemma.

Of course, given our specification:

$$X(p) = \left(\frac{\phi(\cdot)}{\alpha} \right)^{1/(\alpha - 1)}$$

so that the elasticity of demand for the composite good, ε, is a constant and equals $-1/(\alpha - 1)$.

The key parameters of the model are σ, ε, and n. Assume that each variety is produced at a constant marginal cost, c. The profits of the ith firm in the absence of a quota are given by:

$$\pi^1(p^1, \ldots, p^n) = (p^i - c)x^i(p^1, \ldots, p^n).$$

Profit maximization by each firm, taking other prices as given, yields the first-order condition:

$$x^i \left[1 - \frac{(p^i - c)}{p^i} (\mu_i{}^i + \varepsilon \theta^i) \right] = 0 \qquad (1)$$

for the ith firm, where $\mu_i{}^i = -[\partial a^i(\cdot)/\partial p^i][p^i/a^i]$ and $\theta^i = a^i(\cdot)p^i/P$, the share of the ith variety in cost. For this specification we get that

$\theta^i = 1/n$ and $\mu_i^i = (1 - r)(n - 1)/n$, in the symmetric equilibrium. Using this in equation (1) gives the price charged by the producer of a variety in the symmetric equilibrium under free trade, p^F, to be:[8] $p^F = c[\sigma(n - 1) + \varepsilon]/[\sigma(n - 1) + \varepsilon - n]$. Let $nx(p^F, \ldots, p^F) = V^F$.

Now consider the effect of a quota at V. As usual, the price of a license is given by $L(p^1, \ldots, p^n, V)$ defined by the market clearing condition:

$$\sum_{i=1}^{n} x^i(p^1 + L, \ldots, p^n + L) = V \tag{2}$$

if the quota binds, and by zero if it does not. Therefore, if p is charged by all firms in the symmetric equilibrium, while $p(V)$ is the symmetric price needed for total demand to equal the quota, the license price is given by:

$$L(p, V) = \max[p(V) - p, 0]. \tag{3}$$

If the quota is binding, then each firm maximizes:

$$\bar{\pi}^i(p^1, \ldots, p^n) = (p^i - c)x^i(p^1 + L(\cdot), \ldots, p^n + L(\cdot)).$$

This gives the first order condition:[9]

$$x^i \left[1 - (\mu_i^i + \varepsilon\theta^i)\frac{(p^i - c)}{(p^i + L)} \right] + \left[L_i(p^i - c)\sum_{j=1}^{n} x_j^i \right] = 0. \tag{4}$$

The second term enters because of the effect of a change in a firm's price on the price of licenses. Recall that:

$$\frac{x_i^i}{x^i}[p^i + L(\cdot)] = -[\mu_i^i + \varepsilon\theta^i]$$

and

$$\frac{x_i^j}{x^i}[p^j + L(\cdot)] = [\mu_j^i - \varepsilon\theta^j].$$

where $\mu_j^i = [\partial a^i(\cdot)/\partial(p^j + L)]/[(p^j + L)/a^i(\cdot)] = [(1 - r)/n]\mu_i^i(\cdot)$ is defined analogously as the negative of the elasticity of $a^i(\cdot)$ with respect to its ith argument as before and has the same value as before in the symmetric equilibrium.[10] Also, $-\mu_i^i + \sum_{j \neq i} \mu_j^i = 0$ since $a^i(\cdot)$ is homogeneous of

---

[8] As expected, p^F rises with c but falls with σ and ε so that as goods get better substitutes or demand for services gets more elastic, prices fall. p^F also falls with n if $\sigma > \varepsilon$. Also, $\sigma(n - 1) + \varepsilon$ must be positive for p^F to be positive.

[9] Note that goods could be substitutes or complements for each other as $(\partial x^i/\partial p^j)(p^j/x^i) = (\sigma - \varepsilon)/n$ in the symmetric equilibrium. If $\sigma > \varepsilon$ goods are substitutes, while if $\sigma < \varepsilon$, they are complements.

[10] Note that as the arguments of $a^i(\cdot)$ are the license inclusive prices, their elasticities are defined with respect to them, and not the license exclusive prices.

degree zero. The above allows the second term of (4) to be written very simply in the symmetric equilibrium as:

$$\left[L_i(p^i - c) \sum_{j=1}^{n} x_j^{\,i} \right] = \beta \frac{(p - c)}{p} \frac{Lx}{(p + L)} \varepsilon,$$

where $\beta = -L_i p^i/L$, is the elasticity of $L(\cdot)$ with respect to p in the symmetric equilibrium. Moreover, using (2) shows that:

$$L_i = \sum_{j=1}^{n} x_i^{\,j} \Bigg/ \sum_{j=1}^{n} \sum_{i=1}^{n} x_j^{\,i} \tag{5}$$

But with symmetry, $x_i^{\,i} = x_j^{\,j} \; \forall \, i,j$, and $x_j^{\,i} = x_s^{\,r}$ for $i \neq j$, $r \neq s$, so that $L_i = -1/n$, so that $\beta = p/Ln$.

Using the expressions for $\mu_j^{\,i}$ and θ in the symmetric equilibrium gives (4) to be equivalent to:

$$1 - \left[\frac{\sigma(n - 1)}{n} \right] \frac{(p - c)}{(p + L(\cdot))} = 0. \tag{6}$$

Solving for p in (6) gives a solution $p^*(V)$, which corresponds to the intersection of the best response functions assuming the quota is binding in the previous section. Note that in (6), $p + L(\cdot) = p(V)$, the price which when charged by all firms sets demand equal to the quota. This gives, $p^*(V) = p(V)[n/\sigma(n - 1)] + c$, which increases as V decreases. Also note that since $p(V^F) = p^F$ by definition:

$$\frac{p^*(V^F) - p(V^F)}{p(V^F)} = \frac{n}{\sigma(n - 1)} - \frac{p^F - c}{p^F}$$

$$= \frac{n}{\sigma(n - 1)} - \frac{n}{[\sigma(n - 1) + \varepsilon]}$$

$$= \frac{n\varepsilon}{\sigma(n - 1)[\sigma(n - 1) + \varepsilon]}$$

$$> 0.$$

Thus, $p^*(V^F) > p^F$.

We are interested, among other things, in the question of how restrictive the quota has to be for a license price to become positive. As in Section 2 this corresponds to the quota being set so that it is just binding at the symmetric equilibrium, assuming that the constraint is binding, i.e. set at demand when p solves (6) with $L(\cdot) = 0$.

Solving for p in (6) with $L(\cdot) = 0$ gives:

$$p^* = \frac{c\sigma(n-1)}{\sigma(n-1) - n}. \tag{7}$$

Thus, the ratio of the free trade level of imports, V^F, to demand at p^*, denoted by V^*, is:

$$\frac{V^F}{V^*} = \left[\frac{\sigma(n-1) - n}{\sigma(n-1)} \frac{\sigma(n-1) + \varepsilon}{\sigma(n-1) + \varepsilon - n} \right]^{-\varepsilon}.$$

Notice that p^* exceeds p^F, so that V^F exceeds V^*, and as shown above, $p^*(V^F)$ exceeds p^F. Also, as the number of firms or substitutability between their products becomes infinite, competition becomes intense and V^F over V^* goes to unity so that we approach the results of the competitive case. In order to get some idea of the magnitude of V^F/V^*, consider its value for $\varepsilon = 2, \sigma = 2, n = 4$. Here it equals $(1.5)^2$, so that imports must be more than halved in order to make the license price positive.[11]

If auction quotas do not raise revenue, they must reduce welfare as they restrict consumption. For auction quotas to raise welfare, they must raise enough revenue to make up for this consumer surplus loss. Figure 10.4 helps illustrate why it is difficult for this to happen. For simplicity, all firms are assumed to be symmetric and we consider the pure strategy symmetric equilibrium with n foreign firms. On the horizontal and vertical axes we have the output (or average quota) per firm, and price of a representative firm respectively. x^F and p^F denote the Nash equilibrium output and price under free trade. $p^*(V)$ (the Nash equilibrium price in the symmetric equilibrium under a quota assuming that the quota is set at V and is binding) and $p(V)$ (the price at which the quota is binding assuming all firms charge it) are also depicted.

When $V = V^F = nx^F$, that is the quota is set at the free trade level, $p^*(V)$ lies above p^F. In our example, $p^*(V)$ rises as V falls. It intersects $p(V)$ when $V = V^*$, at a price p^* which lies above p^F. When $p^*(V)$ lies above $p(V)$, the equilibrium price with a quota is given by $p(V)$ and the license price is zero as this corresponds to the best response functions, $\bar{B}(\cdot)$, of Section 2 intersecting above the $L(\cdot) = 0$ line. If it lies below $p(V)$, the equilibrium price is $p^*(V)$ and the license price is positive and equals the difference between the two. This corresponds to the best response functions, $B(\cdot)$, intersecting below the $L(\cdot) = 0$ line.

For welfare to rise above its free trade level due to a quota, the license revenues must exceed the consumer surplus loss. For example, the license revenues are zero when the quota is V^* while consumer surplus loss is positive and related to the area EBp^*p^F. A necessary, but not sufficient,

[11] Notice that if σ is small relative to n, V^* becomes negative so that *any* quota gives a zero license price and quotas are always harmful.

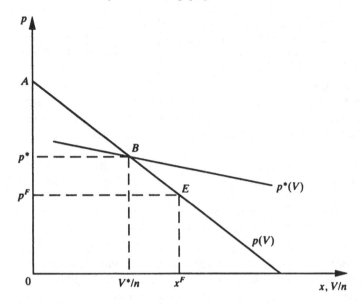

Figure 10.4

condition for welfare to rise with auction quotas is that $p^*(V)$ lie below the free trade equilibrium price for some V. This is evident from Figure 10.4 since this is necessary for license revenue gains to exceed consumer surplus losses. In our example, this cannot be so as $p^*(V)$ is downward sloping and exceeds p^F at $V = V^F$. Even if $p^*(V)$ was upward sloping and did lie below the free trade price at some point, it would have to be very steep for welfare to rise. Thus, any conditions which ensure that $p^*(V)$ does not fall below p^F are sufficient (though not necessary) to ensure that welfare cannot rise with auction quotas.

As a quick aside, let us see how our results so far would change if we had domestic oligopoly and foreign competition.[12] First consider the case where all goods are substitutes for one another. Start from the free trade prices and a quota set at free trade levels. Each domestic firm could make the quota bind by raising its price. It would want to do so, as this raises the license inclusive price of imports and so increases its own demand.[13] This behavior makes the quota bind and creates a positive license price for the quota. However, the presence of positive revenues does not imply that this policy

---

[12] For details of these arguments see Krishna (1988).

[13] The analogy to the effect of a quota with domestic monopoly, analyzed in the classic paper by Bhagwati (1965), should be apparent.

leads to an improvement in welfare. Because foreign supply is competitive, the quota system does not shift profits, so that the gain in revenue comes at the expense of consumer surplus. A quota thus results in a deadweight loss, despite the positive license price and revenue thereby derived.

What if the domestic goods were substitutes for one another, but complements to the imported good, and the quota was set at the free trade level? In this event, domestic firms could make the quota bind by reducing their price, which would raise the demand for imports, and create a positive license price. However, they would have no incentive to do so as this would only reduce their demand relative to that under free trade as the goods are complements. For this reason, a quota at the free trade level has no effect.[14]

4. Conclusion

The analysis of this paper makes a number of assumptions that warrant further discussion. First, it is assumed that the market for licenses is competitive, in order to focus on the strategic response of *producers*. Thus, interesting aspects of strategic behavior in auctions, which is the focus of much of the auction literature, are suppressed. It would be hard to incorporate these aspects. Any model of auctions in the above setting would have to deal with multiple objects and multiple agents. Moreover, it would have to depart from the standard models in auction theory as valuations of licenses *cannot* be specified exogenously as is done for the most part in the auction literature. The value of a license is determined in the market for the good on which the quota is imposed. Thus it depends on the allocation of *all* licenses and the valuations of agents need not meet the usual assumptions made in the multiple object auction literature. Hence, the results of this literature need not hold here. Little is known about such models in general. Krishna (1990a, 1991a) develops some ideas on the endogenous determination of market structure using such models. It is likely that the form of the auction with endogenous valuations is important in determining the allocation of licenses.

Thus, an area where work is needed concerns the determinants of market structure in the market for licenses itself. In this chapter I assume this market is competitive. It is worth exploring when this is likely to occur, when there will be incentives for agents to cartelize this market, and who might have the greatest incentive to do so. Governments often express

---

[14] Variations of such models have also been analyzed in Bhagwati (1965). Krishna (1989b) analyzes the effects of a quota with home monopoly and foreign competition when goods are substitutes or complements. Krishna (1989a) deals with the effects of quotas with international duopoly.

concern about this possibility and limits on the share of licenses any one party can own are often set.[15]

Second, even assuming the market for licenses is competitive, other aspects of the implementation of quota auctions do matter. Here I assume that all quota licenses are auctioned in a competitive market. However, other schemes are used in practice[16] or could be used. For example, all licenses need not be auctioned as done here. By giving away some licenses to producers their incentives to raise price to capture rents can be diluted and this can lead to higher license revenues earned. Krishna (1991a) deals with this issue in the case of foreign monopoly, and Tan (1991) deals with it for the oligopoly case.

While simple models such as these help illustrate why auctioning quotas may not raise more revenue in imperfectly competitive markets, it would be useful for policy purposes to study further the effects of different market structures and implementation schemes on the extent of license rents. This seems to be empirically important as the work of Krishna, Erzan and Tan (1991) suggests that in the MFA (Multi Fibre Arrangement), which restricts world trade in textiles, yarn and apparel, rents do not seem to be going to the holders of licenses alone. This could be due to other sources of market power or details of the implementation processes used in practice, which differ from the simple ones postulated here. Our knowledge of implementation schemes and their effects in implementing quotas is far from perfect, and much work is needed here.

References

Bhagwati, J. N. 1965 "On the Equivalence of Tariffs and Quotas," in R. E. Baldwin, et al. (eds.), *Trade Growth and the Balance of Payments. Essays in Honor of Gottfried Haberler*, Chicago, Rand McNally.

Bergsten, C. F., A. E. Kimberly, J. J. Schott and W. E. Takacs 1987 "Auction Quotas and United States Trade Policy," *Policy Analysis in International Economics*, 19, Institute for International Economics, Washington, D.C., September.

Helpman, E. and P. Krugman 1989 *Trade Policy and Market Structure*, Ch. 4, Cambridge, MA, MIT Press.

Krishna, K. 1988 "The Case of the Vanishing Revenues: Auction Quotas With Oligopoly," NBER Working Paper No. 2723, Cambridge, MA.

1989a "Trade Restrictions as Facilitating Practices," NBER Working Paper No. 1546, *Journal of International Economics*, 26, 251–70.

1989b "What do VERs do?" in J. Nelson and R. Sato (eds.), *Beyond Trade*

---

[15] See for example Bergsten *et al.* (1987).

[16] See Bergsten *et al.* (1987), Appendix B, for a discussion of some of the ways in which quotas are implemented in the U.S.

Friction, New York, Cambridge University Press.

1990a "The Case of the Vanishing Revenues: Auction Quotas With Monopoly," *American Economic Review*, 80, 828–36.

1990b "Auctions with Endogenous Valuations, The Snowball Effect, and Other Applications," NBER Working Paper No. 3483, Cambridge, MA.

1991a "Making Altruism Pay in Auction Quotas," in E. Helpman and A. Razin (eds.), *International Trade and Trade Policy*, Cambridge, MA, MIT Press.

1991b "Auctions with Endogenous Valuations: The Persistence of Monopoly Revisited," Harvard Institute for Economic Research, Discussion Paper No. 1513. Forthcoming in *American Economic Review*.

Krishna, K., R. Erzan and L. H. Tan 1991 "Rent Sharing in the Multi-Fibre Arrangement: Theory and Evidence from US Apparel Imports from Hong Kong," NBER Working Paper No. 3673, Cambridge, MA.

Takacs, W. E. 1987 "Auctioning Import Quota Licenses: An Economic Analysis," Institute for International Economic Studies, University of Stockholm, Seminar Paper No. 390, September.

Tan, L. H. 1991 "Notes on Implementing Quota Auctions," Unpublished Mimeo, Harvard University.

Part V

Trade, growth and dynamics

11 Prices of goods and factors in a dynamic stochastic economy

AVINASH DIXIT

1. Introduction

Of all the important contributions Ron Jones has made to international trade theory, probably the most outstanding is his analysis of the equilibrium effects of changes in the prices of tradable goods on the returns to non-tradeable factors. In Jones (1965), he elucidated the Stolper–Samuelson magnification effect in the Heckscher–Ohlin model. In the process, Jones replaced earlier intricate geometric techniques with the delightfully simple and elegant λ-θ algebra. Jones (1971), together with Samuelson (1971), gave us a general equilibrium formulation of the Ricardo–Viner model, where the relationship between the prices of goods and factors is different from, and perhaps more realistic than, that of the Heckscher–Ohlin model. Jones (1977) and Jones and Scheinkman (1977) were insightful studies of whether and how such relationships extend to models with more goods and factors.

The progress of trade theory in the last two decades has led to formal models of uncertainty and adjustment in a trading economy. Jones' birthday celebration seems a particularly suitable occasion for developing this line of research to examine the relationship between the prices of goods and factors in a dynamic economy with uncertainty.

Comparative statics has been the basic technique for analyzing the effect of changes in the prices of tradeable goods on the returns to non-tradable factors. Goods' prices are exogenous parameters in specifying the general equilibrium of a small open economy. When such exogenous parameters change, the whole equilibrium shifts. Total differentiation, or some other comparative static argument such as revealed preference, allows us to determine the resulting changes in the endogenous variables, including the factor prices.

I thank Lars Svensson for comments on an earlier draft, and the National Science Foundation for research support under grant No. 8803300.

This approach needs re-thinking in a stochastic dynamic setting. If today's output price differs from yesterday's, that is no longer a truly exogenous change, but merely a step in the evolution of a process with a given probability law. The truly exogenous parameters are those that define the stochastic process. It remains true that a chance rise in the price of a good implies a chance increase in the return to the factor specific to (or intensively used in) the production of that good. But the more basic question becomes one of whether owners of this factor are better off if the trend or the volatility of the whole process governing the price of that good changed. In other words, the right comparative statics question is, how do changes in the parameters governing the whole stochastic processes of goods prices affect various aspects of the whole stochastic processes of factor returns?

The analysis would be relatively easy if factors were either costlessly mobile or totally immobile between uses. In these cases, as output prices fluctuate stochastically, those factors that can relocate would do so instantaneously. The equilibrium at each instant would be exactly as described by a static model with the prevailing prices for traded goods. The equilibrium factor prices would be given by the usual formulas. Then the same formulas could be used to map the stochastic process of goods' prices into that of factor prices.

But the case of particular interest in a dynamic stochastic economy is the one where factor mobility has a positive but finite cost. Now owners of factors recognize that the future prices of goods are uncertain. Their investment decisions, and sector location decisions, are made in the light of this knowledge. In particular, the status quo has an option value. Changes are not made unless the current conditions become especially favorable.[1] The equilibrium at any instant is affected by history, and does not coincide with that of a static model corresponding to the currently prevailing prices of goods. The route from goods' prices to factor prices becomes more complicated.

In this paper I shall construct a very simple model of this kind, and use it to carry out some comparative static exercises in the sense described. The problem turns out to be sufficiently hard to force resort to special functional forms. Even then, analytical comparative static expressions seem beyond reach, and the results come from numerical simulations. Therefore this paper is intended as no more than a very tentative exploration, and the conclusions are no more than suggestions that need further research, or hypotheses to be tested in richer models. But I hope

---

[1] See Pindyck (1988), Bertola (1989) and Dixit (1989a, b) for discussions of this feature of irreversible investments under uncertainty. Bertola (1990) constructs a model of a closed economy concerned with issues of investment and growth.

this first attempt proves to be a useful start on what promises to be an interesting new view of the relationship between the prices of goods and factors.

The stochastic process view of comparative statics is not only theoretically more satisfactory, but also more relevant for policy. The cost of factor mobility itself becomes a parameter of interest for comparative statics, with significant policy implications. For example, workers and labor unions in currently depressed sectors often favor restrictions on plant closing. But such policies have repercussions on investment in good times. Labor union leaders with foresight should take this into account, and consider how well their members will do on the average over their lifetime under one set of rules or another. One of the tentative conclusions of the model in this paper is that reducing capital mobility is not in general in labor's interest. Paradoxically, it may be in capital's own interest.

2. The model

The production technology of the model bears very close resemblance to that in the familiar Heckscher–Ohlin and Ricardo–Viner models. This highlights the new issues introduced by dynamics and uncertainty in the simplest possible way.

There are two goods, X and Y. The economy is small and open, good Y is the numeraire, and the price P of good X follows an exogenous stochastic process. Time is discrete, and the process is stationary Markov of the first order; thus the probability distribution of the random price at time $(t + 1)$ is a given constant function of the actual price at time t. In numerical work, I shall assume that $\ln P$ is a random walk with upper and lower reflecting barriers; this is intended to be an approximate description of resource price movements.

There are two factors, capital and labor, and their mobility between sectors is restricted in ways to be specified. When the factor allocations to the sectors are respectively (K_x, L_x) and (K_y, L_y), the outputs are given by the production functions

$$X = F_x(K_x, L_x), \quad Y = F_y(K_y, L_y). \tag{1}$$

These are assumed to have the usual properties of concavity and constant returns to scale. In numerical simulations I use Cobb–Douglas functions,

$$X = A K_x^a L_x^{1-a}, \quad Y = A K_y^a L_y^{1-a}. \tag{2}$$

Note that the constant and the exponent are the same for the two sectors. This preserves a symmetry between the sectors, leaving the trend of the price process as the only possible source of difference between them. This is done deliberately to focus on the new phenomena introduced by uncertainty. Future work can examine the effects of technology differences across sectors.

Capital can move between the sectors at finite cost. To move a unit of capital requires γ units of its output in the sector of its original employment. Once again, this preserves symmetry between the sectors. The parameter γ is allowed to vary over a range of values, to examine the effects of different mobility costs. As for labor, two extreme assumptions are employed. In one, labor is totally immobile between the sectors, and in the other, it is costlessly mobile. This allows us to compare the relative fates of a costlessly mobile factor, a factor that can move at a finite cost, and an immobile factor, in various combinations.

Let L and K be the total amounts of labor and capital. These are held constant, once again to facilitate comparisons with the familiar static models of trade. Now the result of production in one period can be described by a revenue function. When labor is immobile, we have simply

$$R(P, K_x, K_y, L_x, L_y) = P F_x(K_x, L_x) + F_y(K_y, L_y). \tag{3}$$

When labor is costlessly mobile,

$$R(P, K_x, K_y, L)$$
$$= \max\{PF_x(K_x, L_x) + F_y(K_y, L_y) \mid L_x + L_y = L\}. \tag{4}$$

The factor prices, (r_x, r_y, w_x, w_y) in the case of immobile labor, and (r_x, r_y, w) in the case of mobile labor, are given by the partial derivatives of the appropriate revenue function with respect to the factor quantities. Of course, the costs of factor movement must be subtracted from the revenue to find the aggregate disposable income, and the incidence of these costs on factor owners must be specified to arrive at the disposable incomes of individual units.

Turning to demand, I assume a one-period utility function $U(C_x, C_y)$ that is concave and homogeneous of degree one. Utilities are added over time with a discount factor δ. I make the simplest assumption about the intertemporal allocation of consumption, namely to ignore international borrowing and lending. This is again an opportunity for future extension. Now we can write a one-period indirect utility function as $I/\phi(P)$ where I is aggregate disposable income and $\phi(P)$ is a consumer price index. In numerical work I choose the Cobb–Douglas index symmetric between the sectors, namely $\phi(P) = P^{1/2}$.

Now we can consider the dynamics. Each period starts with a realization of the price P. Production occurs using the existing factor allocation (with labor optimized in the case of costless labor mobility). Plans to relocate capital are made, and mobility costs are incurred, but the new allocation does not take effect until the next period. I assume that internal markets in risk-bearing are rich enough to ensure a Pareto optimum. Then the allocation rules must maximize the expected discounted present value of the utility of aggregate consumption. The Bellman value function of this optimization is

$$V(P, K_x) = \max\{I(P, K_x)/\phi(P) + \delta EV(P', K_x')\}, \tag{5}$$

where the maximization is over the choice of the new capital allocation K_x' and $K_y' = K - K_x'$, the expectation is over the distribution of next period's price P' conditional on this period's price P, and the disposable income is found by subtracting the applicable capital adjustment costs from the value of production. Recall that the costs are incurred in units of X-sector output if capital is moving out of the X-sector, and in units of Y-sector output if it is moving out of the Y-sector. Thus

$$I(P, K_x) = R(P, K_x, K - K_x)$$
$$- \begin{cases} \gamma P(K_x - K_x') & \text{if } K_x' < K_x \\ \gamma(K_x' - K_x) & \text{if } K_x' > K_x. \end{cases} \tag{6}$$

For notational simplicity I have suppressed the (unchanging) labor arguments from the revenue function.

It is well known that the solution of such stochastic dynamic programming problems takes the form of a "hysteresis band" in (P, K_x) space.[2] This is a pair of curves such that no capital is relocated when price movements keep the point (P, K_x) within the band formed by the curves, and when a movement takes the point outside the band, just enough capital is relocated to bring it to the nearer edge of band. Unfortunately, analytical expressions for the curves are not available even for the simplest specifications of various functional forms and the price process.[3] Therefore we cannot hope to derive the laws of the stochastic processes for the factor rewards in closed form. The price process must be simulated numerically, and the implications for factor incomes must be inferred from the numerical results. That is what I do next.

3. Numerical simulations

Most of the structure of the simulated model was explained in the previous section. It remains to specify the numerical values of the parameters. Some

---

[2] See Caplin and Krishna (1986a), Dixit (1989a), Bentolila and Bertola (1990).
[3] Bentolila and Bertola (1990) can get farther with analytical results because they consider one industry with an exogenous wage. This would defeat the whole purpose of my general-equilibrium analysis.

will be kept fixed throughout the exercise, and others will be varied over a range to study their comparative static effects. The fixed parameters include the total quantities of capital and labor, $K = 1$ and $L = 2$; when labor is immobile the separate sectoral quantities are fixed at $L_x = L_y = 1$. This again preserves symmetry across sectors in all the features except those arising from the output price uncertainty. Parameters of the production function are also fixed, the constant $A = 1$ and the exponent $a = 0.5$. Future work should examine the consequences of varying these, allowing them to differ across sectors, and should also consider production functions other than Cobb–Douglas. Finally, the discount factor is fixed at $\delta = 0.9$.

Turning to the parameters that are the focus of the comparative statics, consider the output price process first. I assume that the price can take on one of $(2J + 1)$ discrete values

$$P = \exp(\sigma j), j = -J, -(J-1), \ldots, -1, 0, 1, \ldots, (J-1), J \quad (7)$$

It performs a random walk over these values.[4] From any interior point j, the probability of going to $(j + 1)$ is π and that of going to $(j - 1)$ is $(1 - \pi)$. From J, the probability of staying at J is π and that of going to $(J - 1)$ is $(1 - \pi)$. Similarly, from $-J$ the probability of going to $-(J - 1)$ is π and that of staying at $-J$ is $(1 - \pi)$. This is as if there are reflecting barriers at $\pm(J + \frac{1}{2})$. Now at any interior point the trend rate of increase of $\ln P$ is $(2\pi - 1)$, and the standard deviation is σ. I vary π from 0.5 to 0.7; values from 0.3 to 0.5 are automatically covered on interchanging the roles of the sectors.[5] The range of variation of σ is from 0.1 to 0.2.

While σ captures one aspect of price volatility, there is another, namely the size of the range of price variation as measured by J. With $J = 10$ and $\sigma = 0.1$, the price can vary by a factor of e either side of its central value, for a total variation by a factor of 7.3. This seems a reasonable range to constitute the central case of the analysis. I consider variations around it.

Next comes the adjustment cost γ. The central value chosen is $\gamma = 1$. This means that if all the capital, along with a unit of labor, is in one sector, then to move it all to the other sector requires all the output for one period. More intuitively, starting from an initially equal allocation and the price at the central point of its range, a price change of about 30 per cent on either side is needed to bring about any capital relocation. This agrees with the

[4] I consider only the long run averages of factor prices, therefore the initial level of the output price is irrelevant. Discounted present values are affected by the initial price, and future work involving these should allow that as a separate parameter.

[5] Note that perfect symmetry between the sectors means that for every realization of prices $\{P_t\}$, there is an equiprobable realization $\{P_t^{-1}\}$. For this, we need equiprobable geometric steps in the P-process. That is, $\ln P$ should be trendless, or $\pi = 0.5$. We do not need a "Jensen's inequality correction" to make P itself trendless.

consequence of plausible adjustment cost values used elsewhere, for example Dixit (1989a, b). I allow γ to vary from 0 to 5; at the upper end capital mobility is almost eliminated.

For numerical calculations, the values of capital must also be discretized. I divide the range of K, of total length 1, into 20 subdivisions. Thus capital can be moved only in units of 0.05. This has some unfortunate side-effects that I will point out as they arise.

Let the discrete units of capital be indexed by k. With the obvious change of notation from the continuous state variables to their discrete counterparts, the Bellman value function defined in (5) and (6) can be written as

$$V(j,k) = \max_{k'} \{I(j,k)/\phi(j) + \delta[\pi V(j_+,k')$$

$$+ (1 - \pi) V(j_-,k')]\}. \tag{8}$$

Here the steps of the random walk in j are defined by

$$j_+ = \min(j + 1, J), \quad j_- = \max(j - 1, -J), \tag{9}$$

thus taking care of the reflecting barriers. The disposable income $I(j,k)$ is defined by

$$I(j,k) = R(j,k) - \begin{cases} 0.05\gamma \exp(\sigma j)(k - k') & \text{if } k' < k \\ 0.05\gamma (k' - k) & \text{if } k' > k. \end{cases} \tag{10}$$

When reading the expression for the adjustment costs, recall that each step of k represents 0.05 units of K.

This dynamic programming problem is easy to solve numerically. The mapping defined by the right hand side of (6) or (8) is a contraction by the usual argument; see Stokey et al. (1989) for a thorough exposition. Starting from any initial guess, repeated application of the mapping in (8) leads to a fixed point that is the optimum. I employed the simplest initial guess, namely complete stationarity,

$$V(j,k) = R(j,k)/(1 - \delta).$$

The iteration was continued until the average absolute deviation between the matrices $V(j,k)$ in two successive steps became less than 10^{-6}, an arbitrarily chosen tolerance level.[6]

The maximizing capital allocation k' as a function of the initial (j, k) was stored in another array. This set the stage for simulating the price process to

---

[6] This took a little over three minutes on a 16MHZ 386SX PC using the Lahey Fortran compiler.

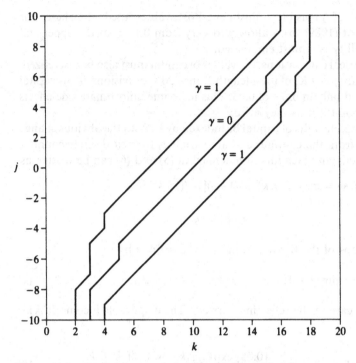

Figure 11.1   Capital hysteresis bands with immobile labor.

generate the implications for the factor returns. Starting from a central location, namely $j = 0$ and $k = 10$, the price process was allowed to run for 100,000 steps, a number that was judged large enough to obtain good averages over time.[7] The corresponding evolution of the optimal capital allocation was traced. At each step of the (j, k) or (P, K_x) process, the factor prices were calculated and divided by the price index to convert them into real magnitudes. This exercise was confined to calculating the long run averages (ergodic values) of these prices, but future work can examine more details of the distribution of these processes.

Note that for tracing such a long process on a computer, we must have a particularly good random number generator, which has an effectively infinite period and is free from high-order serial correlations. I chose the one recommended for this purpose by Press *et al.* (1989, pp. 197–98). For additional security, for each parameter configuration I carried out at least three runs of the price process using different "seeds" for the random number generator. The numbers agreed within 1 percent, usually better.

---

[7] This generally took under two minutes for each run.

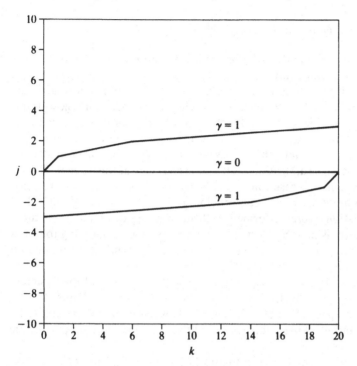

Figure 11.2   Capital hysteresis bands with costlessly mobile labor

The results reported in the tables below are the average values from all the runs for each experiment.

Labor is either costlessly mobile or totally immobile, so the relevant prices are obvious: the marginal products w_x and w_y in the separate sectors when labor is immobile, and the common marginal product w when it is mobile. In the case of capital, which moves across sectors at a cost, it is not immediately clear which is the relevant price to report. I chose three that capture different aspects. The first two, r_x and r_y, are the marginal products of hypothetical units of capital that are for ever confined to sectors X and Y respectively. The third, r_m, is the income of a hypothetical marginal unit of capital that is always the first to move whenever there is any capital relocation, each time paying the adjustment cost.

Now we can proceed to examine the numerical results. In view of the special nature of the model, the functional forms, and the parameter choices, all the results should be regarded as tentative suggestions, and not definitive pronouncements. It would be tedious to repeat this warning every time, but I hope the single statement above suffices to keep readers on the alert throughout.

a. Hysteresis bands for the central case

I begin by describing the equilibrium for the central case. Remember that the discount factor is always fixed at $\delta = 0.9$. Other parameters are: zero trend ($\pi = 0.5$), range $J = 10$, volatility $\sigma = 0.1$, and adjustment cost $\gamma = 1.0$. Figure 11.1 shows the case when labor is totally immobile (one unit in each sector); Figure 11.2 is for the case where labor is costlessly mobile (two total units). In each case the central curve represents the capital allocations that equate the values of its marginal products in the two sectors, that is, the allocations that would come about when $\gamma = 0$. The two outer curves in each case constitute the hysteresis bands for $\gamma = 1.0$. I have chosen to draw the jagged curves joining the actual discrete points where the calculations were performed, instead of trying to fit a smooth curve, because there is no clear principle that governs such smoothing to obtain the optimal policies in going from a discrete dynamic programming problem to a continuous one.

In Figure 11.1, at the central point $k = 10$, the width of the hysteresis bands is $j = \pm 3$, that is, 35 percent in terms of the price. In Figure 11.2 the corresponding width is about 25 percent. This is roughly comparable to the values found elsewhere, for example Dixit (1989b), thus supporting the choice of this central value of γ.

The band is much flatter in Figure 11.2 than it is in Figure 11.1; in this sense there is more capital mobility when labor is also mobile.

b. Changes in adjustment costs

Table 11.1 summarizes the long-run average equilibrium factor rewards when the adjustment cost varies. Because of the symmetry ($\pi = 0.5$), hypothetical units of capital confined to the one sector or the other get the same return ($r_x = r_y$), as do actual units of labor when immobile ($w_x = w_y$). In numerical computations, this was borne out to within 2 percent in each run; the values reported are the averages across runs.

The column labelled "Switches" reports the number of times during a run of 100,000 draws of the price process that the hypothetical marginal unit of capital, which always gets the priority in moving, relocates from one sector to the other. The values reported are averages across the number of such runs performed in each instance (corresponding to different starting seeds for the random number generator). The numbers are rounded, as excessive accuracy would be spurious.

There are two noteworthy aspects of these switches. First, as γ increases, the number of switches falls quite quickly. Even in the central case of $\gamma = 1$, switches occur on the average only once every 60 periods. This is in keeping

Table 11.1 *Effect of adjustment cost changes. Common parameters*: $\delta = 0.9$, $J = 10$, $\sigma = 0.1$, $\pi = 0.5$

Case (a) – Immobile labor

γ	$r_x = r_y$	r_m	$w_x = w_y$	Switches
0.0	0.769	0.770	0.385	37,300
1.0	0.762	0.791	0.387	1,600
2.0	0.766	0.797	0.383	1,060
5.0	0.740	0.813	0.378	370

Case (b) – Mobile labor

γ	$r_x = r_y$	r_m	w	Switches
0.0	0.654	0.940	0.457	7,000
1.0	0.657	0.941	0.455	1,120
2.0	0.660	0.941	0.455	780
5.0	0.670	0.930	0.450	460

with previous findings that even small adjustment costs reduce movement very significantly when there is ongoing uncertainty, because the option value of the status quo becomes large very quickly.[8] Secondly, there are fewer switches when labor is mobile than when it is immobile.[9] This seems to contradict the idea that capital mobility is greater when labor is mobile. But it pertains to a different aspect of movement, namely the number of occasions when any capital is moved. When labor is mobile, the hysteresis band is very flat, and on each occasion when capital relocates, a large number of units of it move. But there are fewer occasions when any relocation is called for. Thus, while j keeps above 3 or below -3, all the capital is in the one sector or the other, and there are no switches.

Turning to the factor rewards, we note several points.

(1) There is little or no fall in capital's average return as the adjustment cost increases, even to the point of reducing capital mobility almost to zero. Note that the hypothetical units confined to one sector or the other (r_x and r_y) do not have any adjustment cost subtracted from them, but the footloose marginal unit (r_m) does. Over some stretches, higher adjustment cost actually helps capital. The marginal unit gains in this way when labor is

[8] See Pindyck (1988), Bertola (1989), and Dixit (1989a, b) and (1991).
[9] The one exception occurs for $\gamma = 5$, by which time both numbers are so small that the instance seems uninteresting.

immobile, and the fixed units when labor is mobile. I have no intuitive explanation for this difference. But the general phenomenon accords with the previous results of Bentolila and Bertola (1990) for the firing costs of labor. They found that at a given wage the industry's long run average employment rises so long as all firms remain in business. Here we have costs of moving capital. The amount of labor (analogous to the number of firms) is fixed. Also, in general equilibrium we keep the quantity of capital fixed and look at the long run average return. With this reinterpretation, the effect is very similar.

(2) Labor is not helped if the mobility of capital is restricted. If anything, it is slightly hurt. The intuition when labor is mobile is relatively simple: a more efficient allocation of a complementary factor is beneficial. When labor is immobile, workers in each sector are helped by having more capital employed there. Thus they want more prompt capital inflow in good times, but slower outflow in bad times. The net effect depends on the curvature of labor demand as a function of the capital stock over the range of capital movement involved. In our example this is such as to make the former effect dominate.

(3) Comparing the cases of immobile and mobile labor, we see that the marginal unit of capital is better off when labor is mobile, but the fixed units are better off when labor is immobile. It is obvious that the marginal unit of capital, which relocates to the sector with a sufficiently high relative price, benefits if it can attract more labor to its current sector. As to the other result, a unit of capital that is restricted to the X-sector benefits from labor immobility when P is low, but is hurt by being unable to attract more labor when P is high. This is similar to the twofold effect of capital mobility on immobile labor mentioned above, but the variation of labor mobility costs in the present instance is the full range from zero to infinity. Here the net effect turns out to be negative. Thus the effect of the mobility of one factor on the return to another immobile factor is likely to be situation-specific.

(4) When $\gamma = 0$ and labor is costlessly mobile, the model is "almost" purely Ricardian. It is Ricardian because the two sectors have equal factor intensity, and it is only "almost" so because capital cannot change its location for one period. Note that the total factor supplies are $L = 2$ and $K = 1$. With Cobb–Douglas production functions, if capital were truly perfectly mobile, we would have $r = 2w$. In fact r is slightly greater than $2w$; once again the innate mobility cost (delay) helps capital.

c. Changes in output price volatility

Table 11.2 shows the effects of changing different dimensions of price volatility. Once again the cases of immobile and mobile labor are

Table 11.2 *Effect of price volatility changes. Common parameters:* $\delta = 0.9$, $\pi = 0.5$, $\gamma = 1.0$

Case (a) – Immobile labor

J	σ	$r_x = r_y$	r_m	$w_x = w_y$	Switches
10	0.1	0.762	0.791	0.387	1,600
5	0.2	0.770	0.792	0.385	3,320
20	0.1	0.922	0.970	0.471	1,400
10	0.2	0.932	0.990	0.475	3,100

Case (b) – Mobile labor

J	σ	$r_x = r_y$	r_m	w	Switches
10	0.1	0.657	0.941	0.455	1,120
5	0.2	0.667	0.941	0.457	2,250
20	0.1	0.744	1.260	0.602	600
10	0.2	0.755	1.270	0.609	1,170

distinguished. In each case, the first line restates the results for the central parameter values. In the second line, the total range of price variation is kept unchanged, but the standard deviation of ln P per unit of time is doubled. This has very little effect on factor rewards; capital restricted to one of the sectors seems to benefit very slightly. The other two lines both correspond to a doubling of the total range of price variation. The third line keeps the standard deviation per unit time unchanged, while the fourth doubles it along with the total range. These changes benefit both factors quite significantly. The probable explanation is that the utility function has no aversion to income-risk, while the revenue function is convex in the price.

d. Changes in output price trend

Table 11.3 shows the effect of a non-zero price trend. As π increases, the X-sector is more favored. The number of switches drops off quite quickly. Most factor returns move as expected, but one feature is worth pointing out. When labor is immobile, the trend away from the Y-sector actually helps the hypothetical unit of capital that is confined to this sector. As most of the capital moves to the X-sector, the unit left behind has all the labor to itself, so its marginal product is high, and indeed increases as π rises. More paradoxical is the finding that for $\pi = 0.55$ and 0.60, we have $r_y > r_x$. But

Table 11.3 *Effect of trend in price process. Common parameters:* $\delta = 0.9$, $J = 10$, $\sigma = 0.1$, $\gamma = 1.0$

Case (a) – Labor immobile

π	r_x	r_y	r_m	w_x	w_y	Switches
0.50	0.762	0.762	0.791	0.387	0.387	1,600
0.55	0.789	0.810	0.811	0.593	0.198	1,900
0.60	0.823	0.833	0.833	0.686	0.140	850
0.65	0.848	0.825	0.851	0.718	0.126	350
0.70	0.863	0.814	0.863	0.733	0.122	40

Case (b) – Labor mobile

π	r_x	r_y	r_m	w	Switches
0.50	0.657	0.657	0.941	0.455	1,120
0.55	0.971	0.341	1.010	0.486	420
0.60	1.080	0.232	1.090	0.522	70
0.65	1.130	0.199	1.130	0.540	10
0.70	1.150	0.184	1.150	0.550	2

the gap is very small, and is probably explicable as either an artifact of discretization or a chance occurrence in stochastic simulation.

4. Suggestions for future research

In conclusion, let me gather together the various restrictive features and loose ends that are worth attention in future research. (1) Even within the confines of this model, I have examined only the long-run averages of the factor prices. Many other aspects of these stochastic processes should be studied. (2) Long-run averages are important, but just as in steady state models without uncertainty, they are flawed as welfare indicators because they neglect discounting and initial conditions. Better measures, presumably based on the function V, should be constructed. (3) The equal-exponent assumption in the Cobb–Douglas production functions preserves symmetry and simplifies numerical calculations, but precludes study of the effects of differences in factor intensities. Since these are so important in static models, a generalization in this respect should be a high priority. (4) More general production functions will allow influences of different degrees of factor substitution in each sector, while more general utility functions will introduce risk aversion and demand-side differences.

(5) A truly dynamic model will have investment and growth of the total capital stock, and intertemporal trade.[10] Of course, all these extensions require much greater computational effort.

The main purpose of this paper has been to introduce the idea that in a stochastic dynamic open economy, the question of the relationship between prices of goods and factors must be reformulated in terms of stochastic processes, and to carry out some tentative explorations along these lines. I hope the results are sufficiently interesting or provocative to generate the needed extensions and generalizations. But it is a pity that the analysis lacks the beauty of the λ-θ algebra of the static model. Perhaps one day the theory of stochastic processes will progress to the point of making it possible to treat this topic with the elegance that a paper truly worth dedicating to Ron Jones should have.

References

Bentolila, Samuel and Giuseppe Bertola 1990 "Firing costs and labor demand: How bad is Eurosclerosis?" *Review of Economic Studies*, 57, 3, (July), 381–402.

Bertola, Giuseppe 1989 "Irreversible investment," working paper, Princeton University.

1990 "Flexibility, investment, and growth," working paper, Princeton University.

Caplin, Andrew and Kala Krishna 1986 "A simple dynamic model of employment," working paper, Harvard University.

Dixit, Avinash 1989a "Entry and exit decisions under uncertainty," *Journal of Political Economy*, 97, 3, (June), 620–38.

1989b "Intersectoral capital reallocation under price uncertainty," *Journal of International Economics*, 26, 309–25.

1991 "Analytical approximations in models of hysteresis," *Review of Economic Studies*, 58, 1 (January), 141–51.

Grossman, Gene and Elhanan Helpman 1991 *Innovation and Growth in the Global Economy*, Cambridge, MA: MIT Press.

Jones, Ronald W. 1965 "The structure of simple general equilibrium models," *Journal of Political Economy*, 73, 6, (December), 557–72.

1971 "A three-factor model in theory, trade, and history," in *Trade, Balance of Payments, and Growth*, eds. J. Bhagwati *et al.*, Amsterdam: North-Holland.

1977 *"Two-Ness" in Trade Theory: Costs and Benefits*, Special Paper No. 12, International Finance Section, Princeton University.

Jones, Ronald W. and José A. Scheinkman 1977 "The relevance of the two-sector production model in trade theory," *Journal of Political Economy*, 85, 5, (October), 909–35.

Pindyck, Robert 1988 "Irreversible investment, capacity choice, and the value of the firm," *American Economic Review*, 78, 5, (December), 969–85.

---

[10] See Bertola (1990) and Grossman and Helpman (1991) for models with different concerns, that have some of these dynamic features.

Press, William H., Brian P. Flannery, Saul A. Teukolsky and William T. Vetterling 1989 *Numerical Recipes: The Art of Scientific Computing*, FORTRAN Version, New York: Cambridge University Press.

Samuelson, Paul A. 1971 "Ohlin was right," *Swedish Journal of Economics*, 39, 2, (December), 365–84.

Stokey, Nancy and Robert E. Lucas Jr. with Edward C. Prescott 1989 *Recursive Methods in Economic Dynamics*, Cambridge, MA: Harvard University Press.

12 Capital market imperfections and the infant industry argument for protection

ERIC W. BOND

This chapter analyzes the role for infant industry protection in the presence of capital market imperfections. A two good, two period model of a small open economy will be presented in which one of the sectors has the characteristics of an "infant" industry. Firms in the infant industry are unprofitable at world prices in the first period. During the first period when losses are being incurred, entrepreneurs learn about the production process. In the second period, firms become profitable (on average) at world prices. The approach to capital market imperfections in this paper is to treat them as resulting from the agency costs associated with external finance when there is private information on the part of entrepreneurs. This model will then be used to examine whether government intervention in support of the infant industry can yield Pareto-improvements.

The traditional treatment of capital market imperfections (Baldwin [1969], Corden [1974]) is to model the capital market imperfection as an exogenously given wedge between the social cost of capital and the rate at which firms can borrow from the private sector.[1] Since the future profits are being discounted at too high a rate by private sector lenders, there will be too little entry into the infant industry. Two main policy conclusions emerge from this literature. The first is that subsidies to the infant sector are desirable, because they make the amount of entry closer to the socially optimal level. The second is that direct intervention in the capital market,

I have benefited from comments from conference participants, as well as from seminars at Australian National, New South Wales, Keio University, Rutgers, Western Ontario and Wisconsin. In particular, comments from Mark Harrison and Ig Horstmann led to significant improvements in previous versions of the paper.

[1] An exception is a recent paper by Flam and Staiger (1991) who analyze the infant industry argument in a partial equilibrium model in which there is adverse selection in credit markets of the type studied by Stiglitz and Weiss (1981). Production subsidies may be welfare improving in their model, because an increase in the price of output raises the average quality of firms being funded by the industry. Their model is static, and does not consider the intertemporal aspects of the infant industry argument that are emphasized here.

such as through subsidized loans, is preferable to indirect intervention in the form of production subsidies or tariffs. Although these indirect interventions raise entry, they also introduce new distortions in the market.[2]

It will be shown in this paper that the policy conclusions may differ markedly from the traditional ones when the capital market imperfection is explicitly modelled. The inefficiencies in the loan contracts in this paper, such as restrictions on the amount that may be borrowed and loan rates that differ from the social discount rate, arise from the efforts of lenders to separate efficient firms from inefficient ones. If it is assumed that the government has the same information about firms as do the private lenders, then the government faces the same informational constraints in trying to separate types of firms when it intervenes in credit markets. The potential gains from government intervention then depend on the government's ability to use its tax/subsidy tools in goods markets or loan markets to relax the selection constraints faced by private sector lenders.[3]

Two forms of private information will be considered in this paper. The first concerns the type of a potential entrant, which may be either entrepreneur or non-entrepreneur. Non-entrepreneurs have a zero probability of success, while entrepreneurs have a probability of success which is revealed during the initial period of losses. A financial contract must provide loans to entrepreneurs to cover first period losses, but it must also impose sufficiently strong penalties on entrepreneurs who fail to discourage non-entrepreneurs from taking the loans. The second piece of private information is the actual probability of success of an entrepreneur at the beginning of the second period. Financial contracts must provide incentives to entrepreneurs who learn they have a low probability of success to drop their projects, rather than continuing the project during the second period.

These two types of information problem provide conflicting forces in the design of contracts. Imposing large penalties on firms that exit after the first period will discourage entry of non-entrepreneurs, but it will also encourage entrepreneurs with a low expected return to stay in the industry during the second period. It is shown that when endowment levels of

[2] Alternatively, learning economies may spill over to affect other firms in the industry, leading to a classic externality argument for government intervention. This would lead to an argument for a production subsidy as the first best policy if the externalities are related to the volume of output. For an extensive discussion of this case, and other forms of the infant industry argument, see Corden (1974, Chapter 9).

[3] This approach is similar to that advocated by Dixit (1989), who analyzes the role for commercial policy as a form of insurance. He examines the competitive provision of insurance in the presence of adverse selection, and then analyzes the role for tax policy by a government facing the same informational constraints.

entrepreneurs are high, contracts can be written that will achieve the efficient consumption allocation and there will be no capital market imperfection. When endowment levels are low, so that entrepreneurs have insufficient collateral, it is not possible to design contracts that yield the first best outcomes. Entrepreneurs with low collateral levels will remain in the industry when they have too low a probability of success, because the risk of loss is shifted onto lenders. Also, entrepreneurs with low collateral levels may be unable to get funding. These two distortions reflect the agency costs associated with external finance. The capital market distortion exists because the cost of externally generated funds is higher than that of internally generated funds for firms whose endowment levels are too low.

It is shown that although national income is below the maximum level when the incentive constraints are binding in the capital market, the competitive equilibrium will be an informationally constrained Pareto optimum if the fraction of non-entrepreneurs in the population is high enough. This means that direct intervention in capital markets, as through the use of low interest loans to firms in the infant sector, cannot yield a Pareto improvement. On the other hand, if the population contains too high a proportion of entrepreneurs, the competitive contracts will not be a constrained Pareto optimum. Pareto improvements can be obtained by taxing the financial contracts of entrepreneurs, and using the proceeds to subsidize those who do not enter the industry. This policy reduces the incentive for non-entrepreneurs to mimic entrepreneurs, and allows more efficient contracts with entrepreneurs to be obtained. Note that in neither of these cases is it desirable to use a capital market subsidy, which is the traditional tool for dealing with infant industries.

It is also shown that there exist circumstances under which indirect taxes, such as production subsidies or consumption taxes, can be used to yield Pareto improvements. This occurs in cases where there are actions taken by the borrowers that differ between types, but which cannot be observed by the lender. Examples include cases where tastes for consumption goods differ between types, or input usages differ across firms. The advantage of the government in this case comes from its ability to tax aggregate consumption or production of a good. If aggregate consumption (production) can be taxed, but individual consumption (production) is unobservable to the lender, then the possibility exists that indirect taxes can lead to Pareto improvements. This represents a sense in which indirect forms of intervention are superior to direct forms of intervention.

Section 1 presents the model and confirms that in the absence of private information, competitive capital markets will yield an efficient allocation. The infant sector technology is an extension of the model used by Bernanke and Gertler (1990) to study optimal financial contracts. In order to focus on the role of capital markets, the production structure in the model abstracts from factor proportions explanations of trade and focuses on the role of technology.[4] Section 2 considers the case of a competitive financial sector when the entrepreneur's type and probability of success are private information. Financial contracts can be made contingent on the state that occurs (success, failure, or exit from the industry), but not on either the type of the borrower or the probability of success. It is shown that first best allocations are attainable for entrepreneurs with endowments that are sufficiently large. The second-best contracts are characterized for the case in which endowments are too low to attain first best allocations, and it is shown that these contracts are a constrained Pareto optimum. In the absence of differences in production decisions between types, it is shown that production subsidies cannot yield a Pareto improvement. Section 3 considers the case in which there are differences in production decisions between types that are hidden from lenders, and shows that production subsidies can be used to obtain a Pareto improvement in this case. Section 4 offers some concluding remarks.

1. The model

In this section, a two period model of a small open economy is presented in which comparative advantage evolves over time. The infant sector consists of firms that are initially unprofitable at world prices. Some of these infant firms will learn that they have a high expected return and will be profitable in the future, while others will learn they are unlikely to succeed and should exit the industry. We first present the production structure of the model, and then indicate how capital markets can achieve the first best allocation when there is no informational asymmetry regarding entrepreneurial ability.

A. The production structure

The home country economy is assumed to consist of a continuum of households, each of which has an endowment of labor, denoted by l, and a type, which is either entrepreneurial (e) or non-entrepreneurial (n). There are two sectors. One sector, x, is a traditional sector in which the technology is widely known and is constant across time periods. The traditional sector employs only labor, and produces under conditions of constant returns to scale, with a_{LX} denoting the requirement of labor per unit of good x. Choosing good x to be the numeraire, the competitive profit

---

[4] Comparative advantage is thus based on differences in exogenously given labor productivities, as in the Ricardian model. Jones (1979) has emphasized the usefulness of the Ricardian model for dealing with questions dealing with the effects of technology on trade.

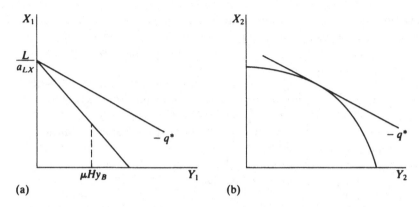

Figure 12.1

conditions ensure that the wage rate will be $w = 1/a_{LX}$ if good x is produced.

The other sector, y, is an infant sector that employs labor and entrepreneurs. Infant sector projects (firms) are indivisible and require an entrepreneur and one unit of labor to produce output. In the first period, the output of all advanced sector projects is low (denoted by y_B) as entrepreneurs learn about the production process and about their entrepreneurial ability. In the second period, the entrepreneur may either succeed and produce a good output level y_G ($y_G > y_B$) or fail and remain at the bad output level y_B. The probability of success, π, varies across entrepreneurs and is only learned by the entrepreneur at the end of the first period. At the beginning of the first period when entry decisions must be made, the entrepreneur knows only the distribution functions $F(\pi)$ for the population of entrepreneurs as a whole. Non-entrepreneurs may organize firms, but their first and second period output level is y_B with certainty. This specification of infant sector technology is similar to that used by Bernanke and Gertler (1990) to study the effect of financial contracts on the exit decisions of firms.

Let L denote the aggregate endowment of labor and H the measure of households. μ is the fraction of households that are type e. Letting N_1 be the number (measure) of infant sector firms organized in period 1, the outputs in period 1 will be $X_1 = (L - N_1)/a_{LX}$ and $Y_1 = N_1 y_B$. The transformation schedule for period 1 is linear as illustrated in Figure 12.1a, due to the fact that all infant sector firms are identical in period 1. It will be assumed that the world price of good y, q^*, is constant across periods and is such that bad project outcomes result in a loss of amount $B^* \equiv w - q^* y_B > 0$. This assumption ensures that it will never be advantageous for non-entrepreneurial households to undertake infant sector projects, so that $N_1 \leq \mu H$ in any efficient production equilibrium. The home country thus has a static comparative advantage in production of good x in period 1.

At the beginning of the second period, entrepreneurs who entered in period 1 must decide whether to continue to produce y based on their observation of π. Let m denote the marginal entrepreneur, which is the lowest value of π for entrepreneurs to stay in the industry. Second period outputs will be given by $Y_2 = (1 - F(m))N_1 E(y \mid \pi \geq m)$ and $X_2 = (L - (1 - F(m))N_1)/a_{LX}$, where $E(y \mid \pi \geq m)$ is expected output of an active firm in period 2, conditional on m being the marginal entrepreneur. The second period transformation schedule is illustrated in Figure 12.1b. The second period production structure has a specific factor element (Jones 1971) since expected returns vary across entrepreneurs depending on what they learned in the first period. Given N_1, second period output is varied by altering m. Differentiating the output expressions with respect to m yields $(dX_2/dY_2) = -1/a_{LX}(my_G + (1 - m)y_B)$. The transformation schedule is concave to the origin because reducing output of y results in exit of firms with lower probability of success.

Second period national income is maximized by having entrepreneurs remain in sector y if expected profits $\pi G^* + (1 - \pi)B^*$ are non-negative, where $G^* = q^* y_G - w$ is the profit if the project is a success. The marginal entrepreneur will be the one for which expected profits are zero, which yields

$$m^* = B^*/(B^* + G^*) \tag{1}$$

If the home country can borrow on world capital markets at rate r^*, the national wealth is maximized by the choice of N^1 that maximizes $(X_1 + q^* Y_1) + (X_2 + q^* Y_2)/(1 + r^*)$.[5] Since output in each period is linear in N_1, the home country will maximize national income by having all entrepreneurs enter in period 1 if the expected profits from entry are non-negative.

$$V_1(m^*) = -B^* + (1 - F(m^*))(p(m^*)G^*$$
$$- (1 - p(m^*)B^*)/(1 + r^*) \geq 0 \tag{2}$$

where $p(m^*) = E(\pi \mid \pi \geq m^*)$ is the average probability of success. It will be assumed in what follows that (2) is satisfied with strict inequality, which guarantees a form of dynamic comparative advantage in good y. Although the home country will not necessarily export good y in period 2, it is still

[5] The assumption that the country can borrow and lend on world capital markets at an exogenously given rate is not crucial to the analysis. Similar results would be obtained if the projects of entrepreneurs were financed by loans from non-entrepreneurs, with the interest rate determined endogenously to clear the domestic loan market.

desirable to have all entrepreneurs enter in period 1 if this condition is satisfied.

B. Household preferences and credit markets with perfect information

We now show that in the presence of perfect capital markets, the national income-maximizing entry and exit conditions characterized above will be achieved by competitive capital markets. Perfect capital markets are defined here to be the case where both the type of the household (e or n) and the value of π (at the end of the first period) can be observed by the lenders.

Entrepreneurs will enter the y sector if the utility of the consumption bundle obtained with entry exceeds that available by employing their labor endowment in the x sector. The expected wealth of a type e household that enters the y sector at the beginning of period 1 is $\Omega^e(l,m) = wl(2 + r^*)/(1 + r^*) + V_1(m)$. Although entry by sector y firms is assumed to be profitable in an expected value sense, firms with $wl < B^*$ will be unable to cover first period losses without some form of external financing. Capital markets have the potential to allow entrepreneurs to fund projects and also finance current consumption out of expected future profits. In order to simplify the analysis and focus on the issues related to the intertemporal smoothing of consumption, it will be assumed that households are risk neutral. Preferences of all households will be given by the risk neutral constant elasticity of substitution (RINCE) preferences introduced by Farmer (1990). For the two-period model analyzed here, these preferences take the form

$$U(c_1, Ec_2) = [c_1{}^\rho + \beta(Ec_2)^\rho]^{1/\rho} \tag{3}$$

where $c_i = h(d_{xi}, d_{yi})$ is a composite of consumption in period i, with d_{ji} the consumption of good j in period i and h being homogeneous of degree one in consumption levels of the two goods. Ec_2 is the expected value of period 2 consumption, β is the rate of time preference, and $1/(1 - \rho)$ is the elasticity of substitution. It will be assumed that β equals the market discount rate $1/(1 + r^*)$. This simplifies the presentation by ensuring that consumption will be fully smoothed when the consumer prices are constant across periods.

In the case of perfect information, lenders can write contracts contingent on the type of the household. For type n households, the wealth constraint will be $\phi_1 c_1 + \beta \phi_2 c_2 = wl(1 + \beta)$, where $\phi_i(q_x, q_y)$ is the minimum cost of a unit of the composite commodity in period i when the consumer price of good j is q_j.[6] Units of the composite commodity will be chosen such that $\phi(1, q_y{}^*) = 1$, which applies when there are no consumption taxes or tariffs. Type n households would then consume wl in each period.

For type e households, a contract will consist of a vector of terms $(\alpha_1\, \alpha_G\, \alpha_B\, \alpha_E\, m)$, where a_1 is the payment from the lender to the entrepreneur in period 1 and m is the minimal value of π for which the project will be continued in the second period. α_E is the payment made by the entrepreneur if the project is not continued, and $\alpha_G (\alpha_B)$ is the payment made by the entrepreneur in the event of a good (bad) outcome when the project is continued. In order for the contract to be feasible, consumption of the borrower must be non-negative in all states, which requires

$$c_1 = wl - B - \alpha_1 \geq 0 \quad c_B = wl - B - \alpha_B \geq 0$$
$$c_E = wl - \alpha_E \geq 0 \qquad c_G = wl + G - \alpha_G \geq 0 \tag{4}$$

Assuming that lenders are large enough that their profits are given by the expected return from the population as a whole, lender profits will be

$$\gamma = \beta[(p(m)\alpha_G + (1 - p(m))\alpha_B)(1 - F(m)) + F(m)\alpha_E] - \alpha_1$$
$$= \Omega^e(l,m) - \beta[(p(m)c_G + (1 - p(m))c_B)(1 - F(m)) + F(m)c_E]$$
$$- c_1 \geq 0 \tag{5}$$

where the second equality in (5) follows from substitution of (4).

A feasible contract will be a *competitive equilibrium* if it yields non-negative profits and there exists no other contract that is preferred by borrowers and earns non-negative profits. Formally, this contract can be obtained as the contract that maximizes expected utility of entrepreneurs (3), subject to the constraints (4) and (5). The solution to this optimization problem yields the following result:

Proposition 1: With no private information in credit markets and competition among lenders, then

(a) All entrepreneurs will enter in the first period and have consumption $c_1{}^* = Ec_2{}^* = \Omega^e(l,m^*)/(1 + \beta)$ in each period.

(b) Only those entrepreneurs with values of $\pi \geq m^*$ will be funded in the second period.

To prove proposition 1, it is convenient to substitute for the contract terms using (5) and to view lenders as offering a contract (C, m), where

---

[6] Since h is homogeneous of degree one in consumption, the expenditure function for c_i will be $\phi(q_{xi}, q_{yi})c_i$. The separability of (3) allows the two stage budgeting procedure of choosing x and y within a period to minimize expenditure for given c_i, and then allocating expenditure between periods to maximize utility.

$C = (c_1, c_G, c_B, c_E)$ is a vector of consumption levels. The profit condition for this case can be expressed as $\gamma = \Omega^e(l, m) - \beta E c_2(m) - c_1$, since borrowers are indifferent over all combinations (c_G, c_B, c_E) yielding a given $E c_2$ and satisfying the non-negativity constraint on consumption. The constrained optimization problem can then be expressed as maximizing $U(c_1, E c_2(m))$ subject to $\gamma \geq 0$. The value of m is chosen to maximize the expected consumption of entrepreneurs, which is equivalent to maximizing $V(m)$. This yields the socially optimal value m^* from (3). The value of c_1 is chosen to allocate consumption optimally between periods, which yields (4). Profits of lenders will equal zero in the optimal policy.[7]

Proposition 1 establishes that competitive financial markets will achieve the allocation of resources that maximizes national wealth when there is no private information. Since the economies of learning are internal to the firm in this model, this result is not surprising in light of earlier discussions by Baldwin (1969) and Corden (1974). However, Proposition 1 serves as a useful benchmark for comparison with cases in which there is private information.

2. Optimal contracts with private information

We now examine the case in which the household's type and the value of π are private information. Since lenders cannot observe π or type, loan contracts can only specify the amount of the loan to be made in the first period α_1 and the payments to be made by the borrower in the second period states α_i ($i = B, G, E$). These contract terms must be designed in such a way that type n households are discouraged from entering the industry, and type e households that discover they have a low π value after the first period will exit the industry. It will be shown in this section that the existence of private information yields two types of inefficiencies in the competitive equilibrium. First, type e households with sufficiently low wealth levels will be unable to obtain financing. Second, households with higher wealth levels may enter the industry, but may be credit rationed and have insufficient incentive to exit the industry. These inefficiencies result from the agency costs associated with external finance.

The incentive constraint introduced by the fact that household type is unobservable is that type n households cannot earn higher utility from

---

[7] Note that due to the assumption of risk neutrality of households, the terms (c_G, c_B, c_E) of the optimal contract can take any values such that (5) is satisfied with $\gamma = 0$ and the non-negativity constraints on consumption are satisfied. If entrepreneurs were risk averse, then the optimal contract would be the one that equalized consumption across states. Thus, the results of Proposition 1 can be extended to the case in which entrepreneurs are risk averse.

starting a project in period 1 and exiting in period 2 than by supplying their resources in non-entrepreneurial activities in period 1.

$$U(wl, wl) \geq U(c_1, c_E) \tag{6}$$

The second constraint is that when π is private information, firms will exit the industry only if the return from exiting and supplying resources in a non-entrepreneurial activity, c_E, exceeds the expected return from staying in, $\pi c_G + (1 - \pi)c_B$. The marginal entrepreneur will be the one that is indifferent between staying and leaving in period 2, which yields

$$m = \frac{c_E - c_B}{c_G - c_B} = \frac{B^* + \alpha_B - \alpha_E}{B^* + G^* + \alpha_B - \alpha_G} \quad \text{with} \quad c_G - c_B > 0 \tag{7}$$

The second condition is required for firms with $\pi > m$ to stay in the industry.

A comparison of (7) with the conditions of Proposition 1 indicates that the first best optimum could be attained with a contract which specified $\alpha_G = \alpha_B = \alpha_E = [B^* + V_1(m^*)(1 + r^*)/(2 + r^*)](1 + r^*)$. Since the contract specifies the same payment by the entrepreneur in all states, this contract does not distort the entrepreneur's decision on whether to continue the project. Furthermore, it can be verified that a type n household would not choose to initiate projects with this contract, since it yields the same present value of consumption as (wl, wl) but a less desirable intertemporal allocation. However, this efficient contract is feasible only if the wealth of entrepreneurs is sufficiently large that income in the bad state $(wl - B^*)$ exceeds the required payment.

The effect of private information about π on choice of contract terms can be seen by referring to Figure 12.2. The set of (c_G, c_B, c_E) that yield Ec_2^* from Proposition 1 and having non-negative consumption in each state form a plane segment in R^3. The triangle in Figure 12.2 is a two-dimensional representation of this plane segment, where each edge of the triangle corresponds to a range of values for which consumption in one state equals 0. Note that the triangle in Figure 12.2 will be larger the greater the labor endowment of the household, and that it will be non-empty for all $l > 0$ since $V_1(m^*) \geq 0$. In order for a first best contract to be attainable when π is private information, the terms must also satisfy (8) for $m = m^*$. The line FG in Figure 12.2 is the intersection of the locus of values of the c_i satisfying (7) for $m = m^*$ with the contract terms consistent with the first best contract. Note that from (7), we are only concerned with the portion of the line where $c_B \leq c_G$, which is the segment HG. The fact that point G must lie on the $c_B = 0$ facet of the triangle can be established by a continuity

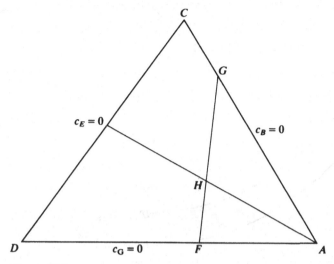

Figure 12.2

argument: at node A $(c_E > c_G = c_B = 0)$ we have $m = \infty$, and at node C $(c_G > c_E = c_B = 0)$ we have $m = 0$.

For a given level of l, the first best contract is attainable only if there is some contract on HG which satisfies the selection constraint (6). This is illustrated in Figure 12.3, which shows the indifference curve for a type n household with endowment l_1. If a type n household mimics a type e and takes a loan, its first period consumption level is $c_1{}^e = wl - B^* - \alpha_1{}^*$. In order to prevent a type n households from imitating type e, the lender can give an entrepreneur who exits a consumption level no higher than $c_E(l_1)$ illustrated in Figure 12.3. This contract will be feasible if the lowest value of c_E consistent with $m = m^*$ (point G in Figure 12.2) is no larger than $c_E(l_1)$. It is shown in the Appendix that as the endowment level falls, the minimum value of c_E that is consistent with providing the correct second period exit incentives $(m = m^*)$ to entrepreneurs falls less rapidly than does the maximum level of c_E required to keep out non-entrepreneurs. This yields the following result:

Proposition 2: There exists an endowment level l^1 such that first best contracts are attainable with private information if $l \geq l^1$.

The first best contracts fail at low endowment levels because the endowment of entrepreneurs serves as collateral for lenders. When collateral levels are low, lenders are constrained in how they can use contract terms to provide incentives to borrowers. We now consider the possibility of second best contracts which allow entry of entrepreneurs, but lead to a lower level

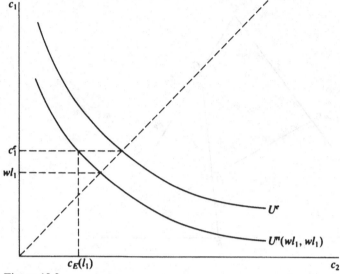

Figure 12.3

of entrepreneurial welfare and inefficient exit decisions in the second period. The basic trade-off in the second best contract involves the choice of α_E. In order to keep type n households from entering in period 1, lenders want to impose penalties as large as possible on firms that exit after one period (high α_E). However, high values of α_E make it more likely that entrepreneurs who observe a low π will stay in the industry. Second best lending contracts must be designed to yield an optimal trade-off between these two elements.

A second-best financial contract will be to choose contract terms

$$\max_{c} U[c_1, (p(m)c_G + (1 - p(m))c_B)(1 - F(m)) - F(m)c_E] \qquad (8)$$

subject to (4), (5), (6), and (7).

In examining this problem, it will be assumed that there are a sufficiently large number of low π values that the present value of having a type e household stay in is negative, $V_1(0) = -B^* + \beta[p(0)G^* - (1 - p(0))B^*] < 0$. This ensures that the second best contract will never have $m = 0$.

The following proposition, which is proven in the Appendix, characterizes the second best contracts for those households with insufficient wealth to obtain the first best contracts.

Proposition 3: The second best contract will have an exit level of entrepreneurs that is less than the socially optimal level and will take all income from entrepreneurs who fail in the second period. The marginal rate of substitution between period 1 and period 2 consumption for entrepreneurs may be either greater or less than the market discount rate.

As noted in the derivation of (8), efficient exit decisions occur if payments are equalized across states. When collateral levels are low the lender is unable to collect from entrepreneurs in the low income (B and E) states. The second best contract takes as much as possible from entrepreneurs in the B state, but takes less than the full amount in the E state to encourage exit from those entrepreneurs with low values of π. The desire to keep out non-entrepreneurs prevents the E payment from being set low enough to achieve efficient exit. In the presence of private information about probability of success, entrepreneurs with low collateral continue low probability projects that are not socially desirable because the losses in the B state are partially borne by lenders.

Finally, note that if agency costs are large enough, there will be no lending at all to households with wealth levels that are sufficiently low. For example, suppose that non-entrepreneurs that enter do not invest all of their loan in the firm, since they know that there is no chance of success in the second period. The consumption of an n type that takes a loan will be $U(c_1^e + z, c_E^e)$, where z is the amount of consumption that is taken out of the project. It is easily shown that if $0 < \rho \leq 1$, there are values of l sufficiently low that it will be impossible to prevent type n from taking contracts intended for type e. This results in too low a level of entry into the industry due to the agency costs resulting from the informational asymmetry.

The characterization of the second best contracts for this case can be compared with those obtained by Bernanke and Gertler (1990), who consider a model in which there is no consumption smoothing role for lenders. This is equivalent to fixing $\alpha_1 = \dot{}$ in the current model. They obtain the result that consumption will be zero in the bad state and that the value of m will be less than the socially optimal level, as in Proposition 3. The difference in the current case is that the ability to vary the size of the first period loan, α_1, gives the lender an additional tool for separating types in this case. This tool will be more powerful in cases where the elasticity of intertemporal substitution is relatively low.

3. Pareto optimal allocations

Section 2 showed that in cases where there is private information about household type and π, there will be a capital market imperfection for entrepreneurs with low wealth levels. In this section, we examine whether government tools such as loan subsidies, consumption or production taxes, and tariffs can be used by the government to effect Pareto improvements. In formulating this problem, it will be assumed that the government faces the same informational constraints as the private sector. Thus, welfare improvements must arise from the government's access to tools that are not available to the private sector lender, rather than from superior information.

We first examine whether the contracts are Pareto optimal, subject to the informational constraints. We derive a condition under which the competitive contracting problem will not yield a Pareto optimum, and show that in this case a Pareto improvement can be obtained by a tax on loan contracts in the infant sector. We then examine whether indirect instruments (consumption taxes, production subsidies, and tariffs) can be used to obtain Pareto improvements. The case for these instruments results from their ability to relax the self-selection constraints in the private sector contracting problem. In order to simplify the analysis, it will be assumed that all individuals have the same endowment level.

A Pareto optimal allocation consists of a contract $C^n = (c_1{}^n, c_2{}^n)$ for non-entrepreneurs and $C^e = (c_1{}^e, c_G{}^e, c_B{}^e, c_E{}^e)$ for entrepreneurs that maximizes the utility of entrepreneurs, subject to the requirement that utility of non-entrepreneurs be at least equal to a specified level U. In addition, the allocations must satisfy the non-negativity constraints on consumption (5), the self-selection constraint (6), the requirement that m be chosen according to (7), and an aggregate resource constraint. The first three of these constraints are identical to those for the case of competitive financial contracts. The aggregate resource constraint requires that the present value of aggregate consumption be no greater than the present value of aggregate income, where μ is the fraction of the population that is type e. This constraint is written as

$$\mu V_1(m) + wl(1 + \beta) - \beta\{\mu[(p(m)c_G{}^e + (1 - p(m))c_B{}^e)(1 - F(m))$$
$$+ F(m)c_E{}^e] + (1 - \mu)c_2{}^n\} - \mu c_1{}^e - (1 - \mu)c_1{}^n \geq 0 \quad (9)$$

In order to determine whether the competitive equilibrium is a Pareto optimum, we consider the social planner's problem for the case in which $U = U(wl, wl)$. The maximization problem for this case is

$$\max_{C^e, C^n} U[c_1{}^e, (p(m)c_G{}^e + (1 - p(m))c_B{}^e)(1 - F(m)) + F(m)c_E{}^e] \quad (10)$$

subject to: (4), (9), (6), (7), and $U(c_1{}^n, c_2{}^n) > U(wl, wl)$.

The only difference between the Pareto optimal problem and the competitive equilibrium problem (8) is that the resource constraint (9) for the former does not require the contracts offered to entrepreneurs to yield zero profits. Profits (losses) from contracts offered to entrepreneurs can be offset by losses (profits) on contracts offered to non-entrepreneurs. Defining λ_R to be the Lagrange multiplier for the resource constraint (9) and letting λ_i $(i = 1, B)$ be the multipliers associated with the non-negativity constraints on consumption as above, the first order conditions for optimal choice of the contract for entrepreneurs will be given by those obtained for the competitive case (A.4) with λ_y replaced by $\mu\lambda_R$. The first order conditions for optimal choice of contract terms for non-entrepreneurs will be

$$\frac{\partial L}{\partial c_1^{\,n}} = \frac{\partial U^n}{\partial c_1^{\,n}}(\lambda_n + \lambda_S) - (1 - \mu)\lambda_R = 0 \tag{11a}$$

$$\frac{\partial L}{\partial c_2^{\,n}} = \frac{\partial U^n}{\partial c_2^{\,n}}(\lambda_n + \lambda_S) - (1 - \mu)\beta\lambda_R = 0 \tag{11b}$$

where λ_n is the multiplier associated with the constraint $U(c_1^{\,n}, c_2^{\,n}) - U \geq 0$.

These conditions require that the marginal rate of substitution for type n equal the discount rate, which involves equal consumption in each period. The competitive equilibrium, in which type n consume wl in each period, will be a constrained Pareto optimum if it satisfies these first order conditions with $\lambda_n, \lambda_R > 0$. Using (A.4c) to solve for λ_R, (11a) can be rewritten as[8]

$$\lambda_n = \frac{(1 - \mu)}{\mu} \frac{p(1 - F)\partial U^e/\partial Ec_2}{[(\partial V/\partial m)\,(m/(c_G - c_B) + p(1 - F))\beta]\,(\partial U^n/c_2)} - \lambda_S \tag{12}$$

The first term in (12) is positive and $\lambda_S > 0$ in a second-best competitive contract. Since $\mu \in (0,1)$, there will be μ sufficiently small that the $\lambda_n > 0$ and the competitive equilibrium will be a constrained Pareto optimum. Similarly, for μ sufficiently large, the competitive contract will fail to be a constrained Pareto optimum. If μ is large enough that the competitive equilibrium fails to be a Pareto optimum, then Pareto improvements can be obtained by transfers between types. Note that this will require transfers from entrepreneurs to non-entrepreneurs, since transfers to non-entrepreneurs will relax the self-selection constraint by making it less attractive for non-entrepreneurs to mimic entrepreneurs. These results can be summarized as:

---

[8] This condition is analogous to that derived by Rothschild and Stiglitz (1976) for the existence of equilibrium in a competitive insurance market with adverse selection. Note that if lenders can offer more than one type of loan contact, a competitive equilibrium will not exist if (12) is not satisfied with $\lambda_n > 0$. An incentive would exist for lenders to offer contracts which involved subsidies between types. However, these contracts would not survive in a competitive market because other lenders would offer more attractive contracts to the profitable type.

Proposition 4: If μ is sufficiently small that (12) yields $\lambda_n > 0$ at the competitive equilibrium, the competitive equilibrium contract is a constrained Pareto optimum and subsidies or taxes to loan contracts will not yield Pareto improvements. If (12) yields $\lambda_n < 0$, then a Pareto improvement can be made by a tax on loan contracts to the infant sector with proceeds being redistributed to all households.

When μ is small, there are a relatively small number of entrepreneurs and transfers to non-entrepreneurs are a relatively expensive way of discouraging entry by non-entrepreneurs because the tax per entrepreneur is high. However, when μ is large transfers are relatively cheap and the government can relax the self-selection constraint by subsidizing non-entrepreneurs.

It might at first seem surprising that the optimal policy involves a tax on infant sector contracts, rather than a subsidy as is usually argued. The market inefficiency here results from the fact that it is too attractive for type n to imitate type e, so that contract terms must be distorted from the first best to discourage entry by type n. A tax on financial contracts which is used to finance a subsidy to all households will have the desired effect of discouraging entry by type n households and relaxing the selection constraint faced by private sector lenders.

We now consider the potential for production subsidies and consumption taxes to be welfare-improving. Taxes and subsidies could potentially yield Pareto improvements if they introduced new instruments beyond those available to lenders. However, it is readily shown that the competitive equilibrium cannot be improved on by the use of production subsidies because the reallocations provided by subsidies are already being provided by financial markets. Let s_i be the production subsidy per unit of infant sector output in period i. The resource constraint requires that

$$\mu V_1(m) + wl(1 + \beta) - \beta \{[p(m)(c_G{}^e + s_2 y_G)$$
$$+ (1 - p(m))(c_B{}^e + s_2 y_B)(1 - F(m))$$
$$+ F(m)c_E{}^e] + (1 - \mu)c_2{}^n\} - \mu(c_1{}^e + s_1 y_B)$$
$$- (1 - \mu)c_1{}^n \geq 0. \tag{13}$$

The consumption level of entrepreneurs in period 1 becomes $c_1{}^e + s_1 y_B$ and that in state i in period 2 is $c_i{}^e + s_2 y_i$ $(i = G, B)$. It is readily seen that the possibility of a period 1 production subsidy introduces no new tools for the planner, since the partial derivative of the Lagrangean with respect to s_1 will be proportional to that with respect to c_1. At the optimal choice of c_1, a production subsidy cannot improve welfare. A similar argument establishes that period 2 production subsidies cannot be welfare improving.

If tastes are identical across households, then a similar argument can be made regarding the effects of consumption taxes. An argument for consumption taxes is obtained if there are differences in tastes between types. Suppose that a price index for the composite good differs across households, with that for household j given by ϕ^j. A given loan by the lender will then be spent in different ways by the borrowers. It can be shown that starting from the constrained Pareto optimum that solves (10), a small change in the price of consumption good y in period 1 will be welfare improving if the tastes of the two household types differ. The intuition underlying this result is that by taxing the consumption good that type n households have a taste for in the first period, the government can make period 1 consumption less attractive for type n's and make it less attractive for them to mimic type e's by taking the loan. This relaxation of the incentive compatibility constraint allows a Pareto improvement. Similarly, differences in the use of inputs across firms in the first period could also be utilized to help separate types.

This form of intervention is quite different from that usually discussed in the literature on policy intervention, where the argument is that direct interventions in the distorted (capital) market are preferred to indirect interventions (production subsidies or consumption taxes), because direct interventions directly target the distortion. In the present model, the indirect distortion works because there are hidden actions of the borrowers that could be used to differentiate consumers but cannot be controlled by the lenders.[9] These actions can be affected by the government, however, through its ability to tax aggregate consumption or production of the good. The ability to achieve welfare improvements results not from an informational advantage of the government, but from an ability to alter actions that lenders cannot use.

4. Conclusions

This paper has developed a two-period model of an infant industry in which there is learning that is internal to the firm, and has examined the allocations obtained by competitive capital markets when there is private information about entrepreneurial ability. The assumptions made here regarding private information have been intended to capture basic types of informational asymmetries that are likely to arise when in cases where firms in a country are entering a new industry. It has been shown how these informational asymmetries can give rise to capital market imperfections, in

---

[9] Greenwald and Stiglitz (1986) discuss the use of taxation to shift incentive constraints. Note that if lenders can bundle loan contracts with the consumption of goods, then competitive lenders can take advantage of differences in tastes to relax incentive constraints. Taxation would then be unnecessary. However, this requires the lender to be able to monitor individual consumption of goods, See Bond and Crocker (1991) for an analysis of this issue in the context of insurance markets.

208   Eric W. Bond

the sense that borrowers may not be able to borrow the amount they want at the market interest rate or borrowers may be denied access to credit entirely. In the present model, these imperfections arise in cases where the wealth of entrepreneurs is too low to allow sufficient collateral to attain first best loan contracts. It has been shown that if the share of entrepreneurs in the population is not too large, then these contracts will be a constrained Pareto optimum and a government that faces the same informational constraints as the private sector cannot raise welfare through the use of subsidies to loans in the infant sector.

Although the results of this paper indicate some role for government intervention with imperfect capital markets under certain conditions, the interventions are more subtle than in the case where the capital market distortion is an exogenously given wedge. The interventions here require substantial information on the part of the government regarding the tastes of households, the input usage of firms, and the composition of the population. This suggests that in using the capital market imperfections argument for protection, the source of the market imperfection should be carefully specified and its implications for government intervention explicitly derived.

Appendix

Proof of Proposition 2: To establish this proposition, it will be shown that there exists an endowment l^1 such that for $l < l^1$ the set of (c_G, c_B, c_E) satisfying the non-negativity constraints on consumption (5), the competitive profit condition (6), and the incentive constraints (7)–(8) for the first best contract is empty.

First, consider the restriction on c_E imposed by the self-selection constraint (7). Using RINCE preferences, (7) can be written as

$$(wl)^\rho(1 + \beta) \geq c_1^\rho + \beta c_E^\rho = (wl + V_1(m^*)/(1 + \beta))^\rho + \beta c_E^\rho$$

(A.1)

where the second equality follows by substituting for optimal first period consumption from (4). The SS locus in Figure 12A.1 is the values of c_E and l at which the self-selection constraint (A.1) holds with equality. Differentiating (A.1) yields

$$\frac{dc_E}{c_E} = \left(1 + \frac{V_1}{\beta(1 + \beta)c_E}\left[\frac{c_1}{c_E}\right]^{\rho-1}\right)\left(\frac{dl}{l}\right).$$

(A.2)

The coefficient on dl/l in (A.2) must be greater than 1, which means that the slope of the locus SS in Figure 12A.1 must be steeper than a ray from the origin. Note also that for $\rho < 0$, the maximum value of c_E consistent with (A.1) approaches 0 as $l \to 0$. For $\rho > 0$, there will be a positive value of l at

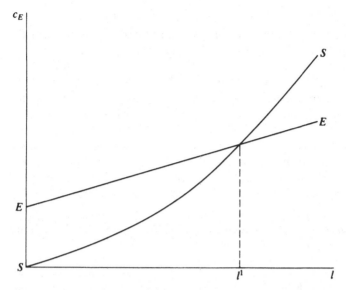

Figure 12A.1

which $c_E = 0$.

We now examine whether the values of c_E required to satisfy self-selection are consistent with zero profits for lenders and efficient exit. Since (A.1) depends only on the payment in the exit state, the first best will be attainable if (A.1) is satisfied for the point on the segment HG in Figure 12.2 with the smallest value of c_E. We now show that point G, which corresponds to $c_B = 0$, yields the smallest value of c_E. For given c_1, total differentiation of the competitive profit condition for lenders (5) yields $(1 - F)[pdc_G + (1 - p)dc_B] + Fdc_E = 0$. Total differentiation of (7) yields $m*dc_G + (1 - m*)dc_B - dc_E = 0$. Solving these two equations for dc_G yields the relationship between c_E and c_B along the locus HG, which is $(p(1 - F) + m*F)dc_E = (1 - F)(p - m)dc_B$. Increases in c_B raise c_E, since the average probability of a success, p, exceeds that of the marginal firm, m. Therefore, the lender should set c_B as small as possible to discourage entry of type n households.

The value of c_E associated with point G is obtained by solving (5) and (7) simultaneously for c_E, using $c_B = 0$. This yields

$$c_E = \frac{m}{\beta[p(1 - F) + mF]} l[V_1(m) + wl(1 + \beta) - c_1]. \tag{A.3}$$

Evaluating (A.3) at $m = m*$ and $c_1 = c_1* = wl + V_1\beta/(1 + \beta)$ in (A.3) yields $c_E = m*[wl + V(m*)(1 + \beta)]/[p(1 - F) + m*F]$. This expression is illustrated by the EE line in Figure 12A.1, which must have a positive vertical intercept and a slope less than 1 $(m^* < p(1 - F) + m^*F)$.

The first best financial contract will be attained for all l for which the EE line (the minimum c_E consistent with efficient exit) lies above the SS locus (the maximum c_E consistent with self-selection). The above discussion established that the SS schedule intersects the horizontal axis at some $k > 0$ if $1 \geq \rho > 0$, so there are no feasible values of c_E satisfying (A.1) for $l \leq k$. If $\rho < 0$, the value of c_E on the SS locus approaches 0 as $l \to 0$. Since the EE locus must have a positive vertical intercept, there must exist a positive l such that the SS lies below the EE and first best contracts cannot be attained. Furthermore, the SS locus is steeper than a ray from the origin and the EE locus is a line with a slope less than one, so these schedules can have only one intersection. This intersection is the desired l^1 of proposition 2.

Proof of Proposition 3: The following lemma allows a simplification of the analysis of the second best contracts.

> *Lemma*: If $V_1(0) < 0$, neither $c_G = 0$, or $c_E = 0$ can hold in a second-best contract which leaves type e households better off than they are by not entering in period 1.

Proof: If $c_E = 0$ and either $c_G > 0$ or $c_B > 0$, then returns from staying in exceed those from exiting for all π and $m = 0$. However, this cannot be optimal since $V_1(0) < 0$. If $c_G = 0$ and $c_E > c_B \geq 0$, then all firms will exit in the second period and $V_1(1) = -B^* < 0$. Entering has negative present value and is dominated by no entry of entrepreneurs. If $c_G = 0$ and $c_B > c_E \geq 0$, then only firms with the lowest value of π would stay in. This yields a lower present value than $V_1(0)$ and cannot be a second-best optimum. The only remaining case is $c_G = c_B = c_E = 0$. Under such a contract, the utility level of type e would equal that of type n who imitated type e, since both would have consumption bundles $(wl - B^* + \alpha_1, 0)$. By (6), this cannot leave entrepreneurs better off than if they did not enter.

Given the result of the Lemma, the Lagrangean problem for the second-best contracts can be set up as:

$$\max_{(C)} U[c_1, (p(m)c_G + (1 - p(m))c_B)(1 - F(m)) + F(m)c_E]$$

subject to:

$$c_B \geq 0 \qquad\qquad\qquad\qquad\qquad\qquad\qquad\qquad \lambda_B \geq 0$$

$$c_1 \geq 0 \qquad\qquad\qquad\qquad\qquad\qquad\qquad\qquad \lambda_1 \geq 0$$

$$\Omega^e(l, m) - \beta[(p(m)c_G + (1 - p(m))c_B)(1 - F(m))$$
$$+ F(m)c_E] - c_1 \geq 0 \qquad\qquad\qquad\qquad \lambda_\gamma \geq 0$$

$$U(wl, wl) - U(c_1, c_E) \geq 0 \qquad\qquad \lambda_S \geq 0$$

where U takes the RINCE form, and m is given by (7). The λ_i denote the multipliers associated with the respective constraints. The first order conditions for a maximum require:

$$\frac{\partial L}{\partial c_1} = \frac{\partial U^e}{\partial c_1} + \lambda_1 - \lambda_\gamma - \lambda_S \frac{\partial U^n}{\partial c_1} = 0 \qquad\qquad \text{(A.4a)}$$

$$\frac{\partial L}{\partial c_G} = \frac{\partial U^e}{\partial Ec_2} p(1 - F) - \lambda_\gamma \left(\beta p(1 - F) - \frac{\partial V}{\partial m} \frac{\partial m}{\partial c_G} \right) = 0 \qquad \text{(A.4b)}$$

$$\frac{\partial L}{\partial c_B} = \frac{\partial U^e}{\partial Ec_2}(1 - p)(1 - F) - \lambda_\gamma \left(\beta(1 - p)(1 - F) - \frac{\partial V}{\partial m} \frac{\partial m}{\partial c_B} \right)$$

$$+ \lambda_B = 0 \qquad\qquad \text{(A.4c)}$$

$$\frac{\partial L}{\partial c_E} = \frac{\partial U^e}{\partial Ec_2} F - \lambda_\gamma \left(\beta F - \frac{\partial V}{\partial m} \frac{\partial m}{\partial c_G} \right) - \lambda_S \frac{\partial U^n}{\partial c_2} = 0 \qquad \text{(A.4d)}$$

where U^e denotes the utility level of a type e household with the contract and $U^n = U(c_1, c_E)$ is the utility of a type n household if it imitates a type e.

The characteristics of second best contracts in proposition 3 are established from the first order conditions (A.4). We first establish that $m < m^*$ in the second best contract. From (7), $\partial m/\partial c_E = 1/D$, and $\partial m/\partial c_G = -m/D$, where $D \equiv c_G - c_B > 0$. Substituting these results in (A.4b) and (A.4d) and combining yields

$$\frac{\lambda_S}{F} \frac{\partial U^n}{\partial Ec_2} = \frac{\lambda_\gamma}{D} \frac{\partial V}{\partial m} \left(\frac{m}{p(1 - F)} + \frac{1}{F} \right). \qquad\qquad \text{(A.5)}$$

In a second best contract, the self-selection constraint for type n households will be binding ($\lambda_S > 0$), which requires that the right-hand side of (A.5) be positive. Therefore, it must be the case that $\partial V/\partial m > 0$ at an optimum. Differentiating (2) yields

$$\frac{\partial V}{\partial m} = -(mG^* - (1 - m)B^*)f(m). \qquad\qquad \text{(A.6)}$$

We then have $\partial V/\partial m \gtreqless 0$ as $m \lesseqgtr B^*/(B^* + G^*)$. In order for (A.5) to be satisfied, we must have m less than the socially optimal level.

The fact that $c_B \geq 0$ must bind at an optimum is obtained by combining (A.4b) and (A.4c), and making use of $\partial m/\partial c_G = -m/D = m(\partial m/\partial c_B)/(1 - m)$, to get

$$\lambda_B = \frac{\lambda_\gamma}{pD} \frac{\partial V}{\partial m}(p - m). \qquad\qquad \text{(A.7)}$$

212   **Eric W. Bond**

Since $m < p(m)$ and $\partial V/\partial m > 0$, the expression on the right-hand side of (A.7) is positive, so $\lambda_B > 0$ at a second best optimum.

The intertemporal allocation in the second best contract is obtained from (A.4a) and (A.4b) to be

$$\frac{\partial U^e/\partial Ec_2}{\partial U^e/\partial c_1} = \frac{\lambda_\gamma[1 + (\partial V/\partial m)(m/(Dp(1 - F)))]}{\lambda_\gamma(1 + r^*) + \lambda_S(\partial U^n/\partial c_1) - \lambda_1}. \tag{A.8}$$

The first best contract involves complete consumption smoothing, which means that the right-hand side of (A.8) equals β. Since $\partial V/\partial m > 0$, the second term in the numerator is positive, which tends to make the right-hand side exceed β ($c_1 > Ec_2$). The second term in the denominator tends to make the right-hand side less than β. Thus, the second best contract may involve either $c_1 \geq Ec_2$ or $c_1 \leq Ec_2$, depending on the importance of the selection constraint and the distortion in the exit decision. If $\lambda_1 > 0$, then $c_1 = 0$ and the second period consumption must be larger.

References

Baldwin, Robert 1969 "The Case Against Infant Industry Protection," *Journal of Political Economy*, 77, 295–305.

Bernanke, Ben and Mark Gertler 1990 "Financial Fragility and Economic Performance," *Quarterly Journal of Economics*, 87–114.

Bond, Eric W. and Keith Crocker 1991 "Smoking, Skydiving, and Knitting: The Endogenous Categorization of Risks in Markets with Asymmetric Information," *Journal of Political Economy*, 99, 177–200.

Corden, W. M. 1974 *Trade Policy and Economic Welfare*, Oxford University Press, Oxford.

Dixit, Avinash K. 1989 "Trade and Insurance with Adverse Selection," *Review of Economic Studies*, 56 (3), 235–41.

Farmer, Roger 1990 "RINCE Preferences," *Quarterly Journal of Economics*, 43–60.

Flam, Harry and Robert Staiger 1991 "Adverse Selection in Credit Markets and Infant Industry Protection," in E. Helpman and A. Razin (eds.), International Trade and Trade Policy, MIT Press, Cambridge.

Greenwald, Bruce and Joseph Stiglitz 1986 "Externalities in Economies with Imperfect Information and Incomplete Markets," *Quarterly Journal of Economics*, 98, 321–36.

Jones, Ronald W. 1971 "A Three Factor Model in Theory, Trade, and History," in Bhagwati, Jones, Mundell, and Vanek (eds.), *Trade, Balance of Payments, and Growth*, North-Holland, Amsterdam.

1979 "Technical Progress and Real Incomes in a Ricardian Trade Model," Ch. 17, *International Trade: Essays in Theory*, Amsterdam, North-Holland.

Stiglitz, Joseph, E. and Andrew Weiss 1981 "Credit Rationing in Markets with Imperfect Information," *American Economic Review*, 71, 3, 393–410.

13 Endogenous real business cycles and international specialization

KAZUO NISHIMURA AND MAKOTO YANO

1. Introduction

This study investigates, from the viewpoint of endogenous real business cycles, the relationship between international specialization and dynamic behavior of multiple countries' economic activities (business cycles) in a two-good, two-factor model in which capital is freely mobile internationally.[1] Among the many areas of international economics to which Professor Ronald Jones has made major contributions are the determination of trade patterns and the international movement of capital. In his early work, Professor Jones investigated world specialization patterns in models in which production factors are internationally immobile (Jones, 1956 and 1961). He then extended his research to the case in which capital is freely mobile internationally. In this setting, he investigated the determinants of capital flows and the roles of tariff and tax policies (Jones, 1967, 1987 and 1989, Jones and Ruffin, 1975, and Jones and Dei, 1983). Through this long sequence of insightful research, Professor Jones has illuminated the critical role that the international movement of capital plays in the determination of a world specialization pattern. We are both graduates of the University of Rochester, the school that Professor Jones has helped to become a center of economic thought, and we are honored to have this opportunity to present our study involving a subject to which he has made such an important contribution.

The relationship between international specialization and international

We are grateful to Taiji Furusawa, Ron Jones, Marc Noland and Jeff Nugent for useful conversations.

[1] The number of studies on endogenous real business cycles has rapidly been rising. So far, those studies have focused on closed economy models (except Nishimura and Yano, 1990). For the study of perfect foresight models, see Benhabib and Nishimura (1979, 1985), Boldrin and Montrucchio (1986), Deneckere and Pelikan (1986). For the study of overlapping generations models, see Benhabib and Day (1982) and Grandmont (1985). For an extensive survey, see Scheinkman (1990).

214   Kazuo Nishimura and Makoto Yano

business cycles has long been considered in the context of what may be called the hypothesis of trade destabilization, the proposition that trade destablizes a (small) less-developed country by making the country overly specialized in a small part of the primary sector, thereby subjecting it to the (larger) business cycles of (more developed) large countries. Although this hypothesis has been studied extensively in the empirical literature,[2] there has not yet been a serious attempt in a rigorous theoretical framework to examine the relationship between specialization patterns in a world economy and dynamic patterns of economic activities.

This study may be thought of as a first attempt to examine this relationship. It investigates output co-movements of different parts of a world economy in relation to world production patterns. While in a static framework Jones (1989) examines the relationship between output co-movements and production patterns, there has not yet been any study that treats this relationship in a dynamic framework. As Scheinkman (1990) points out, one key to explaining output co-movements may lie in the global dynamics of a deterministic economic model. With this consideration, we have built a simple perfect foresight model of trade and capital accumulation and examined output co-movements of countries (see Nishimura and Yano, 1990).[3] In this study, we relate co-movements to production patterns by reconstructing the production side of that model.

In this reconstruction, we intend to capture the historical fact that, often, the specialization of less-developed countries (LDCs) in primary industries, such as mining and agriculture, has been associated with large-scale flows of foreign capital into the LDCs. As Jones (1967) and Jones and Ruffin (1975) demonstrate, those processes of specializations can be described by the standard two-good, two-factor model, in which the international mobility of capital almost always leads one country to be completely specialized. In order to utilize this fact, we transform to a dynamic setting that model, which has widely been adopted in the classical literature on the international movement of capital.[4]

Our study is different from the classic literature in that we allow for

___

[2] As Yotopoulos and Nugent (1976) explain, the recent empirical literature has generally rejected this destabilization hypothesis. Very little evidence, moreover, is found to support the "stabilization hypothesis" either (see Glezakos and Nugent, 1982). Those studies ignore the general equilibrium effect of opening trade, which this study focuses on from the theoretical viewpoint.
[3] The study of capital accumulation in a large-country perfect foresight model of international trade, which focuses on aspects of both trade and finance, was pioneered by Wan (1971). However, the line of approach set forth by Wan has not been followed until recently. For recent studies that deals with such models, see Grossman and Helpman (1989) and Yano (1991).
[4] Most of the early literature, which incudes MacDougall (1960), Kemp (1966) and Jones (1967), was concerned with optimal tax/tariff policy.

international movements of financial capital as well. In our setting, countries are allowed to borrow and lend freely. This aspect of trade has been omitted in the static literature in order "to separate out the question of geographical location of an existing capital stock" (Jones, 1979, p. 174). Here, instead, we focus on the interaction between physical and financial capital in order to consider the relationship between patterns of international specialization, which have traditionally been studied in a static context, and patterns of capital accumulation, which are usually dealt with in a dynamic context.

In what follows, Section 2 presents our model. Section 3 presents a characterization of autarky accumulation patterns. Section 4 characterizes patterns of aggregate capital accumulation in a free-trade equilibrium in relation to specialization patterns of countries. Section 5 relates aggregate accumulation patterns to individual countries' accumulation patterns in a free-trade equilibrium. Section 6 summarizes our results and makes concluding remarks. The appendix provides proofs for several lemmas in the text.

2. Model

The structure of production in this study is a dynamic version of the standard two-good, two-factor model; in the static context, the role of international capital movements has been extensively investigated in this model (see, for example, Kemp, 1966, Jones, 1967 and Jones and Ruffin, 1975). One production factor is a primary good, which may be thought of as labor. The other factor is a produced good (call it good Y). It must be put into production processes one period prior to the period in which labor is employed and outputs are produced. In this sense, we call good Y the capital good.

In order to keep our characterization tractable, we keep the consumption side as simple as possible. For this reason, we assume that only one good, call it good X, is consumed and that utility functions are linear. We call good X the consumption good.

We assume that there are two countries α and β. In each country, labor supply is fixed, time-independent and immobile across countries. In the case of free trade, both goods X and Y are freely mobile between the countries.

We focus on perfect foresight equilibria; in a perfect foresight equilibrium, the present value prices of all future goods and factors are known in the present period. For $h = \alpha, \beta$, denote by $q_{ht} > 0$, $p_{ht} > 0$ and $w_{ht} > 0$ the present value prices of goods X and Y and labor, respectively, in country h in period t. Because goods X and Y are freely mobile between the countries in the case of free trade whereas labor is not, $p_{\alpha t} = p_{\beta t}$ and $q_{\alpha t} = q_{\beta t}$ must hold in a free-trade equilibrium, but $w_{\alpha t} \neq w_{\beta t}$ in general. We require that, in equilibrium, all the price paths are summable:

$$\sum_{t=0}^{\infty} |p_{ht}| < \infty, \quad \sum_{t=1}^{\infty} |q_{ht}| < \infty \quad \text{and} \quad \sum_{t=1}^{\infty} |w_{ht}| < \infty. \tag{2.1}$$

In order to simplify our presentation, we do not explicitly write down each country's production processes by individual sectors' production functions. Instead, we express a country's production technology by a single function and assume that the function satisfies all the properties derived from the two-by-two model. To this end, denote by $x_{ht} \geq 0$ and $y_{ht} \geq 0$ country h's output of goods X and Y, respectively, in period t. Moreover, denote by $k_{ht} \geq 0$ country h's input of good Y (the capital good) in period t. Let $\bar{l}_h > 0$ be country h's labor endowment. Country h's technology is expressed by

$$x_{ht} = f_h(k_{ht-1}, y_{ht}, \bar{l}_h) = g_h(k_{ht-1}, y_{ht}).$$

We make the following assumptions for g_h:

Assumption 1: Function $g_h : D_h \to R_+$, $D_h \subset R^2$, is a concave and continuously twice differentiable function on a closed and convex subset of R^2, D_h.

Assumption 2: Let $g_h{}^1 = \partial g_h/\partial k$, $g_h{}^2 = \partial g_h/\partial y$, $g_h{}^{11} = \partial^2 g_h/\partial k^2$, $g_h{}^{22} = \partial^2 g_h/\partial y^2$ and $g_h{}^{12} = \partial^2 g_h/\partial k \, \partial y$.
 (a) If $y_h = 0$, then $g_h{}^1 > 0$, $g_h{}^2 = 0$, $g_h{}^{11} < 0$ and $g_h{}^{12} = g_h{}^{22} = 0$.
 (b) If $g_h(k_h, y_h) = 0$, then $g_h{}^1 > 0$, $g_h{}^2 = -1$, $g_h{}^{11} < 0$ and $g_h{}^{12} = g_h{}^{22} = 0$.
 (c) If $g_h(k_h, y_h) > 0$ and $y_h > 0$, then $g_h{}^1 > 0$, $g_h{}^2 < 0$, $g_h{}^{11} < 0$, $g_h{}^{22} \leq 0$ and
    $g_h{}^{11} g_h{}^{22} = (g_h{}^{12})^2$.

Assumptions 2a and 2b are concerned with the case in which country h is completely specialized. They are compatible with the properties of a production function of the standard neo-classical type. For the sake of explanation, suppose that h is completely specialized in sector X, i.e., $y_{ht} \equiv 0$. Then, we may express g_h by sector X's production function, say ϕ_{Xh}, as $x_h = \phi_{Xh}(k_h) = g_h(k_h, 0)$. If ϕ_{Xh} is a standard production function, g_h satisfies the properties stated in Assumption 2a. Suppose, instead, that h is completely specialized in sector Y, i.e., $x_{ht} \equiv 0$. In this case, we may write g_h by sector Y's production function, say ϕ_{Yh}, as $0 \equiv \phi_{Yh}(k_h) - y_h = g_h(k_h, y_h)$. If ϕ_{Yh} is a standard production function, g_h satisfies the properties stated as Assumption 2b.

Assumption 2c is concerned with the case in which country h is incompletely specialized, i.e., $g_h(k_h, y_h) > 0$ and $y_h > 0$. The properties stated as Assumption 2c can be derived from the properties of the two sectors' production functions (see Jones, 1965, for a systematic explanation). For the sake of explanation, suppose that h's capital stock increases and that sector Y's output is kept constant. Then, sector X's output must increase ($g_h^1 > 0$), and the marginal product of capital stock must decrease ($g_h^{11} < 0$). Suppose, instead, that h's capital stock is kept constant and that sector Y's output increases. Then, sector X's input must decrease ($g_h^2 < 0$), but the marginal rate of substitution between the sectors cannot decrease ($g_h^{22} \leq 0$). In the two-by-two model, given a relative price of output, the aggregate product $x_{ht} + (p_h/q_h)y_{ht}$ is linear in capital input k_{ht-1}. This is due to the fact that g_h is concave but not strictly ($g_h^{11}g_h^{22} = (g_h^{12})^2$).

An increase in k_{ht-1} affects individual sectors' outputs. This effect is captured by the Rybczynski theorem, which implies that, given a relative price of outputs, an increase in capital stock expands the capital intensive sector and shrinks the labor intensive sector. In order to capture this Rybczynski effect in our setting, we note the following lemma:

Lemma 1: If $g_h^{22} < 0$, the function

$$y_h(k_h, q) = \operatorname*{argmax}_{y_h} [g_h(k_h, y_h) + py_h]$$

is well defined and satisfies

$$\partial y_h/\partial k_h = -g_h^{12}/g_h^{22}.$$

Proof: Follows from the first order condition, $g_h^2(k_h, \eta_h) = -p$.   Q.E.D.

Lemma 1 implies that, given $g_h^{22} < 0$, an increase in k_h increases y_h if and only if $g_h^{12} > 0$. In the light of the Rybczynski theorem, therefore, we may introduce the following terminology.

Remark 1: Sector Y is *capital intensive* if $g_h^{12} > 0$ and *labor intensive* if $g_h^{12} < 0$.

If a factor intensity reversal occurs, $g_h^{12}(k_h, y_h) = 0$ must hold for some (k_h, y_h). For the sake of simplicity, however, we exclude such a possibility by assuming the following:

Assumption 3: If $g_h(k_h, y_h) > 0$ and $y_h > 0$, $g_h^{12} \neq 0$.

In addition to the above assumptions, we make the following assumptions:

Assumption 4: There are $\theta > 0$ and $0 < \sigma < 1$ such that if $k > \theta$ and $(k,y) \in D_h$, $y < \sigma k$.

Denote by $\bar{k}_{h0}$ country h's initial capital stock.

Assumption 5: There is $y > \bar{k}_{h0}$ such that $(\bar{k}_{h0}, y) \in D_h$.

Assumptions 4 and 5 are taken from the standard literature on capital theory (see, for example, McKenzie, 1986). Assumption 4 implies that too large a capital stock cannot be reproduced even if all the productive resources are used for production of the capital good (i.e., $g_h(k,y) = 0$). Behind this assumption, it is implicit that the primary-goods endowments work as a bottle-neck in production processes. Assumption 5 implies expansibility of each country's initial stock.

Optimization on the production side is captured as follows:

$$(x_{ht}, k_{ht-1}, y_{ht}, l_{ht}) = \operatorname*{argmax}_{(x,k,y,l)} [q_{ht}x + p_{ht}y - p_{ht-1}k - w_{ht}\bar{l}_h]$$

$$\text{subject to} \quad x = f_h(k, y, \bar{l}_h), \quad h = \alpha, \beta \quad \text{and} \quad t = 1, 2, \ldots \quad (2.2)$$

Denote by c_{ht} h's aggregate consumption in period t and by $u_h(c_{ht})$ h's period-wise utility function. We assume linear utility functions.

Assumption 6: $u_h: R_+ \to R$ satisfies $u_h(c_{ht}) = c_{ht}$.

Because country h's wealth is $p_{h0}\bar{k}_{h0} + \sum_{t=1}^{\infty} w_{ht}\bar{l}_h$, its consumers' optimization is summarized as follows:

$$(c_{h1}, c_{h2}, \ldots) = \operatorname*{argmax}_{(\zeta_{h1}, \zeta_{h2}, \ldots)} \sum_{t=1}^{\infty} \rho^t u_h(\zeta_{ht})$$

$$\text{subject to} \quad \sum_{t=1}^{\infty} q_{ht}\zeta_{ht} = p_{h0}\bar{k}_{h0} + \sum_{t=1}^{\infty} w_{ht}\bar{l}_h, \quad h = \alpha, \beta. \quad (2.3)$$

(For the moment, we proceed our discussions with the general utility function $u_h(c_h)$, which will be useful for discussion.)

An autarky equilibrium of a country can be defined as follows:

Definition 1: Path $e_{ht} = (c_{ht}, x_{ht}, k_{ht-1}, y_{ht}, q_{ht}, p_{ht-1}, w_{ht})$, $t = 1, 2, \ldots$, is in an *autarky equilibrium* if it satisfies conditions (2.1), (2.2), (2.3) and the market clearing conditions $c_{ht} = x_{ht}$ and $k_{ht} = y_{ht}$, $t = 1, 2, \ldots$.

A free-trade equilibrium is defined as follows:

Definition 2: Path $e_t = (c_{ht}, x_{ht}, k_{ht-1}, y_{ht}, l_{ht}, q_t, p_{t-1}; h = \alpha, \beta)$, $t = 1, 2, \ldots$, is in a *free-trade equilibrium* if it satisfies conditions (2.1), (2.2), (2.3), $p_{t-1} = p_{ht-1}$, $q_t = q_{ht}$ and the market clearing condition $\Sigma_h c_{ht} = \Sigma_h x_{ht}$ and $\Sigma_h k_{ht} = \Sigma_h y_{ht}$, $t = 1, 2, \ldots$.

The existence of an equilibrium in our setting may be proved by following Bewley (1972). Such a proof is not a main subject of this study and is not given here.

3. Accumulation patterns in an autarky equilibrium

This section states the basic result on autarky accumulation patterns on which this study is built. The result directly follows from a result proved by

Benhabib and Nishimura (1985).

We say that a path κ_t, $t = 0, 1, \ldots$, is *monotone* if $(\kappa_t - \kappa_{t+1})/(\kappa_{t+1} - \kappa_{t+2}) > 0$ for all t, *fluctuant* (of period 2) if $(\kappa_t - \kappa_{t+1})/(\kappa_{t+1} - \kappa_{t+2}) < 0$ for all t and *stationary* if $\kappa_t = \kappa_0$ for all t. Then, we have the following:

Theorem 1: Let k_{ht}, $t = 0, 1, \ldots$, be country h's path of capital accumulation in an autarky equilibrium path. If path k_{ht} is not stationary, the following holds:

(a) If the capital good production sector (Y) is capital intensive, the capital accumulation path is monotone.

(b) If the capital good production sector (Y) is labor intensive, the capital accumulation path is fluctuant.

4. Aggregate accumulation patterns in a free-trade equilibrium

Our main focus is on the case in which two countries have different technologies. In the case of free trade, goods are both freely mobile across borders. In such circumstances, in general, at least one country becomes completely specialized (see Jones and Ruffin, 1975). In the present study, therefore, we consider separately the case in which only one country is completely specialized (Case A) and the case in which both countries are completely specialized (Case B). Moreover, Case A is subdivided into the case in which the country is completely specialized in the consumption good sector (Case A.1) and the case in which it is completely specialized in the capital good sector (Case A.2).

This section, to start with, characterizes patterns of aggregate capital accumulation $\Sigma_h k_{ht}$, $t = 0, 1, \ldots$. Theorem 2 below demonstrates that if one country is to be incompletely specialized after the opening of trade, the aggregate accumulation pattern in a free-trade equilibrium will coincide with that country's autarky accumulation pattern (see Case A in Theorem 2). The post-trade aggregate accumulation pattern is, therefore, completely independent of the pre-trade accumulation pattern of the country that is to become completely specialized. If, instead, both countries are to be completely specialized after the opening of trade, the aggregate capital accumulation path will be monotone (see Case B in Theorem 2).

Theorem 2: Let $e_t = (c_{ht}, x_{ht}, k_{ht-1}, y_{ht}, l_{ht}, q_t, p_{t-1}; h = \alpha, \beta)$, $t = 1, 2, \ldots$, be in a free-trade equilibrium.

Case A: Suppose that country α is incompletely specialized (i.e., $x_{\alpha t} > 0$ and $y_{\alpha t} > 0$ for $t = 1, 2, \ldots$) and that country β is completely specialized (i.e., either (1) $y_{\beta t} = 0$ for $t = 1, 2, \ldots$ or (2) $x_{\beta t} = 0$ for $t = 1, 2, \ldots$). Then, the following holds:

(i) If α's capital good production sector (Y) is capital intensive, the aggregate capital accumulation path $\Sigma_h k_{ht}$, $t = 0, 1, \ldots$, is monotone.

(ii) If α's capital good production sector (Y) is labor intensive, the aggregate

220 **Kazuo Nishimura and Makoto Yano**

capital accumulation path $\Sigma_h k_{ht}$, $t = 0, 1, \ldots$, is fluctuant (of period 2).

Case B: Suppose that the two countries are completely specialized in different sectors (for example, $x_{\alpha t} = 0$ and $y_{\beta t} = 0$ for $t = 1, 2, \ldots$). Then, the aggregate capital accumulation path $\Sigma_h k_{ht}$, $t = 0, 1, \ldots$, is monotone.

Our proof of the theorem is based on the well-known fact that a free-trade equilibrium may be thought of as an optimal allocation maximizing an aggregate world utility function (see Negishi, 1960). As the next three lemmas show, the aggregate utility function to be maximized depends on specialization patterns after the opening of trade. The lemmas, which are concerned with, respectively, Cases A.1, A.2 and B in the theorem, require separate proofs that are rather tedious. For this reason, proofs are given in the Appendix.

Let $e_t = (c_{ht}, x_{ht}, k_{ht-1}, y_{ht}, l_{ht}, q_t, p_{t-1}; h = \alpha, \beta)$, $t = 1, 2, \ldots$, be a free-trade equilibrium. Let $k_t = \Sigma_h k_{ht}$.

Lemma 2.A.1: Suppose that $x_{\alpha t} > 0$, $y_{\alpha t} > 0$ and $y_{\beta t} = 0$ for $t = 1, 2, \ldots$.

Then,

$$(k_0, k_1, \ldots) = \operatorname*{argmax}_{(\kappa_0, \kappa_1, \ldots)} \sum_{t=1}^{\infty} \rho^t v_{A1}(\kappa_{t-1}, \kappa_t) \text{ subject to } \kappa_0 = \sum_h \bar{k}_{h0},$$

(4.1)

where

$$v_{A1}(\kappa, \eta) = \max_{(\kappa_h; h=\alpha,\beta)} g_\alpha(\kappa_\alpha, \eta) + g_\beta(\kappa_\beta, 0) \text{ subject to } \kappa_\alpha + \kappa_\beta = \kappa.$$

(4.2)

Moreover, $v_{A1}(\kappa, \eta)$ is continuously differentiable and satisfies the following:

$$\partial v_{A1}/\partial \eta = g_\alpha^{\,2} < 0;$$

(4.3)

$$\partial^2 v_{A1}/\partial \kappa \, \partial \eta = c g_\alpha^{\,12},$$

(4.4)

where $c = g_\beta^{\,11}/[g_\alpha^{\,11} + g_\beta^{\,11}] > 0$.

Lemma 2.A.2: Suppose that $x_{\alpha t} > 0$, $y_{\alpha t} > 0$ and $x_{\beta t} = 0$ for $t = 1, 2, \ldots$.

Then,

$$(k_0, k_1, \ldots) = \operatorname*{argmax}_{(\kappa_0, \kappa_1, \ldots)} \sum_{t=1}^{\infty} \rho^t v_{A2}(\kappa_{t-1}, \kappa_t) \text{ subject to } \kappa_0 = \sum_h \bar{k}_{h0},$$

where

$$v_{A2}(\kappa, \eta) = \max_{(\kappa_h, \eta_h \,; h = \alpha, \beta)} g_\alpha(\kappa_\alpha, \eta_\alpha)$$

subject to $g_\beta(k_\beta, \eta_\beta) = 0$, $\kappa_\alpha + \kappa_\beta = \kappa$ and $\eta_\alpha + \eta_\beta = \eta$. $\qquad$ (4.6)

Moreover, $v_{A2}(\kappa, \eta)$ is continuously differentiable and satisfies the following:

$$\partial v_{A2}/\partial \eta = g_\alpha^{\ 2} < 0; \qquad (4.7)$$

$$\partial^2 v_{A2}/\partial \kappa \, \partial \eta = c g_\alpha^{\ 12}, \qquad (4.8)$$

where $c = g_\alpha^{\ 2} g_\beta^{\ 11}/[g_\alpha^{\ 2} g_\beta^{\ 11} - g_\alpha^{\ 22}(g_\beta^{\ 1} + g_\alpha^{\ 12}/g_\alpha^{\ 22})^2] > 0$.

Lemma 2.B: Suppose that $y_{\alpha t} = 0$ and $x_{\beta t} = 0$ for $t = 1, 2, \ldots$.

Then,

$$(k_0, k_1, \ldots) = \operatorname*{argmax}_{(\kappa_0, \kappa_1, \ldots)} \sum_{t=1}^{\infty} \rho^t v_{B}(\kappa_{t-1}, \kappa_t) \text{ subject to } \kappa_0 = \sum_h \bar{k}_{h0},$$

$$(4.9)$$

where

$$v_{B}(\kappa, \eta) = \max_{(\kappa_h \,; h = \alpha, \beta)} g_\beta(\kappa_\beta, 0) \quad \text{subject to} \quad g_\alpha(\kappa_\alpha, \eta) = 0$$

and $\quad \kappa_\alpha + \kappa_\beta = \kappa$. $\qquad$ (4.10)

Moreover, $v_{B}(\kappa, \eta)$ is continuously differentiable and satisfies the following:

$$\partial v_{B}/\partial \eta = -g_\beta^{\ 1}/g_\alpha^{\ 1} < 0; \qquad (4.11)$$

$$\partial^2 v_{B}/\partial \kappa \, \partial \eta = -g_\beta^{\ 11}/g_\alpha^{\ 1} > 0. \qquad (4.12)$$

We prove Theorem 2 diagrammatically with Figures 13.1, 13.2 and 13.3. Lemmas 2.A.1, 2.A.2 and 2.B imply that, by suppressing the subscripts of utility functions v_{A1}, v_{A2} and v_{B}, path k_t, $t = 0, 1, \ldots$, is optimal in the optimal growth model $\sum_{t=1}^{\infty} \rho^t v(k_{t-1}, k_t)$. Define a value function

$$V(\eta) = \max_{(\kappa_0, \kappa_1, \ldots)} \sum_{t=1}^{\infty} \rho^t v(\kappa_{t-1}, \kappa_t) \quad \text{subject to} \quad \kappa_0 = \eta. \qquad (4.13)$$

In our framework, V is well defined on R_+, concave and differentiable (at least) almost everywhere with $V' > 0$. Note that V' can be thought of as the marginal value of capital at the beginning of a period, which is depicted by curve MV in Figure 13.1. By concavity, curve MV is non-increasing.

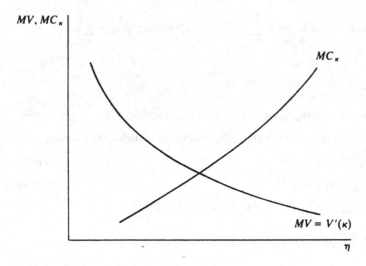

Figure 13.1

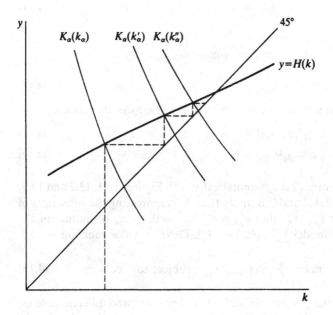

Figure 13.2

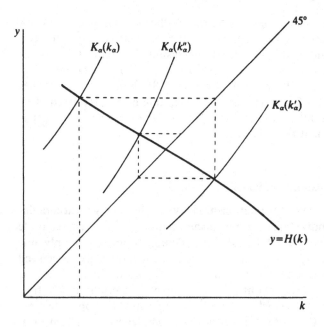

Figure 13.3

Note $v^2 \equiv \partial v(\kappa,\eta)/\partial \eta < 0$ and that $-v^2 > 0$ captures the marginal disutility (cost) of leaving capital stock at the end of a period. Figure 13.1 depicts by curve MC_κ the relationship between p and η in $p = -v^2(\kappa,\eta)$ for a given κ. Curve MC_κ is upward-sloping and shifts continuously as κ changes.

Curves MV and MC_κ have a unique intersection. Thus, the value of η at the intersection can be written as a function of κ, $\eta = H(\kappa)$. Because, by the optimal principle, along any optimal path k_t, $t = 0, 1, \ldots, \eta = k_t$ must maximize $v(k_{t-1},\eta) + V(\eta)$ for any $t = 1, 2, \ldots$, it must hold that

$$k_t = H(k_{t-1}) \tag{4.14}$$

for $t = 1, 2, \ldots$; for this reason, we call $H(\kappa)$ the aggregate accumulation function.

To complete the proof, note that optimal path k_t is monotone if the aggregate accumulation curve $H(\kappa)$ is increasing (see Figure 13.2) and fluctuant of period 2 if $H(\kappa)$ is decreasing (see Figure 13.3). In case B, by (4.12), $\partial v^2/\partial \kappa \partial \eta > 0$. In this case, as κ increases, curve MC_κ shifts downwards. This implies that even if MV has a vertical segment, curves MC_κ and MV cannot intersect on a vertical segment. (If they do, then a change in a beginning-of-a-period stock κ does not affect the optimal choice of an end-of-a-period stock, η; this contradicts the fact that the initial stock is productive). Thus, as κ increases, the intersection between MV and MC_κ shifts to the right along MV, i.e., $H(\kappa)$ is increasing. Theorem 2.B is proved.

To prove Theorem 2.A, suppose that α's sector Y is capital intensive, $g_\alpha^{12} > 0$ (see Remark 1). Then, by (4.4) and (4.8), $\partial v^2/\partial \kappa \, \partial \eta > 0$ in either Case A.1 or Case A.2. Since $H(\kappa)$ is increasing, statement (i) is proved. If α's sector Y is labor intensive, $g_\alpha^{12} < 0$. Then, by $\partial v^2/\partial \kappa \, \partial \eta < 0$, $H(\kappa)$ is decreasing; statement (ii) is proved.

5. Accumulation patterns in individual countries

This section investigates the relationship between the aggregate accumulation pattern and individual countries' accumulation patterns in a free-trade equilibrium. Theorems 3.A.1 and 3.A.2 demonstrate that if only one country is completely specialized, over time, the incompletely specialized country's capital stock generally moves in the same direction as the aggregate capital stock. In contrast, the completely specialized country's stock and the aggregate stock may move in opposite directions. Theorem 3.B demonstrates that if both countries are completely specialized, over time, the capital stock of the country that is completely specialized in the capital good sector moves in the same direction as the aggregate capital stock. The other country's capital stock and the aggregate capital stock may move in opposite directions.

5.1. Case A.1

This is the case in which country β is completely specialized in sector X (the consumption good sector) while country α is incompletely specialized. We first prove that, in a free-trade equilibrium, country α's accumulation pattern coincides with the aggregate accumulation pattern. To this end, we note the following lemma (as is shown in the Appendix, the lemma can be proved as a corollary of Lemma 2.A.1).

Lemma 3.A.1: The function

$$(k_{hA1}(\kappa, \eta); \; h = \alpha, \beta) = \max_{(\kappa_\alpha, \kappa_\beta)} \; [g_\alpha(\kappa_\alpha, \eta) + g_\beta(\kappa_\beta, 0)]$$

$$\text{subject to } \kappa_\alpha + \kappa_\beta = \kappa \tag{5.1}$$

is well defined. Moreover, functions $k_h = k_{hA1}(\kappa, \eta)$, $h = \alpha, \beta$, satisfy the following:

$$dk_\alpha = \frac{g_\beta^{11}}{g_\alpha^{11} + g_\beta^{11}} d\kappa - \frac{g_\alpha^{12}}{g_\alpha^{11} + g_\beta^{11}} d\eta; \qquad (5.2)$$

$$dk_\beta = \frac{g_\alpha^{11}}{g_\alpha^{11} + g_\beta^{11}} d\kappa + \frac{g_\alpha^{12}}{g_\alpha^{11} + g_\beta^{11}} d\eta. \qquad (5.3)$$

Functions $k_{hA1}(\kappa, \eta)$, $h = \alpha, \beta$, capture the optimal allocation of capital input, given aggregate levels of capital input and capital good output, κ and η. For a given k_h, we may depict the relationships between κ and η in $k_{hAi}(\kappa, \eta) = k_h$ by a curve $K_h(k_h)$, which we call h's iso-capital-input curve.

Recall that the direction of the slope of the aggregate accumulation curve $H(\kappa)$ is the same as the sign of g_α^{12}. Therefore, by Lemma 3.A.1, the iso-capital-input curves of α, $K_\alpha(k_\alpha)$, are sloped in the direction opposite to $H(\kappa)$ by $g_\alpha^{11} < 0$ (Assumption 2). Moreover, since $g_\beta^{11}/(g_\alpha^{11} + g_\beta^{11}) > 0$, curve $K_\alpha(k_\alpha)$ shifts to the right as k_α increases. Therefore, as shown in Figures 13.2 and 13.3, country α's capital stock increases if the aggregate capital stock increases and decreases if it is decreased. In other words, country α's capital stock always moves in the same direction as the aggregate capital stock. This establishes the following result:

Theorem 3.A.1: Let $e_t = (c_{ht}, x_{ht}, k_{ht-1}, y_{ht}, l_{ht}, q_t, p_{t-1}; h = \alpha, \beta)$, $t = 1, 2, \ldots$, be in a free-trade equilibrium. Suppose that country α is incompletely specialized (i.e., $x_{\alpha t} > 0$ and $y_{\alpha t} > 0$ for $t = 1, 2, \ldots$) and that country β is completely specialized in the consumption good sector (i.e., $y_{\beta t} = 0$ for $t = 1, 2, \ldots$). Then, the capital stock of country α moves in the same direction as the aggregate capital stock.

The iso-capital-input curves of β, $K_\beta(k_\beta)$, are sloped in the same direction as curve $H(\kappa)$. Moreover, curve $K_\beta(k_\beta)$ shifts to the right as k_β increases. Therefore, if all the iso-capital-input curves are steeper than the aggregate accumulation curve, β's capital stock moves in the same direction as the aggregate capital.

In general, country β's capital stock may not move in the same direction as the aggregate capital stock. (We do not present the example here, for it is beyond the scope of this study.) Figure 13.4 captures the case in which an iso-capital input curve of β is flatter than curve $H(\kappa)$. In this case, the opening of trade has a "J-curve" effect on β's capital accumulation path. In Figure 13.4, as the aggregate capital stock increases, β's capital stock first declines and then starts to increase to the new stationary level.

The above discussion indicates that *only in a limited case, there is a positive correlation between the time series of the two countries' capital stocks. Relative to the aggregate stock movement, in general, the completely specialized country's stock movement does not exhibit the same regularity as that of the incompletely specialized country.*

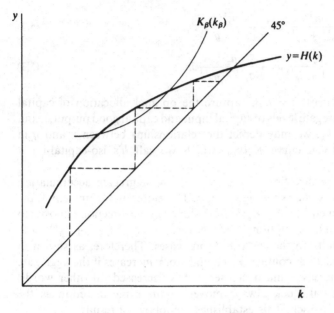

Figure 13.4

5.2. Case A.2

This is the case in which country β is completely specialized in sector Y (the capital good sector) while country α is incompletely specialized. In order to derive a result similar to that in the above section, we note the following lemma (see the Appendix for a proof).

Lemma 3.A.2: The function

$$(k_{hA2}(\kappa,\eta), y_{hA2}(\kappa,\eta); h = \alpha, \beta) = \max_{(\kappa_h, y_h; h = \alpha, \beta)} g_\alpha(\kappa_\alpha, \eta_\alpha)$$

subject to $g_\beta(\kappa_\beta, \eta_\beta) = 0$, $\kappa_\alpha + \kappa_\beta = \kappa$ and $\eta_\alpha + \eta_\beta = \eta$

(5.4)

is well defined. In particular, functions $k_h = k_{hA1}(\kappa, \eta)$, $h = \alpha, \beta$, satisfy the following:

$$dk_\alpha = \frac{1}{|A|}\{[g_\alpha{}^2 g_\beta{}^{11} - g_\beta{}^1 g_\beta{}^{22}(g_\beta{}^1 + g_\alpha{}^{12}/g_\alpha{}^{22})]d\kappa$$

$$+ g_\alpha{}^{22}(g_\beta{}^1 + g_\alpha{}^{12}/g_\alpha{}^{22})d\eta\};$$

(5.5)

$$dk_\beta = \frac{1}{|A|}\{-g_\alpha{}^{12}(g_\beta{}^1 + g_\alpha{}^{12}/g_\alpha{}^{22})d\kappa$$

$$- g_\alpha{}^{22}(g_\beta{}^1 + g_\alpha{}^{12}/g_\alpha{}^{22})d\eta\}; \tag{5.6}$$

$$|A| = g_\alpha{}^2 g_\beta{}^{11} - g_\beta{}^{22}(g_\beta{}^1 + g_\alpha{}^{12}/g_\alpha{}^{22})^2 > 0. \tag{5.7}$$

In Case A.2, the relationship between the aggregate accumulation pattern and the accumulation pattern of the incompletely specialized country becomes somewhat less clear-cut than in Case A.1. This is because, as Lemma 3.A.2 indicates, an increase in aggregate capital input may not result in increases in both countries' capital inputs if the increment is optimally allocated between the countries, i.e., $\partial k_{hA2}/\partial \kappa$ may be negative.

It seems safe, at least from the theoretical viewpoint, to consider it normal that an increase in aggregate capital input is shared by both countries, given an output level of the capital good. For this reason, we say that *the capital usage of country h is normal if $\partial k_{hA2}/\partial \kappa > 0$*. The above discussion indicates that in the case in which the capital usage of each country is normal, the same result as in Case A.1 holds.

Theorem 3.A.2: Let $e_t = (c_{ht}, x_{ht}, k_{ht-1}, y_{ht}, l_{ht}, q_t, p_{t-1}; h = \alpha, \beta), t = 1, 2, \ldots,$ be in a free-trade equilibrium. Suppose that country α is incompletely specialized (i.e., $x_{\alpha t} > 0$ and $y_{\alpha t} > 0$ for $t = 1, 2, \ldots$), that country β is completely specialized in the capital good sector (i.e., $x_{\beta t} = 0$ for $t = 1, 2, \ldots$) and that the capital usage of each country is normal. Then, the capital stock of country α moves in the same direction as the aggregate capital stock.

For the same reason discussed above, country β's stock may move in the direction opposite to the aggregate stock.

5.3. Case B

This is the case in which both countries are completely specialized. Following the above discussion, suppose that countries α and β are completely specialized in the consumption good and capital good sectors, respectively. As a corollary of Lemma 2.B, we have the following:

Lemma 3.B: The function

$$(k_{hB}(k, \eta); h = \alpha, \beta) = \operatorname*{argmax}_{(\kappa_h; h = \alpha, \beta)} g_\beta(\kappa_\beta, 0)$$

subject to $\quad g_\alpha(\kappa_\alpha, \eta) = 0 \quad$ and $\quad \kappa_\alpha = \kappa_\beta = \kappa \tag{5.8}$

is well defined. Moreover, functions $k_{hB}(k, \eta)$, $h = \alpha, \beta$, satisfy the following:

$$dk_\alpha = d\eta/g_\alpha{}^1, \tag{5.9}$$

$$dk_\beta = d\kappa - d\eta/g_\alpha{}^1; \tag{5.10}$$

Recall that, in this case, the aggregate accumulation curve is upward-sloping. By (5.9), every iso-capital-input curve of α is horizontal. As the aggregate output increases, α's capital input increases. These facts imply that α's capital stock moves in the same direction as the aggregate capital stock, which follows a monotone path. This establishes the following result:

Theorem 3.B: Let $e_t = (c_{ht}, x_{ht}, k_{ht-1}, y_{ht}, l_{ht}, q_t, p_{t-1}; h = \alpha, \beta)$, $t = 1, 2, \ldots$, be in a free-trade equilibrium. Suppose that country α is completely specialized in the capital good sector (i.e., $x_{\alpha t} = 0$ for $t = 1, 2, \ldots$), that country β is completely specialized in the consumption good sector (i.e., $y_{\beta t} = 0$ for $t = 1, 2, \ldots$). Then, the capital stock of country α moves in the same direction as the aggregate capital stock.

Again, country β's stock may not move in the same direction as the aggregate capital stock.

6. Summary and concluding remarks

In a simple perfect foresight (deterministic) model of trade, we have investigated patterns of dynamic economic activities (capital accumulation) in relation to patterns of international specialization. A dynamic version of the standard two-good, two-factor model is used to describe the production side of the model. In the case of free trade, the capital good as well as the consumption good is assumed to be freely mobile across borders. Our study is built on the fact that, in such a model, at least one country is completely specialized in a free-trade equilibrium (Jones and Ruffin, 1975).

We have demonstrated that the patterns of dynamic movements of economic activities are related to those of international specialization. In the case in which one country is to be incompletely specialized in a free-trade equilibrium, our results may be summarized as follows:

Conclusion 1: The free-trade accumulation pattern of the aggregate world stock will coincide with the autarky accumulation pattern in the country that will be incompletely specialized. In other words, the free-trade path of aggregate accumulation is monotone if that country's autarky accumulation path is monotone and fluctuant if it is fluctuant.

Conclusion 2: In the free-trade equilibrium, the stock of the country that will be incompletely specialized will move in the same direction as the aggregate stock whereas that of the country that will be completely specialized may not. This holds unambiguously if the latter country will be completely specialized in the consumption good sector but holds only under a certain normality condition if it will be completely specialized in the capital good sector.

These results provide some insights into the hypothesis of trade destabilization. According to the hypothesis, as is discussed in the Introduction, an LDC tends to destabilize its economy by opening trade to the rest of the world.

This hypothesis has often been explained in a small-country context. That is, once a small LDC opens its economy, it becomes subject to prices determined outside of the country. If, in particular, the country has a strong comparative advantage in one particular industry (due to some natural resource conditions, as is often the case), it tends to become "overly" specialized in that sector. As a result, the country tends to become overly volatile to price changes that take place outside of the country, i.e., in "large" developed countries.

This explanation has weakness in that such a country is often not small in the sense of trade theory, i.e., not completely subject to exogenous world prices. Often, on the contrary, such a country is a major producer of the product that it specializes in and, therefore, affects its product's world price significantly; in other words, such a country is often a large country in the trade theoretic terminology.

Our results give some insights into the hypothesis of trade destabilization from the viewpoint of trade between two large countries. In our setting, as Conclusion 1 implies, the post-trade aggregate accumulation pattern is not related to the pre-trade accumulation pattern of the country that is to be completely specialized (for the sake of discussion, let us momentarily call this country a "small country"). The post-trade aggregate accumulation pattern is governed completely by technological conditions in the country that is incompletely specialized (call this country a "large country"). Once trade opens, the accumulation pattern of the "small country" may become totally different from its pre-trade pattern whereas that of the "large country" will be unaffected.

As Conclusion 2 implies, this difference between "small and large countries" is sharper in the case in which the "small country" imports the capital good from abroad than in the case in which it imports the consumption good. This fact seems to suggest the importance of capital in-flow into the "small country" in making that country's accumulation pattern subject to the "large country." In other words, capital goods seem to carry the technological conditions of the "large country" into the "small country" in a more direct manner than consumption goods.

In the case in which both countries are to be completely specialized in a free-trade equilibrium, our main findings may be summarized as follows:

Conclusion 3: The free-trade accumulation pattern in aggregate world stock will coincide with the autarky accumulation pattern in the stock of

230   Kazuo Nishimura and Makoto Yano

the country that will be completely specialized in the capital good sector.

Conclusion 4: In the free-trade equilibrium, the stock of the country that will be completely specialized in the capital good sector will move in the same direction as the aggregate stock whereas that of the country that will be completely specialized in the consumption good sector may not.

References

Benhabib, J. and R. Day 1982 "A Characterization of Erratic Dynamics in the Overlapping Generations Model," *Journal of Economic Dynamics and Control*, 4, 37–55.

Benhabib, J. and K. Nishimura 1979 "The Hopf Bifurcation and the Existence and Stability of Closed Orbits in Multisector Models of Optimal Economic Growth," *Journal of Economic Theory*, 21, 421–44.

1985 "Competitive Equilibrium Cycles," *Journal of Economic Theory*, 35, 284–306.

Bewley, T. 1972 "Existence of Equilibria in Economies with Infinitely Many Commodities," *Journal of Economic Theory*, 4, 514–40.

Boldrin, M. and L. Montrucchio 1986 "On the Indeterminacy of Capital Accumulation Paths," *Journal of Economic Theory*, 40, 26–39.

Deneckere, R. and S. Pelikan 1986 "Competitive Chaos," *Journal of Economic Theory*, 40, 13–25.

Glezakos, C. and J. Nugent 1982 "More on the Cause of Instability in Export Earnings," *Bulletin*, 379–83.

Grandmont, J. 1985 "On Endogenous Competitive Business Cycles," *Econometrica*, 53, 995–1045.

Grossman, G. and E. Helpman 1989 "Product Development and International Trade," *Journal of Political Economy*, 97, 1262–283.

Jones, R. 1956 "Factor Proportions and the Heckscher–Ohlin Theorem," *Review of Economic Studies*, 1–10.

1961 "Comparative Advantage and the Theory of Tariffs: A Multi-Country, Multi-Commodity Model," *Review of Economic Studies*, 161–75.

1965 "The Structure of Simple General Equilibrium Models," *Journal of Political Economy*, 74, 557–72.

1967 "International Capital Movements and the Theory of Tariffs and Trade," *Quarterly Journal of Economics*, 81, 1–38.

1979 *International Trade: Essays in Theory*, North-Holland, Amsterdam.

1987 "Tax Wedges and Mobile Capital," *Scandinavian Journal of Economics*, 89, 335–46.

1989 "Co-Movements in Relative Commodity Prices and International Capital Flows: A Simple Model," *Economic Inquiry*, 27, 131–41.

Jones, R. and F. Dei 1983 "International Trade and Foreign Investment: A Simple Model," *Economic Inquiry*, 449–64.

Jones, R. and R. Ruffin 1975 "Trade Patterns with Capital Mobility," in M. Parkin and A. Nobay (eds.), *Current Economic Problems*, 307–32.

Kemp, M. 1966 "The Gains from International Trade and Investment: A Heckscher–Ohlin Approach," *American Economic Review*, 56, 788–809.

MacDougall, G. 1960 "The Benefits and Costs of Private Investment from Abroad: A Theoretical Approach," *Economic Record*, 36, 13–35.

McKenzie, L. 1986 "Optimal Economic Growth and Turnpike Theorems," in K. Arrow and M. Intriligator (eds.), *Handbook of Mathematical Economics*, North-Holland, Amsterdam.

Negishi, T. 1960 "Welfare Economics and Existence of an Equilibrium for a Competitive Economy," *Metroeconomica*, 12, 92–97.

Nishimura, K. and M. Yano 1990 "Interlinkage in the Endogenous Real Business Cycles of International Economies," *Economic Theory*, forthcoming.

Scheinkman, J. 1990 "Nonlinearities in Economic Dynamics," *Economic Journal*, 33–48.

Wan, H. 1971 "A Simultaneous Variational Model for International Capital Movement," in *Trade, Balance of Payments, and Growth*, J. Bhagwati *et al.* (eds.), North-Holland, Amsterdam.

Yano, M. 1991 "Temporary Transfers in a Simple Dynamic General Equilibrium Model," *Journal of Economic Theory*, 54, 372–88.

Yotopoulos, P. and J. Nugent 1976 *Economics of Development: Empirical Investigations*, Harper and Row.

Appendix

Here, we prove the lemmas that are left without proofs in the text. Let $e_t = (c_{ht}, x_{ht}, k_{ht-1}, y_{ht}, l_{ht}, q_t, p_{t-1}; h = \alpha, \beta)$, $t = 1, 2, \ldots$, be in a free-trade equilibrium. By optimization on the consumption side, consumption path c_{ht}, $t = 1, 2, \ldots$, can be associated with a number $\lambda_h > 0$ (which is often called a marginal utility of wealth or a Lagrangean multiplier) such that

$$\sum_{t=1}^{\infty} \rho^t c_{ht} - \lambda_h \sum_{t=1}^{\infty} q_t c_{ht} \geq \sum_{t=1}^{\infty} \rho^t \zeta_{ht} - \lambda_h \sum_{t=1}^{\infty} q_t \zeta_{ht} \tag{A.1}$$

for any $\zeta_{ht} \geq 0$, $t = 1, 2, \ldots$. We first prove the following:

Lemma 1a: $\lambda_\alpha = \lambda_\beta$.

Proof: By setting $\zeta_{h\tau} = c_{h\tau}$ for all $\tau \neq t$ in (A.1),

$$\rho^t c_{ht} - \lambda_h q_t c_{ht} \geq \rho^t \zeta_{ht} - \lambda_h q_t \zeta_{ht} \tag{A.2}$$

for any $\zeta_{ht} \geq 0$. Thus, for any $t = 1, 2, \ldots$,

$$\rho^t (c_{\alpha t}^F / \lambda_\alpha^F + c_{\beta t}^F / \lambda_\beta^T) - q_t^F (c_{\alpha t}^F + c_{\beta t}^F) \geq \rho^t (\zeta_{\alpha t} / \lambda_\alpha^F + \zeta_{\beta t} / \lambda_\beta^F)$$

$$- q_t^F(\zeta_{\alpha t} + \zeta_{\beta t}) \qquad (A.3)$$

for any $(\zeta_{\alpha t}, \zeta_{\beta t}) \in R_+{}^2$. Suppose $\lambda_\alpha{}^F > \lambda_\beta{}^F$. Then, (A.3) implies that for any t such that $c_{\alpha t}{}^F + c_{\beta t}{}^F > 0$, $c_{\beta t}{}^F > c_{\alpha t}{}^F = 0$. Note that for any t such that $c_{\alpha t}{}^F + c_{\beta t}{}^F = 0$, $c_{\alpha t}{}^F = 0$ since $c_{ht} \geq 0$. By these facts, $c_{\alpha t}{}^F = 0$ for $t = 1, 2, \ldots$. Thus, $0 = \sum_{t=1}^\infty q_t^F c_{\alpha t}{}^F = p_0^F \bar{k}_{\alpha 0} + \sum_{t=1}^\infty w_t^F \bar{l}_F$, which contradicts $w_t^F > 0$ and $\bar{l}_F > 0$. In a similar manner, we may establish a contradiction in the case of $\lambda_\alpha{}^F < \lambda_\beta{}^F$.   Q.E.D.

Let $\lambda = \lambda_\alpha = \lambda_\beta$. Then, by (A.3),

$$\rho^t \sum_h c_{ht}/\lambda - q_t \sum_h c_{ht} \geq \rho^t \sum_h \zeta_{ht}/\lambda - q_t \sum_h \zeta_{ht} \qquad (A.4)$$

for any $(\zeta_{\alpha t}, \beta_{\beta t}) \in R_+{}^2$. Note the following facts:

Lemma 2a: (i) If country h is completely specialized in sector X, i.e., if $y_{ht} = 0$ for $t = 1, 2, \ldots$,

$$q_t g_h(k_{ht-1}, 0) - p_{t-1} k_{ht-1} \geq q_t g_h(\kappa_{ht-1}, 0) - p_{t-1}\kappa_{ht-1} \qquad (A.5)$$

for any $(\kappa_{ht-1}, 0) \in D_h$.

(ii) If country h is completely specialized in sector Y, i.e., $x_{ht} = 0$ for $t = 1, 2, \ldots$,

$$p_t y_{ht} - p_{t-1} k_{ht-1} \geq p_t \eta_{ht} - p_{t-1}\kappa_{ht-1} \qquad (A.6)$$

for any $g_h(\kappa_{ht-1}, \eta_{ht}) = 0$.

(iii) If country h is incompletely specialized,

$$q_t g_h(k_{ht-1}, y_{ht}) + p_t y_{ht} - p_{t-1} k_{ht-1} \geq q_t g_h(\kappa_{ht-1}, \eta_{ht}) + p_t \eta_{ht}$$

$$- p_{t-1}\kappa_{ht-1} \qquad (A.7)$$

for any $(\kappa_{ht-1}, \kappa_{ht}) \in D_h$.

I. Proof of Lemmas 2.A.1 and 3.A.1

Because α is incompletely specialized and because β is completely specialized in X, (A.7) holds for $h = \alpha$, and (A.5) holds for $h = \beta$. Since $g_\alpha(k_{\alpha t-1}, k_{\alpha t}) + g_\beta(k_{\beta t}, 0) = \Sigma_h x_{ht}, k_{t-1} = \Sigma_h k_{ht-1}$ and $k_t = y_{\alpha t}$, by (A.5) and (A.7),

$$q_t \sum_h x_{ht} + p_t k_t - p_{t-1} k_{t-1} \geq q_t(g_\alpha(\kappa_{\alpha t-1}, \eta_{\alpha t}) + g_\beta(\kappa_{\beta t-1}, 0))$$

$$+ p_t \eta_{\alpha t} - p_{t-1}\sum_h \kappa_{ht-1} \qquad (A.8)$$

for any combination of $(\kappa_{\alpha t-1}, \eta_{\alpha t}) \in D_\alpha$ and $(\kappa_{\beta t-1}, 0) \in D_\beta$. Since $\Sigma_h x_{ht} = \Sigma_h c_{ht}$, by (A.4) and (A.8),

$$\rho^t \sum_h c_{ht}/\lambda + p_t k_t - p_{t-1} k_{t-1} \geq \rho^t(g_\alpha(\kappa_{\alpha t-1}, \eta_{\alpha t}) + g_\beta(\kappa_{\beta t-1}, 0))/\lambda$$

$$+ p_t \eta_{\alpha t} - p_{t-1} \sum_h \kappa_{ht-1} \qquad \text{(A.9)}$$

for any combination of $(\kappa_{\alpha t-1}, \eta_{\alpha t}) \in D_\alpha$ and $(\kappa_{\beta t-1}, 0) \in D_\beta$. This implies

$$\rho^t v_{A1}(k_{t-1}, k_t)/\lambda + p_t k_t - p_{t-1} k_{t-1} \geq \rho^t v_{A1}(\kappa_{t-1}, \kappa_t)$$

$$+ p_t \kappa_t - p_{t-1} \kappa_{t-1} \qquad \text{(A.10)}$$

for any (κ_{t-1}, κ_t) at which v_{A1} is well defined. By adding (A.10) through t and by setting $\kappa_0 = \Sigma_h k_{h0}$, the first half of the lemma can be readily proved.

In order to prove the rest of the lemma, write down the Lagrangean associated with (4.2):

$$L = g_\alpha(\kappa_\alpha, \eta) + g_\beta(\kappa_\beta, 0) - \gamma(\kappa_\alpha + \kappa_\beta - \kappa). \qquad \text{(A.11)}$$

The first order condition from (A.11) is:

$$g_\alpha^{\ 1}(k_\alpha, y) = \gamma; \quad g_\beta^{\ 1}(k_\beta) = \gamma \quad \text{and} \quad k_\alpha + k_\beta = k. \qquad \text{(A.12)}$$

Note that $dv_{A1} = d(g_\alpha + g_\beta) = g_\alpha^{\ 1} d\kappa_\alpha + g_\alpha^{\ 2} d\eta + g_\beta^{\ 1} d\kappa_\beta = \gamma d\kappa + g_\alpha^{\ 2} d\eta$. Thus, (4.3) holds by Assumption 2a. Totally differentiating system (A.12) and using Assumptions 2a and 2c, we have the following system:

$$\begin{bmatrix} g_\alpha^{\ 11} d\kappa_\alpha + g_\alpha^{\ 12} d\eta - d\gamma = 0; \\\\ g_\beta^{\ 11} d\kappa_\beta - d\gamma = 0; \\\\ d\kappa_\alpha + d\kappa_\beta = dx. \end{bmatrix} \qquad \text{(A.13)}$$

Since $\partial v_{A1}/\partial k = \gamma$, this implies (4.4). Lemma 3.A.1 also follows from this system.

II. Proof of Lemmas 2.A.2 and 3.A.2

Because α is incompletely specialized and because β is completely specialized in Y, (A.7) holds for $h = \alpha$, and (A.6) holds for $h = \beta$. Since $g_\alpha(k_{\alpha t-1}, y_{\alpha t}) = x_{ht}$, $k_{t-1} = \Sigma_h k_{ht-1}$ and $g_\beta(k_{\beta t-1}, y_{\beta t}) = 0$, by (A.6) and (A.7),

$$q_t g_\alpha(k_{\alpha t-1}, y_{\alpha t}) + p_t k_t - p_{t-1} k_{t-1} \geq q_t g_\alpha(\kappa_{\alpha t-1}, \eta_{\alpha t}) + p_t \Sigma_h \eta_{ht}$$

$$- p_{t-1} \Sigma_h \kappa_{ht-1} \qquad \text{(A.14)}$$

for any combination of $(\kappa_{\alpha t-1}, \eta_{\alpha t}) \in D_\alpha$ and $(\kappa_{\beta t-1}, \eta_{\beta t}) \in D_\beta$ with $g_\beta(\kappa_{\beta t-1}, \eta_{\beta t}) = 0$. Therefore, by (A.4) and (A.14),

$$\rho^t \Sigma_h c_{ht}/\lambda + p_t k_t - p_{t-1} k_{t-1} \geq \rho^t g_\alpha(\kappa_{\alpha t-1}, \eta_{\alpha t})/\lambda + p_t \Sigma_h \eta_{ht}$$

$$- p_{t-1} \Sigma_h \kappa_{ht-1} \qquad (A.15)$$

for any combination of $(\kappa_{\alpha t-1}, \eta_{\alpha t}) \in D_\alpha$ and $(\kappa_{\beta t-1}, \eta_{\beta t}) \in D_\beta$ with $g_\beta(\kappa_{\beta t-1}, \eta_{\beta t}) = 0$. This implies that

$$\rho^t v_{A2}(k_{t-1}, k_t)/\lambda + p_t k_t - p_{t-1} k_{t-1} \geq \rho^t v_{A2}(\kappa_{t-1}, \kappa_t) + p_t \kappa_t$$
$$- p_{t-1} \kappa_{t-1} \qquad (A.16)$$

for any (κ_{t-1}, κ_t) at which v_{A2} is well defined. By adding (A.16) through t and by setting $\kappa_0 = \Sigma_h \bar{k}_{h0}$, the first half of Lemma 2.A.2 can be readily proved.

To prove the second half of Lemma 2.A.2, write down the Lagrangean associated with (4.6):

$$L = g_\alpha(\kappa_\alpha, \eta_\alpha) - \gamma(\kappa_\alpha + \kappa_\beta - \kappa) - \pi(\eta_\alpha + \eta_\beta - \eta) - \mu g_\beta(\kappa_\beta, \eta_\beta).$$
$$(A.17)$$

The first order condition from (A.17) is:

$$g_\alpha^{1}(\kappa_\alpha, \eta_\alpha) = \gamma; \quad g_\alpha^{2}(\kappa_\alpha, \eta_\alpha) = \pi; \quad \mu g_\beta^{1}(\kappa_\beta, \eta_\beta) = -\gamma;$$
$$\mu = \pi; \quad \kappa_\alpha + \kappa_\beta = \kappa; \quad \eta_\alpha + \eta_\beta = \eta; \quad g_\beta(\kappa_\beta, \eta_\beta) = 0.$$
$$(A.18)$$

Note $dv_{A2} = dg_\alpha = g_\alpha^{1} d\kappa_\alpha + g_\alpha^{2} d\eta_\alpha = g_\alpha^{1} d\kappa + g_\alpha^{2} d\eta - (g_\alpha^{1} d\kappa_\beta + g_\alpha^{2} d\eta_\beta) = g_\alpha^{1} d\kappa + g_\alpha^{2} d\eta + \mu(g_\beta^{1} d\kappa_\beta - d\eta_\beta) = g_\alpha^{1} d\kappa + g_\alpha^{2} d\eta$, since $0 = g_\beta^{1} d\kappa_\beta + g_\beta^{2} d\eta_\beta = g_\beta^{1} d\kappa_\beta - d\eta_\beta$ by Assumption 2b. Thus, (4.7) holds under Assumption 2a.

Totally differentiating system (A.18) and using the fact that g_α and g_β, respectively, satisfy Assumptions 2c and 2b, we have the following system:

$$\begin{bmatrix} g_\alpha^{11} d\kappa_\alpha + g_\alpha^{12} d\eta_\alpha - d\gamma = 0; \\ g_\alpha^{21} d\kappa_\alpha + g_\alpha^{22} d\eta_\alpha - d\mu = 0; \\ \mu g_\beta^{11} d\kappa_\beta + d\gamma + g_\beta^{1} d\mu = 0; \\ d\kappa_\alpha + d\kappa_\beta = d\kappa; \\ d\eta_\alpha + d\eta_\beta = d\eta; \\ g_\beta^{1} d\kappa_\beta - d\eta_\beta = 0. \end{bmatrix} \qquad (A.19)$$

Solving this system and rearranging the solution by $g_\alpha^{11} g_\alpha^{22} = (g_\alpha^{12})^2$, we have (4.8). Lemma 3.A.2, too, follows from system (A.19).   Q.E.D.

III. Proof of Lemmas 2.B and 3.B.2

Because α is completely specialized in Y and because β is completely specialized in X, (A.6) holds for $h = \alpha$, and (A.5) holds for $h = \beta$. Since $g_\beta(k_{\beta t - 1}, 0) = x_{\beta t}$, $y_{\alpha t} = \Sigma_h k_{ht} = k_t$, and $g_\alpha(k_{\alpha t - 1}, y_{\alpha t}) = 0$, by (A.5) and (A.6),

$$q_t g_\beta(k_{\beta t - 1}, 0) + p_t k_t - p_{t-1} k_{t-1} \geq q_t g_\beta(\kappa_{\beta t - 1}, 0) + p_t \eta_{\alpha t}$$
$$- p_{t-1} \Sigma_h \kappa_{ht - 1} \qquad \text{(A.20)}$$

for any combination of $(\kappa_{\beta t - 1}, 0) \in D_\beta$ and $(\kappa_{\alpha t - 1}, \eta_{\alpha t}) \in D_\alpha$ with $g_\alpha(\kappa_{\alpha t - 1}, \eta_{\alpha t}) = 0$. Therefore, by (A.4) and (A.20),

$$\rho^t \Sigma_h c_{ht}/\lambda + p_t k_t - p_{t-1} k_{t-1} \geq \rho^t g_\beta(\kappa_{\beta t - 1}, \eta_{\beta t})/\lambda + p_t \Sigma_h \eta_{ht}$$
$$- p_{t-1} \Sigma_h \kappa_{ht - 1} \qquad \text{(A.21)}$$

for any combination of $(\kappa_{\beta t - 1}, 0) \in D_\beta$ and $(\kappa_{\alpha t - 1}, \eta_{\alpha t}) \in D_\alpha$ with $g_\alpha(\kappa_{\alpha t - 1}, \eta_{\alpha t}) = 0$. This implies that

$$\rho^t v_B(k_{t-1}, k_t)/\lambda + p_t k_t - p_{t-1} k_{t-1} \geq \rho^t v_B(\kappa_{t-1}, \kappa_t) + p_t \kappa_t$$
$$- p_{t-1} \kappa_{t-1} \qquad \text{(A.22)}$$

for any (κ_{t-1}, κ_t) at which v_B is well defined. By adding (A.22) through t and by setting $\kappa_0 = \Sigma_h \bar{k}_{h0}$, the first half of Lemma 2.B can be readily proved.

To prove the second half of Lemma 2.B, write down the Lagrangean associated with (4.9):

$$L = g_\beta(\kappa_\beta, 0) - \gamma(\kappa_\alpha + \kappa_\beta - \kappa) - \mu g_\alpha(\kappa_\alpha, \eta). \qquad \text{(A.23)}$$

The first order condition from (A.23) is:

$$g_\beta^{\,1}(\kappa_\beta, 0) = \lambda; \quad \mu g_\alpha^{\,1}(\kappa_\alpha, \eta) = \gamma; \quad \kappa_\alpha + \kappa_\beta = \kappa; \quad g_\alpha(\kappa_\alpha, \eta) = 0.$$
$$\text{(A.24)}$$

Note $dv_B = dg_\beta = g_\beta^{\,1} d\kappa_\beta = g_\beta^{\,1}(d\kappa - d\kappa_\alpha) = g_\beta^{\,1} d\kappa + \mu g_\alpha^{\,1} d\kappa_\alpha = g_\beta^{\,1} d\kappa + \mu d\eta = g_\beta^{\,1} d\kappa - (g_\beta^{\,1}/g_\alpha^{\,1}) d\eta$, since $0 = g_\alpha^{\,1} d\kappa_\alpha + g_\alpha^{\,2} d\eta_\alpha = g_\alpha^{\,1} d\kappa_\alpha - d\eta_\alpha$ by Assumption 2b. Thus, (4.11) follows from Assumptions 2a and 2b.

Totally differentiating system (A.24) and using the fact that g_α and g_β, respectively, satisfy Assumptions 2a and 2b, we have the following system:

$$\begin{bmatrix} g_\beta{}^{11}d\kappa_\beta + g_\beta{}^{12}d\eta_\beta - d\gamma = 0; \\ \mu g_\alpha{}^{11}d\kappa_\alpha + d\gamma + g_\alpha{}^1 d\mu = 0; \\ d\kappa_\alpha + d\kappa_\beta = d\kappa; \\ g_\alpha{}^1 d\kappa_\alpha - d\eta = 0. \end{bmatrix} \tag{A.25}$$

Solving this system, we have (4.12). Lemma 3.B, too, follows from system (A.25). *Q.E.D.*

14 Impact of government on growth and trade

ANNE O. KRUEGER AND
DAVID W. H. ORSMOND

In the 1950s and 1960s, efforts to develop a theory of economic growth proceeded along two main, and largely independent, lines. On one hand, there was a line of research concerned with a theory of economic growth pertaining chiefly to those characteristics believed to be particular to developing countries. On the other hand, neoclassical growth theory was developed, stimulated by the seminal work of Solow.

Initially, the focus of those concerned with the economic growth of the developing countries was primarily upon ways of achieving more rapid capital accumulation in the context of a dual-economy, labor-surplus, model in which a variety of "structural rigidities" and market imperfections were thought to have been responsible for the economic backwardness of developing countries. Attention therefore centered on reasons for backwardness, and the role of government in overcoming market failures.

Neoclassical growth theory, by contrast, was developed on the assumptions that markets function well and that the production function (with at least labor and capital as inputs) had constant returns to scale. Growth in the long run could therefore originate only through technical progress.

Over time, the attention of those seeking a theory of development shifted from a primary concern with capital accumulation in dual economy models to a broader effort to understand the interaction of factor accumulation (including not only physical but also human capital) and government policies in the developing process. This research was stimulated in large part by the experience of developing countries. A key stylized fact was that growth rates were widely divergent among developing countries, and that economic policies – especially with respect to the foreign sector – were one crucial factor that differed between rapidly and slowly growing countries. In the lore of trade and development economists, the fact that Korea's

We thank Ronald W. Jones, T. Dudley Wallace, The Brookings Institution, and participants of the 1991 Interamerican Seminar on Economics (Santiago) for helpful comments.

average annual rate of growth of real GNP rose from under 5 percent in the 1950s to over 10 percent in subsequent decades was associated in part with the shift in the trade and payments regime. By the 1980s, other countries had also experienced large apparent changes in rates of growth and of exports and the empirical regularity appeared confirmed.[1]

By contrast, interest in neoclassical growth models appeared to fade by the late 1960s. The assumption of constant returns to scale evidently implied that economic growth would eventually halt unless new technologies emerged: for any given production function, labor force growth rate, and savings behavior, these models predicted an approach to a steady state per capita income level.

In the mid-1980s, however, Lucas (1988) and Romer (1986) began considering models in which the presence of plausible externalities or increasing returns to scale could explain the continuation of more or less constant growth rates over long time periods. The results were impressive and have led to a revival of interest in growth models, based essentially upon neoclassical premises, but with externalities or increasing returns capable of generating an escape from the "steady state" conclusions of earlier work.[2]

To date, however, the new economic growth models generally assume efficient resource allocation in all economies; sources of differences in growth rates emanate from differences in earlier paths of accumulation and output, but not in the degree to which governmental policies differ or in the efficiency with which resources are consequently allocated. There is a danger that the new economic growth literature and the development economics literature will once again fail to connect.

Recently, Barro (1989 and 1991) began closing the gap by examining the role of governments in new economic growth models, taking into account human capital formation and savings behavior. In his models, government investment expenditures contribute positively to output. Infrastructure is assumed to be effectively provided free of charge to potential users. Barro assumes that more infrastructure augments the productivity of resources in private production. He separates government spending into this "productive spending," from spending on consumption, with the former expected to be positively correlated with growth and the latter negatively. His tests using Summers and Heston's (1988) data from 72 countries bear this out.

In Barro's model, consumption expenditures simply detract from available investible resources. In this paper, we go further, attempting to test the development economist's perceptions of the negative contributions

---

[1] See, for example, Balassa (1989).
[2] For recent extensions, see, for example, Murphy, Shleifer and Vishny (1989) and Romer (1990).

of governmental activities, as well as the positive contributions of other activities, to growth. This paper provides further evidence on the importance of government behavior for economic growth and, in so doing, attempts to start building a bridge between the development economics literature and the new growth theory. The focal point is the recognition that governments do more than spend and tax in manners that maximize social welfare functions: they influence incentives and regulate in ways that affect private behavior, and their spending, even on infrastructure, is not always optimal. A first section outlines some of the stylized facts that have emerged from development economics regarding governmental behavior and its impact on growth. A second section then describes our approach to testing for both positive and negative effects of government activities and describes our data. A third section presents the results. A final section provides some tentative conclusions and suggests further lines of research.

We have been guided in part by Jones's contributions to the evolution of both development theory and to understanding of two-sector models of trade and growth in important ways. He demonstrated how factor market distortions – the result of government interventions that raise the urban wage or lower the cost of capital – could affect the allocation of resources and negatively affect trade (Jones 1971). His contributions to understanding the Heckscher–Ohlin–Samuelson model (Jones 1956, 1965, 1977 and 1979) have provided an analytical underpinning for empirical analysis of the contribution of differences in factor proportions and trade to economic growth.[3] As will be seen below, trade policies – as reflected in our estimates as well as in earlier works in the development literature – do affect growth rates, and an important reason is the opportunities that trade provides for a developing country to use its abundant factors of production effectively.

1. Government policies in developing countries

In practice, many developing countries have adopted economic policies that are highly inimical to economic growth. These include monetary and fiscal policies that result in quadruple digit rates of inflation with in practice an increase in uncertainty and adjustment in relative prices, especially between traded and nontraded goods; expenditure patterns on both consumption and investment that result in a great deal of waste[4]; the

---

[3] See, for example, Krueger (1977).

[4] One of the horror stories emerging from the debt crises of the 1980s was that, in the Philippines, a nuclear power plant built at a cost of $4 billion was never operated. It takes considerable persuasion to convince nonprofessionals that the Philippines were lucky relative to countries where public-sector activities have been the recipients of the most investment, and *do* operate, but fail to cover their operating costs.

construction of parastatal enterprises to undertake manufacturing activities, usually at very high costs; the monopolization of economic activities such as agricultural distribution by the public sector with gross inefficiencies in the delivery of inputs and the collection of outputs; price controls over economic activities; regulation of private investments through licensing; maintenance of overvalued exchange rates and import licensing regimes with strong disincentives for exports and consequent "foreign exchange shortage"; and regulation of the financial system in ways such that real interest rates paid by those receiving funds are strongly negative while many other producers are precluded from borrowing channels.

However, governments also undertake activities that are potentially growth promoting: the construction of essential infrastructure services such as roads, ports, electricity, and telephones; the provision of education and public health facilities; maintenance of law and order; the development of irrigation; and agricultural research and extension services.

In practice, however, not all investment on infrastructure is productive. In part, political-bureaucratic motivations may lead to expenditures and/or employment in infrastructure facilities that are nonoptimal. This can occur because concern is more with maximizing employment than with attaining a social overhead facility at low cost; it can also occur because regional and other political situations cause the location, size, or even sector of the investment to be uneconomic. In developing countries, stories of investments (unmaintained) in four-lane highways without significant traffic, sports stadia, ultramodern airports, new capital cities and in expanding university capacity while leaving many illiterate are too common to ignore. An important issue concerns how criteria can be developed to determine whether government infrastructure activities contribute to or detract from a nation's growth of output.

In addition, government controls, and the incentives they create, affect the output per unit of input, and its growth, in the private sector. That highly overvalued exchange rates, extreme levels of protection, credit rationing, labor market regulations and other measures are important in many developing countries cannot be doubted. Most development practitioners believe, and available evidence suggests, that these practices are important in affecting growth. Again, the question is how to estimate their relative importance.

One question that has arisen repeatedly in the literature on the growth of developing countries has been *why* practices which reduce economic efficiency should also lower the growth rate over time. In the context of a neoclassical framework, after all, economic inefficiencies generated by controls would shrink the production possibility frontier inward and thus affect the level of income; there is no obvious presumed link in theory between the presence of these practices and the growth rate.

Partial answers have been provided. Firstly, controls seem to intensify over time and are thus continuously reducing the productivity of existing and new resources.[5] Secondly, developing countries should be catching up over many years and controls inhibit the process as the approach to the steady-state is greatly slowed down. The new growth theory, with its emphasis on cumulative processes, suggests yet a third reason: if there are externalities in the growth process, anything that slows down the current rate of growth negatively affects the future rate of growth.

A second question is *why* governments would adopt policies inimical to economic growth. Recent advances in the political economy of development policy have suggested a number of answers.[6] In the early development literature, it was implicitly assumed that governments would behave as benevolent social guardians.[7] Experience has shown, however, that governments may instead behave either as "autonomous bureaucratic states" or as "predatory authoritarian states." In the former, the bureaucracy in effect governs and behaves to maximize its power through increasing public employment and the activities undertaken by the state. In the latter, the dictator, or oligarchic ruling group has sufficient political power to extract resources from the economy either directly (through taxation) or indirectly through providing itself services at the expense of the other sectors. There are also governments in which a number of groups compete for political power, and in which the ruling coalition's behavior is constrained by the necessity of maintaining the coalition. In these circumstances, investments and expenditure in particular sectors or regions, or other uses of governmental resources, may in fact be wise investments in maintaining political power despite their low or negative productivity for the economy as a whole.

Findlay and Wilson (1987) modelled the behavior of a predatory government. In their model, the state allocates resources to infrastructure and other goods insofar as it is in its own self-interest to do so. Real national

---

[5] In addition, regulations tend to reduce the flexibility within the economy which may reduce growth to the extent regulations inhibit the realignment over time of inputs between sectors and regions.

[6] See Lal and Myint (forthcoming), and Krueger (forthcoming) for two discussions.

[7] It can plausibly be argued that the motivation of many of the nationalist leaders who led their countries to independence was genuinely idealistic, and that those leaders based their policies on the assumption that their government was and would continue to be committed to maximizing social welfare. Even accepting that motivation, however, it would appear that there has been "bureaucratic capture" of governments in many developing countries, as the administrative apparatus established to implement government controls over the economy created bureaucratic and other interests which then maximized in their own self-interest.

income is a function of private sector inputs and of government expenditures enhancing productivity of the private sector. Findlay and Wilson consider two alternative objective functions the ruler might have. In the first case, the sovereign is constrained by a historically given tax rate and must pay public-sector employees the same wage as is received in the private sector. Subject to this, the sovereign maximizes the surplus, defined as the difference between his tax revenue and his expenditure (when the expenditures indirectly yield additional tax revenue, which is the only reason they are made at all). If this model were correct, the sovereign's expenditures on infrastructure and other investments enhancing private-sector productivity would be suboptimal. In the second version of their model, however, which appears the more plausible, the sovereign's surplus is then spent on other categories of goods – bureaucratic office holders who expand their domain insofar as revenues permit, through, for example, palaces, sports stadia and expanded public employment.

In the Findlay–Wilson model, therefore, government expenditures perform two functions. On one hand, some expenditures enhance the productivity of private sector activity and on the other, some expenditures divert resources from productive uses. Once bureaucratic interests are recognized as a motive in resource allocation, there is no presumption that even investment expenditures will be allocated efficiently. In terms of attempting to estimate the impact of direct government policies, the important challenge is to quantify separately the magnitude of wasteful and of productive expenditures.

Despite the enormous difficulties of segregating various categories of government activities, the presumed importance of the phenomenon in developing countries makes an effort worthwhile. This paper therefore makes a first effort to identify variables that can reflect, at least to some degree, differences in the productivity of different categories of government activities. In addition to those activities that are "directly" reflected in government expenditure accounts, we recognize "indirect" effects on the productivity and growth of private economic activity that arise through controls imposed by the bureaucracy, or the sovereign, over private activity.

2. Quantifying government activities and their effects

The period we cover is from 1976/77 to 1980/81. The choice of time period was determined largely on the basis of data availability.[8] Two other considerations, however, suggest that use of growth rates over that interval makes sense. First, there would be difficulties in using growth rates for the

---

[8] Interestingly, changes in the terms of trade were not a significant determinant of growth over the period and the addition of this variable did not affect the results reported below.

first half of the 1980s because of the differential impact of worldwide conditions on different countries' growth performances. Second, economic policies do change in developing countries.[9]

Our dependent variable is the rate of growth of real GDP over this period, using Summers-Heston (1988) estimates of growth rates. As will be seen, data for proxying unproductive government expenditures are available for at least a few – twenty-six – countries over that period. This group of countries includes eleven relatively developed countries[10] and fifteen developing countries.[11]

We seek to identify the contributions, both positive and negative, of government activities to economic growth. To do so, we need four sets of variables: (1) measures of those government expenditures that enhance private sector output; (2) indicators of those government expenditures that directly reduce private-sector output; (3) indicators of the indirect negative effect of government policies on private sector productivity; and (4) measures of the growth of resources available to the private sector. Here, we describe the measures used.

2.1 *Positive direct effects of government expenditures*

As a potential indicator of the positive product of direct government economic activity the *available* measure – given our negative measure defined below – was the level of output of state-owned enterprises (SOEs). These enterprises cover a range of activities, including provision of power, irrigation and transport (railroads and ports especially) services that presumably enhance private-sector output, although they also include the value added of state marketing boards, and parastatal enterprises engaged in such diverse activities as manufacturing, mining and tourism. Insofar as marketing boards suppress producer prices of agricultural commodities, those activities would not be reflected in measures of the value of their output. Unfortunately, a split between the output of SOEs by major economic activity is not comprehensively available. When public-sector output is produced inefficiently, using a measure of inputs to reflect the negative contribution of government will, we hope, reflect this (see Section 2.2). In the regression results reported below, the variable used is

---

[9] In our sample, Sri Lanka appears to be something of an outlier. A possible explanation may be that in 1977 an election resulted in a change of government, which proceeded to dismantle economic controls and substantially liberalize the economy.

[10] Australia, Austria, Denmark, France, Germany, Ireland, Italy, Netherlands, Portugal, Spain and the U.K.

[11] Benin, Central African Republic, Egypt, Guatemala, India, Kenya, Korea, Liberia, Malawi, Mauritius, Philippines, Sri Lanka, Tanzania, Thailand and Zambia.

public-sector enterprise output as a fraction of nonagricultural GNP.[12] Note that since governments' outputs of nonpriced services are not captured by this proxy, to the extent these contribute to growth, the net direct effect of government is probably biased downward.

2.2 Direct government expenditures that are wasteful

In all models of government behavior, the resources employed by government subtract from those available for private economic activity. For that reason, we use the ratio of public-sector employment to total nonagricultural employment as a proxy for the negative direct impact of government expenditures. Clearly, if the output of state-owned enterprises is a reasonably valid proxy for the positive effects of government expenditures, then a measure of the resources used by government can serve as an indicator of the negative impact of government: estimating the sign and magnitude of the "net" direct effect can then be undertaken by combining the two impacts.[13]

2.3 Indirect negative effects of government

The governmental economic policies that affect the efficiency of private-sector resource allocation may also affect economic growth. Many of these policies have been analyzed and quantified for particular groups of developing countries in the literature.[14]

Two sets of policies whose effects have been shown to be strongly negative are those affecting the trade and payments regime and those which suppress the financial sector. We sought proxies that might reflect the extent to which the credit market and the foreign-exchange market were, in the period under review, distorted by government policies. In the case of the trade and payments regime, we use the percentage premium of the black-market exchange rate[15] relative to the official exchange rate. Although no measure is perfect, there is reason to believe that there is a significant relationship between the height of the black market premium and the restrictiveness of the trade regime.[16] An alternative approach might

[12] There are few available estimates of the values of SOE output on a consistent basis across countries. We use data from Short (1984) and Nair and Filippides (1988). These estimates generally pertain to the 1976–80 period.

[13] No international organization publishes data separately identifying public employment. The most comprehensive data are available in Heller and Tait (1984) and pertain for most countries to 1979 or 1980.

[14] See Little, Scitovsky and Scott (1970) for the first major cross-country analysis. See also Bhagwati (1978) and Krueger (1978, 1983) for trade policies, McKinnon (1991) for financial policies, and Krueger, Schiff and Valdes (1988) for agricultural pricing policies.

[15] Data from *World Currency Yearbook* (formerly Pick's) were collated by Wood (1991). We use Wood's data.

have been to attempt to estimate deviations of real exchange rates from some base year purchasing-power-parity exchange rate. The difficulty with this procedure would have been to attempt to identify reasonably comparable base years across countries.

For the financial market, governments often ration credit through controls upon interest rates and through instructions, or "guidance," as to how banks should allocate their lending across economic activities. There is clearly more scope for such guidance the lower the nominal interest rate relative to the one which would clear the market. To reflect this across countries, we constructed a measure of the real interest rate by taking in general the deposit interest rate deflated by the inflation rate in the estimation period.[17]

Clearly, the expectation is that the estimated coefficient on the real interest rate will be positive: the less negative it is, the less likely is credit to be misallocated across economic activities. For the black-market premium, the coefficient is expected to be negative: a larger premium presumably reflects a more negative effect on output and growth.

2.4 Growth in private sector resources

Here, we seek to be as traditional as possible, and consistent with measures used by Barro and others. The importance of human capital has been recognized by both development economists and the new growth theorists. Indeed, in the works of Romer and others, education may be one source of externalities. Romer (1986) and others believe that growth rates should be positively associated with the initial level of human capital stock. For the countries we include in our estimates, we take the enrollment in secondary school as a proportion of the population age 12–17 in 1965 as our variable.[18]

In general, the initial level of capital stock is expected to be positively correlated with the level of per capita income and, if there are externalities, with growth. The rate of growth of the capital stock ought to be positively correlated with the growth rate. We constructed two measures to take this into account. A real capital stock index was calculated using perpetual inventory methods, taking the 1960 ratio of GDP to investment as having reflected the capital-output ratio at that time, and then adding new investment and depreciating capital for subsequent years, using Summers

---

[16] The magnitude of the premium may also be affected by domestic residents' attempts to diversify their wealth portfolios, rather than the outcome of direct trade controls.

[17] Estimates were also made using the GDP deflator, rather than the consumer price index, as an estimator of inflation. There was no difference in results.

[18] Data were obtained from World Bank (1990).

and Heston data. For the second measure, we took a simple average of real investment to GDP ratios for the 1960–76 period, as used by Barro. Neither variable proved helpful: the signs were negative, sometimes significantly so. It is not clear why this occurred, and the capital stock variable was omitted from the regression estimates reported below.

3. Results

The regression estimates are shown in Table 14.1. The first equation reports the results when the average real rate of growth is related only to the initial (logged) level of average per capita income in 1976/77, public-sector employment, and output of public-sector enterprises. As can be seen, only public-sector employment is significant: a one percentage point increase in the ratio of government employment to the nonagricultural labor force reduces the estimated rate of growth by eight one hundredths of one percent.

The second equation adds proxies for the effects of the trade and payments regime and credit rationing on the growth rate. These variables are highly significant and add greatly to the explanatory power of the estimating equation. In addition, when controlling for employment effects, an increase in the share of state-owned enterprises in nonagricultural output is positively and significantly related to growth. Public employment is significantly negatively related as before. These results are certainly consistent with the hypothesis that direct government activities contain a positive component (output) and a negative component. As expected, a one percentage point higher real interest rate is associated with a 0.24 percent increase in the real rate of growth. The black market premium, also as expected, has a significant negative impact on the growth rate.

Including both direct and indirect effects of governmental activities alone in equation (3) results in an equation capable of accounting for just under 50 percent of the variation in output growth rates, which suggests the importance of both direct and indirect government activities upon the rate of growth. The signs, magnitude, and significance of the direct output effects remain much the same as before and conform again to the Findlay–Wilson hypothesis.

The fourth and fifth equations in Table 14.1 incorporate the human capital variable into the estimation. Education is in general positively related to growth, although it is not significant at the 90 percent level and is unstable for changes in the number of regressors.

Table 14.2 provides estimates of the predicted direct and indirect effects of government activities on per capita output growth in the 26 countries, using the results of equation (3) from Table 14.1. In computing predicted

Table 14.1. *Estimation results: dependent variable GDPPCDOT*

Indep. var.	Regression number				
	(1)	(2)	(3)	(4)	(5)
Constant	4.65	8.52**	3.23***	15.23***	3.56***
	(1.11)	(2.32)	(4.46)	(2.90)	(3.01)
LGDPPC76	−0.10	−0.61		−1.70**	
	(0.21)	(1.47)		(2.27)	
PUBEMP	−0.08***	−0.07***	−0.06***	−0.08***	−0.06**
	(2.86)	(3.34)	(2.94)	(3.74)	(2.79)
SOEGDP	0.04	0.15**	0.13**	0.13**	0.13**
	(0.80)	(2.78)	(2.43)	(2.60)	(2.39)
REALINT		0.24**	0.21*	0.19*	0.22*
		(2.21)	(1.92)	(1.74)	(1.89)
BMPREM		−0.04**	−0.04*	−0.04**	−0.04*
		(2.47)	(2.05)	(2.39)	(2.02)
SECEDN				0.05	−0.01
				(1.72)	(0.36)
Summary Statistics:					
DoF.	22	20	21	19	20
Adj. RSQ	0.30	0.51	0.48	0.55	0.46
F-Stat.	4.62**	6.20***	6.83***	6.16***	5.26***
SSE	81.70	52.22	57.84	45.21	57.48

NB: Numbers in brackets are *t*-statistics
     * significant at 90 percent level
    ** significant at 95 percent level
   *** significant at 99 percent level

Data definitions:
GDPPCDOT: average percentage per annum growth rate over 1976/77 to 1980/81
LGDPPC76: log of average per capita income 1976/77
PUBEMP: percentage share of public to total non-agricultural employment
SOEGDP: percentage share of output of SOEs to total non-agricultural output
REALINT: deposit interest rate deflated by CPI
BMPREM: percentage premium of black over official exchange rate
SECEDN: percentage secondary school enrollments to total in age group

Table 14.2. *Predicted direct and indirect government effects*

	Actual growth rate	Government effects			Diff. actual to pred.
		Direct	Indirect	Total	
Developed Countries:					
Australia	1.6	−0.3	−0.2	−0.5	−1.1
Austria	2.5	0.7	0.3	1.0	−1.7
Denmark	1.7	−0.7	−0.0	−0.8	−0.8
France	2.2	−0.4	−0.6	−1.0	−0.1
Germany	2.8	0.2	0.1	0.3	−0.7
Ireland	3.5	−0.3	−0.7	−1.0	1.2
Italy	4.0	−0.1	−0.5	−0.6	1.3
Netherlands	1.3	−0.6	0.2	−0.4	−1.6
Portugal	3.3	1.6	−1.6	0.1	−0.0
Spain	2.2	−0.3	−0.8	−1.1	0.1
United Kingdom	1.5	−0.3	−0.9	−1.2	−0.6
Developing Countries:					
Benin	−0.2	−3.0	−0.4	−3.5	0.0
Cent. Afr. Rep.	−1.6	−1.0	−1.1	−2.0	−2.8
Egypt	5.5	2.8	−2.3	0.5	1.8
Guatemala	1.7	−0.8	−0.1	−0.9	−0.6
India	1.2	−2.2	0.1	−2.1	0.1
Kenya	1.6	−0.6	−1.8	−2.4	0.8
Korea, Rep. of	3.6	0.1	0.2	0.2	0.2
Liberia	−2.9	−2.0	−3.1	−5.1	−0.9
Malawi	−0.2	−0.2	−3.1	−3.4	−0.0
Mauritius	−0.4	−1.8	−0.5	−2.3	−1.3
Philippines	2.8	−1.2	−0.8	−2.0	1.5
Sri Lanka	4.5	−0.8	−1.5	−2.3	3.6
Tanzania	−0.1	−0.7	−4.9	−5.6	2.3
Thailand	4.5	−0.6	−0.1	−0.6	1.9
Zambia	−4.5	1.1	−5.7	−4.6	−3.1
Simple Averages:					
Developed	2.4	−0.0	−0.4	−0.5	−0.4
Developing	1.0	−0.7	−1.7	−2.4	0.2
Total	1.6	−0.4	−1.1	−1.6	−0.0

Sources: Calculated from regression (3) in Table 14.1
Differences calculated taking the actual less the total predicted value less the constant

growth, the constant term and effects of government activities are included. As is readily apparent, governments appear in many countries to have a large negative impact upon economic growth. The elasticities of public-sector employment and state-owned enterprise output, examined at the means, are negative 1.28 and positive 1.01 percent, indicating that a proportionate rise in both has a relatively small net negative effect upon output growth.

The indirect effects are generally larger than the direct effects (averaging around minus one percentage point) and range from plus 0.3 percent to minus 5.7 percent. The elasticities of changes in the real interest rate and the exchange premium are 0.31 and negative 0.37 percent respectively.

Those countries for which actual growth deviated most from the predicted rate include Sri Lanka, Tanzania, Zambia and the Central African Republic. Sri Lanka, as already mentioned, underwent a strong liberalization program starting in 1977. Tanzania, the CAR and Zambia experienced declines in their growth rates in the early 1980s.

Evaluated at their means, both the direct and the indirect effects of government are more negative in developing compared with developed countries. Indeed, according to these estimates, the difference in actual growth rates between the two groups was more than accounted for by the difference in government policies. Stated another way, the fifteen developing countries for which the relevant data were available experienced on (unweighted) average about 1.4 percent less annual average growth in per-capita income than did the developed countries. If these estimates are used as a basis for computation, if developing countries' governments' activities had been the same as those of developed countries, the former's growth rates would have been 0.5 percentage points higher than the latter's.

4. Conclusions

Equations which use a growth rate as a dependent variable are notoriously difficult because of the inherent problems in specifying the underlying model correctly, and even of estimating the "true" growth rate. The results presented here are highly tentative. Perhaps the surprise should be that any variables were strongly significant, and yet the apparent impact of governmental activities on output growth show up strongly across the forms of the equations used here.

In light of data limitations, these results are clearly preliminary. They strongly point to the need for further research into the combined impact of factor accumulation and government activities upon economic growth. A major barrier to that research is the lack of the relevant data on anything like a comparable basis across countries. We hope that our contribution may stimulate not only further analysis using other sources of data, but also spur the development of better and more consistent data across countries covering the role of government in the economy.

References

Balassa, Bela 1989 "Outward Orientation," in Hollis Chenery and T. N. Srinivasan, *Handbook of Development Economics, Vol. 1*, Amsterdam, North-Holland.

Barro, Robert J. 1989 "A Cross Country Study of Growth, Saving, and Government," NBER Working Paper No. 2855, February.

"Economic Growth in a Cross Section of Countries," *Quarterly Journal of Economics*, 106, 2, 407–43.

Bhagwati, Jagdish N. 1978 *Foreign Trade Regimes and Economic Development: Anatomy and Consequences of Exchange Control*, Ballinger Press for the NBER, Lexington, Mass.

Chenery, Hollis and Alan M. Strout 1966 "Foreign Assistance and Economic Development," *American Economic Review*, 56, 4, 679–733.

Fei, John C. H. and Gustav Ranis 1964 *Development of the Labor Surplus Economy*, Richard D. Irwin, Homewood Illinois.

Findlay, Ronald and John D. Wilson 1987 "The Political Economy of Leviathan," in Assaf Razin and Efraim Sadka, *Economic Policy in Theory and Practice*, Macmillan Press Ltd, London.

Heller, Peter S. and Alan A. Tait 1984 "Government Employment and Pay: Some International Comparisons," International Monetary Fund Occasional Paper No. 24, Washington DC, March.

International Monetary Fund 1990 *International Financial Statistics Yearbook*, Washington, DC.

Jones, Ronald W. 1956 "Factor Proportions and the Heckscher–Ohlin Theorem", *Review of Economic Studies*, 24, October, 63, Reprinted in Jones (1979)

1965 "The Structure of Simple General Equilibrium Models," *Journal of Political Economy*, 73, December, 557–72. Reprinted in Jones (1979).

1971 "Distortions in Factor Markets and the General Equilibrium Model of Production," *Journal of Political Economy*, 79, 3, May–June, 437–59.

1977 "Two-ness in Trade Theory: Costs and Benefits," Princeton Special Papers in International Economics, Princeton. Reprinted in Jones (1979).

1979 *International Trade: Essays in Theory*, North-Holland, Amsterdam.

Krueger, Anne O. 1977 *Growth, Distortions, and Patterns of Trade among Many Countries*, Princeton Studies in International Finance No. 40, Princeton.

1978 *Foreign Trade Regimes and Economic Development: Liberalization Attempts and Consequences*, Ballinger Press for the NBER, Lexington, MA.

1983 *Trade and Employment in Developing Countries: Vol. 3. Synthesis*, University of Chicago Press for the NBER, Chicago.

(forthcoming) *The Political Economy of Economic Policies in Developing Countries*, MIT Press, Cambridge, MA.

Krueger, Anne O., Maurice Schiff and Alberto Valdes 1988 "Agricultural Incentives in Developing Countries: Measuring the Effect of Sectoral and Economywide Policies," *World Bank Economic Review*, 2, 3 (September), 251–73.

Jorgenson, Dale 1961 "The Development of a Dual Economy," *Economic Journal*, 71, September, 309–44.

Lal, Deepak and Hla Myint (forthcoming) *The Political Economy of Poverty, Equity and Growth*, World Bank Comparative Studies, Oxford University Press, Oxford.

Lewis, W. Arthur 1954 "Economic Growth with Unlimited Supplies of Labor," *Manchester School*, 22, 139–91.

Little, I. M. D., Tibor Scitovsky and Maurice Scott 1970 *Industry and Trade in Some Developing Countries*, Oxford University Press, Oxford.

Lucas, Robert 1988 "On the Mechanics of Economic Development," *Journal of Monetary Economics*, 22, 1 (July), 3–42.

McKinnon, Ronald I. 1991 *The Order of Economic Liberalization: Financial Control in the Transition to a Market Economy*, Johns Hopkins, Baltimore, Maryland.

Murphy, Kevin, Andre Shleifer and N. Vishny 1989 "Industrialization and the Big Push," *Journal of Political Economy*, 97, 1003–26.

Nair, Goviudan and Anastasios Filippides 1988 "How much do State Owned Enterprises Contribute to Public Sector Deficits?" World Bank Policy Planning and Research Working Papers, No. 45. December.

Romer, Paul M. 1986 "Increasing Returns and Long-Run Growth," *Journal of Political Economy*, 94, 5 (October), 1002–37.

  1990 "Are Non-Convexities Important for Understanding Growth?" *American Economic Review*, 80, 2, 97–103.

Short, R. P. 1984 "The Role of Public Enterprises in International Statistical Comparisons," in Robert H. Floyd, Clive S. Gray and R. P. Short, *Public Enterprises in Mixed Economies: Some Macro Aspects*, International Monetary Fund, Washington DC.

Solow, Robert M. 1956 "A Contribution to the Theory of Economic Growth," *Quarterly Journal of Economics*, 770, 675–94.

Summers, Robert and Alan Heston 1988 "A New Set of International Comparisons of Real Product and Price Level Estimates for 130 Countries, 1950–85," in *Review of Income and Wealth*, Series 34, No. 1 (March).

Wood, Adrian 1991 "Global Trends in Real Exchange Rates: 1960–84, *World Development*, 19, 4, 317–32.

World Bank 1990 *World Development Report 1990*, World Bank, Washington.

15 Long-run production frontiers for the Jones specific-factors model with optimal capital accumulation

JAMES R. MARKUSEN
AND RICHARD MANNING

1. Introduction

For those of us who received our classroom instruction in international trade theory prior to 1971, the 2×2 Heckscher–Ohlin model of trade constituted our "basic training." The two-good, two-factor model with both factors perfectly mobile between the two sectors was *the* simple general-equilibrium model of factor proportions trade (simple one-factor Ricardian models constituted a technology-based explanation of trade). It is not clear what the justification for this exclusive focus was, but it is certainly true that the four theorems derived from that model constitute an elegant statement of theory: the Heckscher–Ohlin theorem, the factor-price-equalization theorem, the Rybczynski theorem, and the Stolper–Samuelson theorem.

In 1971, Ronald Jones published his paper, "A Three Factor Model in Theory, Trade, and History," in which two goods are produced with three factors, two of which are sector specific and one of which is mobile between sectors. Jones expressed several motivations for this model. First, it removed the "straightjacket" of factor-price equalization, in that factor prices now depend on factor supplies as well as on commodity prices. Second, Jones found the model consistent with recent articles (at the time) in economic history and the theory of capital and international trade.

Gradually, the Jones specific-factors model[1] has become more and more

Richard Manning and I derived some of the basic results in this paper when I was a visitor in New Zealand in 1981 and he was a visitor in Canada in 1982. Years apart interrupted the work, and we picked up the topic when Richard and I were again together in 1989. But the co-authorship was interrupted for good when Richard died of cancer on November 25, 1989. I have completed the present version without him, and the paper is no doubt poorer for it. Richard was a fine scholar and a very dear friend. He is greatly missed. JRM.

Thanks to JoAnne Feeney for comments and suggestions.
[1] Some have referred to this model as a "Ricardo-Viner" model, but neither author formulated a clear statement of such a model and its properties. Further, the model would surely not have attained its present popularity (arguably, it would never have been articulated) without Jones' 1971 paper. I will refer to it as the Jones specific-factors model.

popular, both for pedagogic and for research purposes. The model in my opinion is now used at least as often as the Heckscher–Ohlin model to teach the simple general-equilibrium theory of trade. Several reasons for this popularity are found in later papers by Mayer (1974), Mussa (1974), and Neary (1978). First, the Jones specific-factors (JSF) model does not produce a conflict of interest between workers and capital owners with respect to protection in a given industry. It thus seems far more consistent with observed behavior than the Heckscher–Ohlin (HO) model.

Second, Neary showed that some of the disturbing paradoxes derived by earlier authors are due to the assumption of intersectoral capital mobility. Those results disappear with sector-specific capital, or correspond to dynamically unstable equilibria if the economy adjusts according to a short-run capital specificity hypothesis. Third, Neary argued that some factors are fixed (sector specific) in the short run while factor endowments vary in the long run, leading him to suggest that the HO production model "bears little or no relation to any economically relevant time horizon" (Neary, 1978, p. 509).

The purpose of this paper is to pick up on this last point, and develop a simple dynamic model which is offered as a long-run extension of the JSF. Capital is accumulated endogenously, and the long run is defined as the steady-state equilibrium for given exogenous parameters. Our motivation for the comparison of the Jones model with the steady state is based on the idea that capital is sector-specific (vintage) once created, and therefore that capital can only be shifted by new investment and depreciation. The relevant short-run versus long-run comparison is between the JSF model and the steady state, not between the HO model and the steady state: as noted by Neary, the HO model is relevant to neither the short run nor the long run.

Two versions of the model are presented. In the first, one specific factor is endogenously accumulated, while in the second, both specific factors are endogenously accumulated. In the latter case, the two specific factors need not be identical (i.e., produced with identical technologies and subject to identical depreciation rates) but if they are, the model is also a "longer-run" version of the HO model. In both our versions, capital is optimally accumulated in that consumers maximize the present value of an intertemporal utility function.

With one specific factor accumulated endogenously, the steady-state locus of outputs is constructed from points on the family of JSF production frontiers, one for each level of the endogenous factor K. We show that the steady-state locus of outputs cuts the short-run (the JSF) production frontier at a steady-state equilibrium and that the equilibrium price ratio is equal to the slope of the JSF production frontier at that equilibrium. The direction of trade in the steady state is determined by the ratio of the endowments of the primary factors alone (thus removing one of the ambiguities of the JSF model). Factor-price equalization holds in the steady-state subject to the usual HO restriction of diversification. Comparative steady-state Rybczynski and Stolper–Samuelson relationships differ slightly from the corresponding comparative-statics theorems in the HO model. The long-run responses of outputs to changes in commodity prices and primary factor endowments are shown to be more elastic in the long run than in the short run.

With both specific factors accumulated endogenously, the steady-state conditions imply a unique commodity price ratio at which the economy will produce both goods. This is true regardless of whether or not both capital goods are produced with the same technology. We then show that the steady-state locus of outputs is linear, a result that is a dynamic version of Samuelson's (1951) non-substitution theorem, in that the economy has only one primary factor. Again, the slope of the steady-state locus is not equal to the diversification price ratio, with the wedge between the two dependent on the capital intensities of the two goods, and the technologies for producing the two capital goods. If the latter are identical (production functions and depreciation rates) then the direction of the wedge depends only on the capital intensities of the final goods. In this case we can also provide a contrast among the three frontiers at a particular steady-state solution: the JSF, HO and steady-state loci.

2. One capital good endogenous

Two goods, X_1 and X_2, are produced from three factors: L, which is mobile between sectors, K_1, which is capital specific to X_1, and K_2, which is specific to X_2. K_1 is endogenously accumulated in the long run. To retain the spirit of the JSF model, I will assume that capital is not produced by a separate production function, but rather the capital good is assembled costlessly from the two final goods. Y will denote new production of K_1. p_1, p_2 and q denote the prices of X_1, X_2 and Y respectively. w, r_1 and r_2 are the wage rate and the rental rates on K_1 and K_2 respectively. c_1, c_2, and c_k will denote the unit cost functions for X_1, X_2 and Y respectively. The production functions for the two final goods, the labor supply constraint, and the implied efficient transformation function for given factor supplies are as follows.

$$X_1 = F_1(L_1, K_1) \quad c_1 = c_1(w, r_1) \tag{1}$$

$$X_2 = F_2(L_2, K_2) \quad c_2 = c_2(w, r_2) \tag{2}$$

$$L = L_1 + L_2 \tag{3}$$

$$T(X_1, X_2, L, K_1, K_2) = 0 \tag{4}$$

Let X_{1K} and X_{2K} denote the inputs into the production of new K_1.

$$Y = G(X_{1K}, X_{2K}) \quad c_k = c_k(p_1, p_2) \tag{5}$$

With three goods, one of which is produced only with the other two, countries will generally specialize in two of them unless the production functions for Y are identical, in which case there is an indeterminacy in trade (e.g., you can import Y or import X_1 and X_2 and assemble K_1). To avoid this problem, we will simply assume that Y must be created at home ("assembled on site") so that only X_1 and X_2 are traded. To focus on steady state production and on a meaningful comparison with the short-run production, we will also impose current account clearing on the model (discussed more in Manning and Markusen 1991). The (instantaneous) balance-of-payments constraint then requires that gross production minus capital formation equal consumption.

$$p_1(X_1 - X_{1K}) + p_2(X_2 - X_{2K}) = p_1 C_1 + p_2 C_2 \tag{6}$$

where C_1 and C_2 are the consumption levels of the two final goods. Consumers maximize the standard separable intertemporal utility function

$$V = \int_0^\infty e^{-\rho t} U(C_{1t}, C_{2t}) dt \tag{7}$$

where ρ is the rate of time preference. The time subscript on C will be dropped in what follows. Finally, the equation of motion for the stock variable K_1 is given by the standard equation

$$\dot{K}_1 = Y - \delta K \tag{8}$$

where δ is the constant depreciation rate.

Let μ_1, μ_2, μ_3, λ be the multipliers associated with (4), (6), (5) and (8) respectively. Competitive equilibrium is the solution to the first-order necessary conditions for an interior optimum, maximizing (7) subject to (4), (5), (6) and (8).

$$U_i - \mu_2 p_i = 0 \quad i = 1, 2 \tag{9}$$

$$\mu_1 T_i + \mu_2 p_i = 0 \quad i = 1, 2 \tag{10}$$

$$-\mu_2 p_i - \mu_3 G_i = 0 \quad i = 1, 2 \tag{11}$$

$$\lambda + \mu_3 = 0 \tag{12}$$

$$\dot{\lambda} = (\rho + \delta)\lambda - \mu_1 T_{K1} = 0. \tag{13}$$

From (10) we get the maximization of GNP $= p_1 X_1 + p_2 X_2$ for fixed K_1

(i.e., a tangency between the price ratio and the JSF frontier [Manning and Markusen, 1991]). From (11) we get cost minimization in the production of Y. Maximization of GNP in turn implies that the rental rate on $K_1(r_1)$ is related to the price of each final good by

$$r_1 = -p_i(T_{K1}/T_i) \quad i = 1, 2. \tag{14}$$

From (10), we have $(p_i/T_i) = -\mu_1 \mu_2$ so

$$r_1 = (\mu_1/\mu_2)T_{K1}. \tag{15}$$

By setting (13) equal to zero in the steady state, we get $\mu_1 T_{K1} = (\rho + \delta)\lambda$ and from (12) $\lambda = -\mu_3$.

$$r_1 = -(\mu_3/\mu_2)(\rho + \delta) = (\rho + \delta)p_i/G_i \tag{16}$$

where the second equality follows from (11). Cost minimization and competition imply $p_i/G_i = c_k(p_1, p_2) = q$. We then have

$$r_1 = (\rho + \delta)c_k(p_1, p_2) = (\rho + \delta)q. \tag{17}$$

The rental rate on K_1 is equal to $(\rho + \delta)$ times the price of a new unit of $K(Y)$.

We now turn to the relationship between the supply price ratio and outputs in the steady state. Let X_2 be numeraire so that $p_2 = 1 = c_2(w, r_2)$. The price-equals-unit-cost equation for X_1 can then be written as follows using (17).

$$p_1 = c_1(w, r_1) = c_1(w, (\rho + \delta)c_k(p_1, 1)) \tag{18}$$

$$dp_1 = c_{1w}dw + c_{1r}(\rho + \delta)c_{k1}dp_1$$

$$= c_{1w}dw + \left[\frac{c_{1r}r_1}{p_1}\right]\left[\frac{(\rho + \delta)}{r_1}\right]c_{k1}p_1 dp_1 \tag{19}$$

$$dp_1 = c_{1w}dw + \left[\frac{c_{1r}r_1}{p_1}\right]\left[\frac{c_{k1}p_1}{q}\right]dp_1 = c_{1w}dw + (s_{K_1 X_1})(s_{X_1 Y})dp_1 \tag{20}$$

$$(1 - (s_{K_1 X_1})(s_{X_1 Y}))dp_1 = c_{1w}dw \tag{21}$$

where s_{ij} is the share of (good or factor) i in the production of good j. Since the shares are each less than one, the term in brackets on the left-hand side of (21) is positive, and hence dp_1 and dw are positively related. With p_2 numeraire and K_2 fixed, w depends only on the labor allocation to X_2. An increase in w corresponds to a shift of labor to X_1. Equation (21) thus tells us that the supply price ratio p_1 increases as we move along the steady-state production frontier to greater levels of X_1 output. Thus the price–output relationship is "normal."

Second, note that an increase in p_1 holding K_1 constant increases the labor allocation to X_1 (a movement along the short-run production frontier) and thus increases r_1/p_1, a well-known result of the JSF model. Thus to restore the economy to a new steady-state equilibrium at the new price ratio $(r_1 = (\rho + \delta)c_k(p_1, 1))$ K_1 must rise (the cost function c_k is concave in p_1 by the usual properties). Thus K_1 rises as the price ratio p_1 increases and we move to higher levels of X_1 production along the locus of steady-state outputs.

Now turn to the slope of the steady-state locus and the relationship between that slope and the price ratio (equal to the slope of the short-run JSF frontier) at a steady-state equilibrium. Differentiating (1) and (2), we have the slope of the steady-state locus.

$$dX_2 = F_{2L}dL_2 = -F_{2L}dL_1, \quad dX_1 = F_{1L}dL_1 + F_{1K}dK_1 \quad (22)$$

$$-\frac{dX_2}{dX_1} = \frac{F_{2L}/F_{1L}}{(1 + (F_{1K}/F_{1L})(dK_1/dL_1))} = \frac{p_1}{(1 + (F_{1K}/F_{1L})(dK_1/dL_1))} \quad (23)$$

GNP maximization (for given K_1) implied by (10) in turn implies that the ratio of the marginal products of labor in X_1 and X_2 equals the price ratio p_1. We previously established that K_1 and L_1 move together in the steady-state, so $(dK_1/dL_1 > 0)$. Note finally from (10) that the price ratio is the slope of the relevant JSF production frontier passing through the steady-state equilibrium point. We have the long-run or steady-state marginal rate of transformation (MRT_{ss}) related to the equilibrium price ratio by

$$MRT_{ss} = -dX_2/dX_1 < p_1 = MRT_{jsf} \quad (24)$$

where MRT_{jsf} is the marginal rate of transformation along the JSF production frontier.

The situation is shown in Figure 15.1, where there are two production frontiers through a steady-state equilibrium point A, with associated price ratio $p_1{}^a$. JJ' denotes the JSF production frontier through A, with K_1 being held constant at the steady-state level associated with A. SS' in Figure 15.1 denotes the steady state production frontier. SS' cuts JJ' and its tangent price ratio at A (equation (24)). The two production frontiers coincide on the X_2 axis, since X_2 uses only the two primary factors. The intuition behind the non-tangency of p_1 and MRT_{ss} results from the fact that capital is costly to accumulate. At the tangency point $p_1 = MRT_{ss}$, a small movement up the frontier generates (locally) no reduction in the value of

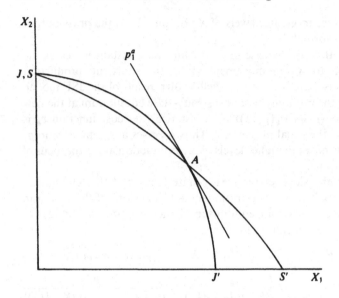

Figure 15.1

gross production but a gain in consumption and utility by consuming the implied reduction in K_1. Thus the tangency point cannot be an equilibrium.

Two other points are of some interest. With respect to the denominator of (23), note first that $F_{1K}/F_{1L} = r_1/w$, and that this denominator can be written as

$$1 + \left[\frac{r_1 K_1}{w L_1}\right]\left[\frac{dK_1/K_1}{dL_1/L_1}\right].$$

Consider a special case where Y is produced from X_1 only. Our result in (17) then implies that the ratio r_1/p_1 is constant at all points on the steady-state locus (c_k is homogeneous of degree one in p_1). But r_1/p_1 is only a function of the ratio in which factors are used in X_1. Thus the K_1/L_1 ratio in X_1 must be constant along the steady-state locus. This in turn implies that factor shares are constant and that the second term in brackets is one. The wedge between p and the MRT_{ss} is constant and larger as the share of capital in X_1 is larger. Second, note that a higher rate of time preference implies a higher rental rate r_1 at a given p_1. At any given price ratio, an increase in ρ implies a deaccumulation of capital and a new steady-state equilibrium interior to the old locus. Different values of ρ generate a family of loci, intersecting on the X_2 axis but otherwise loci corresponding to higher ρ lying interior to those corresponding to lower ρ.

Now consider the long-run versions of the Stolper–Samuelson and Rybczynski relationships, which are themselves modified in the JSF model from the original versions in the HO model (see Jones 1965). Using X_2 as numeraire as before, the price/cost equilibrium conditions are

$$p_1 = c_1(w, (\rho + \delta)c_k(p_1, 1)), \quad 1 = c_2(w, r_2). \tag{26}$$

Holding p_1 constant, we see that there is a unique w that solves the first equation, implying a unique r_2 that satisfies the second equation at constant prices. Suppose that we give the economy more L. With K_2 fixed, the second equation implies that all of the additional L must go to X_1. But then K_1 must be accumulated in exactly the same proportion in order to satisfy the first equation of (26). X_1 must rise more than in proportion to L while X_2 is constant.

$$dX_1/X_1 = dL/L_1 > dL/L > 0 = dX_2/X_2. \tag{27}$$

Now consider an increase in K_2. L must be shifted to X_2 in exactly the same proportion in order to satisfy the second equation of (26), so X_2 must increase in proportion to K_2. But then K_1 must decrease in proportion to the loss of L in X_1, so X_1 must fall.

$$dX_2/X_2 = dK_2/K_2 > 0 > dX_1/X_1. \tag{28}$$

It follows from these results that if two countries have identical technologies and identical rates of time preference, the direction of trade can be predicted by the differences in the relative endowments of the two primary factors between countries. With identical technologies and time preference, the two countries have identical production frontiers if they have identical endowments of L and K_2 (steady state conditions then imply the same value of K_1). (27) then notes that a change in L unambiguously shifts production to X_1 contrary to the ambiguous result in the JSF model. An increase in K_2 shifts production to X_2 which is consistent with the JSF model, although (28) shows that the output response is more pronounced in the long-run ($dK_2/K_2 > dX_2/X_2$ in the JSF model).

Factor-price equalization also holds in the steady state, subject to the usual condition that countries are diversified, as is clear from (26). Commodity prices determine r_1 and w. w in turn determines r_2.

Consider finally the long-run version of the Stolper–Samuelson relationship between commodity and factor prices. By substituting for r_1 from (17), the total differential of the price/cost equation for X_1 is given by

$$dp_1 = c_{1w}dw + c_{1r}(\rho + \delta)c_{k1}dp_1 \qquad (29)$$

$$\frac{dp_1}{p_1} = \frac{c_{1w}w}{p_1}\frac{dw}{w} + \frac{c_1 r_1}{p_1}\frac{(\rho + \delta)}{r_1}c_{k1}p_1\frac{dp_1}{p_1}. \qquad (30)$$

Replacing $(\rho + \delta)/r_1$ with $1/q$, we then get an expression in terms of shares.

$$dp_1/p_1 = s_{L_1 X_1}(dw/w) + s_{K_1 X_1}s_{X_1 Y}(dp_1/p_1) \qquad (31)$$

$$\frac{dw/w}{dp_1/p_1} = \frac{(1 - s_{K_1 X_1}s_{X_1 Y})}{s_{L_1 X_1}} > \frac{(1 - s_{K_1 X_1})}{s_{L_1 X_1}} = \frac{s_{L_1 X_1}}{s_{L_1 X_1}} = 1 \qquad (32)$$

if both X_1 and X_2 have positive shares in the production of Y. Equation (32) gives the result that the wage rate rises more than in proportion to p_1, and this must in turn imply that r_1 rises less than in proportion to p_1 (r_1 must rise by (17)). Labor is drawn away from X_2 so r_2 must fall. We then have a Stolper–Samuelson type result.

$$\frac{dw}{w} > \frac{dp_1}{p_1} > \frac{dr_1}{r_1} > 0 > \frac{dr_2}{r_2}. \qquad (33)$$

Contrast this with the chain of inequalities for the (short-run) JSF model.

$$\frac{dr_1}{r_1} > \frac{dp_1}{p_1} > \frac{dw}{w} > 0 > \frac{dr_2}{r_2}. \qquad (34)$$

In the short run, the specific factor is the big gainer and the effect on labor's real income is ambiguous. In the long run, K_1 is accumulated to the point where its real return is ambiguous and labor is the clear gainer. It is interesting to compare the results of (27), (28), and (33) to those of the original HO theorems, and think of L and K_2 being the two primary factors in the long run, X_2 being intensive in K_2 and X_1 being intensive in L. (33) is then exactly the Stolper–Samuelson theorem. (27) and (28) differ somewhat, however, from the Rybczynski theorem. Reciprocity breaks down in this case because, while (27) and (28) give the changes in outputs in response to endowment changes at constant commodity prices, (33) and (34) do *not* give the changes in factor prices in response to commodity price changes at constant endowments.

A final point that follows from the previous results is that both output responses to price changes and output responses to endowment changes are more elastic in the long run than in the short run. This finding is consistent with the general duality results of Neary (1985), Markusen and Svensson (1985), Neary and Ruane (1988) and Manning and Markusen (1991). The output–price response result is very straightforward, since the long-run response is the sum of the short-run response, and the response due to the change in the capital stock at constant prices. It is clear from our earlier results, for example, that an increase in p_1 increases X_1 at constant K_1 (the short-run effect), but in the long run K_1 increases, generating a Rybczynski-type effect that reinforces the increase in X_1 and the decrease in X_2.

The output–endowment response result is clear from (27) and (28). In the short run X_1 increases less than in proportion to L but increases more than in proportion to L in the long run (27). X_2 increases less than in proportion to K_2 in the short run but in equal proportion in the long run, and it follows that the decrease in X_1 is greater in the long run than in the short run.

3. Both capital goods endogenous

Now consider a situation in which both capital goods are endogenous. In this case we will have a second equation similar to that in (17). Our four pricing equations are now given by

$$p_1 = c_1(w, r_1) \tag{35}$$

$$p_2 = c_2(w, r_2) \tag{36}$$

$$r_1 = (\rho + \delta)q_1 = (\rho + \delta)c_{k1}(p_1, p_2) \tag{37}$$

$$r_2 = (\rho + \delta)q_2 = (\rho + \delta)c_{k2}(p_1, p_2). \tag{38}$$

Add a unit price normalization equation to (35)–(38), arranging it as follows:

$$w = 1 - p_1 - p_2 - r_1 - r_2. \tag{39}$$

Imposing the non-negativity restrictions $(p_1, p_2, w, r_1, r_2) \geq 0$, (35)–(39) then constitute a continuous mapping of a closed, convex, and bounded set into itself, and standard fixed-point theorems apply to ensure existence of an equilibrium price vector. The solution to (35)–(39) may also be unique, implying a single non-zero relative price ratio p_1/p_2 at which the economy produces both goods. I have no uniqueness proof, but I have examined the case where all production functions are Cobb–Douglas and the production function is the same for both capital goods. In this case, a unique non-zero solution to (35)–(39) exists. Let α, β, and γ give the share of labor in X_1, the share of labor in X_2, and the share of X_1 in Y (the identical production function for both capital goods) respectively. r, p_1, and $p_2 = 1$ are then given by

$$r = (\rho + \delta)q = (\rho + \delta)(p_1/\gamma)^{\gamma}(p_2/(1 - \gamma))^{(1 - \gamma)} \tag{40}$$

$$p_1 = (w/\alpha)^{\alpha}(r/(1 - \alpha))^{(1 - \alpha)} \tag{41}$$

$$1 = (w/\beta)^{\beta}(r/(1 - \beta))^{(1 - \beta)}. \tag{42}$$

By combining these three equations we can arrive at an explicit solution for p_1 as a function of the system parameters. The form of this solution is given by

$$p^{(1-\gamma+\gamma(\alpha/\beta))} = [\text{positive constant}], \quad (1-\gamma+\gamma(\alpha/\beta)) > (1-\gamma) > 0. \tag{43}$$

The left-hand side of (43) is a continuous and monotonically increasing function of p_1, running from 0 at $p_1 = 0$ to infinity at p_1 equal infinity. Thus (43) must have a unique solution at a positive value of p_1.

The result in (43) that diversified production is supported only at a single, unique price ratio is simply a special case of Samuelson's "non-substitution" theorem. The manner in which the capital goods are produced essentially reduces the economy to a one-factor economy in the long run, and hence with constant returns, we have the Ricardian property of a single price ratio that supports diversification.[2] In our case however, we know that the price ratio is not in general equal to the slope of the steady-state locus of outputs and hence the latter is not necessarily linear. Taking total differentials of outputs as in (22) and (23), we have

$$dX_2 = F_{2L}dL_2 + F_{2K}dK_2 = -F_{2L}dL_1 + F_{2K}dK_2$$
$$dX_1 = F_{1L}dL_1 + F_{1K}dK_1 \tag{44}$$

$$-\frac{dX_2}{dX_1} = \frac{F_{2L}(1+(F_{2K}/F_{2L})(dK_2/dL_2))}{F_{1L}(1+(F_{1K}/F_{1L})(dK_1/dL_1))}. \tag{45}$$

Marginal rates of substitution are factor-price ratios and, with diversified production, factor prices are constant implying that capital–labor ratios are constant implying that $(dK_i/dL_i) = (K_i/L_i) = k_i$. $F_{2L}/F_{1L} = p$ as in (23). (45) then becomes

$$-\frac{dX_2}{dX_1} = p_1\frac{(1+(r_2/w)k_2)}{(1+(r_1/w)k_1)} = p_1\frac{(1+(r_2K_2)/(wL_2))}{(1+(r_1K_1)/(wL_1))}$$

$$= p_1\frac{(1+s_{K_2X_2}/s_{L_2X_2})}{(1+s_{K_1X_1}/s_{L_1X_1})}. \tag{46}$$

With factor prices fixed in diversified production by the unique price ratio, the right-hand side of (46) is constant and hence the steady-state locus is linear. The relationship between the MRT and p_1 depends both on the factor intensities of the two goods and upon the production functions for K_1 and K_2. A simple case occurs when both capital goods are identical:

[2] A similar but less general result is found in Stiglitz (1970) in a model with one consumption good and one capital good. Stiglitz makes no attempt to relate the result to non-substitution or to note its generality.

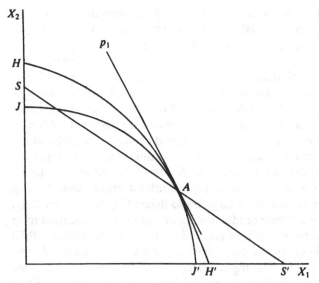

Figure 15.2

$$-\frac{dX_2}{dX_1} < p \quad \text{if both capital goods identical, } X_1 \text{ capital} \qquad (47)$$
$$\text{intensive.}[3]$$

If the capital goods are not identical, then we have a problem in that r_1 and r_2 are not equal and thus the ratio of the factor shares does not in general depend only on factor intensity. But such a result does follow if both final goods are Cobb–Douglas so that the ratio of shares is independent of factor prices. In that case, the right-hand side of (46) is constant and (47) holds if and only if X_1 is capital intensive; i.e., the relationship between the *MRT* and the price ratio is independent of the technologies (subject to (5) of course) for producing the two capital goods.

An outcome with X_1 capital intensive and capital goods identical is shown in Figure 15.2. The price ratio p_1 is tangent to the JSF production frontier given by JJ' and tangent to the HO production frontier for that level of aggregate capital given by HH'. The steady-state locus is given by SS'. Note the result that SS' intersects the X_1 axis to the right of both J' and H', but that S lies between J and H on the X_2 axis. Beginning at A, a movement toward the X_1 axis corresponds to an accumulation of

---

[3] Note the contrast here with fixed propensities models such as Oniki and Uzawa (1965). In the latter case, many results depend crucially on which final good is also the capital good. Here the results need no restrictions on G in (5) and hence are completely robust with respect to the intensity of Y.

aggregate capital in the steady state since X_1 is capital intensive by assumption. For each unit of labor transferred from X_2 to X_1, the increase in K_1 must exceed the decrease in K_2. Thus $S' > H'$ in Figure 15.2. But the movement toward the X_2 axis beginning at A must correspond to a deaccumulation of capital and so $S < H$ in Figure 15.2. The fact that $S > J$ can be seen by considering the move from A along the JSF locus. Since K_2 is fixed, the marginal product of K_2 rises steadily along JJ' as more labor is added to the fixed stock of capital. Once we reach J the marginal product of K_2 is obviously higher. But this same marginal product is constant along SS', and so, beginning at J, we must add to K_2 (this is consistent with total K falling) to reach the steady-state point S. Thus S lies between J and H.

Let me conclude with a few comments about steady-state trading equilibria between countries. In addition to depending upon technology, the slope of the steady state production locus and the diversification price ratio depend upon the rate of time preference. But in the Heckscher–Ohlin tradition, we generally assume that countries have identical and homothetic preferences. The logical extension of this assumption to the dynamic case is that the rate of time preference is the same in the two countries. With this assumption and the assumption of identical production technologies between countries, we would then have that the two countries have identical production frontiers (except for the scale of the labor endowment) in the steady state. Note however that it does not necessarily follow that free trade must involve no trade. Since the price ratio cuts the production frontier, it appears that there is a continuum of trading equilibria possible. Consider Figure 15.3 for example, where two countries have identical labor forces and so have identical production frontiers. One country could produce at point A and the other country at point B, with the common price ratio given by the solution to (39). The two countries trade to $(C^a + X_k{}^a)$ and $(C^b + X_k{}^b)$ respectively (recall from (6) that the value of gross production equals the value of consumption plus gross investment).

Alternatively, assume that both countries are at a common production and consumption point in Figure 15.3, obviously an equilibrium. Now transfer some capital from one country to the other. This generates a Rybczynski effect in both countries such that their production points move to A and B in Figure 15.3 (recall that SS' is a Rybczynski line). But these Rybczynski effects exactly balance, and all commodity and factor prices are preserved at their original levels (i.e., we are in an integrated equilibrium situation). There is no incentive for the country losing capital to accumulate more and no incentive for the gaining country to deaccumulate. The transfer is preserved permanently in differences in instantaneous consumption levels.

The equilibrium shown in Figure 15.3 is thus only one of a continuum

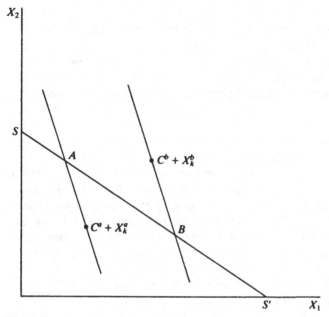

Figure 15.3

constructed by sliding the production points farther apart or closer together. All of the equilibria are "unstable" in that a shock to either country's capital stock will not return the system to its original position. This point may have some interesting implications for the new literature on hysteresis, on the importance of initial conditions, and on economic growth.

4. Summary and conclusions

In this chapter we have provided a long-run extension of Ron Jones's specific factors model (1971) by allowing one or both of the specific factors to be accumulated endogenously according to an optimal program. When one specific factor is endogenous, a number of results are derived. First, the steady-state locus of outputs cuts the JSF production frontier at a steady-state equilibrium point, while the associated price ratio is tangent to the JSF frontier, not to the steady-state locus. The steady-state production frontier is thus neither the envelope of the short-run production frontiers nor is there a tangency between it and the price ratio. Second, output responses to price and endowment changes are more elastic in the long run than in the short run, a finding consistent with the general models of Neary

266   James R. Markusen and Richard Manning

(1985), Markusen and Svensson (1985), Neary and Ruane (1988), and Manning and Markusen (1991). Third, the pattern of trade between two countries with identical preferences (including time preference) and technologies can be predicted by the endowments of the two primary factors. Third, factor-price equalization will hold between two such economies in the steady-state subject to the usual diversification condition. Fourth, modified versions of the Rybczynski and Stolper–Samuelson theorems were derived.

With both specific factors accumulated, we showed that the zero profit conditions reduce to a mapping from the price vector into itself. This suggests a unique price ratio which supports diversified production, which in turn implies that the steady-state locus of outputs is linear. It is, however, possible that multiple solutions to the mapping exist. With all production functions Cobb–Douglas, a unique price ratio exists, and hence the long-run production frontier is linear. The "wedge" between the price ratio and the slope of the long-run production frontier depends on the factor intensities of the two goods and on the technologies for producing the two capital goods. If the latter are identical, then the direction of the wedge depends only on which final good is more capital intensive.

These results with both capital goods endogenous suggest a possibility that is raised at the end of the chapter but not explored in detail here. This is that there may exist a continuum of steady-state free-trade equilibria for two countries with identical preferences and technologies, subject to commodity-price equalization. This finding may be of relevance to recent work on hysteresis, initial conditions and growth.

References

Jones, Ronald W. 1965 "The Structure of Simple General-Equilibrium Models," *Journal of Political Economy*, 73, 557–72.
    1971 "A Three Factor Model in Theory, Trade, and History," in Bhagwati *et al.* (eds.), *Trade, Balance of Payments and Growth: Essays in Honor of Charles P. Kindleberger*, Amsterdam, North-Holland.
Manning, Richard and James R. Markusen 1991 "National Product Functions in Comparative Steady-State Analysis," *International Economic Review*, 32, 613–24.
Manning, Richard, James R. Markusen and James R. Melvin 1992 "Dynamic Non-Substitution and Long-Run Production Possibilities," in Ngo Van Long and Horst Herberg (eds.), *Trade, Welfare and Economic Policies: Essays in Honor of M. C. Kemp*, Ann Arbor, University of Michigan Press, forthcoming.
Markusen, James R. and Lars Svensson 1985 "Trade in Goods and Factors with International Differences in Technology," *International Economic Review*, 26, 175–92.

Mayer, Wolfgang 1974 "Short-Run and Long-Run Equilibrium for a Small Open Economy," *Journal of Political Economy*, 82, 955–68.

Mussa, Michael 1974 "Tariffs and the Distribution of Income: the Importance of Factor Substitutability and Intensity in the Short and Long Run," *Journal of Political Economy*, 82, 1191–204.

Neary, J. Peter 1978 "Short-Run Capital Specificity and the Pure Theory of International Trade," *Economic Journal*, 88, 488–510.

1985 "International Factor Mobility, Minimum Wage Rates, and Factor-Price Equalization: A Synthesis," *Quarterly Journal of Economics*, 100, 551–70.

Neary, J. Peter and Frances Ruane 1988 "International Capital Mobility, Shadow Prices, and the Cost of Protection," *International Economic Review*, 29, 571–86.

Oniki, Hajime and Hirofumo Uzawa 1965 "Patterns of Trade and Investment in a Dynamic World of International Trade," *Review of Economic Studies*, 32, 15–34.

Samuelson, Paul A. 1951 "Abstract of a Theorem Concerning Substitutability in Open Leontief Models," in T. C. Koopmans (ed.), *Activity Analysis of Production and Allocation*, Cowles Commission Monograph 13, New York, John Wiley & Sons.

Stiglitz, Joseph E. 1970 "Factor-Price Equalization in a Dynamic Economy," *Journal of Political Economy*, 78, 456–88.

16 Hysteresis in the trade pattern

GENE M. GROSSMAN AND
ELHANAN HELPMAN

1. Introduction

Writing on "The Role of Technology in the Theory of International Trade,"
Ron Jones (1970, p. 85) asked: "What determines technical change?" Jones
argued (p. 87) that a sensible approach to answering this question would
"entail setting up a distinction between the use of resources to produce [a]
commodity and the use of resources to produce new technical knowledge."
He noted further (p. 87) that "expectations as to the future sales must affect
the quantity of resources devoted to improving the technology." Finally, he
challenged (p. 89) trade theorists to ponder "how transmittable technical
change is from one country to another." Even in idealized circumstances, he
recognized (p. 89), "technical progress in one country may not spill over to
actually affect techniques used in other countries."

Twenty years later, we take up Jones's challenge, using exactly the
approach that he proposed. Our analysis focuses on the issue that Jones
raised concerning the implications for technical change and for patterns of
trade of less than complete international spillovers of the public good that is
technical knowledge.

In Grossman and Helpman (1991, ch. 7) we have studied a world
economy in which countries share in a common pool of general knowledge
capital. A community of industrial researchers in each of two countries
combines knowledge capital with two primary resources (human capital
and unskilled labor) to generate blueprints for new, horizontally differentiated products. The countries manufacture these "high-technology"
products and a homogeneous, traditional good using the same two primary
inputs. Trade entails the exchange of the homogeneous good and some
unique varieties of differentiated products manufactured in one country for
the unique differentiated products of the other. Comparative advantage in

We are grateful to the National Science Foundation, the U.S.–Israel Binational Science
Foundation, and the Pew Charitable Trust for financial support.

the high-technology industry derives from endogenous activity in the research lab.

In this setting, we have established the validity of a dynamic version of the Heckscher–Ohlin theorem. The long-run trade pattern is determined entirely by relative factor endowments. A country that is relatively well endowed with human capital devotes relatively more resources to R&D (which we take to be intensive in its use of human capital), and comes to specialize relatively in producing the goods that require innovative technologies. The country that has an abundance of unskilled labor, on the other hand, specializes relatively in the production of (unskilled labor-intensive) traditional goods. Due to this pattern of specialization, the human capital abundant country enjoys a faster pace of technological progress and a higher rate of output growth than its international trade partner.

But the assumption of a common world pool of public knowledge capital seems at odds with aspects of reality. The concentration of research activities in places like the Silicon Valley and Route 128 near Boston suggests the possibility that technological spillovers may be geographically localized. This would be the case, for example, if highly trained personnel moving between research firms served as the principal conduit for the information exchange. But if knowledge capital stocks are location specific, then not only input prices but also prior research experience may affect a country's competitiveness in the research lab.

In this paper, we study a world economy with national stocks of knowledge capital. Entrepreneurs in each of two countries develop new technologies when expected future profits justify the up-front R&D outlays. Research productivity depends upon the stock of knowledge capital, which accumulates in proportion to local research activity. Our aim in all this is to illuminate the role of history in the determination of world trading patterns. Can a country overcome a late start in research to develop a comparative advantage in high-technology products? Or will the latecomer be forever confined to exporting traditional products? With national stocks of knowledge capital and no exogenous comparative advantage, the answer to this question turns out to be unequivocal.

2. A model of product innovation

The world economy comprises two countries that may differ only in their prior experience in research. The countries are endowed with similar quantities of a single primary factor of production, which we call labor.[1]

---

[1] In Grossman and Helpman (1991, ch. 8) we conduct a more complete analysis that allows also for differences in country size. We shall note in the concluding section how some of our results depend upon the assumption of equally sized countries.

They use this labor to invent new varieties of differentiated products, to manufacture the previously developed differentiated brands, and to produce a homogeneous, "traditional" good. Both types of goods are traded on world markets, so that international trade has both intra-industry and inter-industry components.

Consumers worldwide share the same preferences. The representative household maximizes an intertemporal utility function of the form

$$U(t) = \int_t^\infty e^{-\rho(\tau - t)} \log u(\tau) d\tau, \tag{1}$$

where $u(\tau)$ represents instantaneous utility at time τ and ρ is the subjective discount rate. Instantaneous utility is given by

$$u = \left[\int_0^n x(\omega)^\alpha d\omega \right]^{\sigma/\alpha} y^{1-\sigma}, \quad 0 < \alpha, \sigma < 1, \tag{2}$$

where $x(\omega)$ denotes consumption of differentiated brand ω, y denotes consumption of the traditional good, and $n(t)$ represents the measure of differentiated products available at time t. These familiar preferences imply an elasticity of substitution between every pair of varieties equal to $\varepsilon = 1/(1 - \alpha)$, an elasticity of substitution between the differentiated products and the homogeneous good of one, and an intertemporal elasticity of substitution that is equal to one as well (see, for example, Helpman and Krugman, 1985). They yield static demands of the form

$$x(\omega) = \sigma E p_x(\omega)^{-\varepsilon} \left[\int_0^n p_x(\omega')^{1-\varepsilon} d\omega' \right]^{-1}, \quad \omega \in [0, n], \tag{3}$$

$$y = (1 - \sigma)E/p_Y, \tag{4}$$

where $p_x(\omega)$ denotes the price of variety ω of the differentiated product, p_Y denotes the price of the homogeneous good, and E is aggregate spending. Dynamic optimization requires that spending evolve according to

$$\dot{E}/E = r - \rho, \tag{5}$$

where r is the instantaneous interest rate determined on the integrated world capital market (see Grossman and Helpman, 1989).

The technology for manufacturing the traditional good is common knowledge to producers around the world. This good is supplied competitively by firms that derive one unit of output from each unit of labor input. Together, these considerations imply

$$p_Y = \min(w^A, w^B), \tag{6}$$

$$Y^i = 0 \quad \text{if} \quad w^i > w^j, \quad i = A, B; i \neq j, \tag{7}$$

where w^i is the wage rate in country i, $i = A, B$, and Y^i is the aggregate output of traditional goods there. By contrast, the technologies for the differentiated products are proprietary information. No firm can produce any such good until it has developed a design and perfected the necessary production techniques. The introduction of new products requires the allocation of resources to R&D, as we shall describe below. Once a firm has developed a blueprint, it can assemble the brand with one unit of labor per unit of output.

At a point in time, the number of firms with the ability to produce varieties of differentiated products is given by history. The firms engage in (static) price competition. Since firms that manufacture an identical product earn zero profits in a Bertrand competition, there will be no costly imitation undertaken in the equilibrium that we describe. Thus, no brand has more than a single producer. Each producer behaves as a monopolist in its own submarket. Facing the demands in (3), the (small) purveyor of a unique variety in country i maximizes profits by setting the price

$$p_x^i = w^i/\alpha, \tag{8}$$

which is a fixed mark-up over the local unit production cost. With this price and the demands in (3), the n^i monopolists in country i attain an aggregate market share in the differentiated products industry equal to

$$s_x^i = n^i(p_x^i)^{1-\varepsilon} \Big/ \sum_j n^j(p_x^j)^{1-\varepsilon}. \tag{9}$$

Each monopolist in country i captures instantaneous profits given by

$$\pi^i = (1 - \alpha)\sigma s_x^i E/n^i. \tag{10}$$

Entrepreneurs develop new blueprints using labor and the existing stock of public knowledge capital. The knowledge capital stock K^i in country i reflects the accumulated wisdom in applied science and engineering in the local research community. The greater is the level of understanding of basic scientific principles, the smaller is the quantity of labor needed to invent a new product. In particular, we assume that an entrepreneur located in country i can learn the technology for dn new products per unit time by allocating dn/K^i units of labor per unit time to research activities. Therefore, the measure of products known to some firm in country i expands according to

$$\dot{n}^i = K^i L_n^i, \quad i = A, B, \tag{11}$$

where L_n^i is the aggregate amount of labor devoted to R&D.

We follow Romer (1990) in assuming that knowledge capital accumulates as a byproduct of industrial research. This specification captures the notion that new research builds upon earlier ideas, and that researchers often make discoveries in the course of developing new products that have widespread applicability, but with benefits that are difficult to appropriate. We assume that each research product makes a similar contribution to the public stock of knowledge capital. But, whereas in our previous work (Grossman and Helpman, 1990; 1991, ch. 7) we took these spillovers to be global in reach, here we make the opposite extreme assumption. That is, we confine the spillover benefits from research to the local community in which they are generated.[2] This makes the stocks of knowledge capital specific to each country, and the accumulation of knowledge capital proportional to the local research effort. More specifically, we take

$$K^i = n^i, \tag{12}$$

since n^i reflects the cumulative amount of research activity that has been undertaken in country i. By making productivity in R&D depend upon the state of knowledge, and this a function of prior research experience in a particular location, we have introduced the potential for history and initial conditions to influence the equilibrium outcome.

We allow entrepreneurs to enter freely into R&D. Let v^i be the market value of a blueprint held by a producer in country i. Then an entrepreneur can attain v^i by bearing the product development cost, w^i/K^i. No R&D takes place in country i when the research cost exceeds the benefit, whereas unbounded demand for labor results when the benefit exceeds the cost. Thus free entry implies, in the light of (12), that

$$v^i \le w^i/n^i, \quad \text{with equality when } \dot{n}^i > 0. \tag{13}$$

We equate the value of a blueprint with the present discounted value of the profits that accrue to its owners. That is,

$$v^i(t) = \int_t^\infty e^{-[R(\tau) - R(t)]} \pi^i(\tau) d\tau. \tag{14}$$

where $R(t) \equiv \int_0^t r(\tau) d\tau$ is the cumulative discount factor applicable at time t. Differentiating (14) with respect to t, and rearranging terms, we find

$$\pi^i/v^i + \dot{v}^i/v^i = r. \tag{15}$$

This "no-arbitrage condition" equates the sum of the dividend rate and the

---

[2] Reality undoubtedly lies between these extremes. A more plausible specification might include, for example, lags in the diffusion of knowledge that are shorter within a country than between countries. See Grossman and Helpman (1990) for an analysis of this intermediate case.

rate of capital gain on blueprints (a perfectly safe asset in the present context) to the rate of return on a consumption loan.

We close the model by specifying the market clearing conditions for goods and factors, and by choosing a numeraire. In the market for traditional goods, the value of supply equals the value of demand, or

$$p_Y(Y^A + Y^B) = (1 - \sigma)E. \tag{16}$$

In the market for differentiated products, each country must produce aggregate output that matches in value the total amount of spending devoted to its varieties, i.e.,

$$p_x^i X^i = \sigma s_x^i E, \tag{17}$$

where $X^i = n^i x^i$ is the total quantity of differentiated products manufactured in country i. Finally, in the factor markets, we must have aggregate derived demand equal to the exogenous labor supply L in each country; i.e.,

$$g^i + X^i + Y^i = L, \tag{18}$$

where $g^i \equiv \dot{n}^i/n^i$ is the rate of new product development in country i, and also the aggregate employment in R&D there.

As in all economies that lack a monetary sector, there is nothing here to determine the path of nominal prices. We are free to choose any normalization of prices that we wish, and our choice will have no bearing on the equilibrium allocation. Accordingly, we set

$$E(t) = 1, \quad \text{for all } t. \tag{19}$$

This choice of numeraire turns out to be convenient, because when combined with (5) it implies equality between the *nominal* interest rate and the subjective discount rate at every moment in time. We record that

$$r(t) = \rho, \quad \text{for all } t. \tag{20}$$

3. Steady states

In this section, we identify all steady-state equilibria that may emerge as long-run outcomes of the innovation process decribed in Section 2. Then, in the following two sections, we analyze the equilibrium dynamics that lead to one or another of these steady states.

A steady-state equilibrium (or "balanced growth path") is characterized by a fixed intersectoral allocation of resources in each country. Using (6)–(9), (16)–(17), and (19), we may rewrite the labor market clearing conditions (18) as

$$g^i + \alpha\sigma s_x^i/w^i + (1 - \sigma)s_Y^i/w^i = L, \tag{21}$$

where $s_Y{}^i = Y^i/(Y^A + Y^B)$ is the market share of country i in the traditional manufacturing sector. From this and the fact that the market shares are bounded by zero and one, we see that a constant intersectoral allocation of resources requires constant rates of innovation, constant wage rates, and constant market shares in each country.

Let us consider now the several possible long-term outcomes. First, R&D may be concentrated in a single country, while traditional goods emanate from both locations. Since the latter goods are competitively priced, both countries can supply them only if their wages rates are the same; i.e., $w^i = w$. Then, if country j innovates and country k does not, the former country captures in the long run all but a negligible share of the world market for differentiated products. With $s_x{}^j = 1$ and $g^k = s_x{}^k = 0$, (21) implies

$$g^j + \alpha\sigma/w + s_Y{}^j(1 - \sigma)/w = L, \tag{22}$$

$$s_Y{}^k(1 - \sigma)/w = L. \tag{23}$$

Also, we can differentiate the free-entry condition (13), which holds as an equality for country j, and substitute the result, together with the expressions for profits for firms operating in country j (10), for the nominal interest rate (20), and for spending (19), into the no-arbitrage condition (15), to derive

$$(1 - \alpha)\sigma/w = \rho + g^j. \tag{24}$$

Then (22)–(24), together with $s_Y{}^j + s_Y{}^k = 1$, determine the long-run wage rate common to the two countries, the long-run rate of product development, and the long-run market shares in the industry producing traditional goods. For the feasibility of this allocation, we require $s_Y{}^i \geq 0$, $i = j, k$. From the solution to the system, this implies

$$L/(L + \rho) \leq (1 - \sigma)/\sigma. \tag{25}$$

In other words, a steady-state equilibrium of the type just described can arise only if the budget share of the differentiated products is not too large.

A second type of steady-state equilibrium also has R&D concentrated in one location, but it has the production of traditional goods concentrated as well. Suppose that only country j innovates and only country k produces traditional goods. This requires $w^k \leq w^j$. The labor market clearing conditions that apply in the steady state now read

$$g^j + \alpha\sigma/w^j = L, \tag{26}$$

$$(1 - \sigma)/w^k = L, \tag{27}$$

while the long-run no-arbitrage condition analogous to (24) takes the form

$$(1 - \alpha)\sigma/w^j = \rho + g^j. \tag{28}$$

From these it is simple to calculate that $w^k \leq w^j$ if and only if

$$L/(L + \rho) \geq (1 - \sigma)/\sigma. \tag{29}$$

Notice that (29) is just the opposite inequality from (25). The innovating country specializes its long-run manufacturing activities in the production of differentiated products when the share of these goods in total spending is relatively large.

A third type of steady-state equilibrium involves equal rates of innovation in the two countries, and the production of traditional goods in both locations. With $g^j = g^k = g$, and $w^j = w^k = w$ (as required by the condition of competitive pricing in the traditional manufacturing sector), the steady-state labor market clearing conditions become

$$g + \alpha\sigma s_x^i/w + (1 - \sigma)s_Y^i/w = L, \quad i = j, k, \tag{30}$$

while the no-arbitrage conditions that apply to the value of firms in either location read

$$(1 - \alpha)\sigma s_x^i/w = \rho + g, \quad i = j, k. \tag{31}$$

From (31) we see that $s_x^j = s_x^k = 1/2$. Then (30) implies $s_Y^j = s_Y^k = 1/2$. In this case, long-run resource allocations are the same in both countries.

This exhausts the possibilities for feasible, steady-state outcomes. It is not possible, for example, for the countries to develop new products at different rates in the long run, because then the no-arbitrage condition for the slower innovating country would require its wage to approach zero along with its market share in the differentiated products industry. But a zero wage would imply a zero price of traditional goods, and thus infinite demand for these products. Also, both countries cannot innovate at the same rate with only one of them producing traditional goods, because then the two labor markets could not both clear.[3]

---

[3] If both countries innovate at the same rate, both employ equal quantities of labor in R&D. Also, the no-arbitrage conditions require $s^j/w^j = s^k/w^k$, when $g^j = g^k$. But then both countries employ similar quantities of labor in manufacturing differentiated products. Since the countries are of equal size, the labor markets cannot both clear if one uses labor in the production of traditional goods and the other does not.

We see that, for any set of parameter values, there exist exactly *three* different steady-state equilibria. In two of these, the R&D activity is concentrated in a single country, while the remaining country specializes (almost entirely) in the production of traditional goods.[4] In the third equilibrium, the countries allocate their resources similarly in the long run, and achieve equal rates of innovation. It can be shown, however, that this "interior" allocation is globally unstable (see Grossman and Helpman, 1991, ch. 8). That is, unless the countries happen to begin with the same prior experience in research and thus equal stocks of knowledge capital, the world economy can never reach the equilibrium in which both countries innovate. Moreover, if this equilibrium ever is attained, any slight perturbation that causes the countries to innovate at different rates for even a brief moment puts the world economy on a path that diverges from the initial steady state. In the light of this instability, we shall focus our attention henceforth on the equilibria that have geographic concentration of research activity.

The question that faces us now is: which country innovates? In principle, either country could play the role of the innovator, since the countries have similar endowments and similar natural abilities. But one of them may inherit a head start in the technology race, for reasons of historical accident, or otherwise. Can the other country overcome its initial deficiency in knowledge capital? Will there be multiple equilibria supported by self-fulfilling expectations? Or does history seal a country's fate? We answer these questions in the sections that follow.

4. Equal-wage trajectories

We begin with the case in which $L/(L + \rho) \leq (1 - \sigma)/\sigma$, so that the two long-run equilibria of interest involve production of traditional goods in both countries. We will show that, if the world economy is large enough, then there exists an equilibrium trajectory characterized by cross-country wage equality at every moment in time, and R&D activity that is always concentrated in a single country. Along this trajectory, only the country that inherits the larger stock of knowledge capital can play the role of the innovator.

Let us conjecture the existence of an equal-wage trajectory, and begin to investigate its properties. The issues having to do with existence will become clear as we proceed. We let $\bar{n}^i$, $i = A, B$, denote the initial numbers of differentiated products and the initial stocks of knowledge capital in the two countries. For concreteness, we take $\bar{n}^A > \bar{n}^B$. It follows immediately

---

[4] It also manufactures a negligible quantity of the unique varieties that its firms knew to produce to begin with.

that if $w^A = w^B$ all along the equilibrium path, then only country A can engage in research. For, if wage rates are equalized, so too are per-brand profits (see (9) and (10)). Then (14) implies $v^A = v^B$; i.e., blueprints have the same value in either location. But if R&D offers the same reward everywhere, the capital market will finance the efforts of entrepreneurs only in the location where research costs are lowest. Initially, country A is the lower cost innovator, because researchers there are more productive and factor prices are everywhere the same. But then country A widens the technology gap over time, and so the concentration of R&D activity is self-perpetuating.

Along an equal-wage trajectory, the wage rate is guided by the no-arbitrage condition that applies to blueprints held by firms in country A. Using (15), (8), (19), (20), and $v^A = w/n^A$ (which follows from (13) and the fact that $g^A > 0$), we have

$$\dot{w}/w = g^A + \rho - (1 - \alpha)\sigma s_x^A/w. \tag{32}$$

Next we sum the labor market clearing conditions (21) that apply for $i = A$ and $i = B$, to derive

$$g^A = 2L - [1 - (1 - \alpha)\sigma]/w. \tag{33}$$

Finally, we combine (32) and (33) to obtain

$$\dot{w} = w(\rho + 2L) - [1 - (1 - \alpha)\sigma] - (1 - \alpha)\sigma s_x^A. \tag{34}$$

In Figure 16.1, the line segment DE shows combinations of the wage rate and the market share of country A in the differentiated products industry that imply no change in the wage rate, per (34). This line has been drawn only for values of $s_x^A \geq 1/2$, because with $w^A = w^B$, (9) implies that $s_x^A = n^A/(n^A + n^B)$, and we have seen that country A innovates only if $n^A > n^B$. The arrows in the figure show the direction of movement of the variables at all points. The market share of country A always is rising for $1/2 \leq s_x^A < 1$ (provided that g^A in (33) is positive), because this country expands through time its share in the total number of differentiated products, and the terms of trade do not change.[5] The wage rate rises above DE, and falls below it. We see that a unique trajectory leads to the steady-state equilibrium at E.

The figure also shows the constraints on the wage and the market share that must be satisfied for there to exist a momentary equilibrium with equal wages. Feasibility requires non-negative allocations of resources to all activities. For non-negative employment in the R&D sector of country A, we need the right-hand side of (33) to be non-negative. This restricts us to

---

[5] Differentiating (9) with respect to time, and noting $p_x^A = p_x^B$, $g^B = 0$, and (33), we find $\dot{s}^A = s^A(1 - s^A)\{2L - [1 - (1 - \alpha)\sigma]/w\}$, which is positive for $0 < s^A < 1$ and $g^A > 0$.

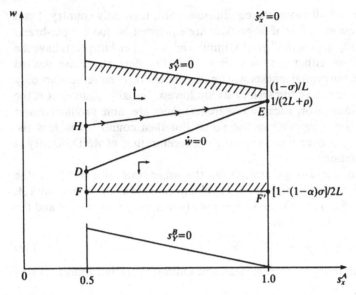

Figure 16.1

the region above the horizontal line FF'. Provided that L is sufficiently large, point F lies below point D, and this constraint does not bind.[6] For $s_Y^B \geq 0$ and $s_Y^A \geq 0$, we must have

$$0 \leq wL - \alpha\sigma(1 - s_x^A) \leq 1 - \sigma, \tag{35}$$

in the light of the expression for s_Y^B that derives from (21) and $g^B = 0$. This confines us to the region bounded by the lines labelled $s_Y^A = 0$ and $s_Y^B = 0$. The former line lies everywhere above point E, when $L/(L + \rho) \leq (1 - \sigma)/\sigma$. The latter line lies everywhere below the horizontal line through F, and thus never binds when $g^A \geq 0$. We conclude that an equal-wage trajectory with *positive* innovation exists, whenever

$$(1 - \sigma)/\sigma \geq L/(L + \rho) \geq 1 - (1 - \alpha)\sigma.$$

We have established conditions under which a productivity lead in R&D will be self-sustaining for country A. Of course, the same conditions apply to country B, if that country happens to inherit the larger knowledge base. Moreover, neither country can overcome an initial productivity disadvan-

---

[6] More precisely, this requires $L/(L + \rho) \geq 1 - (1 - \alpha)\sigma$. If this condition is not satisfied, then part of the trajectory HE *may* pass below FF', in which case there will be no innovation if the countries begin with nearly equal numbers of differentiated products. If the entire trajectory HE lies below FF', as will occur if $2L/(2L + \rho) > 1 - (1 - \alpha)\sigma$, then the world economy experiences no innovation, regardless of the initial product shares.

tage along a trajectory that maintains wage equality. Thus, the equal-wage trajectories exhibit a strong form of *hysteresis*. Events in history that may have provided one country with a head start in the accumulation of knowledge will have long-lasting effects.[7]

Along the equilibrium trajectory HE, the economies follow very different paths of economic development. In country A, the rate of innovation rises through time. The rising wage increases costs in all activities, but the accumulating stock of knowledge capital makes the cost of research rise less quickly than other costs. Therefore, resources move from the manufacturing sectors into R&D. Country B, on the other hand, experiences no technological progress, and sees its labor force drift from the differentiated products industry to the traditional manufacturing sector. As a result, its pattern of trade becomes more and more skewed over time.

One should be careful, however, in attaching normative significance to these findings. Along the equilibrium trajectory, residents of the two countries earn similar labor incomes, because their wage rates are the same. They face similar investment opportunities, because world capital markets are integrated. And they enjoy similar consumption opportunities, thanks to international trade. It follows that households with similar levels of initial wealth fare equally well along any equal-wage trajectory.

5. Unequal-wage trajectories

We turn now to the case in which $L/(L + \rho) > (1 - \sigma)/\sigma$. For such parameter values, the intersection of the $s_Y{}^A = 0$ line in Figure 16.1 with the vertical axis at $s_x{}^A = 1$ lies below the point E. Thus, the equal-wage trajectory must pass into the region where the constraint $s_Y{}^A \geq 0$ becomes binding. As country A comes to dominate the world market for differentiated products, the fulfillment of the demands for labor by the manufacturers of these goods and by research firms leaves less and less to spare for the traditional manufacturing sector. Eventually, the traditional sector releases all of its resources, and still the combined labor demand of the remaining two activities continues to grow. At that moment, the wage rates in the two regions begin to diverge.

The eventual, or perhaps immediate, divergence in wage rates does not alter the main conclusions from the previous section. In particular, it continues to be the case that, in the international technology race, a country that begins ahead, stays ahead. No country can ever overcome an initial deficit in knowledge capital. In the long run, the country that trails initially loses all of its production base in the differentiated products industry.

[7] Markusen (1991) obtains a similar result in a two-period model. Related findings are reported by Krugman (1987) and Feenstra (1990).

To establish these claims, let us suppose that the opposite were true. Then there must come a time when the lagging country (call it country B), trails by only a small amount in the technology race. Since we assume that country B overtakes country A, the rate of knowledge accumulation in the former country must be higher than that in the latter. Suppose that $w^B < w^A$ at that moment when $n^B = n^A - e$, for e small and positive. Since $g^B > g^A$, country B employs more workers in R&D at that moment than country A. With $w^B < w^A$ and the number of brands produced by each country almost equal, country B also employs as much or more labor in the production of differentiated varieties.[8] Finally, if $w^B < w^A$, country B devotes labor to traditional manufacturing, while country A does not. Therefore, at the moment when $n^B = n^A - e$, if $w^B < w^A$, country B allocates more labor to every use. This contradicts the assumption that the countries are of equal size.

The remaining possibility is that $w^B \geq w^A$ when $n^B = n^A - e$. Then entrepreneurs in country B, with lower productivity in the research lab and no factor cost advantage, must face higher costs of product development than their counterparts in country A. The entrepreneurs in country B can attract financing under these circumstances only if their prospective reward from developing a new product exceeds that which is available to entrepreneurs in country A; i.e., only if $v^B > v^A$. But firms in country B can have greater value than those in country A only if per-brand profits are higher in the former country than in the latter over some finite interval of time. During this time, which presumably would come after country B had taken the technological lead, the wage rate in country B would need to be lower than that in country A. But then country B would experience the greater derived demand for labor by manufacturers of differentiated products, and only country B would use labor for producing traditional goods. Again, this contradicts our assumption that the countries have equal labor supplies under the hypothesis that country B introduces new products more quickly. It follows that the wage in country B cannot be greater than, equal to, or less than that in country A at the moment when $n^B = n^A - e$. We reject the hypothesis that country B can eliminate its knowledge deficit.

When $L/(L + \rho) > (1 - \sigma)/\sigma$, the country that conducts R&D does not also produce traditional goods in the steady-state equilibrium. Let us investigate the equilibrium dynamics in a regime in which country A alone innovates and country B alone produces traditional goods, in order to see whether the steady state can be reached along a trajectory that everywhere maintains this pattern of international specialization.

---

[8] The differentiated products industry employs $\alpha \sigma s_x^i / w^i$ units of labor in country i. With $w^B \leq w^A$ and $n^B \approx n^A$, equation (9) implies $s_x^B / w^B \geq s_x^A / w^A$.

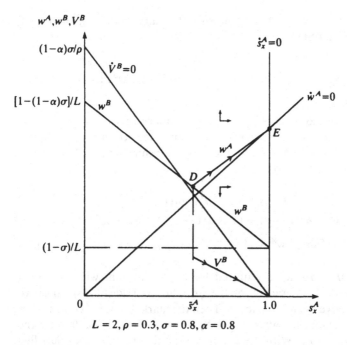

$$L = 2, \rho = 0.3, \sigma = 0.8, \alpha = 0.8$$

Figure 16.2

Using the expression (10) for per-brand profits in country A, the free entry condition (13) that applies in that country, and the expressions for spending (19) and the interest rate (20), we can re-express the no-arbitrage condition (15) that applies to the value of brands produced in country A as

$$\dot{w}^A/w^A = g^A + \rho - (1 - \alpha)\sigma s_x^A/w^A. \tag{36}$$

Then we can substitute for g^A using the labor market clearing condition (21), with $s_Y^A = 0$. This yields the following differential equation for the wage rate in country A:

$$\dot{w}^A = w^A(L + \rho) - \sigma s_x^A. \tag{37}$$

We use (37) in Figure 16.2 to plot the combinations of the wage rate and the market share of the innovating country that imply a constant value for w^A. Above the line labelled $\dot{w}^A = 0$ the wage in country A rises, while below the line it falls.[9]

Next we determine the evolution of the market shares in the differenti-

[9] Figure 16.2 has been drawn for a particular set of parameter values. These are: $L = 2$, $\rho = 0.3$, $\sigma = 0.8$, and $\alpha = 0.8$.

ated products industry. Differentiating (9) and noting $g^B = 0$ and $\varepsilon = 1/(1 - \alpha)$, we obtain

$$\dot{s}_x^A = s_x^A(1 - s_x^A)\left[g^A - \frac{\alpha}{1 - \alpha}(\dot{w}^A/w^A - \dot{w}^B/w^B)\right].$$

The labor market constraint for country B implies $\dot{w}^B = -\alpha\sigma\dot{s}_x^A/L$ when $g^B = 0$, while the labor market constraint for country A implies $g^A = L - \alpha\sigma s_x^A/w^A$. Substituting these relationships and (37) into the expression for $\dot{s}_x^A$, we find

$$\dot{s}_x^A = \frac{s_x^A(1 - s_x^A)[1 - \sigma + \alpha\sigma(1 - s_x^A)]}{(1 - \alpha)(1 - \sigma) + [1 - \alpha(1 - s_x^A)]\alpha\sigma(1 - s_x^A)}$$

$$\times [\alpha\sigma s_x^A/w^A + (1 - 2\alpha)L/\alpha - \rho]. \tag{38}$$

When $(1 - \alpha)L > \alpha\rho$, as is required for an equilibrium with sustained innovation, the term in brackets on the far right-hand side of (38) is positive at all points above the $\dot{w}^A = 0$ locus. Then the market share of country A is rising in this region, for all $s_x^A < 1$. We have indicated this fact by the arrows in Figure 16.2. With these dynamics, only one trajectory (labelled DE) leads to the steady-state equilibrium at point E.

The trajectory DE represents an equilibrium path, provided that it implies no contradiction of the assumptions upon which its construction was based. For example, the assumption that country B performs all manufacturing of traditional products requires the wage in that country not to exceed the wage in country A (see (7)). From the labor market clearing condition for country B (21) and the hypothesis that $g^B = 0$, we calculate

$$w^B = [(1 - \sigma) + \alpha\sigma(1 - s_x^A)]/L. \tag{39}$$

The line labelled w^B in the figure shows the relationship between the wage in country B and the market share of country A in the differentiated products industry. The equilibrium path must not cross below this line, as will be the case if the initial market share exceeds $\tilde{s}_x^A$.

The construction of DE relied also on the assumption that country B performs no research. To justify this assumption, we must check that R&D always is unprofitable in country B. The profitability of research hinges on a comparison of research rewards, v^B, and research costs, w^B/n^B. No research takes place when $v^B < w^B/n^B$, or when $V^B < w^B$, where $V^B \equiv n^B v^B$ is the aggregate value of firms operating in country B. To locate V^B in the figure, we first calculate how this value changes through time, as dictated by the no-arbitrage condition. Making the usual substitutions of (10), (19) and (20) in (15), we find that when $g^B = 0$,

$$\dot{V}^B = \rho V^B - (1 - \alpha)\sigma(1 - s_x^A). \tag{40}$$

Thus, V^B must approach zero in the long run, or else it will rise without bound. The latter possibility is excluded by the valuation equation (14), since per-brand profits are bounded from above. For V^B to approach zero, its initial value must fall below the $\dot{V}^B = 0$ schedule (derived from (40)) in Figure 16.2. Then, the value of firms in country B follows a trajectory such as the one labelled V^B in Figure 16.2. The parameter values that were used in drawing the figure locate this trajectory below the w^B line for all $s_x^A \geq \tilde{s}_x^A$. In this case and others like it, the assumption that country B performs no research is well justified.

We conclude that, for the parameter values used in the figure, if country A inherits a fraction of the world's differentiated products that affords it an initial market share in this industry in excess of $\tilde{s}_x^A$, then the trajectory labelled DE in Figure 16.2 represents an equilibrium growth path. Along this path, the wage in country A always exceeds that in country B, and country A captures an ever growing fraction of world sales in the differentiated products industry. The long-run pattern of trade in this case entails (net) exports of differentiated products by country A and exports of traditional goods by country B.

What happens if the initial market share of country A in the differentiated products industry happens to fall short of the critical level $\tilde{s}_x^A$? In this case, country B will not be able to satisfy all of world demand for traditional goods and also produce its unique varieties of differentiated products. During an initial phase of the dynamic equilibrium, the wage rates in the two regions must be equal, and country A must contribute some of world supply of traditional goods. Only later, when the market share of country B in the differentiated products sector becomes sufficiently small, does the divergence in wage rates take effect, and with it the cessation of traditional manufacturing in the innovating country.

One last possibility can arise for parameter values different than those that underlie Figure 16.2. In Figure 16.3 we have drawn a case where the path of aggregate firm values passes above the line w^B, for a range of market shares in excess of $\tilde{s}_x^A$. In this case, the trajectory DE will not be feasible during an initial phase of the dynamic equilibrium (when the market share of country A is less than $\hat{s}_x^A$), because the implied wage rates and brand values make R&D a profitable activity in country B. Instead, the equilibrium has an initial period with active research in both countries, but with more rapid innovation taking place in country A than in country B.

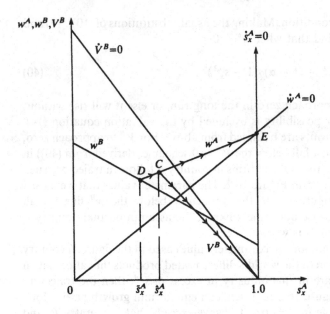

Figure 16.3

During this period, the lower factor costs that prevail in country B, and the higher profit rates that result from this cost advantage, offset the country's productivity disadvantage in the research lab. But the disadvantage grows over time, as country A accumulates knowledge capital more quickly, and eventually R&D becomes unprofitable in country B. This occurs when the economy reaches point C in the figure, whereupon R&D ceases in country B and the economy proceeds along the path leading to the steady state at E.

We can summarize our findings as follows. When $L/(L + \rho) >$ $(1 - \sigma)/\sigma$, then the long-run equilibrium necessarily involves the concentration of R&D activity in the country that inherits the larger stock of knowledge capital, and the concentration of traditional manufacturing in the other country. Depending upon parameter values and the initial difference in knowledge capital, the entire transition to the steady state may be characterized by this same pattern of specialization, or else there may be an initial phase with traditional manufacturing in the country that does none of this activity eventually, or with active R&D in the country that fails to innovate in the long run. In any case, the country that begins ahead in the technology race enjoys faster growth in real output all along the equilibrium trajectory, and a discounted value of (lifetime) labor income that exceeds that of its trade partner.

6. Subsidies to R&D

We have seen that initial conditions fully determine long-run outcomes when technological spillovers are confined to the country in which they are generated. In all cases, a country that begins ahead in the research race realizes faster output growth at every moment in time and exports technology-intensive goods in the long run. We ask now whether the government of an initially lagging country can use policy intervention to change its ultimate fate, and whether such policies that "tip" the equilibrium can be justified on grounds of social welfare.

For the purpose of illustrating this potential use of policy, we introduce an R&D subsidy in the country that begins with the smaller stock of knowledge capital. Under this policy, the government (of country A, say) pays a fraction z of all research expenses. Despite the policy intervention in the market, wage rates may nonetheless be the same in both countries all along the equilibrium trajectory. We will concentrate our formal analysis on this case. With wage rates equalized at all points in time, the value of brands produced in the different countries must also be equal. Thus, R&D activity will be concentrated in the country that has the lower *private* cost of research. This will be the lagging country A, whenever $(1 - z)/n^A < 1/n^B$, or when $s_x^A = n^A/(n^A + n^B) > (1 - z)/(2 - z)$. For values of z approaching one, this inequality must be satisfied.

When, in an equal-wage regime, entrepreneurs in country A conduct research with the support of their government, free entry implies

$$v = (1 - z)w/n^A. \tag{41}$$

Then $\dot{v}/v = \dot{w}/w - g^A$, and the no-arbitrage condition becomes

$$\frac{\dot{w}}{w} = g^A + \rho - \frac{(1 - \alpha)\sigma s_x^A}{(1 - z)w}. \tag{32'}$$

The labor market clearing conditions are the same as before, so (33) continues to give the rate of product development as a function of the wage rate. Substitution of this expression into (32') gives the differential equation for the wage rate that applies in a subsidy regime, namely

$$\dot{w} = w(\rho + 2L) - [1 - (1 - \alpha)\sigma] - (1 - \alpha)\sigma s_x^A/(1 - z). \tag{34'}$$

Using (34'), we can find the combinations of the wage rate and the market share which imply a stationary wage. These values are depicted by the line segment CE' in Figure 16.4. The line has been drawn only for market shares in excess of $s_x^A = (1 - z)/(2 - z)$, because the assumption that entrepreneurs in country A conduct research requires s_x^A to be at least

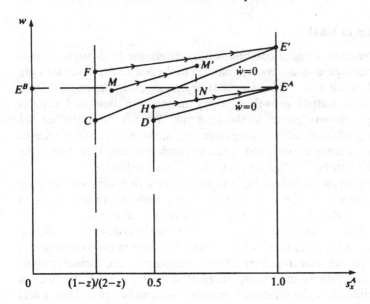

Figure 16.4

this large. Above the line the wage rises when a subsidy is in effect, while below the line it falls.

If the subsidy is permanent, the world economy converges to a steady state at point E' along the trajectory labelled FE'. The subsidy allows country A to replace country B as the increasingly dominant producer of differentiated products. Point E' lies above point E^B, the steady-state equilibrium that would obtain in the absence of the subsidy. This means that the subsidy raises the long-run wage rate. Then, from (33), we see that it increases the long-run rate of innovation as well.

The subsidy need not be permanent, however, for it to induce a long-run equilibrium with country A dominant in the world market for differentiated products. All that is required for this outcome is that the subsidy remain in effect until country A has overcome its knowledge deficit. Let us suppose, for example, that the government in country A announces a temporary subsidy for R&D that will expire on date T. Before time T, equation (33') guides the movement in the wage rate. But once the subsidy has been removed, equation (33) must apply. We know, moreover, that there can be no jump in the value of blueprints at time T. Otherwise, investors would stand to make infinite capital gains or losses. It follows from this that the wage must fall discretely at time T, so that the private cost of innovation equals the value of a blueprint both before and after the policy change.

We can use Figure 16.4 once more to describe the equilibrium trajectory that obtains with a temporary subsidy. In the figure, we have reproduced from Figure 16.1 the saddle path that leads to the steady-state equilibrium at point E^A. Recall that the economy follows this path when, in the absence of government policy, country A has an initial advantage in research productivity. With the subsidy in place, the world economy travels at first along the trajectory labelled MM' (where M gives the initial product share of country A). By time T, the point labelled M' is reached. Then, the government removes the subsidy, and the wage falls by z percent, to the level indicated by point N. Thereafter, the economy follows the saddle path trajectory to the long-run equilibrium at point E^A. How can we be sure that the wage drop at time T will leave the economy on the saddle path trajectory? Clearly, the initial wage at point M must be chosen "correctly," so as to ensure this outcome.

Evidently, temporary government policies can turn a stagnant economy into a growing one, and reverse entirely a country's long-run pattern of trade. This finding reflects again the hysteretic properties of the equilibrium dynamics. Temporary shocks can have permanent effects when "initial conditions" matter.

Would a government that is motivated by concerns for social welfare choose to implement such policies? In the situation described by Figure 16.4, the anwser is "probably not." The equalization of wage rates both with and without the subsidy means that the policy has no effect on the terms of trade. The subsidy's effects on national welfare stem from the induced effects on the equilibrium rate of innovation and the efficiency with which any research is carried out, and from the budgetary implications of the policy.

The subsidy causes research activity to relocate from a place where knowledge capital is relatively abundant to one where it is initially scarce. This raises the resource cost of achieving any given rate of innovation, with adverse consequences for welfare in both countries. The subsidy has an ambiguous effect on the world rate of innovation. The direct effect of the inducement works to promote product development, but the indirect effect associated with the rise in the resource cost of this activity works in the opposite direction. If the aggregate rate of innovation falls, then residents of country A certainly lose from the policy, because the free market equilibrium has a pace of technological progress that is already sub-optimally slow.[10] Even if the rate of innovation rises, the residents of country A may not gain from this, because the benefits of faster product

---

[10] Due to the positive externalities that are generated by industrial research and the non-competitive pricing of the differentiated products, the market allocates fewer resources to R&D than is socially optimal.

development are shared globally under a free-trade regime, whereas the fiscal costs of the subsidy are borne entirely at home.

An important message emerges from this discussion. In a world economy with international trade in goods and assets, the growth rate of domestic output provides a poor measure of national welfare. A country that specializes its production activities in sectors that offer little prospect for technological progress may nonetheless benefit as much as others from the advances that are made in the more progressive sectors of the world economy. Here, commodity trade offers the residents of the non-innovating country the opportunity to consume the complete range of innovative products, while asset trade provides these households with the opportunity to reap high rates of return on their savings.

But even in this context, there do exist circumstances under which a subsidy to R&D in the technologically lagging country might be justified on grounds of national welfare. Consider, for example, the scenario of Section 5, where parameter values are such that the steady-state equilibrium cannot support equal wage rates in the two countries. We recall that, in this case, the long-run wage rate is higher in the country that captures the R&D activity. Thus, a policy that "tips" the equilibrium such as the one described above may effect an increase in labor income relative to the level that would obtain in the absence of policy. Then, national welfare may be increased by the intervention as well. This argument for policy is similar to the one offered by Frank Graham (1923), which has been formalized in Ethier (1982). Ethier showed, in the context of a static, two-sector model of trade with increasing returns to scale in one sector, that a country might benefit from policies that ensure local production of the increasing returns good.[11]

7. Concluding remarks

The stark findings of this chapter – that initial conditions fully determine long-run trading patterns, and that a deficit in the technology race can never be overcome – are partially the result of the parsimonious way in which we have posed our question. In particular, we have studied the endogenous creation of comparative advantage in two entirely symmetric economies. The only way in which these countries have been allowed to differ is in their initial stocks of knowledge capital. In such a setting, if knowledge capital were globally accessible, then the cross-country pattern of specialization and trade would be completely indeterminate. We have

[11] We note that a lagging country might also benefit from R&D subsidies in situations where opportunities for foreign portfolio investment are limited. Then the subsidy could be used to promote the local accumulation of knowledge, which would then raise the rate of return on domestic savings.

sought, without success, to find an equilibrium path along which the initially lagging country "picks itself up by its bootstraps." Unlike some other contexts, optimistic expectations are not enough to support the overturning of adverse initial conditions.

But this does not mean that history alone will rule in high-technology trade when countries differ in their underlying structures. For example, in Grossman and Helpman (1991, ch. 8) we have argued that a large country may overcome an initial deficit in knowledge capital, even if technological spillovers are national in scope. The large country may be able to meet all of world demand for the traditional good, and still have enough resources left to undertake more research than its trade partner. If so, then this country can begin with a low wage that compensates for its productivity disadvantage in the research lab. Then knowledge capital will accumulate there more quickly than abroad, until the large country overtakes the smaller one in the high-technology race. A similar result would undoubtedly apply when, in a multi-factor world economy, a country that is well endowed with a factor that is used intensively in research, happened to begin with a deficiency in knowledge capital. Such a country would have a natural tendency to specialize in R&D, and its initial productivity disadvantage could be offset by a factor cost advantage. In general, both initial conditions and country attributes will matter in the determination of long-run trade patterns.

We close by repeating our warning about the normative interpretation of our results. Not only have we shown that, in some circumstances, a country that begins behind in the technology race will never be able to catch up, but also that, in many of these cases, the failure to do so has no adverse implications for the well being of the populace. The integration of world product and capital markets makes it possible for the residents of one country to avail themselves of the benefits of technological strides taken abroad. By having access to imports of innovative products, these residents can enjoy the same set of consumption opportunities as residents of the country where the inventions occur. And by having the ability to trade in international asset markets, they can enjoy the same set of investment opportunities as well. While the welfare analysis does suggest cases where a country might want to promote its local entrepreneurs in their global technological competitions, it hardly provides a blanket endorsement of such policies.

References

Ethier, Wilfred J. 1982 "Decreasing Costs in International Trade and Frank Graham's Argument for Protection," *Econometrica*, 50, 1243–68.

Feenstra, Robert C. 1990 "Trade and Uneven Growth," National Bureau of Economic Research Working Paper No. 3276.

Graham, Frank 1923 "Some Aspects of Protection Further Considered," *Quarterly Journal of Economics*, 37, 199–227.

Grossman, Gene M. and Helpman, Elhanan 1989 "Product Development and International Trade," *Journal of Political Economy*, 97, 1261–83.

1990 "Comparative Advantage and Long-Run Growth," *American Economic Review*, 80, 796–815.

1991 *Innovation and Growth in the Global Economy*, Cambridge, MA, MIT Press.

Helpman, Elhanan and Krugman, Paul R. 1985 *Market Structure and Foreign Trade*, Cambridge, MA, MIT Press.

Jones, Ronald W. 1970 "The Role of Technology in the Theory of International Trade," in Raymond Vernon (ed.), *The Technology Factor in International Trade*, New York, NY, Columbia University Press for the National Bureau of Economic Research.

Krugman, Paul R. 1987 "The Narrow Moving Band, The Dutch Disease, and the Competitive Consequences of Mrs Thatcher: Notes on Trade in the Presence of Dynamic Scale Economies," *Journal of Development Economics*, 27, 41–55.

Markusen, James R. 1991 "First Mover Advantages, Blockaded Entry, and the Economics of Uneven Development," in E. Helpman and A. Razin (eds.), *International Trade and Trade Policy*, Cambridge, MA, MIT Press.

Romer, Paul M 1990 "Endogenous Technical Change," *Journal of Political Economy*, 98, S71–S102.

Index